Selected Essays

Selected Essays

Viacheslav Ivanov

Translated from the Russian
and with notes by Robert Bird

Edited and with an introduction
by Michael Wachtel

NORTHWESTERN UNIVERSITY PRESS / EVANSTON, ILLINOIS

Northwestern University Press
Evanston, Illinois 60208-4210

First paperback printing 2003

Printed in the United States of America
10   9   8   7   6   5   4   3   2   1

ISBN 0-8101-2083-6

Library of Congress Cataloging-in-Publication Data

Ivanov, V. I. (Viacheslav Ivanovich), 1866–1949.
    [Essays. English. Selections]
    Selected essays / by Viacheslav Ivanov ; translated from the Russian and
with notes by Robert Bird ; edited and with introduction by Michael Wachtel.
        p. cm. — (Studies in Russian literature and theory)
    Includes bibliographical references and index.
    ISBN 0-8101-1522-0 (cloth : alk. paper)
    1. Symbolism (Literary movement)—Russia.   I. Bird, Robert, 1969–
II. Wachtel, Michael.   III. Title.   IV. Series.
PG3467.I8 A23 2001
891.709′15—dc21

                                                            2001000081

Contents

Part IV. Pilot Stars

Editor's Introduction

The essays in this volume, many of which have never before been translated into English, allow the Anglophone reader access to the world of ideas of one of the most wide-ranging and seminal figures of Russian intellectual history. Viacheslav Ivanov (1866–1949), dubbed "Viacheslav the Magnificent" by his contemporary, philosopher Lev Shestov, was not simply the preeminent thinker of Russia's Symbolist movement but more generally a protean force who guided and galvanized prerevolutionary Russian culture. In Ivanov's essays, one recognizes the fundamentally syncretic spirit of the age. This is the prose of a poet who refuses to recognize traditional boundaries, who navigates intrepidly through Western culture (be it antiquity, humanism, or hermeticism), history and myth, theology and politics. His essays thus serve as a window into an entire epoch and its aesthetic, social, and spiritual preoccupations.

It will be helpful to begin by sketching Ivanov's biography, for his education and personal experiences put him in an ideal position to reconcile the diverse currents that ran through Russian culture in the two decades that preceded the revolution. Ivanov was born in Moscow, to a family of relatively modest means. His father, a land surveyor and civil servant of low rank, died early, leaving his wife to bring up their only child. She imbued in her son a fervent religious sense as well as an appreciation for literature and art. Ivanov's extreme piety was severely tested in his last year of gymnasium when, according to his own account, he "suddenly" became an "extreme atheist and revolutionary."[1] This crisis lasted several years, causing confusion and severe depression, but it ultimately led to a reaffirmation of faith and a lifelong fascination with religious questions. Spiritual struggles notwithstanding, the young Ivanov proved to be a student of exceptional abilities. His extraordinary facility with ancient languages impressed his schoolteachers and then the foremost professors in Moscow, who supported his decision to continue his studies abroad in preparation for an academic career.

As a newly married twenty-year-old, Ivanov set off for Germany and matriculated in ancient history at the university in Berlin, joining one of the last groups of participants in the seminar of the venerable Theodor Mommsen. At this time, ancient history was inseparable from classical philology, and students were held to extremely high standards of linguistic proficiency as well as historical knowledge. Not only were dissertations routinely written in Latin (Mommsen would later complain that Ivanov's was "affected" [*verkünstelt*]), but the occasional class was even *conducted* in Latin. Ivanov appears to have thrived in this environment. His lengthy stay in Berlin not only gave him a specialist's command of classical sources, but also a firm grasp of German language and culture (in particular, the works of Goethe and Schiller), a tradition that left an indelible mark on his later work.

After nine semesters of study, Ivanov departed for Italy (by way of Paris) to research and write a dissertation on Roman tax farming, a subject then at the center of studies of antiquity. What was supposed to be a stay of a few months extended to three years, as Ivanov immersed himself in the world of Roman antiquity and, more important, began a passionate affair with Lidia Dimitrievna Zinov'eva-Annibal that would lead to his divorce and remarriage, and to a decision to leave the academic world behind and become a poet. Zinov'eva-Annibal was a woman of considerable talents (she was studying singing at the time she met Ivanov, and she was later to become a prose writer and playwright).[2] Much of Ivanov's poetry is directly or indirectly inspired by her, many of his theoretical writings (especially about theater) bear the imprint of her influence, and his mystical (religious) conception of love clearly reflects their relationship. As Ivanov expressed it in his "Autobiographical Letter": "Through each other we discovered ourselves—and more than only ourselves: I would say that we found God."[3] In short, an event in the physical world led to a metaphysical revelation. In the language of Ivanov's essays, this represented the path *"a realibus ad realiora"* (from the real to the more real). This famous formulation was for Ivanov not simply a theoretical postulate, but—as was so frequently the case in his work—a macrocosmic conviction derived from microcosmic (i.e., personal) experience.

Ivanov had been writing poetry since his school days, but had initially considered this nothing more than an avocation. During the years in Berlin, he had become increasingly serious about his poetic calling. This resolve was strengthened in 1895, when his first wife visited Vladimir Solovyov, the brilliant and idiosyncratic mystic philosopher and poet. Upon reading Ivanov's verses, Solovyov expressed unqualified approbation. Solovyov provided a living link to Dostoevsky, and it would be hard to say which of these towering figures would ultimately influence Ivanov more.

Ivanov and Zinov'eva-Annibal spent almost a decade in Western Europe, much of the time in Geneva (where he found time to study Sanskrit at the university under the tutelage of Ferdinand de Saussure). He now concentrated primarily on his poetry, which itself drew heavily on ancient philosophy and myth. While no longer pursuing scholarship for academic purposes, Ivanov intensively studied the cult of Dionysus, eventually reading (in the summer of 1903) a highly successful series of lectures on the subject at a short-lived Russian university in Paris.[4] One of the listeners was Valery Briusov, the self-appointed leader of the Russian Symbolist school, who sensed in Ivanov a valuable comrade-in-arms. Briusov's conception of Russian Symbolism as an extension of French Symbolism was distant from Ivanov's own, but such fundamental disagreement did not prevent the two from working closely to establish Symbolism as the reigning tendency in Russian literature in the first decade of the twentieth century.

The Paris lectures had been preceded by the publication of the thirty-six-year-old Ivanov's first book of verse, entitled *Pilot Stars*. Comprising poems written over the previous fifteen years, it was a remarkably mature debut volume. Nonetheless, it was greeted with utter incomprehension by Russian critics who were wholly unprepared for such demanding poetry. In retrospect, one can sympathize with their confusion. Not only did Ivanov furnish his poems with imposing epigraphs from a host of languages (all of which he knew well) and in a variety of alphabets, not only did he experiment in grafting classical Greek meters and syntax onto Russian verse, but he reveled in obscure archaisms and recondite allusions to antiquity. This was not poetry for a mass readership (and even the learned Briusov suggested that Ivanov expand the section of explanatory footnotes).[5] But it only encouraged Briusov to enlist Ivanov's aid in creating a Symbolist platform in the journal *Libra,* which was destined to become the mouthpiece of the Russian Symbolists. Many of Ivanov's early critical essays were written for publication in this journal.

In 1905, Ivanov and his wife moved back to Russia permanently. They chose to live in St. Petersburg, and their apartment ("The Tower," as it came to be known among contemporaries) quickly established itself as the center of the capital's intellectual life. The legendary Wednesday gatherings, beginning late in the evening and extending far into the night, brought together poets, artists, and philosophers for readings, criticism, and philosophical debate. Ivanov was in his element as the master interlocutor at these symposia, using his vast erudition to instruct and inspire. The list of visitors to these Wednesday events included virtually every significant poet of the time (not only the Symbolists but also the Acmeists and Futurists, some of whom had their public "debuts" there), as well as a host of leading figures from other areas of Russian culture, such as the stage director Vsevelod Meyerhold, the philosopher Nikolai Berdiaev, the artist Mstislav Dobuzhinsky, the historian Michael Rostovtseff, and even the Marxist revolutionary Anatoly Lunacharsky (who later, as the first Soviet minister of enlightenment, would facilitate Ivanov's emigration).

In these years, Ivanov occupied a position of unquestioned authority. He continued to write poetry, which was now received enthusiastically by a small audience sympathetic to his artistic goals. He was an active participant in Russia's "religious renaissance," heatedly discussing theological issues with a group of religious thinkers independent of the official church. His critical essays, written in a lofty style and demonstrating an unparalleled depth and breadth of knowledge, were studied as quintessential Symbolist statements. As Osip Mandel'shtam wrote to Ivanov apropos of the latter's collected essays: "Your book is beautiful like the splendor of great architectural creations and astronomical systems. Every true poet, if he could write books on the basis of the exact and immutable laws of his work, would write like you."[6]

In 1907, a personal tragedy befell Ivanov and interrupted his gregarious lifestyle. Zinov'eva-Annibal died suddenly after tending to children during an epidemic of scarlet fever. The next two years marked an extremely dark period in his existence, as he immersed himself in mysticism in an effort to achieve a reunion with his wife. This was a time of occult visions, when the border between dream and reality became increasingly evanescent. Suffering from his loss, Ivanov still participated (albeit less energetically) in cultural debates, writing a number of impassioned defenses of Symbolism which to this day are considered the most cogent formulations of the Russian Symbolist program. He also continued to hold the Wednesday symposia, which though different in tone without Zinov'eva-Annibal's spirited participation, attracted an equally illustrious group of visitors.

Ivanov eventually emerged from his prolonged depression by "rediscovering" his late wife in the person of Vera Shvarsalon, Zinov'eva-Annibal's daughter by a previous marriage. Their union led to a son (born in France in 1912) as well as a shift to a simpler, if no less mystical poetic idiom. Upon returning to Russia in 1913, Ivanov took up residence in Moscow, where he associated with a group of critics, philosophers, and religious thinkers (which included such luminaries as Mikhail Gershenzon, Pavel Florensky, Vladimir Ern, and Sergei Bulgakov), and befriended the pianist and composer Alexander Scriabin. A close working relationship developed between Ivanov and Scriabin, which proved of enormous creative significance to both of them. While Symbolism was no longer the reigning tendency in Russian artistic life, Ivanov was still regarded as one of Russia's most profound and eloquent thinkers, and his judgments carried considerable influence.

With the revolution, Ivanov's fortunes worsened considerably. Soviet cultural policy represented the antithesis of the symposial spirit that he had done so much to foster. As Ivanov himself later put it: "I was born free, and the silence there [i.e., in Soviet Russia] leaves an aftertaste of slavery."[7] However, Ivanov's difficulties were not only intellectual. His third wife died in August 1920, exhausted from the privations of the winter of that year, and he sought refuge for himself and his two children in the south, eventually landing a position at the newly founded Soviet university in Baku. After four difficult years there (during which he nonetheless found time to complete and publish a lengthy scholarly monograph on *Dionysus and Pre-Dionysianism*), Ivanov finally secured permission to leave the Soviet Union. He departed for Rome in 1924, remaining in Italy until his death twenty-five years later.

Ivanov was never an émigré in spirit, however. Rather than joining the Russian community abroad, he actively sought to participate in the intellectual life of the West. He converted to Roman Catholicism in 1926, which he viewed as an extension rather than a rejection of Russian Orthodoxy. (This decision was in a sense preordained by the philosophy of Vladimir Solovyov.) In the emigration, Ivanov proved himself the consummate European, writing essays for leading journals in sophisticated German, Italian, and French. Though his reputation never reached the heights that it had in Russia, these essays attracted a highly literate, if small coterie of admirers, including Martin Buber, Ernst Robert Curtius, Charles Du Bos, Gabriel Marcel, and Giovanni Papini. In the Soviet Union, however, his works were not republished for decades, and it quickly became inadvisable—if not wholly impossible—to study them. His name became a footnote to other, more "acceptable" currents in prerevolutionary literature. With the fall of the Soviet Union, Ivanov became the beneficiary of renewed attention. His books were republished, and he has repeatedly been the subject of essays, monographs, and conferences.

Nomenclature notwithstanding, Russian Symbolism owed far less to French Symbolism (with which, according to Ivanov, it shared "neither a historical nor ideological basis")[8] than it did to German Romanticism and to the great poets and prose writers of nineteenth-century Russia.[9] It was not so much an artistic movement as a comprehensive worldview, an attempt to give aesthetics a spiritual foundation. The Russian Symbolists sought to preserve the insights and achievements of past civilizations and to build upon them. They viewed human creativity as a continuum, celebrating "Symbolist" tendencies in the art and culture of civilizations distant both temporally and spatially. (In characteristically provocative fashion, Ivanov begins his excursus at the end of "Thoughts on Symbolism" with the exclamation, "So Dante is a Symbolist!") According to Symbolist conviction, divisions between various fields of knowledge and artistic disciplines were artificial: poetry was intimately linked not only to painting, music, and drama, but also to philosophy, psychology, religion, and myth. The intellectual cross-fertilization that took place at Ivanov's "Tower," in short, was a social manifestation of central Symbolist tenets.

Not surprisingly, then, the Symbolists tended to be proselytizers. They devoted considerable energy to studying world literature and immersing themselves in philosophy, rediscovering little-known poets and thinkers. In a mere two decades, the Symbolists expanded immeasurably the horizons of the Russian reading public. They indefatigably translated foreign works of poetry, prose, and philosophy, carefully prepared new editions of unjustly neglected Russian poets, wrote critical and philosophical essays on their precursors and contemporaries, taught and lectured extensively. Ivanov's activities were in this sense typical: in addition to writing poetry and theoretical essays, he translated Aeschylus, Alceus and Sappho, Goethe and Novalis, Byron and Baudelaire, Dante and Petrarch. He authored critical essays on most of these poets as well as on Pushkin, Gogol, and Dostoevsky. He wrote on music and painting and also produced two lengthy scholarly treatises on Dionysus. He taught Homer and German Romanticism in a university setting, and lectured to young poets on verse form, history, and technique.

Such varied activity might give the impression of eclecticism, of a collection of intellectual interests without an organizing principle. However, the Symbolist worldview was considerably more than a hodgepodge of ideas and slogans from a variety of historical epochs. Ivanov and his fellow Symbolists sought, in proto-Structuralist fashion, to delineate the features that linked antiquity to modernity. Fundamental truths, they insisted, were unchangeable. It was the task of each generation to recognize those truths and apply them to a new historical reality. Ivanov's interest in earlier civilizations had nothing to do with novelty seeking; rather, he studied ancient cultures in order to demonstrate how their underlying beliefs resonated with present-day concerns. To give an obvious example: Ivanov's view of Russia's historical calling ("On the Russian Idea") is clearly indebted to his thorough knowledge of conceptions of statehood in ancient Rome.

In reading Ivanov's essays and poetry, one is invariably struck by his ability to discern likeness. This quality separates him decisively from Nietzsche, whose status as "renegade" scholar turned philosopher and poet would seem to offer an obvious point of comparison. Ivanov read Nietzsche attentively, as his frequent references attest. However, where his German counterpart saw irreconcilable differences, Ivanov found similarities. If, for Nietzsche, Christianity represented a betrayal of Dionysian principles, Ivanov found in Christ a continuation of Dionysian pathos. Without going so far as to equate the two—though he was often accused of precisely this— Ivanov saw the "suffering god" as a forerunner to Christ, with Dionysian religion being a kind of spiritual preparation for the Christian message. Where Nietzsche viewed the Greek world as a battleground of Apollonian and Dionysian elements, Ivanov emphasized the possibility of their combination and reconciliation. In the tradition of Vladimir Solovyov, Ivanov ultimately understood Nietzsche as a Christian thinker in spite of himself. This explains why he applies New Testament concepts to Nietzsche's fundamentally anti-Christian worldview: "Inspired by Dionysian intoxication, Nietzsche was aware that for the illumination of our earthly image (for he willed no less) our heart must change, that within us there must occur some profound transformation, the transfiguration of our entire emotional makeup, the re-tuning of the entire range of our feelings, a rebirth like the state denoted in the original language of the Gospels by the word 'metanoia,' which is what allows one to see the 'kingdom of heaven' on earth" ("Nietzsche and Diony-sus" in this volume, p. 183).

Ivanov certainly shared Nietzsche's fascination with mythology and his advocacy of a "new myth." According to Ivanov, the symbol (and hence Symbolism itself) must be grounded in myth. Genuine poetics was there-fore always mythopoetics, which—whether consciously or not—was always linked to prior myth. In Ivanov's words, "Old myths naturally turn out to be kin to new myths."[10] One should emphasize the word "naturally" here. It is not necessary that the artist consciously base his work on old myths (though this was certainly possible) as much as that great art unavoidably emerges from myth, even if the poet or audience is unaware of the source.[11] In gen-eral, the Symbolists followed the German Romantics in celebrating myth as a not strictly rational means of cognizing reality. But Ivanov went further, seeing myth as profoundly religious in nature and therefore essentially true, not a merely psychological phenomenon (for which he castigated the ap-proach of C. G. Jung). It was not the creation of an individual, but the con-viction of a community. This belief in the correct "instincts" of the people, so crucial to Ivanov's thinking, links him both to the German Romantics and, somewhat surprisingly, to the Russian radical critics of the 1860s, whose calls to "go to the people" are echoed in some of Ivanov's own for-mulations, albeit with the accent placed on spiritual rather than political action. For Ivanov deplored the distance that separated the poet from the masses and looked longingly back to ancient Greece, where the people flocked to a theater that had not yet lost its religious dimension and could therefore offer dramas that functioned as a cathartic rite. (It would be diffi-cult to overestimate the importance of drama—and performance in general—for Ivanov's conception of art.) Indeed, Ivanov argued that Symbolism could bridge the gap between the intelligentsia and the people only by returning art to its mythical (religious) origins.

While Ivanov's thorough knowledge of ancient myth and careful as-similation of Western culture and scholarship would seem to disqualify him from the ranks of the Slavophiles, he nonetheless accepted some of their important presuppositions. One was a belief—given its most memorable expression by Dostoevsky—in the Russian people as possessing a special destiny, seen both as a religious and cultural calling.[12] On the one hand,

Russia was a symbol for Christ himself (as in Fedor Tiutchev's influential poem "These poor settlements," cited frequently and fervently by Dostoevsky) and a "Christ-bearing nation" (see the conclusion of Ivanov's "On the Russian Idea"). On the other hand, Russia was considered a supranational entity, the nation characterized by an openness to the highest aspirations of other nations. According to Ivanov's conception of Slavophilism, a belief in "holy Russia" does not mean that other nations are inferior, for each nation has its own "angel."[13] Nor does it imply an uncritical acceptance of Russia as it exists, for Ivanov was all too cognizant of his country's failings. In fact, Ivanov rejects any notion of a "national idea" that is predicated on a state (i.e., a political entity) or motivated by a sense of national superiority. By situating his image of Russia as an aspiration rather than a realization, he steers clear of the radical Slavophilism that posits Russia as the sole hope and salvation of Western civilization (Dostoevsky's conception, expressed most directly in his "Pushkin Speech" of 1880).

Another Slavophile concept of enormous significance to Ivanov was the untranslatable *sobornost'*.[14] To the Slavophiles, *sobornost'* denoted the special quality of the Orthodox Church, which—they claimed—created a unity based on unanimity (not on coercion or the curtailment of freedom). Ivanov takes this religious concept and applies it to aesthetics (or, one might argue, he places aesthetic issues within the sphere of this religious concept). *Sobornost'* fits in neatly with Ivanov's understanding of the ideal relationship of artist and audience, which is predicated on eradicating individualism and creating in its place a true community of believers. The audience must receive the artwork not as a heterogeneous group of disconnected individuals, but in sympathetic response to the author's conception.

Sobornost' is but one of the myriad connections of art and religion that lie at the core of Ivanov's Symbolism. Theurgy is another, and here the source was Vladimir Solovyov. Solovyov had argued, forcefully but vaguely, for a "theurgic art" (in Ivanov's formulation: "art that achieves the transfiguration and transformation of life").[15] Taking Solovyov's ideal as a practical goal, the Symbolists urged "life-creation" (*zhiznetvorchestvo*).[16] Accordingly, the poet was not simply a creator of books, but of life itself, for life and literature were constituted in essentially the same way. For Ivanov, a believing Christian, it was important to fit the potentially dangerous implications of this artistic credo within the parameters of an Orthodox worldview. Ivanov could not countenance an artist-tyrant who acted in accordance with his personal will to power (the contrast with Nietzsche is explicit in Ivanov's own argumentation).[17] He insisted on a more responsible type of creativity, a creativity that expressed (or "reflected," to use a Goethean image that Ivanov particularly admired) divine will: "The artist triumphs if he convinces us that the marble desired his chisel."[18] The true poet, he insisted, did not invent, but rather discovered. Such is the essence of Ivanov's conception of

"Realistic Symbolism," which he opposed to the subjective "Idealistic Symbolism" of the French Symbolists.

It is worth noting how closely this aesthetic program parallels the Orthodox Christian division of seers into genuine mystics (with their visionary insight into the mysteries) and heretics (who claim their personal fantasies as religious truth). In both cases, the problem of verification becomes central: how can one discern a Realistic Symbolist (objective, mystic) from an Idealistic Symbolist (subjective, heretic)? For Ivanov, this issue was not as complicated as it may seem to us. The genuine poet allowed himself to be guided by myth (which was necessarily true), thus appealing to the people, who were always ultimately capable of distinguishing what was genuine. The poet had access to realms of knowledge often hidden from his compatriots, yet this knowledge never entailed the rejection of reality (as it so often did for the German Romantics). Rather, in the spirit of Dostoevsky, Ivanov viewed the earth itself as a path to the divine. Only if the artist shows "reverence for lower reality and obedience to the will of the earth" will his message be the "good news" of Christ.[19] The artist possesses the ability to recognize the ideal within the earthly, "to reveal the noumenal in the clothing of the phenomenon" ("Lev Tolstoy and Culture" in this volume, p. 203).

Ivanov was a canonical thinker, and it is important to realize this, lest one dismiss his allusiveness as mere pretension. Ivanov cites frequently, and not simply because he could anticipate an erudite audience. Citation was for him both an act of piety and an immersion into a source of timeless authority. It is therefore as essential an element of his style as his complicated syntax, lengthy rhetorical periods, and extended metaphors. It has been recognized that the vast majority of Ivanov's allusions are to authors with whom he is in agreement, while his polemics tend to be hidden.[20] The list of favorite authors is easily established: Plato, Aeschylus, Dante, Goethe, Pushkin, Dostoevsky, and Solovyov—with a second tier peopled by Homer, Petrarch, and Novalis. For Ivanov, these writers were "pilot stars," capable of setting on course anyone who gazed knowledgeably—and receptively—upon them. Even within this pantheon of exemplary authors, Ivanov refers repeatedly to a relatively small number of passages. This is most certainly not a result of insufficient familiarity with his sources (quite the contrary: if one patiently tracks down all references, there can be little doubt that he knew these writers' works thoroughly). Rather, it is because these select passages seemed to Ivanov to contain a precise formulation of an essential truth. He repeats them consciously, like a participant in a religious rite who fully believes in the power of incantation.

Ivanov's favorite text is surely the most canonic of books—the Bible. As a believer, Ivanov naturally understood the Bible as the ultimate authority, a source of indisputable truth. What deserves emphasis is how frequently biblical references are used to explicate an essentially aesthetic program.

This is not a "secularization" of religious doctrine, however, but rather the "sacralization" of aesthetics. Ivanov views the artistic process not simply as being analogous to divine activity, but as being in genuine concord with it. In fact, with his sense of seamless continuity, he traces the artistic act back to origins that predate the Judeo-Christian tradition. While Ivanov insists that his central notion of religious art be understood broadly ("not some definite content of religious beliefs, but a form of the personality's self-determination in its relation to the world and to God"),[21] there can be no doubt that he privileges the New Testament.

Another characteristic element of Ivanov's essayistic style is his use of autocitation. Once again, this is less a case of authorial hubris than a reflection of basic Symbolist principle. Ivanov's theoretical essays were often conceived of as glosses on his poetry. In some cases (e.g., "Thoughts on Poetry"), an entire essay develops the implications of a brief yet programmatic lyric poem. In others, individual lines of poetry are so neatly intertwined with the highly metaphorical texture of the prose as to be almost indistinguishable. However, there is every indication that Ivanov considered poetry to be superior to prose, which used logical syllogism and scholarly argumentation to make the poet's inspired vision more accessible.

Ironically, Ivanov's reputation has always rested primarily on his essays rather than on his verse. This is most easily explained by the semantic and linguistic difficulty of much of the poetry, which offers challenges that few readers are prepared to accept. The essays, their allusiveness notwithstanding, are considerably more direct in their message and therefore easier to comprehend and respond to. Ivanov's views often provoked intense dispute, sometimes even among his comrades-in-arms within the Symbolist camp. Today's readers will surely feel uncomfortable with some of his assumptions and beliefs. Yet one need not always agree with these essays to admire them. Ivanov's skill as an essayist lay in his ability to reconcile diverse ideas from seemingly distant realms, to move among these realms with ease. One of his favorite Goethe citations comes from the "Prologue in the Theater" that introduces the first part of *Faust:* "Wer vieles bringt, wird manchem etwas bringen" (roughly: He who brings much will bring something to many). Ivanov himself brought a lot; his diverse readers rarely found the same thing, but they invariably found something of importance. Whether discussing literature or music, the destiny of the Russian people and its religious calling, or the crisis of contemporary society, Ivanov set the tone of contemporary discussion. Indeed, it would be difficult to name any significant Russian cultural figures contemporary to Ivanov who developed their thoughts independently of him. Osip Mandel'shtam discovered the "yearning for world culture" that he ascribed to Acmeism; Velimir Khlebnikov found justification for his "neoprimitivist" theories. Nor did his influence entirely cease with the advent of the Soviet regime and its policies of forced oblivion: in the "discredited" Ivanov, the Soviet outsider Mikhail Bakhtin found the notion of dialogue and, in the West, Ernst Robert Curtius borrowed and extended Ivanov's mystical conception of memory.

In presenting these essays in English translation, then, our intention is not only to demonstrate the breadth of Ivanov's interests, but also to re-create the context from which Russian modernism arose. For this latter reason, we have not included any of the essays written in emigration. Intellectually and ideologically speaking, there is no radical change that distinguishes the later essays from the earlier ones, but—with the exception of the book on Dostoevsky[22]—this work had a considerably smaller impact. Moreover, much of it was written—or translated almost immediately—into German, Italian, or French, making it more accessible to a Western audience. The present volume contains Ivanov's most influential essays (in particular, those on Russian Symbolism) as well as his statements on major Russian cultural figures (Tolstoy, Scriabin) and intellectual currents ("On the Russian Idea," "On the Crisis of Humanism"). Written over a period of almost fifteen years, they inevitably reflect changes in Ivanov's views and therefore cannot be said to represent a completely consistent or comprehensive "system." Nonetheless, an overarching vision lends continuity to all of Ivanov's work, be it in the form of verse, essay, or scholarship. Individual issues may at times be resolved with different emphasis, yet the larger concerns remain intact (e.g., culture as a unifying force, the spiritual roots and aims of art, the theurgic calling of the artist). Ivanov's method—his ability to bring together disparate fields of knowledge—was inextricably linked to his message. And that method comes through clearly in each of his essays, regardless of the specific subject under consideration.

Michael Wachtel

Abbreviations and Translations

Apollo
Apollon (St. Petersburg, 1909–17).

By the Stars
V. I. Ivanov, *Po zvezdam: Stat'i i aforizmy* (St. Petersburg: Ory, 1909).

Collected Works I, II, III, IV
V. I. Ivanov, *Sobranie sochinenii,* 4 vols. (Brussels: Foyer Chrétien Oriental, 1971–84).

Cor Ardens
V. I. Ivanov, *Cor Ardens,* 2 vols. (Moscow: Skorpion, 1911–12).

Das alte Wahre
W. Iwanow, *Das alte Wahre: Essays* (Berlin and Frankfurt: Suhrkamp Verlag, 1955).

Furrows and Boundaries
V. I. Ivanov, *Borozdy i mezhy: Opyty esteticheskie i kriticheskie* (Moscow: Musaget, 1916).

The Golden Fleece
Zolotoe runo (Moscow, 1906–9).

Hellenic Religion
V. I. Ivanov, *Ellinskaia religiia stradaiushchego boga.* Page proofs c. 1917. The Rome Archive Viacheslav Ivanov.

IMLI
Institut mirovoi literatury (Moscow).

IRLI
Institut russkoi literatury ("Pushkinskii dom," St. Petersburg).

Libra
Vesy (Moscow, 1904–9).

Notes of Dreamers
Zapiski mechtatelei (Moscow, 1919–21).

Peterson, *The Russian Symbolists*
Ronald E. Peterson, trans. and ed., *The Russian Symbolists: An Anthology of Criticial and Theoretical Works* (Ann Arbor, Mich.: Ardis, 1986).

Pilot Stars
V. I. Ivanov, *Kormchie zvezdy* (St. Petersburg: Tipografiia A. S. Suvorina, 1903).

RGB
Rossiiskaia gosudarstvennaia bi-
blioteka (Moscow).

RNB
Rossiiskaia natsional'naia bi-
blioteka (St. Petersburg).

The Tender Mystery
V. I. Ivanov, *Nezhnaia taina. Lepta*
(St. Petersburg: Ory, 1912).

Transparency
V. I. Ivanov, *Prozrachnost'*
(Moscow: Skorpion, 1904).

Works and Days
Trudy i dni (1912–17).

Selected Essays

PART I

Symbolism

The Symbolics of Aesthetic Principles

The ascending, spiraling line, the elation of impulse and overcoming, is dear to us as a symbol of our finest self-affirmation, our "mighty decision: to strive untiringly to the highest being."

> Du regst und rührst ein kräftiges Beschliessen,
> Zum höchsten Dasein immerfort zu streben. . . .
> (Goethe, *Faust,* II.1)[1]

A soaring eagle; a breaking wave; the tension of a column and challenge of a tower; a four-cornered obelisk reaching toward the heavenly monad, narrowing in its ascent and refracted in its supreme proximity to the world's boundaries; the mysterious ladders of the pyramids, rising from the four corners of the earth to a single pinnacle; the *sursum corda*[2] of mountain peaks, formed of the earth's constant flight from the worldly, petrified like a snowy, radiant throne in the detached triumph of final achievement:[3] these are the images of that very "sublime" that calls to our buried self: "Lazarus, come forth!"[4] which calls to our limited self with Augustine's testament: "Transcend yourself" (*transcende te ipsum*).[5] For just as Iazykov wrote,

> . . . genius trembles in joy
> Perceiving its own majesty,
> When another genius's flight
> Burns and shines before it—[6]

so also the sight of ascent awakens divine echoes of daring will in our dungeon depths and elevates us with a suggestion of our "forgotten, and self-forgetting" might.[7]

And when on the highest steps of this ascent there occurs a visible change, a transubstantiation of what has ascended from the earth, although native to the earth, then the soul is pierced by triumphant exultation, the prophetic joy of transcendent freedom.[8] Such was Tiutchev's final cry at the sight of a rainbow:

> It embraced full half the sky
> And was *exhausted* in the heights,—[9]

and upon seeing Mont Blanc:

> And there, in triumphant peace,
> Since the morning clouds departed,
> The White Mountain shines,
> Like an *unearthly revelation*.[10]

The "sublime" in aesthetics, insofar as it is represented by ascent, is an essentially religious phenomenon that thereby transcends the bounds of aesthetics. Concealed within it is the symbolics of a theurgic mystery and a mystical antinomy, whose holy formula and mysterious hieroglyph is "he who bears God battles with God."[11] Yet radiant receptivity to God is itself not sufficient for all gifts of grace to descend to the soul; some gifts demand a readiness to battle with God;[12] when the Divinity offers such a gift, it whispers to the soul: "Come and take it!" Israel's righteous battle with God wrenches forth a blessing.[13] He who offers up a sacrifice draws the divine down to himself and becomes a God-bearer. The God-battling and God-bearing pathos of ascent is resolved in a sacrificial act. This is the pathos of tragedy; tragedy, in turn, is a sacrificial rite.

Indeed, the labor of ascent is an act of separation and dissolution, of spending and giving, of detachment from one's own and from one's self for the sake of what hitherto was alien, and for the sake of a new self:

> Dare to ascend as the throne of the earth,
> Strain your winged impulse,
> Believe your spirit, and celebrate
> White rupture with the green dale.[14]

This labor contains a love of suffering, the free self-affirmation of suffering. Suffering itself can be defined generally as impoverishment and exhaustion through individuation.[15] And redemptive suffering for the world is itself no less than the individuation of a sacrificial victim who has taken upon himself *alone* the sins of the entire world. The world is governed by a collective responsibility of living forces, composed equally of guilt and goodness; sacrifice is when one pays by one's own self for the universal collective responsibility. Whoever separates himself from the world for the sake of the world, dies for the world; he must exhaust himself and die, just as a seed will not grow if it does not die. . . .[16] Our seven-colored rainbow[17] rises above the luxuriously colored earth, filling us with ecstasy as we receive the sacrificial seal; it

> . . . embraced full half the sky
> And was *exhausted* in the heights.

Ascent is a symbol of the tragic element that appears when one of the participants in the Dionysian chorus is separated from the dithyrambic throng. The impersonal element of the orgiastic dithyramb gives rise to the sublime image of the tragic hero, who is revealed as an individual personality and is condemned to death precisely for being separated and exposed. For the dithyramb was originally a sacrificial service, and he who stepped into the middle of the circle was the sacrificial victim.

In any ascent—*"incipit Tragoedia."*[18] Yet tragedy itself signifies the outer death and inner triumph of human self-affirmation. The idea of tragedy is at once the idea of heroism and the idea of humanity; the word for this double idea is theomachy.

As an essentially tragic principle, ascent is preeminently human. It is animated by a will and thirst for the impossible. The Divine desired the impossible from out of the abundance of its limitlessness. And the impossible came to pass: the Divine forgot itself and was perceived as separate within the world of limits. Who will lead it out from these limits? That age-old Eros of the Impossible, the most divine heritage and seal of the human spirit.

II

But a detached, pure rupture with the verdant dale is not yet beauty. The divine good also descends in joy. When Beauty reaches the thrones beyond the clouds, it turns its countenance back toward earth and smiles at the earth.

> And while, half in sleep,
> Our lower world, shorn of strength,
> Is filled with fragrant luxury,
> It sleeps in the noontime dark:
> Upon high, *above* the *earth,*
> Still deeply cast into sleep
> Like *native gods* the icy peaks *play*
> With the fiery azure of the sky.
> (Tiutchev)[19]

Here the impression of beauty is achieved not only by reconciling but also by opposing the heavenly and the worldly. Beauty is achieved by the smiling joy and community shared by the divided whole. Thus, according to Theognis, when the heaven dwellers descended to the wedding feast of Cadmus and Harmony, the Muses sang that "the beautiful is dear";[20] thus sang the Muses, and in joy did the gods echo their praise for the graces of the beautiful.[21]

"When might becomes merciful and descends to the visible,—Beauty is what I call such a descent," says Zarathustra.[22]

The charm of the beautiful is first drawn to us by the downward turn of the ascending line. It is beautiful when a flower inclines toward the earth like a wreath, and Narcissus is beautiful above his mirror of water. Beauty is the tilt of branches and the inspiration of a summer shower from a sudden cloud. And the shadow of a many-eyed mystery endows the night with beauty.[23]

We are captivated by the sight of ascent being resolved in descent. The firmament kisses and graces us with the universal good news of beauty;[24] the rainbow reconciles and assures us. The dome and arc order our soul. All gazes burn when they turn toward the setting sun: but it is the sunrise itself that mysteriously initiates the ecstasy of the sunset.

Both the triangular pediments, the "eagle" (*aétoma*) of the Greek portico,[25] and Raphael's pyramidal groups are harmonious.[26] Beethoven's astral adagios fall to earth in a solar, sparkling spray, which is resolved in scintillating scherzi.[27] The round dances of Naiads and the rhythms of the Muses have an intoxicating effect due to the flowing vibrations of rise and fall:

> Look how the shining fountain
> Is gathered up like a living cloud;
> Look how its moist smoke flames
> And breaks up in the sun.
> And elevated to the sky like a ray,
> It touches the holy height,
> And is fated to fall back down
> To the earth as fire-hued dust.
> (Tiutchev)[28]

Descent is the symbol of a gift. He who bears the gift of heavenly moisture is beautiful when he descends from the heights: the bearded Dionysus appears in such a guise in some ancient marbles, dressed in a wide *stola* and carrying a shallow cup in his hand;[29] Dionysus is the god of moisture, fertilizing and enlivening the earth with ambrosial intoxication, enrapturing with wine the hearts of people. . . . "And only the gift is dear. It is worth living only for the sake of the gift. . . ."[30]

Laughter, this "joy of overcoming," is either murder or earthly mercy. A smile is inspired mercy. Graceful Beauty wears a smile.

Ascent is rupture and separation; descent is the return and good tidings of victory. The one is "glory in the highest"; the other is "peace on earth."[31] Ascent is a "No" to the Earth; descent is "the meek ray of a mysterious 'Yes.'"[32]

We who are born of the earth are able to perceive Beauty only in the categories of earthly beauty. The Soul of the Earth is our Beauty. Thus there is no beauty for us if we break the commandment: "Remain faithful to the Earth."[33]

8

Our perception of the beautiful is formed when we perceive an in-spired victory over earthly decay together with a new turn toward the bos-om of the Earth. For us these delights are like the Mother's own breathing: sighing out toward Heaven, she once again breathes Heaven itself into her breast. Her sighs are heavy, and her breathing is light. Beauty is light. "The Divine approaches with a light step. . . ."[34]

And the moments when we delight of beauty convince us that

> The wings of the soul rise above the Earth,
> But do not abandon the Earth. . . .
> (Vl. Solovyov)[35]

Thus, each time Beauty descends to the earth with the gifts of Heaven, it signifies the eternal betrothal of the Spirit to the World Soul, appearing before us as an endlessly renewed archetype and promise of universal Transfiguration.

> I wear a ring,
> And my face—
> Is the meek ray of a mysterious "Yes."[36]

There is no doubt that beauty and the good are inwardly identical. Beauty and the good share the same hidden principle: its name is descent. The spirit rises out of the limits of selfhood only to descend into a personal sphere that already lies beyond the narrow self. It is as if the divine sun draws up the moisture of feeling into a cloud, from which it then waters the earth. This ascent and descent is the psychological basis of the good; it is only justice that is directed along the horizontal line, the line of equality, which justice has come to love.

There is no pride in descent, this principle of both beauty and the good. In contrast, ascent, taken as an abstract principle, is somehow haughty and cruel. A kind feeling—even if it be for the strongest and high-est—is still descent. This is why goodness is beautiful even when directed at might, for it is still descent and assumes as a preliminary condition that the weakest be elevated into a sphere above that of might. The allegretto of Beethoven's Seventh Symphony would elicit tears even from the eyes of children. But what is this allegretto? Is it God's tears for the world? Or man's tears for God?

The beauty of Christianity is the beauty of descent. The Christian idea has given man the most beautiful tears: man's tears over God. Beauti-ful are the tears of the myrrh-bearing women. . . .[37]

This ascent and descent is the ladder of Jacob's dream. It is the mu-tual mystery-working of kindred spirits, who move and enliven both the earthly and heavenly spheres, exchanging with each other the pails of the world's moisture. This is what Faust contemplates in the hidden writing of

9

the Macrocosm: "how heavenly powers ascend and descend, extending to each other the golden pails!"

> Wie Himmelskräfte auf und nieder steigen,
> Und sich die goldnen Eimer reichen![38]

III

But descent is not always the grace of peace, the return of grace and a joyful reunion. There is also descent as rupture. There is "rapture on the edge of a gloomy abyss,"[39] which Pushkin knew in moments of transcendent insight:

> A gaze that, sinking, will not return:
> To know the depths
> Of the soul's eddy
> (The soul that stopped, and fell
> To the hanging vine
> That whispers with Horror!)—
> "This is you! . . ."[40]

Who? Dionysus, the god of descent understood as rupture, Dionysus the divine sacrifice, the adolescent who looks into the dark mirror and is dismembered by the Titans that suddenly surround the infant.

> And in the abyss, like Maenads,
> The greedy streams of separation dart . . .
> And my white mountains
> Are like a lunar dream. . . .[41]

Follow the powers that are cast down and seethe in the bottomless depths, into the chasm yawning with the murky eyes of madness! . . .

> Follow! follow! follow!
> (Briusov, "A Vision of Wings")[42]

This is the spellbinding insistence and powerful voice of the abyss.

Such, after the "sublime" as defined above, and after the "beautiful," the principle of which is the grace of descent, is the third, demonic principle of our aesthetic agitation: it is known as the chaotic. Its images are the interrupted spring that winds into the depths; the cascading waterfall; the magic of chasms and dark wells; the monstrous mysteries of underground and underwater depths; the larvae of labyrinthine wanderings; and the lightning masks of tempest-tossed elemental forces.[43] This is not the kingdom of sun-gold and diamond-white elevation into the azure, nor that of pink and emerald returns to the earth. It is rather the dark-purple kingdom of the netherworld.

Any aesthetic experience draws the spirit out of the limits of the personal. The ecstasy of ascent affirms the suprapersonal. Descent, as a principle of artistic inspiration (in Pushkin's sense),[44] turns the spirit toward what lies outside the personal. The chaotic is impersonal, as is revealed in the psychological category of frenzy. It completely abolishes all limits.[45]

This kingdom does not know borders and boundaries. All forms are destroyed, the limits abolished, countenances shift and disappear; there is no personality. Only white foam covers the greedy tumult of the waters.[46]

The deep roots of gender nest within these depths of pregnant night, and here gender is not divided. If ascent is masculine, and descent corresponds to the female principle; if Apollo shines in the former and Aphrodite smiles in the latter; then the chaotic sphere is the realm of the androgynous, masculine-feminine Dionysus. This is where becoming unites both genders with the groping touch of dark conceptions.

This realm is truly a shore "beyond good and evil."[47] It is the demonism of the elements, not the demonism of evil. It is a fruitful womb, and not diabolical ossification. The Devil lights his fires in the icy valleys, and as he ignites them he envies what is consumed by the fire—but he is unable to warm himself by its flame.

The terror of descent into the chaotic summons us with the mightiest of calls, the most imperative insistence: it calls us to lose our very selves.

> We are souls of Chaos. Descend and look
> Into the empty cloud of our nighttime eyes! . . .
> Relinquish to us, O mortal, your earthly breast,
> Relieve and cast off your captivity![48]

And the mightiest of arts, Music, sings to us powerfully with the voices of the depths' nighttime Sirens. It raises us out of its vortex (as "chaos gives birth to a star")[49] with the spiraling line of the sublime and returns us cleansed and invigorated to the earth with the good descent of Beauty. As Antaeus is exhausted by his separation from the earth,[50] so would we be impoverished if we were permanently detached from the "ancient," "native" chaos.[51] Somewhere deep, deep below us, "inseparable springs sing us a song of native sound. . . ."[52]

> Midnight and Day know their hour.
> (Bal'mont)[53]

The rhythm of nature must be the rhythm of our lives. All of our building is only the rebuilding of limits. All limits become false. But there is no limit for the living. "Chaos is free, chaos is true. . . ."[54]

Lift high the fluttering banner! Excelsior![55] The crowd below will cry to you from behind: "Apostate! Traitor! Fugitive!" Your holy path remains behind you after you reveal it in your daring. And the banner is raised. . . .

11

But when fulfillment suddenly flows in with miraculous power,
The heart again betrays happiness, spilling the pure nectar.
The strings of redemption will cry out and fall silent in a live complaint. . . .
Again there is rupture and frenzy, and Bacchus is dismembered! Evoe! . . .[56]

From our earthly perspective descent seems to mean that the private is absorbed by that which is held in common. The first instant of Dionysian cleansing is necessary and holy. It marks unification with the nether god of the depths who says Yes to Nature as it is. It is necessary to accept everything into oneself as it exists in the greater whole, and to encompass the *entire* world in one's heart. The source of all strength and all life lies in this temporary emancipation from the self and this opening of the soul to the living streams that flow from the world's very depths. Man can find his preeternal, true will only after he has surrendered his personal will and lost his self; only then does he become the passive tool of the god that lives within him, his bearer, his thyrsus-bearer, god-bearer. Then, for the first time, he says a true "yes" to his inner god, a suprapersonal "yes" no longer to the world, but to the supraworldly; and it is only then that one wills creatively: for to will creatively is to will will-lessly.

Ancient intuition combined all three principles of the beautiful in the image of Aphrodite, "born from foam."[57] Like a universal flower growing upward to the heavens, the goddess "Aphrogenia" or "Anadyomene" rises from the foaming chaos. Born from the vortex, "Urania" or "Asteria" rises and soon embraces the heavens. And the "golden-throned" one now turns her merciful countenance toward the earth; "smiling," she draws near the mortals with a light step. . . . And on bent knee the enamored world glorifies the divine descent of the "*All-popular*" (*Pándēmos*).

Two Elements in Contemporary Symbolism

I. SYMBOLISM AND RELIGIOUS ART

The symbol is a sign, or signification. That which it denotes or signifies is not any particular idea. One cannot say that the serpent, as a symbol, means only "wisdom," while the cross, as a symbol, means only: "the sacrifice of redemptive suffering." Otherwise, the symbol would be a simple hieroglyph, while the combination of several symbols would be a visual allegory, an encoded message that can be read if one finds the key. If the symbol is a hieroglyph, then it is a mysterious hieroglyph, for it has many denotations, many meanings. In various spheres of consciousness, one and the same symbol may acquire varying significance. Thus, the serpent can simultaneously signify the earth and incarnation, sex and death, vision and knowledge, temptation and sanctification.

Like a ray of sunlight, the symbol cuts through all planes of being and all spheres of consciousness, signifying different essences in each plane, performing a different function in each sphere. Truly, like all that descends from the divine womb, the symbol is also a *seméion antilegómenon*, a "sign which will be spoken against" or "object of dispute," to use Simeon's words about the Infant Jesus.[1] At each of the points at which the symbol intersects the sphere of consciousness like a descending ray, it is a sign, the meaning of which is visually and fully revealed in a corresponding myth. Therefore, the serpent of one myth represents one essence, while in another myth it represents another essence. But the entire symbolics of the serpent, all denotations of the serpentine symbol, are united in the great cosmogonic myth, within which each aspect of the serpent-symbol finds its due place in the hierarchy of the planes of divine all-unity.

Symbolics is a system of symbols; Symbolism is art based on symbols. Symbolism fully asserts its guiding principle when it discloses to consciousness things as symbols and symbols as myths. By revealing symbols (i.e., signs of another reality) in the things of the reality around us, art shows this reality to be significant. In other words, art allows one to become conscious of the connection and meaning of everything that exists not only in the

13

earthly realm of empirical consciousness but also in other realms. Thus, true symbolic art touches upon the domain of religion, insofar as religion first and foremost is the awareness of the connection of everything that exists and the awareness of the meaning of all life. This is why one can speak of Symbolism and religious art as phenomena that are interrelated in some way.

By religious art we mean only one of its aspects, only one of its multiform energies that manifests itself in artistic activity. Art was religious only when and only insofar as it directly served the ends of religion. Craftsmen of such art were, for example, the makers of heathen idols, medieval icon painters, and the anonymous builders of Gothic churches. These artists were possessed by a religious idea. But when Vladimir Solovyov says, regarding artists of the future, that "not only will they be possessed by the religious idea, but they themselves will possess it and consciously guide its earthly incarnations,"[2] he poses these *theurgists* a task even more important than that performed by ancient artists, and he understands artistic religious work in an even more sublime sense.

It is to the artist, the conscious successor of the creative efforts of the World Soul, the theurgist, that the following testament is addressed:

> Heir to the creating Mother, call forth
> The transfiguration of the universe.[3]

But how can man use his own creative work to facilitate universal transfiguration? Should he people the earth with the creations of his own hands? Should he fill the air with his own harmonies? Should he force the rivers to flow in the banks marked out for them, and the branches of the trees to spread according to a predetermined plan? Should he imprint his own ideal on the face of the earth, his plan on the forms of life? Will the theurgical artist be the tyrannical artist of whom Nietzsche dreamed, the artist-enslaver who is to revalue all aesthetic values and smash the old tablets of beauty, following only his own "will to power"? . . . Or will he be the kind of artist that "a bruised reed shall he not break, and smoking flax shall he not quench."[4]

We believe that the theurgical principle in art is the principle of least violence and most receptivity. The supreme testament of the artist is not to impose his own will onto the surface of things; rather, he must intuit and proclaim the hidden will of essences. As a midwife eases the process of labor, so must he make it easier for things to reveal their beauty;[5] he is called to remove with sensitive fingers the film that obscures the birth of the word. He will train his hearing, and then he will hear "what things say"; he will sharpen his vision and will learn to understand the meaning of forms and see the reason of phenomena.[6] His creative touch will become tender and prophetic. Under his fingers the clay will mold itself into the image it had awaited,[7] and words will mold themselves into harmonies that are primor-

14

dially established in the element of the language.[8] Only such an openness of spirit can make the artist the bearer of divine revelation.

This is why we defend realism in art, by which we mean the principle of being faithful to things as they are, both in phenomenon and in essence. In our view, aesthetic idealism is less fruitful, less suited for the purposes of religious creative work. By idealism, we mean the assertion of creative license in combining the elements that are obtained by artistic observation and clairvoyance. Rather than following the rule of being faithful to things, idealism follows the postulates of a personal aesthetic worldview, and it is faithful to beauty as an abstract principle. We are not speaking directly of philosophical realism or philosophical idealism; nor are we discussing whether in the final analysis creations of idealistic art might not correspond to real truth to the same degree as works of realistic art, and if they might, then under what conditions. Choosing a purely descriptive method, we are considering the worldview of the artist that is immanent to creative work. We hope to establish that only the realistic worldview, as the psychological basis of the creative process and as the first impulse to creation, assures the religious value of the artistic work. In order that he might "consciously govern the earthly incarnations of a religious idea," the artist must first of all believe in the reality of that which is to be made incarnate.

II. THE SIGNIFYING AND TRANSFORMATIONAL ELEMENTS OF CREATIVITY

In all artistic epochs, the paths and development of art seem to us to be directed by two inner moments, two tendencies, which are deeply ingrained in its very nature. If we view man's mimetic capacity, his aspiration to imitate what he has observed and experienced, as a certain constant substratum of artistic activity, as its psychological "material basis" (*hulē*, as Aristotle would say), then the dynamic elements of creation, its formational energies, its moving and formative energies would manifest themselves in two equally primordial needs, of which the first we shall call the need to signify things, and the second the need to transform them.

Thus, in our opinion, imitation (*mímēsis*) is an essential ingredient in artistic creation, the main drive that man uses insofar as he becomes an artist in order to satisfy two essentially different needs and demands: to signify things, to reveal them simply in form and sound, or *emmorphosis*, on the one hand; and to effect their transformation, or *metamorphosis*, on the other.

Man yields to the desire for imitation either to evoke in others the closest or most commensurate representation of some thing, or else to create a representation of a thing that is indubitably different than the thing itself, intentionally incommensurate to it, but more pleasing and desirable. From the very beginning, realism and idealism accompany the tasks and

15

aspirations of artistic activity; and however they might become intertwined with each other, whatever reciprocal combinations they might enter into, both are everywhere distinct, as forms of a feminine, receptive type (realism) and of a masculine, initiative type (idealism).

Realism, as the principle of signifying things (*res*), appears in many forms and various images, depending on the degree to which the artist's mimetic power is tense and active in the act of signification. When imitativeness (*mímēsis*) becomes dominant, we speak of naturalism; when imitativeness is at its most relaxed, we have before us a phenomenon of pure symbolics. The combination of a few lines in the picture of a savage or a child is sufficient for the clear signification of a man, a beast, or a plant. The simple naming of things or listing of objects is by itself an element of poetry, from Homer to the inventories of André Gide.[9] But naturalism, hieroglyphic symbolism, and nominalism all belong to the sphere of realism, because the artist, having a thing as his object, is engulfed by the sense of its real being. When he uses his magic to evoke the thing in the imagination of other people, he does not impart anything subjective into his signification.

Since, in regard to his object, he is purely passive, purely receptive, the realistic artist sets himself the task of faithfully accepting the object into his soul and communicating it to the soul of another. By contrast, the idealistic artist either returns things different from how he received them (having reworked them not only in a negative sense, through abstraction, but also in a positive sense, by endowing them with new features suggested by the associations of ideas that arose in the process of creation), or else he provides combinations that are not justified by observation, the offspring of his autarchic, capricious fantasy.

The principle of signification naturally dominates the earliest art; and the ritual-ceremonial, hieratic character of archaic art makes it primarily symbolic, since its object is the things not of earthly but of divine reality. This is symbolic realism, aimed at creating objects that correspond absolutely to divine things and are therefore capable of serving as their fetishes. The idealistic leaven is not yet palpable in the act of artistic creation, or at least it is active only unconsciously. The aspiration to animate symbolics by approximating the observed reality, this more active awakening of the mimetic capability, leads art to a point of equilibrium between signification and transformation, where the artist can already dare to proclaim that his ideal of the divine thing is a perfect likeness of the thing itself.

Thus, Pheidias tempted the Greeks to recognize the Zeus he created as a true icon of Olympian beauty.[10] According to popular opinion, whoever beheld Pheidias's idol could no longer be unhappy in life. In other words, the blessed contemplation of this image granted such sanctification, it bestowed a power of such might and grace, that the viewer became almost equal to those initiates who saw the light of the Eleusinian Mysteries, which freed man from sadness forever.[11] Likewise, many centuries after Pheidias, the Florentine commune was agreed in its belief that the countenance of the Mother of God had been truly revealed to the world by Cimabue.[12] Insofar as these examples hold, art still served the ends of true signification, and the artist was still femininely receptive to the revelation that was made incarnate in the religious consciousness of the nation.

But once an artist steps onto the path of idealism, he must inevitably continue along the sloping plane of personal daring. Sooner or later, he will renounce the principle of symbolic signification for the beauty of his own "*ideal*," which has freely blossomed in his soul. This he will communicate to the crowd as a work of *his own* fantasy, as his own "*creation*," so as to captivate them with the sight of beauty, *only* beauty, which might not even exist in reality either here or on high, but which is thus more dear, like a migrant bird from fairy-tale lands. Sooner or later, the artist will arise and proclaim himself a deceptive Siren, a magician who arbitrarily summons forth deceptions that are dearer than a mass of low truths;[13] sooner or later, he will raise this revolt against truth out of his distrust for the hidden possibilities of achieving it in beauty.

When Plato reproaches art for modeling itself not on the ideas of things but on the things themselves, thereby becoming an organ only of man's mimetic capability,[14] he can be understood in two ways, depending on the degree to which we agree to consider him a realistic or idealistic philosopher. Since Plato's ideas are *res realissimae* (things in truth), he demands that art provide such a close signification of these things that the accidental features of their reflection in the physical world would fall away like scales that obscure true vision (i.e., he demands symbolic realism). However, insofar as Plato's ideas, in the interpretation of later thinkers, turn into "concepts" (*Begriffe*) in the sense of formal logic or epistemology,[15] aesthetics begins to see Plato as a proponent of idealistic art, of a free creativity that has ridden itself of the need to account for the data of both observed and intuited reality, of the duty to be faithful to the things that are known through an experience that is equally external and internal.

III. THE ANCIENT IDEALISTIC CANON AND MEDIEVAL MYSTICAL REALISM

Beginning with the fourth century, ancient art mainly adopted the banner of "free creativity" or idealism. The former canons of religious symbolics were replaced by purely aesthetic canons. Religion dictated the necessity of clothing female figures as a symbol of the blossoming mystery that guards the feminine divine, in contrast to the naked descent of the masculine rays of the heavenly world; but this hieratic dress was now removed from the three sister Graces and Aphrodite. On the other hand, the correlations of the parts of the human body were strictly measured and the proportions thereby established were proclaimed aesthetically obligatory.

The predictable consequences of artistic idealism and the academic canon, which we shall analyze below—the phenomena of aesthetic individualism and experimentalism, of a departure from the natural and an aspiration toward the artificial—soon took their toll in Hellas, which was modernized by the Sophist movement. We know the Decadent Agathon from Aristophanes' parody;[16] we know what the new dithyramb was, this Wagnerian "endless melody" of antiquity;[17] and an enormous amount of material allows us to trace the love for the artificial from Socrates' preference for city strolls over country ones[18] to Trimalchio's Feast and *The Golden Ass*.[19]

Nevertheless, Greco-Roman antiquity did not know individualism in our sense. It only had a foretaste of the goodness of the grains and the poisons of the chaff that could only sprout on a historical soil that had been plowed by Christianity. For Christianity revealed the mystery of the image and affirmed the personality once and for all. Like some fine darkness, the breath of the still-living Pan wafted over classical antiquity;[20] and, in the cosmic languor of this morning mist that was gradually filled with the sun, man did not fully belong to himself; he could not yet see the full depth of his inner contradictions and conflicting emotions; he was still an atom of the universal whole, often in spite of his rebellious consciousness, and thus he was with all the organic mystery of his being, which had not yet fully woken to reality.

The Middle Ages were primarily a period of signifying art. The religious worldview, as all-encompassing and harmonious as a Gothic church, determined the rightful place of each thing, both of earth and of heaven, in the deliberately complex architecture of its hierarchic concord. Cathedrals truly grew as some kind of "forests of symbols."[21] Painting served as a universal book for the cognition of divine things. The hieroglyphic symbol came to the aid of any creative plan that failed to find in the empirical observation of nature the plastic combinations of elements of visual experience needed to signify what cannot be depicted: a scroll with the words of the Annunciation was extended to the Virgin from the Archangel's lips; and the infant, leaping in his mother's womb, was depicted as playing on the violin in Elisabeth's womb.[22] Dante desired to see his *Divine Comedy* interpreted in four senses, which together disclose the single real mystery.[23] And in order that there be nothing arbitrary or subjective in art, a melody that might be taken as an accidental outpouring of individual emotion was confirmed in choral unison, where each participant sang one and the same melody, as if assuring the listener that not a sound had been added or taken away from the true song inspired by the angels.

This is why the art of the Middle Ages so idiosyncratically mixes true naturalism with symbolic and fantastic qualities: the concept of realism unites

18

the fantastic and the naturalistic, if only we dare to give the term "realism" the meaning that rightfully belongs to it (i.e., that of an art that demands from the artist only a correct copy, an exact duplicate, true to the original communication of what he observes, of what he is informed, and of the extent to which he is informed).

Signifying art was to yield its dominance to idealistic art only with the appearance of the individualism and skepticism that heralded the beginning of modern history. The Renaissance had an idealistic understanding of classical antiquity, seeking in it emancipation from medieval barbarism: beautiful Helen, summoned from the palace of the Mothers by Faust's magic key, was a phantom (*eídolon*), a shadow of the ancient Helen, and the whole world that she illuminated became for man a magic haze.[24] And in the center of this enchanted world stood the charmer, the "I," the human personality, which had become conscious of its "I" and its full rights, and also its hopelessness in the sense of its inability to transcend the bounds of the self-determining intellect.[25] Plato's philosophy was understood idealistically; the world was peopled not by real gods but by phantom projections of human capacities into infinity, and divine realities were evicted from the world, and all of this in a soul that loves beauty, that has acknowledged aestheticism as the highest spiritual aspiration. All of this would also make art idealistic, an art that transforms reality in its reflection instead of reflecting reality in its real transformation. In the light of the idealistic freedom of self-determining reason, all that was left to the old realism of religious thought, mystical experience, and symbolic art was more or less, sooner or later, to become a superstition, or else a tradition that had lost its vital meaning and become purely formal.

Representatives of the early Renaissance in art still continued the medieval quest for heavenly beauty, Aphrodite Urania, but earth's historic destiny, its daylight epoch, which hides distant stars from our eyes and sends daring seekers to clearly visible horizons, desired earthly incarnation and called to Urania to descend from heaven and present herself to earth in the beautiful, sensible forms of universal Aphrodite. Beginning with Raphael and Bramante, there is a canonic beauty of incarnation, and it is here that contemporaries first recognized the genuine return of pagan antiquity.[26] Tied by the heritage of the ancient type and rule of beauty, limited by the possibilities of a visible nature that, albeit disguised and creatively transformed, according to Leonardo's principle, by new combinations of the elements of sensible perception,[27] was still essentially the same physical nature, artists easily and quickly developed stable canons for their craft and bequeathed them to culture as the constant and immutable (today we would say: academic) norms of art. Under the name of classicism, these norms were fated to put the stamp of "Parnassus," sacred to all who revere the Muses, on all European art beginning with the sixteenth century. Through all the metamorphoses of the Renaissance, Baroque, Rococo, Empire, and other derivatives, these norms were fated to crystallize within consummate, contained boundaries the soul of the changing epochs of the single culture that flows from antiquity.

IV. REALISM AND IDEALISM IN MUSIC AND DRAMA

Thus, we have ascertained the two principles that direct artistic activity: the principle of signification and that of the transformation of real things. Further, we found that the first of these principles triumphed in the art of the Middle Ages, whereas the latter principle was dominant in the art that began with the blossoming of the Renaissance. In order to extend this characterization to the art that encompasses the last four centuries, we shall use the proposed distinction between the two principles to analyze in a cursory and general way: on the one hand, the paths of modern music, which indicate art's ever-growing tendency toward idealism; on the other hand, the paths of drama, which exhibit elements of maximal resistance to this reigning tendency.

We have defined unison as the means of lending an objective character to melody, of removing from its aesthetic appreciation the impression of an arbitrary musical mood. Polyphony in music corresponds to the moment of equilibrium between the signifying and inventive principles of art, a moment we see in Pheidias's art. Every participant of the polyphonic chorus is individual and, as it were, subjective. But the harmonic restoration of the structure of chords fully confirms the objective purposefulness of the seeming discord. Both the choral or polyphonic, the orchestra and the church organ, formally serve as a defense of musical objectivism and realism against invasion by the forces of subjective lyrical arbitrariness, and to this day their aesthetic enjoyment is closely linked to the way they calm our, one might say, musical conscience by the collective [*sobornyi*] authority of general animation, supported harmoniously by voices or instruments.

The chorus and orchestra, or the organ that replaces the orchestra, are forms of agreement and unanimity about the musical idea, a *consensus omnium de re communi*.[28] But the epoch of subjectivism makes itself known by battling for a musical monologue, and the invention of the clavichord or piano was a purely idealistic substitution, replacing the effect of symphony with that of the individual monologue, which contains within itself and reproduces by its own power the entire polyphonic plenitude of universal harmony. Instead of an aural world, as an expression of the real universal *will*, there is an analogous aural world as *representation*, or the creation of an individual will.[29] It goes without saying that the musical monologue (examples of which in the nineteenth century are by Chopin and Schumann), like the "new dithyramb" in Greece, presently dominates almost the entire realm of

20

music and that, as the musical monologue is emancipated from traditional forms of harmony and thematic finish, idealistic subjectivism in music has reached its extreme limit. In contrast, earlier composers would variously moderate the impression of pure subjectivism, even in the monologue, by strictly adhering to the structural canons of composition and by introducing symbolically marked choral passages into the monologue, such as are abundant in Beethoven's sonatas, for example. One of the most powerful means of creating a polyphonic effect within the monologue itself was the fugue.

We see that music has developed in accordance with the idealistic tendency of the artistic development of the epoch on the whole: individualism and subjectivism are defeating objectivism and realism, understood as the principle of signifying a thing independent of the individual consciousness of the given thing.

Let us take a look at drama, which in modern history has replaced the medieval spectacles of universal and holy events as reflected in miniature and purely signifying forms on the stages of the mystery plays. We know that classical French tragedy is one of the triumphs of the transformational, decorative, idealistic principle. Calderón, however, is different. In him everything is but a signification of the objective truth of divine Providence, which governs human destiny. A pious son of the Spanish church, he was able to combine all the daring of naive individualism with the most profound realism of the mystical contemplation of divine things.[30]

And Shakespeare, of course, is also different. Shakespeare was a visionary of the earthly world and a clairvoyant of the spiritual world; Shakespeare was a realist who hardly even had time to glance at and denote all the mysterious things he saw clearly, but who had neither the opportunity nor the will to express his inner self. Romanticism is inextricably tied to Shakespeare in its ancestry and its development. It is for good reason that we see the Romantics' turn away from the idealistic canon and their love for the Middle Ages. Their turn away from the artificial toward nature, from generalizations toward the particular, from the invention of the abstract type toward the discovery of a concrete type is based deep in the mystery of the equivalence of creative energies. Most significant in their creations was the combination of fantastic and trivial elements; their constant fragmentariness and unevenness; their play at contradiction and eccentricity; and their profound sense of humor, which derives from the contrast of two *res:* that which is embodied in worldly reality and that which is sought outside of this reality—a sense of humor that is so alien to the classical beauty that in Baudelaire's poem says: "Look, I do not laugh, I never cry."[31] Romanticism is one of the many different types of realism. The Romantic is the one who has set off to seek the "blue flower," understood as *res intima rerum,* the inner reality of things.[32] Thus, the literary genre of "novel" [*roman*], in which realism is triumphant, also shares a name with Romanticism: the

21

Romantics Balzac and Hoffmann were realists, while the realists Dickens and Dostoevsky were Romantics.

Such are the two balancing and competing principles of artistic activity in their own nature and in the history of the art that precedes our own: on the one hand, the principle of signifying, discovering, and transfiguring a thing; and, on the other hand, the constructive principle of invention and transformation. The former affirms the thing as possessing being, whereas the latter affirms the thing as worthy of being. The former aspires to objective truth, the latter to subjective freedom. The former is self-subordination, the latter self-determination. The former is realism not only as an aesthetic norm but also as the epistemological basis for a worldview (in the philosophical sense this appears now as naive realism, now as mystical realism). The latter is idealism, not only as a cult of ideal form but also as the philosophical conviction that autonomous reason has a normative function. The former attempts to grasp the phenomenon as symbol; the latter creates symbols that generalize phenomena. The former plants in the aesthetically receptive soul an embryo of new intuitions, new movement, new life, introducing a certain dynamic principle; the latter fills the soul with a consummate image, it inspires an Olympian dream, it is the words of Jehovah after a day of Creation: "it is good," the tranquillity of the static, and the rest of the seventh day.[33]

What follows is intended to reveal the presence of both types of creativity in the so-called Symbolism of today. We believe that our understanding of contemporary Symbolism depends directly on the degree to which our eye is accustomed to distinguishing two essentially distinct, heterogeneous phenomena in this complex cultural-historical entity. Two infants lay in the cradle of contemporary Symbolism, just as two twins, the future founders of the city, slept long ago in the cradle abandoned among the reeds of the flooding Tiber: willful Remus, who subsequently leapt across the holy furrow that his brother had dug around the Palatine, the *moenia Romae*;[34] and Romulus, who was called to further and more profound historical deeds by his very virtue of self-limitation and renunciation of the *ego* for the sake of the *res*.[35]

V. REALISTIC SYMBOLISM

Baudelaire's poem "Correspondances" has been acknowledged by the pioneers of modern Symbolism to be the fundamental doctrine and, as it were, profession of faith of the new poetic school. Baudelaire says:

> Nature is a temple. Out of its living columns are sometimes torn vague words. In this temple man passes through a forest of symbols; they accompany him with kindred, knowing gazes.

Like long echoes, which mix in the distance and merge there into a gloomy, deep unity, as vast as night and light; like long echoes fragrances, colors, and sounds respond to each other.[36]

Thus, the poet discloses the real mystery of nature, which is wholly alive and wholly based on hidden correspondences, relations, and echoes of what seems to our moribund ignorance to be divided and in conflict, which seems to be both arbitrarily near and lifelessly mute. A multivoiced eternal word sounds forth in nature for those who are able to hear it.

The proclamation of objective truth as such must be acknowledged as realism. And since the poem also describes the real essence of nature as symbol with other new symbols (the temple, columns, the word, the gaze, and so on), we must ascribe it to the type of Realistic Symbolism. Thus, we find in the very cradle of contemporary Symbolism a pure example of signifying creativity, taking this term as defined above.

The roots of this type will become obvious from the comparison of this sonnet with several passages from Balzac's mystical-Romantic stories "Lambert" and "Seraphita." In the story "Louis Lambert" we read:

> Everything that belongs to the realm of sight on account of being endowed with form may be reduced to a few original bodies, the principles of which exist in air or light, or in the principles of air and light. Sound is a transmutation of air; all colors are transmutations of light; every fragrance is a combination of air and light. Thus, the four manifestations of matter to man's senses—sound, color, smell, and form—have a single origin. . . . Thought, which is akin to light, is expressed by a word that is sound.[37]

In another place in the same novella, Balzac says:

> Perhaps fragrances are ideas. Nothing is impossible in the marvelous transmutations of human substance.[38]

And in "Seraphita" we find the following comparison:

> They discovered the principle of melody as they heard the hymns of heaven which evoked the sensations of color, fragrance, and thoughts, and which reminded them of the innumerable details of all creations, just as an earthly song can resurrect the smallest memories of love.[39]

In another context, Balzac speaks of this subject in the following way:

> It occurred to me that the colors and foliage of trees contain within themselves a harmony that is revealed to our consciousness, enchanting our eye, just as musical phrases evoke thousands of recollections in the hearts of those who love and are loved.[40]

> I know where the singing flower grows, where shines the light that speaks, where fragrant colors sparkle and live.[41]

In the story "Seraphita," we encounter the very name "Correspondances" as a term that signifies the interaction of higher and lower worlds in the sense of Jakob Boehme and Swedenborg.[42]

These are the sources of the poem, which has served as a symbol of faith for the new poetical school: a mystical study of the hidden truth of things, a revelation about things more prescient than the things themselves (*res realiores*),[43] concerning being as perceived by mystical cognition, more essential than essentiality itself. And these revelations were taken by the Symbolist and Decadent Baudelaire from the creations of the realist and Romantic Balzac.

But if this example makes obvious the connection that links the type of contemporary Symbolism that we have termed realistic with both the literary movement of realism as well as with the school of Romanticism (which, in the person of such Romantics as Novalis, abounds in analogies of mystical symbolics), then, on the other hand, it nourishes these roots in the art of Goethe. The meaning of the symbol for the ends of art was a question that intensely occupied Schiller at the time he was assimilating Kant's philosophy;[44] and although Schiller himself remained primarily an idealist, Goethe, whom he informed of all the conclusions of his Kantianism, used the concept of the symbol in his own, Goethean, objective-epistemological, and at the same time mystical sense, mightily enriching all of his own creative work with it. Goethe[45] says that he has been given "the veil of Poetry from the hands of Truth" (der Dichtung Schleier aus der Hand der Wahrheit),[46] as if repeating a verse by the old, vatic poet from the age of signification, Dante:[47] "mirate la dottrina che s'asconde sotto 'l velame dei versi strani" (wonder at the teaching that is hidden beneath the veil of strange verses).[48] And a contemporary poet of the Realistic-Symbolist type hears something congenial in the testaments Goethe bestows on the artist in his *Wilhelm Meisters Wanderjahre:*

> Just as nature in its variety reveals the one God, so in the expanses of art there breathes creatively a single spirit, a single meaning of the eternal type. This is the sensation of truth, which arrays itself only in beauty and boldly rushes toward the ultimate clarity of the brightest day.[49]

And further:

> Let the artist always see before him the joyful rose of life, abundantly surrounded by its sisters, encircled by the fruits of Autumn, in order that it arouse with its open mystery the sensation of its inner life.[50]

Only the Realistic Symbolist poses himself the task of evoking an unmediated comprehension of the inner life of what truly is, removing the coverings by depicting the open sacrament of this life. He sees the deepest, true reality of things, *realia in rebus,* and does not refuse phenomenal being a relative reality, insofar as it contains the more real reality that is hidden within it and signified by it. "Alles Vergängliche ist nur ein Gleichnis"— "All that is transient is only a symbol."[51] Goethe approaches idealistic art by making the only fully legitimate and, for realism, equally acceptable and holy demand (let us recall that Plato's ideas are *res*), the insistent demand that the general type be revealed and affirmed in the transient and unstable variety of appearances: "in the expanses of art there breathes creatively a single spirit, a single meaning of the eternal type."

VI. IDEALISTIC SYMBOLISM

But, apart from elements of Realistic Symbolism, modern poetry has from the very beginning also exhibited marked features of Idealistic Symbolism, which is essentially heterogeneous to the former. Baudelaire's poem "Correspondances" continues thus:

> There are fresh smells like a child's body, sweet like an oboe, green like meadows; and there are other, corrupt, luxurious, and victoriously triumphant, which spread around the charm of immortal things; such are amber, musk, benzoin, and incense; they sing the delights of the spirit and the ecstasy of feelings.[52]

Does not the poet here abandon his main idea about nature's harmonious correspondence as the mystical principle of its hidden life and the open mystery of its phenomenal incarnation?[53] Does he not dwell on examples and details, desiring no more than to tempt us to sense in our memory a series of fragrances and combine them with a series of visual or aural perceptions through some insistent associations? Experiencing this parallelism of sensual impressions will we not achieve only the enrichment of our perceiving "I"? We gain no insight into the meaning of this parallelism as it regards the riddle of nature's inner life. But we have become more sensitive, more refined; we have made an experiment and are encouraged to experiment further, most of all in the realm of the artificial. Even the very concept of psychological experimentation is by definition a concept of artificial experience. The mystery of the thing, the *res*, is almost forgotten; albeit the festive luxury of our "I," which is cognizant and tastes of all things, is royally multiplied. Solomon ordered that the temple be built, and gave himself over to pleasure; he sang his beloved, his own sister, a song of songs, and drowned in the bliss of his harem.[54]

Here, we glimpse Baudelaire's second face, that of a Parnassian. Baudelaire's Parnassianism had its greatest impact on the entire technical and formal side of his poetry. His canonically correct and strict verse of a wonderful mint, his measured, confident stanzas, his love for metaphor, which often remains only a rhetorical metaphor without being transubstantiated into symbol, his terseness,[55] his conservatism with respect to techniques of external poetic and musical depiction, the dominance of the plastic over the musical in a line that feels as if it had been produced in Benvenuto Cellini's workshop, all of this is the heritage of Parnassian aesthetics. To this, Verlaine opposes his testament of faithfulness to the spirit of music and song:[56]

> De la musique avant toute chose;
> Et pour cela préfère l'impair,
> Plus vague et plus soluble dans l'air,
> Sans rien en lui qui pèse ou qui pose.[57]

Baudelaire would not have been able to "wring the neck of eloquence," according to Verlaine's testament ("prends l'éloquence et tords-lui son cou"),[58] or even theoretically to desire to achieve a verse that would create an undefined impression and that would "dissolve in the air"; Baudelaire wished his verse to have the weight of metal and the pose of a statue. His beauty is the marble idol of the famous and purely Parnassian poem "La Beauté."[59]

The traditions of Parnassus begat modern Symbolism's preference for the artificial over the natural. The search for the rare and exotic also derives from Parnassian traditions.[60] All that Decadence affirmed radically and took to its end, to the extreme, it inherited from Parnassus in a moderate, reasonable dosage, or in embryonic form. Decadence as such is only an imaginary revolt against the canons of idealistic, classical art. However, it is itself profoundly idealistic and even canonic; at least it immediately undertook to develop formulas and charters of art, respecting poetic mastery (*la maîtrise, die Mache*) above all else.

What did Decadence assimilate from the element of symbolic art? It immediately strove for symbols and discovered that the aforementioned realistic symbolics already existed; it brushed up against realistic symbolics and passed it by, developing another form of subjective, idealistic symbolics. Here is an example. The pouring of golden sand is an image not alien to religious symbolics: it concerns supreme states of mystical contemplation. How then does Viélé-Griffin utilize it?[61] For the glorification of a chimera, for the apotheosis of illusion. A handful of sand is sufficient for the poet to imagine himself the owner of piles of gold. He is capable of turning the gloomiest days of the most inconsequential existence into "spiritual eternity" (*éternité spirituelle*).

Thus, on the one hand, we see the canon of the Renaissance and classicism, the new Parnassus, the classical ancient heritage and the profound, but smug, consciousness of the decline and increasing decrepitude of the noble genealogy of this heritage, the purely Latin self-determination of modern art as the art of late scions and royal epigones, and the purely Alexandrian concept of the beauty of fading, of the luxurious and refined delight of flowering corruption. On the other hand, we see the springs of medieval mysticism, now concealed underground, and an attentiveness to their deep roar, the presentiment of a new revelation of the open mystery concerning the inner life of the world and its meaning, realism, Romanticism, and the Pre-Raphaelite Brotherhood.[62] Both of these currents have flowed into the veins of modern Symbolism and have made it a hybrid, two-faced phenomenon, an as yet undifferentiated unity, leaving it for the destinies of its further evolution to discover a discrete expression for each of the two principles, which although merged externally, are locked in internal conflict.

VII. THE CRITERIA FOR DISTINGUISHING THE TWO ELEMENTS

The distinguishing criterion is given in the very concept of the symbol. The concept of the symbol is understood completely differently depending on which of the two elements is dominant in a unified Symbolist movement. For Realistic Symbolism, the symbol is the goal of artistic revelation: each thing, insofar as it is inner reality, is already a symbol; the more directly and closely the thing participates in absolute reality, the more profound, the less analyzable it is in its final content. For Idealistic Symbolism, the symbol, since it is only a means of artistic depiction, is no more than a signal that is supposed to establish the interaction of separate individual consciousnesses. In Realistic Symbolism, the symbol is, of course, also the principle that connects separate consciousnesses, but their union in *sobornost'* is achieved by their common mystical vision of an objective essence, a vision that is the same for everyone. In idealistic realism, the symbol is an arbitrary sign exchanged by conspirators of individualism, a secret sign that expresses the solidarity of their personal self-consciousness and their subjective self-determination.

For Idealistic Symbolism, symbols are a poetic means by which people mutually infect each other with a single subjective experience. The former means of verbal communication were incapable of articulating the results of the accumulated psychological wealth, the previously unknown feelings, and the emotional stirrings, incomprehensible to earlier generations, which were suffered by the "last people," as the Decadents so misguidedly loved to call themselves. Therefore, it was still necessary to find for this subjective content associative and apperceptive equivalents that would be able to evoke in the perceiver, through something like a reverse chain of association and apperception, analogous emotional states. Combinations of visual, aural, and other sensible images were supposed to affect the listener's soul in such a way that there would sound in it a chord of sensations corresponding to the chord that inspired the artist. This method is Impressionism. Idealistic Symbolism uses impressionability. On the contrary, Realistic Symbolism, in its final content, presupposes a clairvoyant vision of things in the poet and postulates the very same clairvoyance in the listener. Its method is not Impressionism but pure symbolics or, if you prefer, hieroglyphics. It says: "The world of spirits is not closed; your feelings are closed, your heart is dead."[63]

The pathos of Idealistic Symbolism is illusionism. The phenomenal is all the illusion of Maya; beneath the veil of the shrouded Isis, perhaps, there is not even a statue but only emptiness, *le Grand Néant* of the French Decadents.[64] "Let us analyze the wonderful patterns of the veil; after all we did not catch the most captivating lines, the most magical combinations. Know, initiate, that we ourselves weave this veil. Thus, be attentive to the new, sweet deceptions of the hierophant of the Sirens. The name of poetry is Chimera." Thus speaks Idealistic Symbolism. It speaks to modernity, which is glad to listen to it; for modernity is concerned with two things only: materialistic sociology and nihilistic psychology.[65] Modernity only objects that Decadence is indifferent to social questions. On the other hand, this psychology triumphs in the cenacles of the Decadents.[66] Psychiatrists correct us: "no, it is psychopathy." For our purposes, this is the same thing. What is important in regard to our discussion is that Idealistic Symbolism has dedicated itself to the study and depiction of subjective emotional experiences without worrying about what lies in the objective sphere that transcends our individual experience. Idealistic Symbolism aims to preserve its own soul, i.e., its refinement and enrichment for its own sake. The spirit of Dionysus—which demands the squandering of the soul as such, the loss of the subject in the great subject and its restoration through the perception of the latter as a real object—does not breathe in Idealistic Symbolism.

Idealistic Symbolism is a musical monologue. In contrast, Realistic Symbolism, in its ultimate essence, is a chorus and a round dance. The pathos of Realistic Symbolism stretches from Augustine's *transcende te ipsum* to the motto: *a realibus ad realiora.*[67] Its alchemical enigma, its theurgical attempt at religious art, is the affirmation, cognition, and revelation in reality of another, more real reality. This is the pathos of mystical aspiration toward the *Ens realissimum,* the Eros for the divine. Idealistic Symbolism is the intimate art of the refined; Realistic Symbolism is the reclusive art of a visionary seeing of the world and a religious act for the world.[68]

Idealistic Symbolism is a step on the path toward the great universal idealism that Dostoevsky prophesies in the epilogue to *Crime and Punishment,* when he says that there will be a time when people stop understanding each other due to the negation of generally obligatory real norms of concord in thought and feeling, and, therefore, due to the extraordinarily developed inner life of each personality as it travels the paths of isolated, solitary individualism. The individualism, we might add, that is proclaimed by Idealistic Symbolism is not even individualism of character, such as we find in the practical rather than theoretical individualists of times past, in the Borgias and Napoleons. It is rather the individualism of psychology, the cult of the transient, because peripheral experience of our impressionability, this clearest expression of the modern *mania psychologica,* which has truly eclipsed for us the concept of character and has turned the life of personality into a sheer flow of conflicting feelings and into a stream of changing affects. Formally and most immediately, Idealistic Symbolism will canonically broaden the old canons or will commonsensically cast aside the elements that resist strict aesthetic canonization and will create a new Parnassus.

Realistic Symbolism will reveal the myth within the symbol. Myth can only grow from out of the symbol, understood as reality, like an ear of wheat from a seed.[69] For myth is the objective truth concerning what is. Myth is the purest form of poetry that signifies. Thus, Plato claims that in the harmony of the anti-individualist world he desires, the task of the poet, "if he wants to be a poet, is to create myths."[70] Is myth still possible? Where is the creative religious soil on which it might blossom? But why do we not ask more immediately: is Realistic Symbolism possible? Where is the faith in *realiora in rebus?* We believe that Realistic Symbolism does exist. If Realistic Symbolism is possible, then myth is also possible.

VIII. REALISTIC SYMBOLISM AND MYTHOPOESIS

We have established that Idealistic Symbolism has its origin in the ancient aesthetic canon through the mediacy of Parnassus, while Realistic Symbolism has its origin in the mystical realism of the Middle Ages through the mediacy of Romanticism and with the participation of Goethe's symbolism. We have defined the principle of Idealistic Symbolism as psychological and subjective, the principle of Realistic Symbolism as objective and mystical. For the former type, the symbol is a means; for the latter, it is an end. Mythopoesis allows us to reach the desired end of achieving the most symbolic revelation of reality. Realistic Symbolism goes by way of the symbol toward myth; the myth is already contained within the symbol and is immanent to it; contemplation of the symbol reveals the myth within the symbol.

Mythopoesis grows out of the soil of Realistic Symbolism. Idealistic Symbolism is able to give forth new copies of ancient myths; it can adorn and modernize them; it can breathe into them new philosophical and psychological content. But though it can galvanize an ancient myth in such a fashion or, if you wish, raise it to a "pearl of creation," it, in the first place, will not create a new myth, and, in the second place, it robs the old myth of life, leaving us with a moribund form or phantom reflection. For myth is a reflection of realities and any new interpretation of a genuine myth is its distortion. A new myth, on the other hand, is a new revelation of those very realities. Just as an apprehension of absolute truth that someone attains in secret cannot avoid becoming universal as soon as it is announced even to a few, so must a commensurate signification of the truth concerning things that has been revealed to a percipient spirit be universally accepted as something important, true, and necessary, becoming a true myth in the sense of a generally accepted form of aesthetic and mythical perception of this new truth.

When we approach what serves as a surrogate for myth in the art of the idealistic type, we study the soul of the artist, his subjective world. Insofar as this world is analogous to our own, we can appreciate the work as answering the inner needs of our time and uttering for us what had been on the tips of our tongues. By contrast, in true myth we see neither the personality of its creator nor our own; rather we believe directly in the truth of the new intuition. A work of Idealistic Symbolism, even when maximally universal, is only an invention that sums up the efforts of our search. Myth that has grown out of the symbol (understood as the signification of a reality that, although hidden, is recognized as truly being) is a discovery that puts an end to the search itself until that same knowledge is made more profound by further insight into a meaning that lies even deeper within it.

For in those distant ages when myths were truly created, they answered the needs of inquisitive reason by signifying *realia in rebus.*[71] In ancient times man called the sun the Titan Hyperion or radiant Helios, not to adorn the concept of the sun or to color its perception in a certain way, but rather to signify it more accurately and truly than if it had been depicted as a bright disk that did not resemble man. By representing the sun as an indefatigable Titan or a young god with a cup in his hands, ancient man asserted that it was something more real than a visible disk. Subsequently, another mythopoet came along and, disagreeing with his predecessor, argued that the sun was not Helios and Hyperion together but only Helios, while Hyperion was his father. Then new mythopoets appeared, saying that Helios was Phoebus. Finally, still later, the Orphics and mystics came and declared that Helios was that very Dionysus who had hitherto been known only as Niktelios, the night sun. These researchers of the hidden essence of a single *res* quarreled over all this, each seeking to say about this same *res* something more profound and real than his predecessor, each ascending in this fashion from less to more substantial knowledge of the divine thing. The essence of mythopoesis is most typically revealed in those instants of hesitation when man awaits the blossom of a myth that will be not invention but discovery. He does not know what precisely the hidden essence of religious magnitude will be—though its existence is established, it has not yet been revealed to mystical consciousness or has been lost and forgotten by it. Hence the inscription "to the unknown god" on the Athenian altar; hence the dedication "to god or goddess" on the Palatine altar.[72]

From this it follows that myth is created by the clairvoyance of faith and is a prophetic dream, a nonarbitrary vision, an "astral" (as the ancient seers of being said) hieroglyph of the final truth of that which is in truth. Myth is a recollection of a mystical event, of a cosmic sacrament. Truly heaven descended to earth, loving it and fructifying it, as Aeschylus relates when he speaks of the shower of Uranus that poured onto supine Gaea.[73]

In Sergei Gorodetsky's *Iar'*, there are certain poems—not the best— in which the young poet, anticipating the mystery of myth, perspicaciously sketches its origin ("The Great Mother"):

> You came as a golden empress,
> And turned your face toward heaven,
> Blushing at Dionysus's mysteries.
> And the ears of the wheat for our daily bread
> Lifted up their rosy faces,
> In order that their grains might ripen with you.
> You will leave, golden empress,
> Vespertine shadows will spill forth;
> But the rye, communicant of secret visions,
> Will be true to the scarlet instant,
> And an old woman, breaking the loaf,
> Will tell the tale of the Firebird's feathers.[74]

A real mystical event, in this case the marriage of Demeter and Dionysus, has occurred on a higher plane of being. It is preserved in the memory of the ears of wheat because the soul of the things of the physical world (in the verses cited above, the soul of the rye) is truly a communicant of the secret visions and deeds of the divine plane. And the man who communes of the bread becomes in turn a communicant of those same primordial mysteries that he recalls with the vague and merely signifying memory of otherworldly events: this vagueness of recollection is the most profound essence of myth. Clear insight into the mystery of the marriage between the Logos and the Soul of the Earth cannot occur in popular myth; and the old woman, breaking the bread, will only tell a "tale" of the Firebird's feathers that is distant and unfaithful, despite all of its signifying truth.

Thus does the poet believe, thus does he know with his intuitive cognition. Mythopoesis is the creation of faith. The task of mythopoesis is truly the "evidence of things unseen."[75] And Realistic Symbolism is a revelation of what the artist sees as reality in the crystal of lower reality. It is just such a visionary seeing that we find in Tiutchev, whom we recognize as the greatest representative of Realistic Symbolism in Russian literature.

Everything that Tiutchev says he announces as a hierophant of hidden reality. The yearning of the night wind and the languor of waking chaos, the deaf-mute language of dim lightning bursts and the voices of the currents playing in the moonlight; the mysteries of daytime consciousness and the consciousness of sleep; the bodiless world at night, swarming audibly but invisibly, and the living chariot of the cosmos sailing freely into the heavens' temple; the ubiquity of living soul and living music in a nature that is ready to respond to the kindred voice of man; the Heavenly King on the cross-roads of the native land, who walked all through it in a slave's visage under the burden of the cross:[76] for Tiutchev all of these are proclamations of objective truths; all of this is already myth. Characteristic for Tiutchev, precisely as a representative of Realistic Symbolism, is the light tinge of poetic wonder, kindred to the "philosophical surprise" of the ancients,[77] this shade of wonder that is, as it were, experienced by the poet when he turns his gaze to the simple things of the reality that surrounds him and that, of course, is communicated to the reader together with a vague consciousness of some new riddle or the presentiment of some new comprehension (cf., for example, the poem "On a quiet night, in late summer, how the stars in heaven glow . . .").[78] Pushkin rarely dwells on this initial moment of perception, where what is perceived excessively dominates the perceiver: he instantly overcomes this opposition and, in the act of depiction, enters into full harmony with what he depicts—he is a true "classic."

For Vladimir Solovyov, the objects of his poetic inspiration were inner events of his personal life, understood on the astral plane (to use the language of astrologists and alchemists). He only portrayed what had occurred, as a real myth of his personality: such, for example, is his long poem "Three Meetings" and the many lyrical poems devoted to communion with the departed.[79] Vladimir Solovyov posits the theurgical task as the highest task of art. By the theurgical task of the artist, he means a world-transfiguring revelation of supernatural reality and the emancipation of true beauty out from beneath the coarse coverings of matter.[80] Solovyov spoke in this sense in his speeches on Dostoevsky: "artists and poets must once again become high priests and prophets, but now in another, even more important and sublime sense: not only will they be possessed by the religious idea but they themselves will possess it and consciously govern its earthly incarnations."

Hence follows the first condition of the mythopoesis we have in mind: the emotional labor of the artist himself. He must not create outside of his connection to divine all-unity; he must train himself to realize this connection in his art. And myth, before being experienced by all, must become an event of inner experience, personal in its arena, suprapersonal in its content.

Attempts to approach myth in contemporary poetry are, of course, far from the theurgical goal that we have defined as mythopoesis. For us these attempts are significant as symptoms of a turn, or rather solstice, of the modern soul toward another worldview, at once realistic and psychic. It is not the folkloric themes that we find valuable but the return of the soul and its new, albeit timid and accidental, brush with "the dark roots of being."[81] It is not the religious mood of our lyre nor its metaphysical aspiration that is fruitful but the first, still obscure and deaf-mute realization of the suprapersonal and suprasensible connection of what is, a realization that has shone in moments when dislocated consciousness falls into utter despair, when the beautiful kaleidoscope of life begins to be horribly distorted, becoming a diabolical masquerade, and when the whimsical dream has begun to turn into a stifling nightmare.

IX. MYTH, CHORUS, AND THEURGY

The question of the chorus is inextricably linked to the question of myth and to the affirmation of the principles of Realistic Symbolism. The chorus is in and of itself already a symbol, a sensible signification of the concord and unanimity of *sobornost'*, the visible evidence of a real connection that brings isolated consciousnesses together into a living unity.[82] The chorus cannot arise without a *res*, a universally significant reality outside of the individual and above the individual. Around the altar, whether visible or invisible, the choral procession takes place. Therefore, one can say that the chorus sings myth, whereas myth is created by the gods. The chorus is desirable insofar as religious consciousness or the cognition of absolute reality is desirable. If there is this cognition, this reality, then the chorus necessarily, inevitably will be. If this cognition, this reality has been lost, then there will be no chorus.

Ancient tragedy was the triumph of myth. The weakening of the signifying, realistic principle in art and the rise of idealistic art coincided with the fall of religion and the fall of the chorus in antiquity. We have on more than one occasion raised the question of the chorus in regard to the fate of drama.[83] The chorus is a postulate of our aesthetic and religious *credo*, but we are far from intending or desiring that it be re-created artificially. We do not want to purchase it at a discount, as a purely aesthetic phenomenon. We will not ask ourselves whether the chorus is possible at the present time: we would thus be asking whether religious reality still exists in contemporary consciousness.

In our view, the search for a new theater and the dissatisfaction with the existing one indicate the instinctive efforts of religious intuition. Through theater we would like to approach supreme, absolute reality: hence our exhaustion with illusionism. All contemporary theater rests on illusion: not only an outer but also an inner illusion. An actor, author, or director is triumphant when he successfully creates out of such an illusion by hypnotizing the viewers into identifying with the hero of the drama; the viewers must experience a part of the hero's life; they must themselves become the hero for an evening. It was not this way in choral drama: the viewers participated in the rite by identifying not with the hero-protagonist but with the chorus, from which the hero emerged. The viewers were perhaps participants in the hero's tragic guilt, but they also restrained him from it, opposing their voice to the hero's daring in the collective [*sobornyi*] court of the chorus; they did not offer sacrifice, and least of all did they experience the illusion of temporary sacrifice and harmless, hour-long heroism. Rather, they partook of the sacrifice, in the round dance of celebrants of the sacrifice, and they returned from the realm of Dionysus truly cleansed, having experienced a liturgical event of inner experience.

Today it is not so. At a concert (as the justly irate Andrei Bely has noted, supposedly of music),[84] we experience all the potential of our heroism between two intermissions and just manage to obtain faith in it and in ourselves, and then return self-satisfied to the utterly unheroic everyday world; the exact same thing, we might add, occurs with us at the theater. But, of course, we cannot blame the Dionysus of music and stage for our discord or dishonesty; we can blame only our spirit of idealistic aestheticism. However that may be, as long as we remain this way, we can speak of chorus and myth only theoretically, as it were, as if we had no presentiment that some great change is at hand and at the doors.[85] But, perhaps as a result of this very presentiment, we personally do not agree with those who hold that we should just wait (at least in the realm of drama) for other people to come, fresher and more honest, who will bring their own myth if they need it, and their own chorus. We contend that, when the guest comes, artists will answer for not having filled their lamps with oil.[86] For the myth of which we speak is not an artificial creation of nonspontaneous creativity, as is usually and complacently thought.

On the contrary, the time is coming when science will have to recall certain truths that have been clearly understood by researchers of myth and symbol—for instance, in the time of Creuzer.[87] Antiquity on the whole is incomprehensible unless one takes account of the great, international, and most ancient (in root and rudiment) organization of mystical unions, guardians of inherited knowledge, and mysteries through which man was reborn. It is not only in the famous mysteries, such as the Eleusinian or Samothracian, that we encounter traces of this organization but also in most of the priestly communities that arose in the shadow of the glorious temples. Disciples of philosophers joined together into societies similar to the cultic *thiases*;[88] discipleship was already esotericism, whether one speaks of Egypt or India, of the ancient Pythagoreans or Neoplatonists, or, finally, of the Essenes and the apostolic community.[89] These theurgists and, as the Hellenes often said, "theologians" were the organizers of religions from time immemorial. If we are unable to follow Creuzer in ignoring the influence of popular poetic and religious creativity on the origin of myths, we will nonetheless be forced to admit sooner or later that a quantitatively significant share of myths—and perhaps as concerns religious content the most important part—was refracted through the theurgical medium, and the theurgists grafted the remaining part onto the young shoots of popular belief and ritual.

In esoteric communities, for example in Eleusis, myths were created that were alien to popular myths, just as they were created in Plato's academy and in Platonic schools; myths were also created in temples. And insofar as they became the property of the uninitiated and were revealed to the crowd, they were not called myths but rather holy tales (*hieroi logoi*), and it was only on the lips of the crowd, with its elaborations or distortions, in its universal visage, that they became myths in the full sense of the term. For a myth in the full sense is absolutely universal. In some cases (as in the myth of Zagreus), it is possible to trace how the holy tale, related after long having been kept secret from the people, little by little occupied in the general religious-mythological worldview a place equal to that of primordial myths, despite the very contradictions and innovations entailed in disclosing an unheard-of secret concerning eternal gods.

These historical analyses are intended to limit the absolute character of the usual view of mythopoesis as a spontaneous act of popular creativity. If it is possible to speak, like Vladimir Solovyov, of the poets and artists of the future as theurgists, it is also possible to speak of the mythopoesis that will issue from them or through them. According to Vladimir Solovyov, it is therefore necessary that the religious idea first of all possess them as it once possessed the ancient teachers of divine rhythm and harmony; and then it is necessary that "they themselves possess it and consciously govern its earthly incarnations."

Contemporary art intersects with the religious problem through Realistic Symbolism and the mythopoesis that is organically linked to it. At first glance, the religious problem appears to be twofold: the preservation of religion on the one hand, and the possibility of religious creativity on the other. In reality there is only one problem. Without inner creativity the life of religion cannot be preserved, for it would be dead already. On the other hand, religious creativity is by its very nature the preservation of religion, unless it degenerates into the creation of surrogates and likenesses of religion, into the imitation of its forms so as to clothe a nonreligious idea in them. Religion is the connection and knowledge of realities. Art, drawn into the religious sphere through the magic of the symbol, will inevitably fall prey to the temptation of clothing an irreligious essence in hieratic forms, unless it holds to the motto of Realistic Symbolism and myth: *a realibus ad realiora.*

The Testaments of Symbolism

A thought expressed is a falsehood.[1] When Tiutchev made this paradoxical acknowledgment, exposing the symbolic nature of his own verse, he also unintentionally uncovered the very root of the new Symbolism: the conflict between the necessity and the impossibility of expressing oneself, a conflict that is painfully experienced by the modern soul.

Thus, Tiutchev's own poetry does not so much *communicate* directly to his listeners his inner world of "mysteriously magic thoughts," as it brings them to *participate* through signification in its own fundamental mysteries. The will to discover and disclose leads to a violation of the law of "concealed" speech. The vengeance exacted for this violation is the distortion of what is revealed, the disappearance of what is disclosed, the falsehood of the "expressed thought . . ."

> Stirring them up, you disturb the springs:
> Feed on them, and be silent.[2]

Yet, instead of selfish jealousy, dreamy pride, or distrust, these lines express a realization of a universal truth, namely the discrepancy that has arisen between the spiritual growth of the personality and the external means of communication: the word is no longer equal in strength to the content of inner experience. Any attempt to "express" it kills it, and the listener receives into his soul not life, but the dead veils of a life that has departed.

Since it is impossible to illustrate this discrepancy with purely psychological examples, let us analyze an abstract concept—for example, the concept of "being," as both expression and expressed. Regardless of the epistemological view of "being" as a cognitive form, one must acknowledge that it refers to a variety of inner experiences. Being is represented to consciousness in ways that can vary greatly, so that anyone who believes he has been granted a partial revelation of the "mystical" meaning of being will sense that there is an "expressed falsehood" in the verbal attribution of this very "being" to objects of theoretical apprehension, as this word is usually understood. At the same time, he will sense that it would also be false to deny these objects what language has signified by the symbol "being." "It is ridiculous," such a theorizer would say, "to affirm at once that the world is, and that God is, if the word 'is' means the same thing in both cases."

How, then, should one view the use of such ambiguous verbal terms to construct not only judgments but also syllogisms? A *quaternio termino-rum*[3] will invariably accompany any attempt to use the data of suprasensi-ble[4] experience in a logical way. And is the formal logic of word-concepts even applicable to the material of concept-symbols? Meanwhile, our living language is a mirror of external, empirical cognition, and its culture is ex-pressed by the augmentation of the logical element to the detriment of the purely symbolic or mythological energy, which once wove the most tender natural tissue of language, and which now is the only thing capable of restoring truth to the "expressed thought."

II

It is in the poetry of Tiutchev that Russian Symbolism was first created as a consistently applied method and inwardly defined as double vision. It was here that the need for a different poetic language was first felt.

In both his consciousness and his creative work, the poet experiences a certain dualism: the splitting, or rather doubling, of his spiritual persona.

> O, wise soul of mine!
> O, heart so full of fear!
> O, how you beat upon the threshold
> Of this seemingly double being! . . .
>
> So, you are the home of two worlds.
> Your day is pain and passion,
> Your dream prophetically vague
> As the spirits' revelation.[5]

Such is self-consciousness. Poetic creation is also divided between the "outer," "daylight" world, which "embraces" us in the "full splendor" of its "manifestations,"[6] and the "mysterious, nighttime" world. The latter both frightens and attracts us, for it is our own inner essence and "ancestral heri-tage";[7] it is a "bodiless, audible, and invisible" world, woven, perhaps, "of thoughts emancipated by sleep."[8]

The same symbolic dualism of day and night, as the worlds of sensi-ble "manifestations" and suprasensible revelations, can be found in Nova-lis.[9] Both Novalis and Tiutchev breathe more freely in the nighttime world, which grants direct participation in "life divinely universal."[10]

But the discord that divides the two worlds is not final; discord only appears to the consciousness that is earthly, personal, and imperfect:[11]

> Is there enmity between them?
> Is not the sun the same for both?
> And while dividing, does it not
> Join them in a static medium?[12]

In poetry, these worlds are together. Today we call them Apollo and Dionysus, we know their unconfused and undivided nature, and in each true creation of art, we sense their actual biunity.[13] But in Tiutchev's soul, Dionysus is more powerful than Apollo, and the poet must seek salvation from the charms of Dionysus at Apollo's altar:

> He bursts out from his mortal breast
> And thirsts to unite with boundlessness.[14]

In order to preserve his individuality, man limits his thirst for union with "boundlessness," his striving toward "self-oblivion," "destruction," "confusion with the world of sleep";[15] and the artist turns to the clear forms of daylight being, the patterns of the "gilt-woven veil," which the gods have thrown over the "mysterious world of spirits," "the nameless abyss," i.e., the abyss that does not find its name in the language of daylight consciousness and external experience. . . . And yet the most valuable instant in experience and the wisest instant in poetic creation is its immersion into that contemplative ecstasy in which there are "no barriers" between us and the "bared abyss" that opens up in Silence.[16]

> There is a certain hour of universal silence,
> And at this hour of revelation and wonder
> The living chariot of the cosmos
> Glides freely into the heavens' sanctuary.[17]

The kind of creation we call symbolic becomes possible only now, in this noumenal openness: whatever consciousness retains of the phenomenal world is "suppressed by oblivion,"

> And only the virginal soul of the Muse
> Is disturbed by the gods in its prophetic dreams.[18]

Such is the nature of this new poetry, this somnambulist proceeding around the world of essences under the veil of night.

> Night comes, and with sonorous waves
> The elements beat against their shore . . .
> And that's its voice: it compels and implores us.
> The magical boat comes to life in the harbor . . .

Amidst this dark "immeasurability," double vision is revealed within the poet.[19] "Like demons deaf and dumb,"[20] the lights of the Macrocosm and Microcosm wink at each other. "What is above is also below."[21]

> The firmament, burning with the glory of stars,
> Looks mysteriously out of the depths;
> And we sail further, bounded on all sides
> By a flaming-bright abyss.[22]

In the symbol of "The Swan," we also find poetry represented as the reflection of a double mystery, the world of appearances and the world of essences:

> Between a double abyss
> It nurtures your visionary sleep,—
> And you are everywhere surrounded
> By the full glory of the starlit firmament.[23]

So poetry should provide the "visionary sleep" and "full glory" of the world, reflecting the world in the "double abyss": of external-phenomenal and inner-noumenal apprehension. The poet would like to have another, special language, so as to illustrate the inner world.

> How can the heart express itself?
> How can another understand?
> Can he understand what gives you life?[24]

But there is no such language; there are only hints and also the charm of a harmony capable of suggesting to the listener an experience similar to the one which no words can express.

> This is the play and sacrifice of private life!
> Come and reject the illusion of sensation,
> And dive, awakened and willful
> Into this life-giving ocean!
> Come and wash your suffering breast
> With its ethereal stream:
> And partake of life divinely universal
> If only for an instant.[25]

The word-symbol becomes a magic insistence that brings the listener to *participate* in the mysteries of poetry. Thus is it also for Baratynsky: "holy poetry" is "the mysterious power of harmony," while the soul of man is its "communicant." . . .[26] How far this view is from those eighteenth-century views (found as late as Pushkin) on the adequacy of the word and its sufficiency for *reason*, on the unmediated communicability of "beautiful clarity," which might always be transparent if only it did not prefer to deceive![27]

III

Symbolism in modern poetry is the first vague reminiscence of the holy language of high priests and magi. At one time, they endowed the words of the popular language with a special, mysterious meaning, which was revealed only to them since they alone knew the correspondences between the hidden world and the bounds of generally accessible experience. They knew gods and demons, people and things by names other than the ones by which the people called them; and it was in this knowledge of true names that they saw the basis of their power over nature. They taught the people to mollify terrible forces by affectionate and flattering evocation, to call the left side "the best side," to call the Furies "the good goddesses," and the lords of the underworld "the bestowers of wealth and all abundance." But they kept to themselves the heritage of some names and verbal signs, and they alone understood that "mixing bowl" (*krater*) means the soul, that "lyre" means the world, that "cave" means birth; that "Asteria" means the isle of Delos, while "Skamandrios" is the youth Astyanax, Hector's son;[28] and (long before Heraclitus and the Eleatics, of course) they knew that "to die" means "to be born," and "to be born" means "to die";[29] that "to be" means "to be in truth" (i.e., "to be as gods");[30] and that "thou art" means "divinity is in you";[31] and that the nonabsolute "to be" of popular usage and worldview (*dóxa*) refers to the illusion of real being or potential being (*mè ón*).[32]

According to contemporary epistemologists,[33] any logical judgment contains a third, hidden, normative element in addition to subject and predicate, a certain "yes" or "let it be so," by which the will affirms truth as value. Although our general outlook is wholly alien to these philosophers, we can nonetheless be helped by this theory to understand the religious-psychological moment in the history of language. This moment allowed the concept of "being" to be used in establishing a connection between subject and predicate, a usage that first realized the integral makeup of a grammatical sentence ("pater *est* bonus").[34] The words of primitive, natural speech were placed one against the next like the Cyclops' boulders;[35] the appearance of a *copula* that might cement them together was the beginning of the artificial cultivation of the word. And since in ancient times the verb "to be" possessed the holy meaning of divine being, one might suppose that the wise men and theurgists of those times introduced this symbol into every spoken judgment so that it might sanctify all future cognition and foster or rather sow in people the sense of truth as a religious and moral norm.[36]

In this way the original "shepherds of the peoples" mastered a speech that was called "the language of the gods." The transfer of this conception and definition onto poetic language signified the religious-symbolic nature of the melodious, "inspired" word. When the poets themselves rediscovered that poetry is "symbolism," this itself was a reminiscence of the ancient "language of the gods." For, if one believes Schiller,[37] when the poet returned to earth after tarrying in the palaces of Olympus, he found that not only had the material world been divided up without him and that the singer had no part or share of earthly things but also (and Schiller was still unaware of this) that all the words of his native language had been confiscated by the lords of life and co-opted into everyday use by life's common needs. And all that was left to the poet was to recall the language he had been granted to converse with the heaven dwellers, and in this way, he became temporarily inaccessible to the understanding of the crowd.

Symbolism forebodes that hypothetically conceivable, fully religious epoch of language, when it will embrace two separate forms of speech: speech about empirical things and relations, and speech about objects and relations of an order revealed only in inward experience, that is, the hieratic speech of prophesying. The former speech (the only one we are presently accustomed to) will be logical speech, a speech having analytic judgment as its fundamental inner form. The latter kind of speech is currently entangled with the former in an incidental fashion, just as holy golden mistletoe encircles the congenial oaks of poetry but strangles the gardens of science with parasitic growths; on pastures of inspired contemplation such speech rises as lush ears of native corn, but it is like foreign chaff on fields turned by the plows of exact thought; this latter is mythological speech. The main form of mythological speech will be "myth," understood as a synthetic judgment with a concept-symbol as its subject, and a verb for its predicate: for myth is the dynamic aspect (*modus*) of the symbol, viewed as movement and mover, as action and active force.[38]

IV

Symbolism is poetry's recollection of its original, primordial tasks and means.

In the poem "The Poet and the Crowd," Pushkin depicts the Poet as a mediator between the gods and people:

> We are born for inspiration,
> For sweet sounds and prayers.[39]

The gods "inspire" the messenger who brings their revelations to the people; people communicate through him their own "prayers" to the gods; the "sweet sounds" are the language of poetry, the "language of the gods." The argument is not between a worshiper of abstract, lifeless beauty and pragmatists of life who accept only what is "useful"; the argument is rather between the "high priest" and the crowd. The crowd no longer understands the "language of the gods," which is now dead and, for that reason alone, useless. It demands from the Poet an earthly language, for it has lost or forgotten religion and is left only with utilitarian morality. The Poet is always religious because he is always a poet. But now he only strums his sacred strings "with a distracted hand," for he sees that there are no longer any listeners around him.[40]

Pushkin's poem is executed strictly in the style of antiquity, which did not know the formula "art for art's sake." Some have wrongly seen it as a proclamation of the artist's right to a kind of creative work that is irrelevant to life, shutting itself off from life in its own separate world. Pushkin's Poet is mindful of his destiny—to grant a religious order to life, to interpret and reinforce the divine connection of what truly is, to be a theurgist. When Pushkin speaks of Greece he perceives the world like a Hellene and not like a modern Hellenizing aesthete; his words concerning the divine nature of the Belvedere marble are not an irresponsible, purely verbal affirmation of some "cult" of beauty in a godless world, but a confession of faith in the living mover of the harmony that supports the world.[41] And the expulsion of the "uninitiated" is not a rhetorical metaphor.

Poetry strove to become an incantatory magic of rhythmic speech, mediating between the world of divine essences and man. The melodious word bent the will of exalted kings, provided race and tribe with the help of the netherworld hero whose praises were "sung," warned of the inevitable charter of the Fates, and imprinted the god-given laws of morality and legal order in unshakable utterances (*rhēmata*). By affirming in people reverence for the divine, the melodious word affirmed the universal order of living forces. Truly, the lyre's charms formed stones into city walls, and it is no mere allegory to say that rhythms were able to heal ailments of soul and body, to grant victories, and to quiet internecine strife.[42] Such were the immediate tasks of ancient poetry: hymnic, epic, and elegiac. The means for achieving these tasks was the "language of the gods," the word's system of enchanting symbolics,[43] with its musical and orchestic accompaniment.[44] These very elements formed the basis of original, "syncretic," ritual art.

In the following phenomena, we find expressions of Symbolism's reminiscence of this epoch of poetry, which is all but forgotten historically, but unforgettable in the powerful current of ancestral heritage:

1. The new demands of personality have dictated a rediscovery of the symbolic energy of the word that religious tradition and the national soul's power of preservation have saved from long centuries of enslavement to external experience;
2. The idea of poetry as the source of intuitive cognition, and of symbols as the means of realizing this cognition;
3. The emerging self-determination of the poet not only as artist but also as a personality bearing an inner word, as an organ of the world soul who signifies the hidden connection of what truly is, as a visionary and creator of life's mysteries.

It is therefore not surprising that cosmic themes have come to dominate the content of poetry; that ephemeral and elusive emotions have acquired an echo of "world weariness"; that aestheticism bequeathed to us a refinement of outer perceptivity and inner sensitivity that has served as valuable experience in the search for a new apprehension of the world; and that the cognition of the irreality of phenomena has come to be seen as the universal tragedy of the isolated personality.

V

Any evaluation of Russian "Symbolism" depends largely on the degree to which one correctly understands both the international nature of the Symbolist literary phenomenon and the essence of the Western influence on our recent poets, who commenced their activity with a vow of fidelity to the highly significant, yet highly ambiguous summons that resounded in the West. Close study of our "symbolic school" will demonstrate that this influence was ultimately superficial, and that its borrowing and imitation was youthfully rash and, in essence, fruitless. It will also show that all that is genuine and vital in Russian poetry of the last one and a half decades is deeply rooted in native soil.

There was only a short interval of pure aestheticism, nihilistic in its worldview, eclectic in its tastes, and pained in its psychology. It served as a boundary between the appearance of the so-called Symbolist school and the preceding epoch, when our national genius found great representatives in its religious reaction against a wave of iconoclastic materialism. Leaving aside the creative work of Dostoevsky, which lent lasting definition to the paths of our spirit but which does not belong to the sphere of the rhythmic word, let us recall the native names of Vladimir Solovyov and the singer of *Evening Fires*.[45] In cast of mind and artistic method, Tiutchev precedes both of these poets in the ancestral succession of our poetry's symbolic tradition; he is the true forefather of our true Symbolism.

Tiutchev was not the solitary founder of the movement, which we believe is destined to express the inner sanctuary of the national soul. Of Tiutchev's contemporaries, the Russian Muse first found ethereal harmonies of mystical emotion on Zhukovsky's lyre. After Zhukovsky, Pushkin's genius was like a diamond of rare purity and play, which could not help but refract the blinding, albeit fragmented, rays of inner experience, illuminating all of life in its facets. Baratynsky's meditative and silently solemn melody seems the voice of a dark memory that speaks of some distant living knowledge, which had revealed the secret book of the world soul to the poet's once-visionary gaze. Gogol knew the tremor and delight of the second sight given to the "lyric poet," but he was fated to remain only a frightened spectator of life, which wrapped itself before him in the magically rippling veil of an intricate myth in order to conceal the final meaning of its symbolics from his wise spirit. Finally, there was Lermontov, who was both seraphic (as was said in the Middle Ages) and demonic (a word Goethe often used), who yearned for a mysterious meeting and songs other than the "tedious songs of the earth," a "wondrous desire"[46] that oppressed him equally whether in furious rebellion or prayerful compassion: Lermontov was the first Russian poet to tremble at a premonition of the symbol of symbols, the "Eternal Feminine," the mystical flesh of the eternally born Word.[47]

However, the motifs we have noted in their lyric poetry notwithstanding, it would still be incorrect to call these poets—as we do Tiutchev—Symbolists in the strictest sense of the word. In our view, the distinguishing marks of purely symbolic art are the following:

1. The artist must consciously express a parallelism between the phenomenal and noumenal; harmoniously discover a correlation between what art depicts as outer reality (*realia*) and what it intuits in the outer as the inner and higher reality (*realiora*); and signify correspondences and correlations between the phenomenon (which is "only a likeness," "*nur Gleichnis*")[48] and its intellectual or mystically envisioned essence, which throws before itself the shadow of the visible event;[49]
2. A mark inherent to truly symbolic art (even in cases of so-called unconscious creation, which does not conceptualize the metaphysical connection of what it depicts) is a special intuition and energy of the word, which therefore appears to the poet as a cipher of the inexpressible; the word accepts into its sound many echoes of unknown origin and, as it were, echoes of native underground springs, and thus it serves as both boundary with and exit into boundlessness, as both letters (generally comprehensible writing) of outer experience and hieroglyphs (hieratic transcription) of inner experience.[50]

The historical task of the modern symbolic school was to reveal the nature of the word as symbol, and the nature of poetry as the symbolics of true realities. It cannot be doubted that the school has failed to fulfill its double task. But it would be unjust to deny it several initial achievements, primarily within the bounds of the first part of the problem. Particularly indisputable is the significant role the Symbolist pathos has played in the shift in the system of spiritual values that comprise intellectual culture as a worldview, a shift we are all experiencing.

VI

A generalizing study could handily distinguish two consecutive moments within the history of our modern Symbolism. Their characteristics allow us to oppose them as thesis and antithesis, and to postulate a third, synthetic moment. The synthetic moment should conclude the period under discussion with some definitive achievements in the series of pressing goals we have outlined.

44

The pathos of the first moment was comprised of the artist's sudden realization that the world is not small, flat, and bare, not measured and calculated. It was revealed to him that there is much in the world of which yesterday's wise men did not even dream, and that there are paths and breaches into its mystery from the labyrinth of the human soul, if only—and the first heralds thought that this was the final word on the matter—if only man could learn to dare and "be as the sun," forgetting the distinction he had been granted between the permissible and impermissible.[51] The artist learned that the world is magical and man is free. This optimistic moment of Symbolism is typified by a trust in the world as datum. These new argonauts of the spirit discovered harmonious correspondences in the world, and other, even more enigmatic and captivating correspondences seemed to await them, since to know such correspondences meant to gain mastery over them.[52] Although Vladimir Solovyov's teaching on the theurgical meaning and purpose of art was still not fully understood, it already rang in the poet's soul as an imperative summons, like Faust's promise "to strive untiringly to the highest being" ("zum höchsten Dasein immerfort zu streben").[53] The word-symbol promised to become a holy revelation or wonder-working "mantra" that would take the spell off the world. Within their lives and creative work (necessarily in a labor of life, as in a creative labor!), artists were to achieve an integral incarnation of the worldview of mystical realism or "magical idealism," as Novalis termed it.[54] But first these artists had to pass the religious and moral challenge of the "antithesis." The current discord, if not disintegration of the former phalanx shows clearly how difficult it was to overcome this challenge and what sacrifices it cost . . . O, insane Vrubel', peace to your glorious and suffering shadow![55]

Each line of the foregoing indicates that Symbolism did not want to be and could not be "only art." The Symbolists would be sounding brass or a clanging cymbal[56] if they had been unable to experience the crisis of war and the liberation movement together with the whole of Russia.[57] But it was important for them to suffer through this common ailment; for the national soul was ill and they were to transform the refined poisons of the illness in their sensitive and insane souls. After this the world no longer seemed to them a Golconda of magical wonders,[58] or a solar lyre awaiting the inspired fingers of the lyre-playing wonder-worker. Instead, it has seemed a pile of "ashes" illuminated by the Gorgon's deadly gaze.[59] Cries of final despair resounded in the works of Zinaida Gippius, Fedor Sologub, Aleksandr Blok, and Andrei Bely.[60] Sunlike, free man emerged as a worm crushed by the "datum" of chaos, while he weakly insisted on affirming in himself the god that had been overthrown by reality.[61] The knight of the "Beautiful Lady" dreamed that she was a "cardboard bride."[62] The image of the long-awaited Woman began to bifurcate and merge with the image of the whore that was revealed to him. In the name of a religious acceptance of the Earth, eternal

45

under the cover of decay, they proclaimed the religious nonacceptance of "the world";[63] the fact that this most painful sore was called by its proper name angered those who did not accept the world, their anger sharpened by the pain of their discord. People began to be jealous of torment and, seized by panic, to be afraid of the words that burned their souls in silence. Positive religious feeling assured us that an "irreconcilable No" was the necessary path to the exposure of a "blinding Yes."[64] And erstwhile artists, like Aleksandr Dobroliubov and Dmitry Merezhkovsky, shook the ashes from their feet to bear witness against the temptations of art, striving to achieve religious action on another field of endeavor.[65]

What was in store for those who remained artists? For artistic work, any tarrying in the "antithesis" was tantamount to a denial of the theurgic ideal and an affirmation of the Romantic principle. The reminiscence of former radiant visions found support in their souls only as a reminiscence, losing the vitality of real presence; it could only console their ailing souls with dreamy melodies about something distant and unrealizable. The conflict between illusion and reality could only cultivate Romantic humor.[66] Another possibility was to follow the example of Leonid Andreev and go about uttering threats and curses;[67] but this would not be art and would soon lose any efficacy and soundness, even if the artist commanded Byronic strength.

It was easier and more feasible to leave the vicious circle of the "antithesis," to renounce the skill of flying beyond the clouds and attaining suprapersonal feelings, and capitulate before the existing "givenness" of things. This process of losing one's wings quite predictably leads these tranquilized Romantics to naturalism, which, while still at the limits of Romanticism, is usually colored by an everyday, descriptive humor; in the sphere of poetry, it leads to the elegance of the jewel polisher's craft, which lovingly elevates into a "pearl of creation" anything it finds "beautiful" in this, in all likelihood, most literary of worlds. This craft promises a pleasant blossoming in Russia. And it will be well served by the enthusiastic study of the poetic canon that is currently under way.

"Parnassianism" would have a full right to exist if only it did not distort all too often the natural characteristics of poetry, especially lyrical poetry. It is too inclined to forget that lyric poetry is by its nature far from a depictive art, such as the plastic arts and painting. Rather, like music, it is an art of motion, active rather than contemplative, and, in the final analysis, lyric poetry creates life not icons.[68]

VII

The appeal to the formal canon is generally fruitful, providing one undertakes a genetic study of traditional forms rather than a scholastic and dogmatic one; it is harmful only when the appeal deviates toward lifeless, academic idolatry and epigonism. With regard to the tasks of Symbolism, the appeal to the formal canon has a particular purpose: it exerts a cleansing effect on art; it exposes the inelegance and falsity of innovations introduced without inner justification; it casts away everything incidental, temporary, and alien; it instills rigorous taste, artistic exactitude, the sense of responsibility, and a careful restraint in dealing with tradition and innovation; it brings the Symbolist poet face-to-face with his true and final goals; and, finally, it develops in him an awareness of his living ancestry and his inner connection with past generations, making him truly free for the first time within the hierarchic coordination of creative efforts, granting experience to his daring and awareness to his striving.

But the outer canon is as fruitless as any norm if it cannot bring the principle of harmony into the elemental agitation of living forces. It is as helplessly tyrannical as any norm if its harmonizing principle does not enter into organic connection, one might say into marriage with the elemental force that seeks harmony, if instead it seeks with violence to coerce and enslave the elemental force. We believe that the future paths of Symbolism depend on whether the elemental force we would call the "inner canon" achieves victory and mastery in the artist's soul.

By "inner canon" we mean that which the artist experiences as a free and integral recognition of the hierarchic order of real values, which form in their harmony the divine all-unity of final Reality. In the artist's creative work, the inner canon is the living connection of properly coordinated symbols, from which the artist weaves a precious veil for the World Soul, creating, as it were, a nature that is more spiritual and transparent than the multicolored peplos of natural being.[69] As soon as forms are correctly combined and coordinated, art instantly becomes vital and significant: it turns into a signifying vision of the interrelations that innately tie forms to higher essences; into the holy, visionary action of love, which conquers the division of forms; into a theurgic, transformational *"Let it be."*[70] When this mirror is turned onto the mirrors of fragmented consciousnesses, it restores the original truth of what is reflected, amending the guilt of the first reflection, which had distorted the truth. Art becomes the "mirror of mirrors" (*speculum speculorum*); due to this very reflective quality, everything becomes a symbolics of united being, where each cell of the living, fragrant tissue creates and glorifies its own petal, and each petal illuminates and glorifies the glowing center of the unknowable flower: the symbol of symbols, the Flesh of the Word.[71]

Symbolism still contemplates symbols in the discrete correspondences that have been disclosed and, as it were, torn from the connection of the whole. It has not yet gained full vision; it still "sees passersby as trees."[72] Symbolic forms shall no longer exist in the symbolics of final achievements that are reached through the "inner canon"; there shall be one form, one image as symbol, granting the vindication of all forms. Fet, "looking straight from time to eternity," sang about this in his swan song, while he "flowed like smoke, and melted," attaining a clear vision of the "Sun of the World":

> And motionless upon fiery roses
> The living altar of the cosmos censes;
> Within its smoke, as in creative dreams,
> All power shakes, in dreams eternity appears.

> And all that darts along abysses of space,
> And every ray, of matter and of spirit,
> Is but your reflection, O Sun of the World,
> And but a dream, an ephemeral dream.[73]

Dionysianism can only be confused with inner anarchism and amorphism if one has scarcely managed to be taken up into the Dionysian eddy.[74] When the Maenad loses herself in the god, she stops with hand extended, ready to accept and carry whatever the god grants, whether it be a torch or a *thyrsus* with the head of her son,[75] a sword, or a flower. She is fully and impersonally obedient to the other's will. Her silent word is "Come! Let there be!"[76] . . . "Thus you too, meeting god: o, heart, stop! o, heart, stop! . . . At the final threshold, o, heart, stop! o, heart, stop! . . . O, heart, stop. . . ."[77]

The "inner canon" denotes an inner labor, the labor of *obedience,* made in the name of that to which the poet has said "yes," to which he has betrothed himself with the golden ring of the symbol:

> My wedding ring has sunk
> To the purple sea bed:
> O violent storm, show
> In the azure depths—the Face![78]

And from whence does the World Soul answer the poet? From the dark-blue crystal of unspeakable distances? From the sky-blue halo of inexpressible intimacy?

> I wear a ring,
> And my face—
> Is the meek ray of a mysterious "Yes."[79]

The fate of the symbolic poet depends on this connecting act, which entails the utter surrender of the will and the religious ordering of all essence. Symbolism thus obligates.

Up to now, Symbolism has complicated life and complicated art.[80] From now on, if it is fated to *be,* it will *simplify.*[81] Before, symbols were uncoordinated and dispersed, like a deposit of precious stones (and this is why lyric poetry was dominant); from now on, symbolic works will be like monolithic symbols. Before, there was "symbolization"; from now on, there will be *symbolics.* The integral worldview of the poet will reveal within itself this integral and united symbolics. The poet will find religion in himself, if he finds *connection* in himself.[82] And "connection" is "obligation."

In the terminology of aesthetics, the connection of free coordination means: the *"grand style."* The ancestral, inherited forms of the "grand style" in poetry are epic, tragedy, and mysterium, the three forms of a single tragic essence. If symbolic tragedy indeed becomes possible, this will mean that the "antithesis" has been overcome: the epic negatively affirms the personality by renouncing the personal, giving positive affirmation to the principle of *sobornost'*. Tragedy is the resurrection of the personality. Tragedy is always realism, always myth. Mysterium is the abolition of the symbol as likeness, and of myth as reflection; it is a crowning and triumph achieved by passing through the gates of death. Mysterium is victory over death, the positive affirmation of personality and its action; it restores the symbol as incarnate reality, and restores myth as an actual *"Fiat,"* "Let it be! . . ."

We conclude with several words to young poets. In poetry everything that has poetic sincerity is good. One need not want to be a "Symbolist." Only in solitude can one reveal the Symbolist in oneself—and even then it is better to try to conceal this from others. Symbolism obligates. The old scholastic stamps have been worn away. Something new can be purchased only at the price of an inner labor of personality. With regard to the symbol, one should remember the testament: "Do not take in vain."[83] And even he who does *not* take the symbol in vain—like an artist who knows nothing of *"realiora"*—he should work for six days, completing all of his work in these days, so that he might leave one, seventh day in the solemn sense interpreted above,

for inspiration,
For sweet sounds and prayers.[84]

Thoughts on Symbolism

Amidst the silent hills I met a shepherd
Who blew into a long alpine horn.
His song flowed pleasant to the ear, but this
Rich horn was but an instrument to waken
A captivating echo in the mountains.
And every time, creating little sound,
The shepherd would await the mountain echo,
It flowed among the steep ravines in such
A harmony, so inexpressibly sweet,
It seemed: an invisible chorus of spirits
Upon otherworldly instruments translated
The language of the earth by speech of heaven.
And then I thought: "O genius! Like this horn
You must sing earthly songs, and in men's hearts
Awaken other songs. And blessed is he who hears."
Above the mountains then a voice gave answer:
"So nature is a symbol like this horn.
She sounds for echoes. The echo then is God.
Blessed is he who hears both song and echo."[1]

I

If, as a poet, I am able to *paint* in words ("poetry is like unto painting"; "*ut pictura poesis,*" as classical poetics expressed this thought in the words of Horace, who was himself following ancient Simonides);[2] to *paint* so that the listener's imagination reproduces what I depict as distinctly and as vividly as I see it, and so that the things I name are represented to his soul as palpably textured and vitally colorful, whether shaded or radiant, whether in motion or static, in accordance with the nature of their visual appearance;

if, as a poet, I am able to *sing* with magical force (for "it is not enough that poems be beautiful: let them also be sweet and capriciously attract the soul of the listener wherever they desire"—*non satis est pulchra esse poemata, dulcia sunto et quocumque volent animum auditoris agunto*—as classical poetics described this tender violence in the words of Horace);[3] if I am able to *sing* so mellifluously and powerfully that the listener's soul becomes enamored of the sounds and follows my flutes obediently, yearning with my desire, is saddened with my sadness, ignited with my ecstasy, so that with the harmonious beating of his own heart he might answer each shudder of the musical wave that bears the melodious poem;

if, as poet and sage, I command the knowledge of things; if I instruct the listener's reason and educate his will, while giving pleasure to his heart;

—but if I am a poet crowned with this threefold crown of melodious power, yet, despite this threefold charm, am still unable to compel the very soul of the listener to sing together with me in a voice different than my own, not in the unison of its psychological surface but in the counterpoint of its innermost depths, to sing of what is deeper than the depths I show and higher than the heights I disclose, if my listener is but a mirror, but an echo, only accepting, only accommodating; if the ray of my *word* does not seal my *silence* and his silence with the *rainbow* of a secret *covenant:*[4]

then I am not a *symbolic* poet . . .[5]

II

If art per se is one of the most powerful means of human union, then one could say of symbolic art that the principle of its efficacy is union par excellence, union in the immediate and profoundest meaning of the word. In truth, symbolic art not only unites but also connects. Two are connected by a third, higher element. The symbol, this third element, can be likened to a rainbow that flares up between the ray of the word and the moisture of the soul that reflects the ray. . . . And Jacob's ladder begins in each work of truly symbolic art.[6]

Symbolism connects consciousnesses in such a way that they give birth together "in beauty." According to Plato, the goal of love is "to give birth in beauty."[7] Plato's depiction of the paths of love is a definition of Symbolism. In its growth the soul ascends from a state of attraction to a beautiful body up to the love of God. When an aesthetic phenomenon is experienced erotically, the artistic creation becomes symbolic. The enjoyment of beauty, like an attraction to corporeal beauty, becomes the initial step in an erotic ascent. When a work of art is experienced in this way, its meaning is inexhaustible. The symbol is the creative principle of love, the guiding Eros. An ancient, naively profound Italian song speaks of what then occurs between the two lives—the one made incarnate in creation and the one that partakes of it creatively (*creatively,* for Symbolism is art that turns the perceiver into a *participant* in the creative act): in this song two lovers arrange a meeting in order that the third, the god of love, might himself appear with them at the appointed hour:

Pur che il terzo sia presente,
E quel terzo sia l'Amor.

So that the third is also present,
So that the third is Love.

III

L'Amór / che muove il Sóle / e l'altre stélle—"Love, which moves the Sun
and other Stars. . . ."[8] Here, in the concluding verse of Dante's *Paradise,* the
images form a myth, and wisdom is taught by the music of the verse.

Let us analyze the musical structure of this melodic verse. Its three
rhythmic waves are accented by the caesurae and in turn accent the words:
Amor, Sole, Stelle; for it is on them that the *ictus* falls. As a result of this
word arrangement, the radiant images of the god of Love, the Sun, and the
Stars seem blinding. They are divided by the valleys of the rhythm, the indeterminate and dark *muove* (moves) and *altre* (other). Night yawns in the
intervals between the radiant outlines of those three ideas. Music is made
incarnate in a visual phenomenon; the Apollonian vision appears above the
gloom of Dionysian disturbance: the Pythic dyad is undivided and unconfused.[9] Thus, the starlit firmament is boundlessly and powerfully imprinted
on the soul. The soul becomes the contemplator (epoptes)[10] of the mysteries, but it is not deprived of the guidance of a teacher who could explain to
the consciousness what it has contemplated. Some hierophant, standing
above the soul, proclaims: "Wisdom! You see the movement of the radiant
sphere, you hear its harmony: know then that this is Love. Love moves the
Sun and other Stars."[11]—The hierophant's holy word (*hieròs lógos*) is the
word as *lógos.*

Thus, Dante is crowned with the threefold crown of melodious power.
But this is not all that he achieves. The startled soul not only perceives, not
only repeats the prophetic word: the soul finds within itself its own, complementary word, and out of its mysterious depths the soul painlessly gives
birth to this word. The powerful magnet magnetizes the soul: it itself becomes a magnet. The universe is revealed within it. Whatever it sees above
itself in the heavens is opened within it below.[12] Love is within the soul: for
it now loves. *Amor . . .*—this sound affirms the magnetic state of the living
universe and also causes the soul's molecules to arrange themselves mag-
netically. And within the soul is the sun, and the stars, and the hum of the
harmonious spheres, moved by the power of the Divine Mover. The soul
sings its own melody of love in harmony with the cosmos, just as Beatrice's
melody sang in the soul of the poet when he uttered his cosmic words. We
must therefore analyze Dante's verse not only in its own right, as an object
of pure aesthetics, but also in its relation to the subject, as the agent of
heartfelt emotion and inner experience. This verse not only appears to be

full of outer musical sweetness and inner musical energy, but it is also polyphonous, since it causes additional musical vibrations and awakens certain palpable overtones. This is why it is not only an artistically perfect verse but also a *symbolic* verse. This, then, is why it is divinely poetic. Moreover, the individual words of the verse are pronounced so powerfully in the given connection and given combinations that they themselves are symbols, and therefore the verse is composed from symbolic elements; thus the verse represents a synthetic judgment in which an active verb (moves the Sun and the Stars) is found for the symbol-subject (Love). Thus, we see before us a *mythopoetic* crowning of Symbolism. For myth is a synthetic judgment in which the predicate verb is attached to a subject-symbol.[13] The holy word, *hieròs lógos*, turns into the word as *mythos*.

If, having described the effect of the concluding words of *The Divine Comedy*, we dared to evaluate it according to the religio-metaphysical hierarchy of values, we would have to call this effect *theurgic*. And—within the category of analysis sketched above, which is actually far from obligatory for the aesthetics of symbolic art—this example would serve to verify for us the hypothesized identity of true and supreme Symbolism and theurgy, an identity that has already been proclaimed on more than one occasion.

IV

Thus, I am not a Symbolist if I am unable to awaken through an imperceptible hint or influence incommunicable feelings in the listener's heart. These feelings are similar at times to primeval recollection ("and long in the world it suffered, full of a wondrous desire; the tedious songs of the earth could not replace the sounds of heaven"),[14] at times similar to a distant, vague presentiment, at times to the tremor felt at someone's familiar and desired approach. Moreover, we experience both this recollection and this presentiment or presence as an incomprehensible expansion of our personal makeup and empirically limited self-consciousness.

I am not a Symbolist if my words do not arouse in the listener a feeling of connection between his "I" and what he calls his "not-I," a connection between things that are empirically divided; if my words do not immediately convince him of the existence of hidden life where his reason did not suspect any life at all; if my words do not move in him an energy of love for what he had previously been unable to love because his love did not know how many mansions it had.[15]

I am not a Symbolist if my words are equal to themselves, if they are not an echo of other sounds, about which, as of the Spirit, you know not whence they come and whither they go[16]—and if they do not awaken an echo in the labyrinths of souls.

V

In this case, I am not a Symbolist—for my listener. For Symbolism denotes a relation, and a symbolic work cannot exist by itself, just as an object cannot exist removed from its subject.

Abstract aesthetic theory and formal poetics analyze the work of art in itself; therefore, they do not know Symbolism. One can speak of Symbolism only if one studies a work in its relation to the perceiving subject and the creative subject, understood as integral personalities.[17] Hence, it follows that:

1. Symbolism lies outside of aesthetic categories.
2. Every work of art can be evaluated from the viewpoint of Symbolism.
3. Symbolism is tied to the integrity of the personality, both that of the artist himself and that of the person experiencing the artistic revelation.

It is obviously unthinkable that a Symbolist be a craftsman;[18] it is similarly unthinkable that a Symbolist be an aesthete. Symbolism deals with man. Thus, it restores the word "poet" in its old meaning of poet as personality (*poetae nascuntur*)[19] in opposition to the common usage of our day, which tries to reduce this lofty name to the meaning of "an artist-versifier acknowledged as talented and skillful in his technical field."

VI

Is the symbolic element obligatory in the organic composition of a perfect creation? Must a work of art be effective symbolically in order to be called perfect?

The requirement of symbolic efficacy is no more obligatory than the demand of *ut pictura* or *dulcia sunto*. . . .[20] What formal feature is ever absolutely necessary in order that a work be called artistic? Since such a feature has never been named, there cannot yet be a formal aesthetics.

But there are schools of thought. And each is distinguished by the particular, supraobligatory, so to speak, demands that it freely imposes upon itself, as the rule and vow of its artistic order. In this way, the symbolic school demands from itself more than other schools.

Clearly, the very same demands might also be satisfied unconsciously, without any rule or vow. Each work of art may be tested from the viewpoint of Symbolism.

Since Symbolism denotes the relation of the artistic object to a double subject (creative and perceiving), whether or not any particular work is symbolic depends to a large degree on our perception. For example, we can take symbolically Lermontov's words: "Out from under a mysterious, cold demimasque your voice sounded forth to me . . . ,"[21] although, in all likelihood, the author of these verses considered these words to be equal to themselves in their logical capacity and content, and he had in mind a mere meeting at a masquerade. On the other hand, by studying the relationship of a work to the integral personality of its creator, we can also establish its symbolic character independent of our own perception. In any case, the following confession of Lermontov appears to us to exemplify this:

> The word newborn
> Of flame and light
> Will meet no response
> Amidst worldly noise.[22]

One clearly sees the poet attempting to express an inner word by means of an outer word, and despairing of the accessibility of the latter to the perception of those who are listening; this perception, however, is necessary in order that the word-flame, word-light not be engulfed by darkness.[23]

Symbolism is magnetism. A magnet attracts only iron. Iron molecules are normally in a magnetized state. And whatever is attracted by a magnet becomes magnetized. . . .[24]

So, we Symbolists do not exist—if there are no Symbolists listening. For Symbolism is not only creative activity but also creative cooperation, not only the artistic objectification of the creative subject but also the creative subjectification of the artistic object.

"Is Symbolism dead?" our contemporaries ask. Some answer, "Of course it is dead!" It is for them to know whether Symbolism has died for them. We, however, the dead, bear witness by whispering to those feasting at our funeral repast that death does not exist.

VII

But if Symbolism has not died, it certainly has matured! It is not the power of its standard-bearers that has grown and strengthened, I mean to say, but the holy laurel branch in their hands, the gift of the Heliconian Muses, who commanded Hesiod to proclaim only the truth—their living standard.[25]

It was not long ago that many took Symbolism to be a technique of poetic depiction akin to Impressionism, so that one could formally delegate it to the department of stylistics that is concerned with tropes and figures. If I imagine that I am reading some fashionable textbook on the theory of literature—quite possible, although as of yet unwritten—I see the following note for pupils, coming after the definition of metaphor: "If a metaphor is developed over the course of the entire poem instead of being contained in a single distinct utterance, then it is proper to call such a poem symbolic."

We have also come far from the Symbolism of poetic puzzles,[26] the literary technique (again, only a technique!) comprised of the art of evoking a series of images capable of arousing associations, the sum of which makes one guess and perceive with particular force an object or experience that has intentionally been repressed; instead of being named directly, it is supposed to be deduced. This genre, which in the period after Baudelaire was the favorite of the French Symbolists (with whom we have neither a historical nor an ideological basis to connect our task),[27] does not belong to the sphere of Symbolism as we describe it. Not only because it is a mere technique: the reason lies even deeper. In this case, the poet seeks to impart to the lyrical idea an illusion of volume in order to condense and materialize the content while gradually reducing its volume. We were becoming carried away by reveries of *dentelle, jeu supreme,* and so on, and Mallarmé only wants our thought, having described wide circles, to descend right into the single point he has marked.[28] For us, Symbolism is, on the contrary, an energy that liberates from the bounds of the given, imparting to our souls the motion of an unfolding spiral.

In contrast to those who have called themselves "Symbolists," we seek to be true to the calling of art, which depicts the small and makes it great, and not vice versa. For such is the humility of art, which loves the small. It is more characteristic of true Symbolism to depict the earthly than the heavenly: it considers the power of the echo to be more important than the volume of the sound. *A realibus ad realiora. Per realia ad realiora.*[29] True Symbolism does not tear itself from the earth; it wants to connect the roots to the stars; it grows as a stellar blossom from nearby, native roots.[30] It does not falsify things; when it speaks of the sea, it means the earthly sea, and when it speaks of the snowy heights ("and for how many ages have the snowy heights shown white, yet the dawn still sows fresh roses on them"—Tiutchev),[31] it means the peaks of earthly mountains. As art, it strives for one thing: for the elasticity of image, its inner vitality and extension in the soul where it falls, like a seed that must grow and give forth grain. Symbolism in this sense is an affirmation of the extensive energy of the word and art. This extensive energy does not seek but rather avoids intersecting with spheres heteronomous to art, for example, with religious systems. Symbolism, such as we affirm it, is not afraid of a Babylonian captivity in any of these spheres: it is unique in realizing the active freedom of art; it is also unique in believing in art's active power.

There were some who called themselves Symbolists but did not know (as Goethe, the distant father of our Symbolism knew long ago)[32] that what Symbolism speaks of is marked by universality and *sobornost';* they led us by paths of symbols along bright meadows so as to return us to our dungeon, to the cramped cell of the lesser "I." As illusionists, they did not believe in the divine expanse and knew only the expanse of fantasy and the charm of a languorous dream, from which we awoke in prison. True Symbolism pursues a different goal: the emancipation of the soul (*kátharsis,* as an event of inner experience).

Excursus: On Sect and Dogma

. . . So Dante is a Symbolist! What does this mean for the self-determination of the Russian symbolic school? It means that we are abolishing ourselves as a school. We are abolishing ourselves, not because we have disavowed something and have decided to set out on a new path: on the contrary, we remain fully true to ourselves and the activity we have begun. But we do not want a sect; our confession is universal [*sobornyi*].[33]

Indeed, a real Symbolist is concerned, of course, not with the fate of what is usually called a school or movement (as defined by chronological limits and the names of its leading participants); he is concerned with establishing some general principle. This principle is the Symbolism of any true art. We are convinced that we have achieved this goal, that Symbolism is from now on affirmed forever, even if with time it turns out that we who affirmed it were at the same time its least worthy proponents.

I shall allow myself by way of explanation a comparison from the history of Church dogma, for it most graphically shows the significance of reaching a conclusive formulation of guiding ideas. When the Fathers of the First Ecumenical Council proclaimed *homoousia,* the acceptance of this particular dogma and the unconditional rejection of the opposite (i.e., *homoiousia*) became an essential feature of Orthodox consciousness and its decisive distinction from heretical consciousness.[34] How then were the people who proclaimed this teaching of faith to regard the ecclesiastical teachings of their predecessors? Of course, they would regard them as teachers who had long marked out and prepared the true confession, or else who had held to it in silence. Symbolism is undergoing a similar process.

An aspiration to achieve a symbolic grounding of art can be clearly observed in the history of artistic consciousness ever since the time of Goethe. This aspiration has appeared with particular intensity and clarity in modern Russian literature. I will limit myself to mentioning Tiutchev in the sphere of verse and Dostoevsky in the area of prose. It is of their victories, and not those of our contemporaries, that I speak when I speak of the triumph of Symbolism. It is not our school, not our skills and canons that I defend. By praising Symbolism, I believe that I am proclaiming a dogma of artistic Orthodoxy. And if I express myself in such a way, I hope that I will not be accused of disrespect toward the source from which I take my comparison; for art is truly a sacred possession and *sobornost'*.

It would be logical to call objections raised against this dogma heresy. There are various types of aesthetic heresy; for example, the heresy of social utilitarianism is still alive, however surprising one might find its vitality to be, and in my opinion, it has found its most recent supporter in Russia in the person of Dmitry Merezhkovsky.[35] But he is too experienced a man that one might easily believe in the healthy sincerity of his demagogic catcalls about the similarity between Tiutchevism and Oblomovism, and of other such comparisons and considerations. What is interesting is not the content of this sermon but its psychology: how is the very phenomenon of Merezhkovsky psychologically possible, the phenomenon of a Symbolist who seeks to arouse suspicions against Symbolism? The answer to this question adds a telling feature to the characterization of Symbolism as a whole, and this feature bears positive significance, despite all its moribund monstrosity in this particular case. Symbolism must always strive to transcend its own bounds. The image and likeness of higher realities are imprinted on the symbol, and they comprise its living soul and motive energy; the symbol is not a dead mold or an idol of this reality but its half-animated bearer and participant. However, it is only half alive and would like to come fully to life; it would like to merge integrally with the very reality it signifies. The symbol is a word becoming flesh but unable to become it fully; should it become flesh, it would thereby stop being a symbol and become this same theurgic reality. Symbolism's Eros for action is holy; Symbolism craves a task that is not mortal and human but rather immortal and divine. Merezhkovsky, for his part, imagines the wine of his religious pathos to be new, and he would pour it into the ancient skins of old-fashioned irreligious radicalism of the time of Belinsky and the 1860s.[36]

The other, most widespread aesthetic heresy is the misconception of "art for art's sake." This view, that art must be totally sundered from the roots and inner heart of life, rears its head in periods of decline, in periods of superficial aestheticism; it rests, in essence, on a misunderstanding. I shall briefly express my attitude toward this heresy.

The only task, the only object of any art is Man. Not the good of man but his mystery. In other words, man, taken on the vertical axis, in his free growth inward and upward. The word Man with a capital letter determines the content of all art; it has no other content. This is why religion has always found a place in grand and true art; for God is on the vertical axis of Man. Only the narrow-minded good that lies on the horizontal axis of Man finds no place in art, and a desire for utilitarianism immediately puts a stop to all artistic activity. The closer we look into the essence of heresies, the more evident becomes the truth of the correct aesthetic confession of faith.

Manner, Persona, Style

I

The first and easiest achievement for an original talent is the acquisition of a unique *manner* and a personal *tone,* distinctly characteristic of it alone. External uniqueness itself bears witness to the inner independence of the creative gift. No mere skill is capable of creating this characteristic feature, which appears spontaneously, unintentionally, naturally, and without artifice, and which, of course, precedes the negative achievement of the perfection of form, its model flawlessness and strict purity. On the other hand, inner artistic independence is unfailingly expressed in external individuality: however deep, meaningful, and creatively novel the world perception of the artist might be, it is the sure mark of a weak talent if it is impersonal in its means of expression.

When speaking of a poet's development, his first and half-unconscious experience must be acknowledged to be an attentive hearkening to the vague music that sounds somewhere in the distant depths of his soul, to the melody of new words, as yet unspoken by human lips, but already predetermined within the poet himself, or of something that is not yet even words, but merely the faint rhythmic and phonetic schemes of a word that has been conceived, but not yet carried to term, which is as yet unborn. This morphological principle of artistic growth already bears within itself, as in a seed, future individuality as new "tidings."

The second achievement is the acquisition of an artistic *persona.* Only when the artist finds and reveals his persona can we fully say of him: "He has brought a new word," and demand nothing further of him. But this achievement is the hardest, and often an entire life is spent consolidating it. When the artist is at this stage of his path, he knows only too well that, however we might judge the independent calling of art, its independence from life, and its incommensurability with an individual personality, for a true creator, life and art are nevertheless the same: even if Apollo does not call the poet to holy sacrifice every day, each time he calls the poet, he demands the entire man.[1] All too often at this stage, "a tragedy begins" for the artist: *incipit tragoedia.*[2]

At times, an unexpected opposition is revealed between the image of creative incarnation found by the poet and the principle of form within the inner word: the morphological principle of artistic maturation may lead the organism to a metamorphosis incomprehensible to itself. Shedding skins like a snake, the artist begins to feel burdened by his previous coverings. The insistent inner call to new becoming engenders in him dissatisfaction with what he has achieved and affirmed. He sacrifices his previous manner, often without having exhausted all of its possibilities. If he is insufficiently magnanimous to make this act of self-renunciation, he often remains at the stage of his initial uniqueness; but a stagnant manner becomes *mannerism.* This easily proves the relative smallness of his talent. A great talent experiences this self-renunciation in various ways. There are talents of grace who pass with divine ease, painlessly and unperturbed, through the path of this second incarnation on earth that we call artistic creation. There are other talents for whom the search for a personality means a break with art, or else a transition into a realm of forms so transcendent to art that any attempt to realize them seems to border on artistic madness (Vrubel').[3] The power that makes the artistic personality healthy and saves him in his search for a new morphological principle of creative life is truly the power of the healing god Apollo: it is *style.*

But if in order to find a new persona it is necessary to sacrifice manner, then, in order to find one's own style, it is necessary to be able partially to repudiate one's persona. Manner is a subjective form; style is an objective one. Manner is immediate; style is mediated: style is achieved by overcoming the identity between personality and creator, by objectifying the personality's subjective content. The artist, in the strict sense of the word, only begins at the instant marked by the triumph of style.

He who has mastered an original manner sees the creative process as the reworking of the outer datum of perception by the subject's inner energies. For the artist who possesses style, there exist two kinds of datum: that of outer perception and that of his inner reaction to perceptions; as an artist, he himself is free of both and freely utilizes each without becoming identified with his own subjective "I." His activity becomes normalized insofar as he, by rejecting individual arbitrariness and an isolating autarchy, freely subordinates himself to the objective principle of beauty as the general category of human union. At the same time, his activity becomes normative insofar as that which is affirmed in his creation, arising from subordination to the general norm, acquires the character of an objective value. But such lofty achievements are purchased at the heavy price of self-limitation ("in der Beschränkung zeigt sich erst der Meister"),[4] and for self-limitation one needs selfhood, one needs a persona, and the attempt to pass from manner directly to style ("le style, c'est l'*homme*"),[5] without having defined oneself as a persona, creates not style but *stylization*. For its part, stylization relates to style as mannerism to manner.

The next and yet higher acquisition, which bestows the final crown on the artist, is the *grand style*.[6] It demands the ultimate sacrifice of personality, the integral surrender of self to the objective and universal principle, either in its pure idea (Dante), or in one of the auxiliary and subordinate forms by which divine all-unity is affirmed (such is, for example, true nationality). Pushkin's greatness was revealed in the way that, not content with style, he strove toward and at times approximated the hallowed limits of universal art.[7] Imitation of the grand style without fulfilling the preliminary steps—first artistic individualism and then style creation—can only produce something low and vulgar.

II

Attempts to establish a durable canon that would define the conditions of "perfection" for poetic works belong to the distant past. We moderns, with our "historical sense,"[8] now know well what such attempts are worth. Aristotle was possible only after Sophocles, and he had already forgotten much of what had animated the religious creative work of Aeschylus. Horace was the theoretician of the young neoclassicists of the Augustan age. Boileau had to misunderstand Ronsard fatally.[9] Our theoretical programs have turned into a personal confession of faith; an example is Verlaine's "L'art poétique."[10] Our lot, apparently, is aesthetic anarchism, or else eclecticism. . . . "Sing sorrow, sorrow: but good win out in the end!" as Aeschylus says.[11]

However, such is the reality, as musicians well know. Once, the principle of music was order; music issued from the assumption of concord between the order of humanity and that of the world, and it strove to bring the conflicting forces into concord. Now, the principle of music has become pure kineticism, a becoming without any goal. Hence the atrophy of elements of closure and internal completeness, such as the melodic period. Hence also the disregard for consistent thematic development as a logical principle that signifies the full cycle of experience, the completing of which leads to overcoming and catharsis, and, consequently, restores the static norm. Fragmentariness, atomism, and alogism have become slogans in music. The struggle with logism naturally concludes with the triumph of psychologism. Psychologism, which is not based on normative self-determination, causes irritability and irregularity; the music of modern man is music *à court haleine*.[12] If a composer turns to the universal, his cosmic schemes turn out to be a projection of his psychology. His flight, impulsive and hopeless, is like the flight of a bird over a boundless sea, a bird that is already tired and still cannot see land on the horizon; classical music, in contrast, seems a smooth circling of eagles in the heights over a motionless peak. For no art can expose as directly and immediately as music whether or not an artist believes in God. Thus, in our day, music is doing underground, destructive work in the realm of our "subconscious."

Hence the chaos we observe in the sphere of musical art and musical tastes, within which one principle stands out: the struggle for the predominance of one's own individual will and anarchy. The strongest man triumphs, and the strongest is he who has best answered the demands of the evolutionary moment, the "spirit of the time."[13] The spirit of the time has been expressed most directly by our "Futurists," who have charted, in a significant triangle, a self-loving *Ego* which helplessly pretends to significance.[14] But why, however, does it "helplessly pretend"? Because, scattered into atoms of experience by psychologism, the *ego* does not even denote "character." In its musical emanations, it disintegrates into a boundless series of atrophied musical themes, none of which finds resolution. Each theme compensates for the inadequacy of its own inner development and justification only by brilliant and exquisite harmonization. In other words, we seek to enrich each instant with the fullest possible content, sometimes more than it can naturally accommodate, in order to betray it immediately for the next one. Everywhere component parts are forced together, while the whole remains disconnected and therefore powerless. But disconnectedness is the guiding principle of the ailing modern soul and of its immediate, involuntary confessions in music. It is as if you see before you some kind of flight, directed into the distance, under the threat of pursuant horror, a flight along thorns and cleats, each one of which stings sharply, but the burning pain of each instant is erased by the sting of the next. *Sic desperati. . . .*[15]

Is it necessary to explain that there is nothing more repugnant to the spirit of Dionysus? But it is precisely Dionysus who has sent this malady down upon us. For he in grace brings "true" madness down onto people and it is also he who, when angered, brings down "untrue" madness.[16] In order to approach Dionysus, one needs strength; he raises this strength to abundance and overflowing. Dionysus does not take possession of the weak; he destroys them. The approach of this god is dangerous;[17] it is unwise to rush toward him; one must stand and wait, preparing oneself in fear for the desired and fearful meeting.[18] The personality must fortify itself, gather itself into a unity; unity is achieved only by religious self-determination, only by the subordination of all internecine component parts to the supreme unity of the religious principle. We, however, begin not with obedience, but with a challenge. We educate ourselves as slaves raise slaves—in rebellion, and not as kings educate future masters—in submission. Whenever we try to be wise and cautious, we cowardly begin to act like slaves, since we are incapable of religious obedience. This cowardly reaction seeks salvation from old idols. Our relation to art becomes the piety of Old Believers;[19] creativity is replaced by superstitious imitation and calculated restoration: unchecked psychology turns into sedate archeology. *Sic laudatores temporis acti....*[20]

Of all the arts, poetry, especially lyric poetry, is closest to music. What has been said concerning music may be applied to poetry as well, although with some qualifications. Music is more immediate and free, and therefore more symptomatic. Much that is unthinkable in the daylight of the word is possible in the musical twilight. The word, by its very essence, cannot be alogical. The clear norm of consciousness is immanently present in the word. The word by its very nature partakes of *sobornost'* and, consequently, is moral. It is destroyed if certain logical and moral boundaries are transgressed. The word heals; there are demons and chimeras that cannot bear being named, which disappear at the sound of their name. The force of evil turns the word into its instrument by means of euphemisms. Therefore, the sickness of the age can appear in lyric poetry only in concealed form. In lyric poetry, it is futile to seek clear proofs of psychological anarchism and atomism. On the other hand, an inner lack of principle will lend it the hypocrisy of soulless eclecticism. In order to avoid this, we know no other means than the subordination of the inner personality to a single, supreme determining principle. This is the inner canon. The days are upon us when an artist, if he does not desire to be religious, "will lose even what he would keep," i.e., will also cease to be an artist.[21] At the same time, as the reader would be well advised to note, by religion we mean not some definite content of religious beliefs, but a form of the personality's self-determination in its relation to the world and to God.

III

The peculiarity of the cultural moment we are experiencing is that, at the present time, both series of theses and conclusions, the aesthetic series and religious-ethical series, are becoming intertwined and entering into interaction. With every instant of our own creative work, we affirm the truth of our assurances that art, in our eyes, is autonomous and not subject to any law (or *telos*) of any neighboring and coordinated cultural sphere. We know by the experience of artists how an artistic creation is engendered from "the spirit of music"[22] and how it is carried to term and born by the regular action of the forces that conditioned its conception. We know how negligible is the freedom of a creator who cannot change the action of these forces, and how independent of his intention and will is the independent life of the work. We, therefore, are the first who are ready to express surprise at the coincidence of the two series charted above. But we differ from those who do not understand this connection, or who pretend not to understand, by our submissive acceptance of something we did not invent, but which has been determined by the eternal stars which assign to each era particular demands and trials and which prepare for each era its own dangers and promises.

Indeed, how can we rid ourselves of soulless eclecticism except by imbuing all our creative work with the breath of a living soul? And where can one find this living soul if not in an integral personality? And how is an integral personality possible if, having doubted its substantial unity, since it had not affirmed such unity by an act of will, it knows no other self-determination than a modal one—if all of it, in each lived instant, is not a *res* but only a *modus?* How can one make art vital if it seeks to evade life? If, on the other hand, it has remained in life, then it, of course, incorrectly sees its calling only in the passive reflection of life. Then it becomes dominated by the mimetic element, an element which, in Plato's just opinion, is precisely the original sin of art, its negative pole.[23] "The artist is not an ape," we might say, repeating the words of an ancient tragic poet of Aeschylus's school, which he applied to a famous actor of his time who was leading a tragedy of Sophocles into psychologism and naturalism.[24] In order for art to be vital, the artist must live; and to live does not mean to dream in an arbitrary and groundless manner (in other words, to negate life by covering it with the misty charms of sleepy illusion, the miragelike projections of our human, all-too-human, desires and our small, petty passions). In the age of Decadence, snobs and desperate souls proclaimed: "give us flowers, give us flowers, to close up the black hole"—*le néant,* or, if you please, *le Grand Néant.*[25] We no longer wish to be costume designers for skeletons, torchbearers in the funeral procession that accompanies to the graveyard of history the entire holy family of sisters: Love, Faith, and Hope, together with their mother, Wisdom.[26] For of the gifts that the Muses did not deny us, the best gift is artistic intuition and a prophetic faith in the truth of resurrection.

Likewise, to live does not mean to experience, merely to experience the datum of life as if observing an experiment. Such a man either begins to ape the datum like a neurasthenic or else is utterly reduced to a vague moan of suffering caused by that which is being experienced, so that the datum itself is indistinguishable in his creative work from his reaction to it. For suffering is an irritation that has crossed the threshold separating it from pleasure; the weaker the force of resistance on the part of the perceiver, the quicker the irritation turns into pain. If a personality is only passively perceptive and not energetically active, art inevitably falls victim to a pained psychologism. Art will be vital if the artist lives actually and actively. "Whoever lives, enlivens": a sign of genuinely actual life is its will to vivify, to awaken the vital forces of others. Thus, truly vital art is the result of an integral personality that is equal to itself in all psychological modi, a personality that cannot but realize its unity in respect to living unities and, together with them, cannot but submit to all-encompassing unity in a joyful

affirmation of its individual and universal being. The more integral and en-
ergetic the personality, the more vital is its universal feeling; only weakness
alienates from the whole; strength fortifies the connection, and a normal
man is directly concerned with everything, not only with everything human
but with everything up to the stars themselves. In other words, to live means
to find in oneself a religious (connecting, coordinating, and obligating)[27]
form of relation toward the greater whole, independent of the content of
the ideas and concepts, beliefs and hopes, with which consciousness might
desire or be able to fill this form.

Although art remains an autonomous sphere, due to the correspondence developed above between the aesthetic series and the series of living
values and insofar as it intuits its correlation to other cultural spheres, art
may take from the analysis of general cultural life warnings and initiatives.
Although art is not obliged to make use of these, they are fruitful and, perhaps, salvific for it when it encounters inner difficulties or hazards on its
separate, independent path. The inner difficulty or hazard that modern art
has encountered has already been indicated above. It is most of all the lack
of character or, to say the same in technical transcription, the lack of style
in modern art.

The masses, whose name "is legion, because they are many,"[28] com-
plaining about the displeasure they feel and the bankruptcy they suspect in
all modern art as such, often ask: "why do we, who seem so insensitive to
poetry, receive true pleasure from rereading Pushkin?" No matter how much
stubborn obtuseness and dull self-confidence, autosuggestion and imitation,
and, finally, laughable misconceptions regarding Pushkin might be contained in such declarations, there is nonetheless a certain truth at the basis
of their verdict. A man of the masses essentially knows two kinds of art. One
is deeply intimate and immediately responds to his sorrows and joys, the
demands and needs of his emotional range; he is aesthetically undemand-
ing toward this kind of art and is practically always grateful to it. And there
is another kind of art for him, which he is capable of respecting—and at
times even of loving—as Art with a capital letter, despite his extremely
vague comprehension of it. Unconsciously, he is extremely demanding toward this second kind of art and is mostly correct in his recognition of it.
This is art of a style that is generalized to the borders of grand style.

It is this very style that the masses miss in modern art. And they fail
to find it because modern artists have not yet outgrown the standards of
limited individualism. They have their own emotional range, and the common man has his own. The two orbits barely come into accidental contact
with each other. Grand style, and a style that approximates it, does not know
such a delimitation and division into "yours" and "mine." As a general style,
it encompasses each individual orbit. Moreover, it is oriented with regard to
the general national consciousness in such a way that the universal norm is

its axis and passes through its center, thus inevitably coinciding with the axis of general national consciousness, since the latter has not moved from its foundations, has not betrayed its universal sanctuary. An outer symptom of this faithfulness of orientation is the poet's language, which grows through him and gives forth new blossom and fruit, which is joyfully accepted by the entire nation and acknowledged by it as its native heritage. It is as if around the axis there glimmers a unique, colorful illumination: this is the *modus* of the national comprehension and experience of the universal norm. The poet naturally accepts such a national coloring into his range if the latter is correctly oriented. Such are some of the simplest conditions of true style.

When we conduct a clear evaluation of the entire sum of cultural phenomena, we see that it is possible to remain within the bounds and context of one of the series defined above in order to find in consciousness a means of overcoming the dangers that threaten art. We can demonstrate this with the example of lyric poetry: based on the foregoing considerations of the nature of style, we shall try to find the criterion of lyric "perfection" as it might appear to the modern consciousness, which is attempting to overcome the deviations it comprehends and does not wish to submit to the formulas of ancient or modern fashion.[29] Moreover, we shall at first limit our analysis to the purely aesthetic series.

IV

If we hold to the old and generally correct division of poetry into three genres—epos, lyric, and drama—we will be able to arrive at the distinguishing features of these three genres from the presence of the two basic elements that are subject to artistic depiction: the extrapersonal datum and its inner reworking by the personality. The epos is distinguished by the depiction of only the first of the two elements, that of the extrapersonal datum. In the epos, the personality of the artist renounces its activity, becoming but a passive mirror of what is perceived (the extrapersonal datum), and all of its poetical actuality passes into pure reincarnation. The stronger this actuality, the more vital is the datum of the depicted world that it has saturated. In contrast to the epos, which is formally limited to the sphere of the datum alone, tragedy is essentially concerned only with the personality. The task of tragedy is to reveal the duality of personality, to show the personality to be in division and conflict with itself. Elements of the extrapersonal datum serve only to concretize this inner disintegration of personality into two conflicting forces. Tragedy does not arise out of the simple collision of personality with the datum; it is necessary that one part of the personality become the ally of this datum, with the other part becoming its enemy. The sacrifice of Polyxena touches and horrifies; but that of Iphigenia is tragic, since the father is sacrificing the daughter, and the daughter is sacrificing her life.

66

The distinguishing mark of lyric poetry is that both elements are represented in it, and necessarily in their interrelation and interaction. The task of lyric poetry is to reveal the reworking of the datum by the personality. Works that are lyric in form, but which set forth only the datum, combined with a passive and purely receptive relation of the personality toward it, are in their essence not lyric but rather epic. Works that are lyric in form, but which set forth only the inner disintegration of the personality and the contradictions of its will, are also in their essence not lyric but rather tragic monologues. Both the former and the latter belong, however, to poetry, something that can in no way be said in regard to two other types: meditations, albeit even very sublime ones, and rhetoric, albeit of extreme grandiloquence, both of which types are clothed in lyric form. In the former case (in so-called philosophical poems), we are dealing not with the struggle between the energies of will that condition a tragic conflict but rather with the interrelation of concepts, which are brought into harmony through dialectical development. In the latter case, we see not the personality's inner reworking of the datum, which comprises an event for the personality and summons all of its creative forces, but rather the personality's purely external reaction to the datum, a reaction that leaves the personality inwardly unchanged and impenetrable.

The period of manner in the artist's development is characterized by the datum predominating over the personality or the personality predominating over the datum. Neither the one nor the other is given sufficiently full expression; nonetheless, the activity of reworking is palpably signified by the very forms by which the emotional process is incarnated in the word. The period of style, on the contrary, is marked by a distinct division between the element of the datum, depicted or signified with epic transparence and impartial exactitude, and the element of personal attitude toward this datum as such, that is, taken in its genuinely characteristic capacity and content. A strict balance between the extrapersonal datum and the personal reaction to it is observed in a work that has style.

In the period of an artist's life when he is occupied with acquiring and expressing his persona, it is typical and natural to observe that the balance dictated by style has been violated in favor of the personal element. Lyric poetry becomes subjective to a degree that is incommensurate with style. Nonetheless, it would be ridiculous to condemn this imperfection as an artistic fault, for so often it is bursting with vital forces and beautiful in its premonition of ultimate beauty. But while he is still seeking his persona, one can still demand from the artist that he observe a certain moderation in the subjectivism of his perception and in its verbal expression. One cannot grant the subjective lyric poet the right to distort the datum beyond recognition or to absorb it into himself so that the depiction of the outer world turns into an incoherent nightmare. One cannot grant him the right to call things by names uncharacteristic of them and to attribute to them uncharacteristic features. The rape of the datum must not be considered lyrical subjectivism.

True, the very concept of the datum is only conditionally objective. It is what is subjectively perceived as given. "Darum pfuscht er auch so: Freunde, wir haben's *erlebt.*"[30] So, we are deprived of the possibility of verifying the conscientiousness of the perceiver's statements concerning what he perceives; and as far as the ability of following the perceiver on the paths of his subjective perception is concerned, this ability is, in its turn, subjective. Here we would seem to lose a reliable criterion, if only we did not have numerous tangential means for determining the degree of reliability of whoever is acting as the witness of his own experience. But, let us suppose that we are convinced of this reliability; then we have the right to present our witness with a new demand, a new inquiry.

We have the right to inquire of him, insofar as he desires to show us his persona, whether he really seeks to determine it, whether he is really creating his integral personality or rather dissipating and scattering it. Is his character being formed before us, or is it rather decomposing? Is he not infecting us with miasmas of decay? And if these questions are pronounced beyond the threshold of aesthetic analysis,[31] then this is only because the poet himself is the first to have stepped over the threshold of art, which demands respect for the things of the world common to us all, which requires that one fulfill a certain measure of objectivism, and which symbolically signifies the recognition of objective norms. A genius has no reason to be afraid of such limitations, of such obedience, but playing at genius ("das genialische Treiben")[32] will reject them with disdain.

So, we who want modern art to ascend to style should make the following demand of modern lyric poetry. Before all else, it must reach a clear distinction between the contents of the datum and the personality, and avoid mixing the colors of the one and the other into a confused haze. We demand that the psychologism of rebellious individuality not triumph over the logism of the universal idea, that lyric poetry carry inwardly the principle of order and union with divine all-unity, and not the principle of disorder and isolation. Finally, we demand that lyric poetry not crawl into the underground out of a fear of life.[33]

On the Limits of Art

When so many days had passed that exactly nine years had elapsed since that first appearance of my lady, on the last of those days it occurred: the wondrous one appeared before me in clothes as white as snow, between two noble women who were older in years. She walked along the street and cast a glance in the direction where I, overcome by timidity, was standing. And in her ineffable benevolence, which now has been rewarded in eternal life, she greeted me with such sympathy that I seemed to witness the bounds of blessedness. The hour of the sweet salutation was precisely the ninth hour of that day; and her words then reached my ears as if for the first time and I experienced such sweetness that I left the crowd as if drunk. Escaping to the solitude of my chamber, I gave myself over to thoughts of the merciful one; and while I was contemplating her a pleasant sleep came over me, and a wondrous vision arose in my slumber. I dreamed that a fire-colored cloud obscured my chamber and that one could make out in it the image of the Master, whose visage would horrify anyone who dared to behold him; yet he himself was merry and jubilant; and it was wondrous. And I seemed to hear his words, incomprehensible to me except for a few, among which I caught the phrase: "I am your lord." And it was as if I saw a naked woman sleeping in his arms, barely covered with a blood-red cloth; taking a deeper look I recognized her as the woman of the kind salutation, who had granted me her greeting of good will on that memorable day. And it seemed that in one hand he held something burning with flame, and it was as if he said: "Behold your heart." And for some time he remained thus, and then it seemed as if he was waking the sleeping woman, mastering her with the force of his will, bidding her to taste of what he held in his hand, and she ate timidly. After this his joy soon turned into a bitter plaint; and with a plaint he lifted the woman into his arms, and together with her he appeared to fly up to heaven. And this brought down upon me fear and such anguish that my light sleep could not contain it; it dispelled my sleep and I awoke. And waking I fell into meditation and found that it was the fourth hour of night when the vision appeared; so it is clear that it appeared in the first of the last nine hours of night. And considering what I had seen, I thought to relate it to the many glorious troubadours of the time; and, as I had myself acquired the art of harmonious

words, I resolved to compose a sonnet in which I would hail all who had faithfully given tribute to Love and relate to them all that I had beheld in sleep,
asking them to interpret my vision. And then I began this sonnet:

Hail to all who compassionately give tribute,
Pure servants of Amor, the Sovereign of hearts!
Whoever reads this scroll and gives answer
Will be a friend to me, his brother in faith.

She had completed a third of her journey through the celestial sphere,
She whose path grants light to all stars,
When he of whom there is no equal came before me
Jubilant, and bound my breast with fear.

He bore a heart; my flesh did flame;
And I saw my Lady beneath a light cover
In the Master's embrace.

He awoke the frightened woman from oblivion
And bid her eat of the crimson victuals;
And with a plaint he soared into the lands beyond the stars.

This sonnet is divided into two parts: in the first part, I send my greetings
and request an answer; in the second part, I define what must be answered.
The second part begins with the verse: "She had completed a third of her
journey through the celestial sphere."[1]

In this third chapter of Dante's *New Life,* we find a twofold testimony:
the testimony of a man concerning the life of his heart and his inner experience, and the testimony of an artist concerning the appearance of an artistic creation that is immediately communicated. There is no doubt as to the
authenticity and sincerity of these direct and guileless testimonies, just as
there is no doubt that Dante was both a man with a profound emotional life
and a great artist. What then do we see? Is not the ecstasy described here
one of the highest ascents of his spirit into a realm of suprasensible consciousness, such that man cannot return without having been enriched by
the fruits of this ascent, and which marks the rest of his life as an indelible
and decisive event? And is it not clearly evident how this rapture, which lifts
him so powerfully above the earth, releases him, as it were, from its eagle's
claws and then surrenders him whole to his native vale, returning to him
with great care his ordinary shell of earthly emotions as he follows the steps
of descent? Then he is suddenly overcome by thoughts and concern for
other people, by the desire to bring these others tidings, which he himself
recognizes as important without being able to comprehend them: now he
himself consciously descends to the depths of the vale. And here, in his sonnet, we find something new that was not present in his vision, while the vision itself is reduced to its defining features, as if condensed into flesh or
compressed into a crystal; the contours of the vision are sharper and bolder,

and it is related in a voice and tone that is firm, intrepid, impassive. And how much is wholly concealed or passed over! And see how all that in the vision remained shrouded in fog and vaguely alarming, elusive and unconscious, has become more conscious and qualitatively poorer in these magnificent verses!

This presents a clear illustration of what is to be developed conceptually in the following exposition: that when creating a work of art, the artist descends from spheres that he, as a spiritual man, attained in his ascent. It follows that there are many who ascend but few who are able to descend, i.e., there are few true artists.[2] I might add that the example I have cited is especially revealing here because the poet intentionally minimizes the distance between the levels of ascent and descent. He considers himself obliged to preserve strict precision in the communication of what he has seen and forbids himself even the slightest degree of invention, meticulous in his concern that his creation wholly correspond to his experience.

Let us look more closely at the process: erotic ecstasy gives rise to a mystical epiphany; then this mystical epiphany gives rise to a spiritual conception that is accompanied by the vivid calm of the enriched and gladdened soul; and this calm gives rise to a new musical agitation that draws the spirit to the birth of a new form of incarnation. The musical agitation yields to a poetic dream in which recollections are mere material for contemplating the Apollonian image that is to be reflected in the word by the harmonious body of a rhythmical creation, until, at last, the desire that is ignited by contemplating the Apollonian image gives rise to the verbal flesh of the sonnet. All of the moments I have enumerated are clearly designated by our witness: (1) the mighty wave of the Dionysian storm; (2) the Dionysian epiphany, or vision, which resolves the ecstasy and which must not be confused with the artist's Apollonian dream; (3) the cathartic calm that is conditioned by an integral and consummate experience of ecstasy. Dante the artist is wholly absent from these three initial moments, in which is manifested only the primordial and fundamental basis of his soul. This engenders in him not only the artistic but all the other revelations and mysteries of his spirit. This is the general element of his genius, but not his purely artistic genius itself. There follows: (4) a new Dionysian state unlike the preceding one, which when compared in intensity to the previous one is like a strong swell on the sea as opposed to a storm; it is preeminently musical and can be separated from the preceding three moments not by hours but by years; this is the state of which Pushkin said, "the soul is oppressed by a lyric agitation, it trembles and sounds forth";[3] (5) the Apollonian dream, memory's dream of the epiphany that the artist has glimpsed, a dream that reveals to him the ideal image of his yet-to-be-incarnate creation; for, according to Pushkin, the soul that trembles and sounds forth immediately "seeks, as if in *slumber*, to pour out at last in a free expression"; (6) and (7) as soon as the Apollonian dream clearly appears to the soul, a new "lyrical agitation" and "sounding" arise that draw the artist to his ultimate realization, to the materialization of his dream fantasy; there appear "easy rhymes rushing head on" and verses that "flow freely," and the dream becomes the flesh of the word. These four latter moments are characteristic of the artist as such and are the stages of descent.

The creation of forms is thus made manifest at three points: (α) in the mystical epiphany of inner experience, which may be either a clear encounter

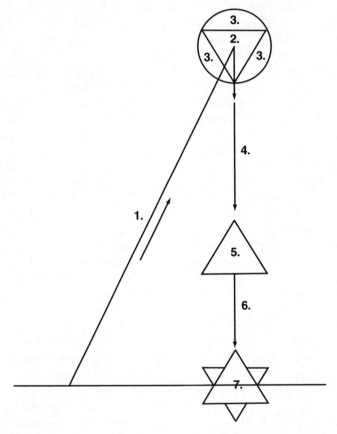

The ascending line, 1–3. The conception of the work of art: (1) Dionysian agitation; (2) the Dionysian epiphany [α]—an intuitive vision or comprehension; (3) catharsis, conception.

The descending line, 4–7. The birth of the work of art: (4) Dionysian agitation; (5) the Apollonian dream [β]—the mirror image of the intuitive moment in memory; (6) Dionysian agitation; (7) artistic incarnation [γ]—the World Soul's assent to accepting the intuitive truth that is mediated by the artist's creative work (the synthesis of the Apollonian and Dionysian principles).

or a face-to-face vision of higher realities only in exceptional cases, and which remains beyond the bounds of the artistic-creative process proper; (β) in the Apollonian vision of a purely artistic ideal, which is that very dream of poetic fantasy that artists customarily call their creative "dreams"; (γ) in the ultimate incarnation of dreams in meaning, sound, and visual or tangible matter. Each of these stages of form-creation is achieved by experiencing a Dionysian agitation that is essentially consubstantial but which adopts various forms and acts with various degrees of violence. On the whole, Wagner is correct when he says in his *Meistersinger:*

> Remember this single testament:
> The poet is born to be a seer of dreams;
> And all the art of harmonious words
> Is the interpretation of vatic dreams.[4]

Let us compare a single sonnet by Petrarch to the testimony of Dante that we have studied. Petrarch's poem is similar to Dante's in the form of its visionary exposition of a lyrical idea, but it is without a doubt more Apollonian with respect to the experience that engendered it and therefore more representative for the study of the purely artistic element. This is his thirty-fourth sonnet on the death of Laura:

> My mind was enraptured beyond the limit of the universe
> By my yearning for her who has been taken from the earth;
> And I passed through the heavenly gates
> Into the third circle of souls. How less haughty
>
> Did she appear to me in imperishable beauty!
> Giving me her hand, she uttered: "I am the one
> Who urged your passion. But this bother
> Did not last long, and I was granted
>
> Ineffable quiet. Around me I lack only you
> And the lower veil that you loved,
> But you shall come. Be faithful, I am your light."
>
> Why did you remove your hand, that the word fell silent?
> O, if only your sweet greeting still rang,
> Then I would never again see earthly day![5]

Petrarch did not give us an autobiographical commentary to this sonnet. We see that it is full of profound feeling. But it is permissible to doubt whether the vision he describes was as vivid an epiphany as Dante's vision; all the more so since Petrarch himself with the words "levommi il mio penser" indicates the appearance of an image within the bounds of the thinking consciousness. However this may be, the partially ecstatic state that precedes his Apollonian dream is fully palpable. Even if this ecstasy did not grant him sufficiently defined forms, all the more vivid and vital did the

Apollonian vision appear to his spirit, gathering within itself, as in a transparent crystal, the rays of his sublime inner experience, which raised him to the realm where one contemplates the purest revelations of love. The Apollonian dream that he attains at the height of his devotional activity is so beautiful that, when clothed in the impeccably beautiful flesh of the word, it is vividly felt to be a certain sacrificial renunciation of something that by its very nature cannot be made incarnate, that is inexpressible in human words, but which is undoubtedly innate to the image of imperishable beauty he has seen. By admitting that he would not have woken again in the flesh unless the harmony he heard had fallen silent, the poet himself testifies that he perceives the communication of his experience through earthly words to be a descent. Thus, Petrarch proclaims himself to be descending in his role as artist; if we, however, sense ourselves to be ascending into the higher spheres, carried aloft above the earth by his lyrical charms, and if we believe that we see even that elusive and unspoken something, illuminated by a heavenly beam and filled with heavenly harmony, which Petrarch did not express and at which he merely hinted, this is to be expected and means only that the artist descends in order to show us the path of ascent:

> Do not imagine that while melting in the heavens
> We are severed from the earth.
> A holy path leads
> To supernal dreams.[6]

II

To take and to give: life consists in the exchange of these two energies. In spiritual life and activity, they correspond to ascent and descent. Goethe's words "to strive tirelessly to the highest being" can be considered as a general formula of the spiritual life, understood as the growth of the personality.[7] Whoever stops, telling the moment "wait,"[8] falls. With respect to the spiritual path, a fall is a negative value; in contrast, both ascent and descent are positive. Ascent is growth conditioned by nutrition, or a strengthening that requires the consumption of hitherto alien energies: it refers to "taking."

Ascent is normal; it is human. It shows its humility by postulating hunger and imperfection; its pride is the anticipation of present possibilities as future achievements. Descent, on the contrary, does not follow a spiritual norm, but seeks either to destroy it and become chaotic, or to create it and become normative; it can be bestial or divine, or finally, in its purely human form, regal. It shows its humility by a certain renunciation of its riches, in the abnegation of its achievements; its pride is dissipation, the return from present achievements to the new possibilities of the path it has traveled.

Ascent is the law of self-preservation in its dynamic aspect, which can turn into self-destruction when its natural static state is violated. Descent is the law of self-destruction halted in its action by a static moment; it is a crystalline sediment in the personality that threatens it with petrifaction. In general, ascent is the accumulation of strength, while descent is its radiation. Spiritual apprenticeship as such cannot be anything but constant ascent; but the wholeness of life demands ascent and descent in equal measure. Danger and daring are characteristic of both kinds of motion; but there is more danger and daring in descent than in ascent. On the other hand, descent, when correct and true, is more sacrificial and more full of grace.

These general considerations do not relate directly to the aesthetic sphere. Let us cast a glance at their relevance to aesthetics.

We experience a perception of beauty when we discern a certain primordial dualism in the sphere of a given phenomenon while simultaneously contemplating the eventual overcoming of this dichotomy, which can be distinguished only analytically, in perfect synthetic unity. Moreover, the elements of the dualism that we seek to surmount are essences or energies correlated as the material substratum and the formative principle. Such a definition requires that the formative principle be active, while the material substratum must be not only passive but also malleable, in the sense that its very nature must present both an ability and readiness to assume a form that, as it were, fills it inwardly, instead of being imposed superficially from outside. The perception of the beautiful is destroyed by the impression of violence being committed on the material substratum: a work of art wants to imitate nature, whose forms are revelations of the inner processes of organic life, so that Goethe is correct when he says, "what is given on the outside exists within."[9] Therefore, a perception of beauty is a perception of vitality, and a work of art, to be sure, can create an impression of the greatest immobility, like a crystal (which itself, however, is frozen life), but it cannot create an impression of death or the primordial absence of life. In the latter case, we would have a mechanical product but not a "creation," which is the word we use to denote the analogy between the task of the artist and a natural organism.[10]

One consequence of the foregoing is, for example, the demand, profoundly justified in an aesthetic sense, that the material of a work of art be palpable and, as it were, faithful to itself, that it express its willingness to accept the forms that the artist grants it. Thus, one who sculpts in wood should not imitate the technique of one who sculpts in marble, but rather work over the wood with special techniques congenial to the organic fabric of wood fibers. Matter comes to life in a work of art to the degree that it affirms itself, not in the state of stagnant sleep, but in a state of awareness reaching to its ultimate depths; through this it accepts the image of freely assenting to the creator's conceptions. The artist triumphs if he convinces us that the marble desired his chisel; he naturally lives in a unity of soul with the matter he forms; he naturally imagines it to be alive and is in love with it, trusting it to such a degree that he does not hesitate to tell it his most intimate and distant thoughts. He is convinced that the matter will always be able to understand him and will always respond with love. This is the pathos of the aphorism by Michelangelo that opens his collection of sonnets and canzones:

> Non ha l'ottimo artista alcun concetto
> Ch'un marmo solo in se non circoscriva
> Col suo soverchio, e solo a quello arriva
> La man che obbedisce all'intelletto.[11]

"The best artist does not have a conception that any single slab of marble could not contain within its surface, and the hand that is guided by genius reaches only to the borders of this marble." But the participation of matter in the genesis of a work of art is limited to its assent to the form it is given, by this joyous acceptance of the idea imprinted upon it. Matter is revealed to spirit but does not ascend to it; it is spirit that descends to matter. The artist's thought, which he envisions as being realized in the spirit, is made incarnate in assenting matter through descent. The formative principle is the descending principle, just as matter is the accepting principle. Thus, there is no place for ascent in the creation of beauty. Nietzsche also understood that beauty is descent, and he says through the mouth of Zarathustra: "When might becomes merciful and descends to the visible—Beauty is what I call such a descent."[12]

Thus, the artist's activity is a kind of daring and simultaneously a kind of sacrifice, for he, insofar as he is an artist, must descend, while the general law of spiritual life, which wants to be life in truth and in a constantly growing force, is ascent to the highest being.[13] Hence the contradiction between the artist and the man: the man must ascend, while the artist must descend. How can this contradiction be resolved? In certain types and certain eras, it was resolved and is resolved just as in everyday life, very simply. One could even say that for all modern history, beginning with the Renaissance, due to the weakening of religiosity and the disintegration of what was previously a synthetic culture, this type of artistic psychology has become absolutely dominant. The practical resolution of which we are speaking is found in the separation or divorce of the artist and man within the creative personality: the one does not know what the other is doing.[14] However, when the man inquires of the artist, or the artist of the man, more often than not this path leads to an irreconcilable inner discord within the personality similar to that once experienced by Botticelli, and which in Russia was experienced by Gogol or Lev Tolstoy.[15] But, for the most part, when the artist feels that the meaning of his own life and its highest peaks are in his artistry, he simply considers the man within him to be the inferior and therefore neglected part of his being, illuminated by artistic genius; then there naturally arises within him the illusion of ascent through artistry. The "idle loiterer, priest only of what is beautiful"[16] usually feels himself to be the most insignificant "of all the insignificant children of the world,"[17] while in moments of creative illumination, he feels himself sanctified and sacerdotal. But then the very instant when "the prophetic eyes, like the eyes of a frightened she-eagle"[18] open wide is a moment of sudden flight, relative to which the purely artistic work of creative realization and materialization again appears to be descent.[19]

III

The relationship between artist and man has proven more complex for some contemporary poets. The general revelation of the symbolic nature of art called them to develop it in such a way that its dormant energies of intuitive insight and suprasensible efficacy might radiate more freely and more powerfully. This relationship became more complex as a result of these artists' unique personal qualities and life experience: their view of things appears to have been complicated from the beginning by some new apperceptions that granted them the experience (whether actual or illusory is another question; most likely it was part actual, part illusory) of a kind of double vision.[20] They believed that these new apperceptions revealed to them unexpected and distant connections, correspondences, and correlations among things. These people were predisposed to mysticism, which was to flare up in new generations because of general and distant historical factors; their souls had a mystical cast. On the whole, they remained faithful to themselves even at times when their minds and wills experienced doubt and disbelief. Due to this predisposition, artistic creativity and what they imagined to be suprasensible intuition naturally merged, which lent their art a unique tint and wrapped their truly mystical experience in the cocoon of a poetic dream. They thought that this would initiate new possibilities for art as such, that art was the very sphere where the new knowledge of universal essences could be achieved, given, on the one hand, the static crystallization of previous religious revelation and, on the other, the inability of scientific thought to answer the riddles of the universe.

It is therefore not surprising that representatives of the movement under discussion did not distinguish, or thought that they did not distinguish, the man, understood as the bearer of inner experience and of various epistemological and other spiritual values, from the artist, the interpreter of man. And even if the man and the artist became more or less separated, then these poets experienced the separation as emotional discord and as a kind of apostasy from the holy possession entrusted to them. "We were prophets and wanted to become poets," Aleksandr Blok reproachfully says of himself and his comrades as he describes the states of this discord and the "hell" of the artist who is only an artist.[21] By contrast Valery Briusov, enamored of so-called pure art and addressing himself to the naively direct Bal'mont, once exhibited his desire for such "hell" by exclaiming: "We are prophets, you are a poet."[22] In fact, all of these figures were true poets; measuring their prophecy lies beyond our competence and the matter at hand. But while they were poets, they were not artists in the full sense of the word, and they were not artists precisely insofar as they introduced into their art their "I," which strove toward the light but was unorganized, human, even immature and captive. As people, they were in the main faithful to the spiritual testament of ascent, and in every way possible, they demonstrated their striving for supreme being whenever they appeared with their "tidings for the world."[23] They created whenever they strove; they created insofar as they strove; and they imported this "boundless" (like the *ápeiron* of the ancient thinker),[24] unlimited, and formless element directly into their art in its raw state, so to speak. In them, the artist ascended instead of descending, because it was the man who was ascending, and in their consciousness the artist was identical to the man.

But "the master first shows himself in limitation,"[25] and if the disciples of the Muses were fated to achieve mastery, they had to acknowledge this limitation sooner or later. It is of limitation that I speak, however, not of renunciation. For those who have ever drunk from its chalice (which for some is bitter at the edges and sweet within, while for others it is the other way around), to repudiate Symbolism would essentially mean "to exchange a crown for a wreath,"[26] even if the "crown" was more a promise than a sure prize. In the language of the Symbolists, this would be to repudiate their "bride," their holy possession, to which they were betrothed with the ring of the symbol. This would mean to descend from the mountainous and difficult path to nearby and fertile valleys in order to rest under one's fig tree. Capua inspired horror in Hannibal.[27] The conditions for the only possible limitation were at last designated by the formula: "the inner canon." This limitation denotes the integral subordination of the artist to the general laws of immortal, pure, virginal, self-directed, autocratic, universal, divinely infantile art, and at the same time an integral acceptance of the law of the ascending spiritual path upward and of man's unceasing ascent to the highest being. Whoever in addition to this ascent can also encompass artistic descent, let him do so.[28]

But when the problem is posed in this way, one must wonder what remains of the Symbolist formula that I myself have proposed: *a realibus ad realiora.*[29] Does this not express ascent from the knowledge of simple realities to the knowledge of things more real than that first reality? Or is the growth of this knowledge not its ascendant progression? So is this formula annulled in order to be replaced by a new, contrary one: from the more real to the real, *a realioribus ad realia?* Not in the least! By the earlier formula we mean: art—insofar as it is true art—serves to raise from the real to the more real those who enjoy it and perceive it correctly. But when speaking not of the efficacy of art but of the conditions and process of artistic creativity, it is necessary to say: "from the more real to the real." The *realiora* that are revealed to the artist ensure that the simple reality he depicts will be inwardly true and that it will be possible to coordinate it correctly with the higher realities. As a man, the artist must inhabit the higher realm to which he attains through ascent, in order that, when he turns toward the earth and enters onto lower steps of reality, he might show these latter to be genuinely existing and bring about their genuine actuality.

The artist sees the very actuality of everyday realities only from the higher level of consciousness, for it is only then that he rules over reality. Thus, the creator of the novel *Madame Bovary* looks down on the life he depicts from some frigid and indifferent realm; in this realm, all of the passions that simmer below have already been surmounted in principle and all moral weaknesses have been renounced, right up to a refusal to provide an aesthetic evaluation of the things selected with such care.[30] This realm lays low over the earth, and from there everything, right down to the smallest detail, is clearly visible, as are all living things' hidden emotions. However, the higher things that are raised above this realm, and the hidden things that are concealed in corporeality below, remain utterly invisible to both Flaubert the artist and Flaubert the man. And yet it is only when the poet abides in the plane of this suprasensible impassivity, and only when he descends from above to the smallest details of lesser realities, that these latter, without idealization, become not insignificant, but more important and significant than if they had been depicted by one who was himself encumbered by the gray nets of their cobweb charms. For if a realist depicts reality from anywhere but the realm of the more real, his depiction will always remain the merely dreamy fantasy of a subjective spirit immersed in an illusory emotion; it will never possess either true objectivity or the magic force of life that populates our emotional atmosphere with the demonic offspring of a genius imagination,[31] whose effects remain palpable far beyond the sphere of the given works or art, such as Hamlet, Werther, the Bronze Horseman, or Chichikov.[32]

IV

Now, however, we must make a significant reservation. There is one realm of art that is exceptional in many respects. It belongs to poetry, and here the greatest strength is required of the poet and the least tension required of the artist. In this realm, the poet who encompasses two personalities, namely those of the poet and the artist, gives foremost expression to the former of these hypostases. This realm of poetry is the lyric. Here descent is least of all palpable; the lyric can be realized aesthetically, even in the poet's very ascent. Everything that the spirit experiences and learns in this ascent may pour directly into the elements of song. Neither the final mastery of new experiences of ascent nor their full assimilation and comprehension is necessary for the lyricism of emotion to find itself an artistically sufficient form. It is in this realm that the Symbolists were able to create in the easiest and most artistic manner at the very time that they were in ascent. And since they always declared themselves to be in ascent it is not surprising that the lyric dominated so decisively over other genres in their literary work and that, if attempts at epic or drama occurred in their art, that they were usually colored by this selfsame all-consuming lyricism. In this way, the natural talent itself of these poets forced them to achieve a natural self-limitation, thus saving their works for art.

Thus it was, but this is not entirely how it should be. The form of Symbolism we have described did not have to be its norm. The poet had to be a poet in full, and therefore he also had to be an artist, specifically an artist as much of drama and epic as of the lyric. We desire to affirm Symbolism not as legend and not as historical fact (history has affirmed it anyway) but in light of the general tasks of art and of the art of the future. We have no reason to fear for the revelations of Symbolism, insofar as they were true revelations. But, if art must be the bearer of these revelations, we find it important first and foremost that Symbolism be art in full measure. Art, however, is always descent. Art will be symbolic, i.e., truly full of content and energy, to the degree that the inner canon is realized by the artist, whether consciously or unconsciously.

The outer canon is the rules of art understood as technique. It is unified in the sense that it encompasses general and natural foundations that derive from the very nature of the given art. Thus, poetry is a verbal art and therefore must preserve the holy possession of the word, without substituting inarticulate onomatopoeia and without distorting its natural, organically regular structure. In another sense, there is absolutely no single outer canon but a multitude of them, and Shakespeare's art does not cease to be art for contradicting the rules of the French tragedians.[33] One might say that in each individual case, the artist chooses or establishes an outer canon for each new work. Sound criticism should only observe whether, within the bounds of the work being judged, the artist himself has not violated the technical norms that he set himself for the realization of his work. This should be sufficient to explain the concept of the "outer canon."

What I have called the inner canon relates not at all to the artist as such but to the man; consequently, it relates to the Symbolist artist, insofar as Symbolism is understood not in the sense of an external method, but in the inner and, in essence, mystical sense. For this kind of Symbolism is founded on the principle of accumulating spiritual knowledge of things and on the general surmounting of the personal principle, not only in the artist as such, and not only at moments of purely artistic creation, but in the artist's very personality and in all of his life, by means of a supraindividual, universal principle. The inner canon is the law of organizing the personality in accordance with universal norms, the law of vivifying, strengthening, and realizing the connections and correlations between individual being and collective [*sobornyi*], universal, and divine being. The deeper and more independent this ascent is, the clearer will creativity be realized not as its auxiliary moment but as its holy sacrifice.[34] Creativity would not be a sacrifice if it were a new spiritual acquisition: on the contrary, it surrenders strength and radiates energy; it is anguish and suffering in the realm of higher spirituality; it is the responsibility and, as it were, a kind of sin of incarnation; but at the same time, it is a certain redemptive sacrifice, and sweet and passionate sacrifice. The moment of descent, this moment of sacrifice, passion, and incarnation, reveals preeminently the erotic nature of creativity: erotic not in the Platonic sense, for Plato's Eros is the Eros of ascent and the son of Hunger,[35] but in the divinely creative sense, that of Dionysus or Zeus, for it is in this way that Zeus is poured onto Danae as a golden rain or that he overwhelms Semele in storm and flame.[36]

I must add that, according to the definition of the beautiful given above, artistic descent consists essentially of the effects of the formative principle, consequently—of the principle of form. The task of the artist is not to communicate new revelations but to reveal new forms. For if his task was to impose onto the plane of lower reality some alien content taken from the plane of higher realities, then we would not observe the mutual penetration of the descending and receptive principles, such as creates the phenomenon of beauty. What we have termed the material substratum would only be outwardly and superficially covered with an element foreign to it, and in the best case, it would only be clothed in it, as if in a transparent blue mist or golden aura, but the matter would not express its inner assent to being clothed in this manner; it would experience the violence and coercion of mystical idealization. For to idealize things is to do violence to them. No, the descending principle in artistic creativity is the hand that obeys genius, of which Michelangelo speaks; it only forms the material substratum, revealing and realizing the lower reality that is naturally and gratefully open to receiving consubstantial higher life.

Enriched by the epistemological experience of higher realities, the artist knows features and organs of lower reality that are hidden to the naked eye and by means of which this lower reality combines and connects itself with another reality; these are the sensitive points at which lower reality touches "other worlds."[37] The artist notes these points, which can be determined only by means of higher intuition and mystically, and if they are correctly marked, they issue forth and radiate lines of coordination between the small and the great, the individual and the universal. Each microcosm, which in its norm is similar to the macrocosm, contains the artist within itself, as a raindrop contains the image of the sun. Thus form becomes content, and content—form; thus, descending from the most real and mysterious to the real and clear (for it is fully incarnated insofar as it achieves realization when brought to the greatest clarity), the artist raises those who perceive his artistry *a realibus ad realiora*.

V

Most people in our day and age would probably agree that art serves knowledge and that the kind of knowledge represented by art is in a certain sense superior to scientific knowledge. The object of knowledge is known through the mediation of art differently than by scientific method: in some ways it is more limited and disordered, in others more vital and essential. The knowledge of the artist is included in the concept of intuition as one of its varieties, incapable of being replicated by its other types. The strength of intuitive ability is recognized as one of the distinguishing marks of artistic genius.

If we turn more closely to the epistemological activity of the artist, we first of all distinguish in it a moment during which the artist is present within a certain lower reality, which enriches him with its experiential knowledge and consciousness, in the sense that he feels this reality from within. But even for a simple depiction of reality as it is experienced by the artist during this first moment of his presence within it, it is necessary that he remove or distance himself from it by passing into a realm of consciousness that lies outside of it. What might this realm be like? The spirit may experience it as a void of sorts; the more independent and distant is the artist's experience of it with respect to the previous reality, the more energetically will the creative process reflect the pole of consciousness lying outside this reality, and the more clearly will its artistic apprehension flare up. For each apprehension, as a kind of philosophical Eros, combines an immanent presence within the object of knowledge and its transcendent contemplation. The creative spirit's withdrawal to a realm transcendent to reality, which liberates it from the will's connections to reality, is for the artist the first step toward awakening his intuitive powers, while for the man within him, it is itself a kind of spiritual ascent, even if it reveals itself to him only in its negative form—in the form of freedom from his previous entanglement in the reality he experienced. He is already located in something more real than previous reality, even if he is aware of this more-real something only as a realm of hollow indifference. And when he undertakes the incarnation of his creative intention, he will descend from such a more-real something to his previous habitation, with the magic mirror of an art that has been alienated from it, if only for a single instant.

But the creative spirit that alienates itself from the previously experienced world does not always perceive the newly accessible realms as a barren desert. In order to ascend into this desert, he must pass through a layer of mirages, deceptive hallucinations, and tempting but empty mirror images that reflect the selfsame reality that he has left behind, and which is now refracted in the shifting veil of his own passions and desires: this realm borders directly on the lower plane, and descent therein makes the artist's work only dreamy, capriciously fantastic, and whimsically misty. Such an artwork will contain neither the intuitive knowledge of things nor the immediate, elemental consciousness of the reality that the artist has already left; only the artist himself will be reflected in such a work, in all his emotional limitation and isolation. He, however, who by alienating himself from the world has ascended to the genuine void, to the bleak desert, can receive revelation of the contours of higher realities lying beyond the desert, which are like the first shells of the world of incorporeal ideas; such revelation occurs first in a kind of symbolic hieroglyphics, and then in a less mediated, face-to-face vision.[38] It is here, on the edge of the desert, that the springs of true intuition gush forth. When one reaches these bounds, it is first of all revealed to him that the lower reality from which he ascended and to which he shall again descend is something essentially alien to the world he is currently experiencing, but that it is encompassed by it (this higher world) as if it rested in its womb. Correct ascent restores to the spirit its earthly homeland, while mere dreamy flights into the aforementioned membrane of mirages serve to isolate him. Correct ascent is the only thing that can restore for the artist the reality of the lower world, that can make him a realist.

When the artist descends from the realm of higher realities into the vale of lower reality, he perceives the latter as being embraced by the higher realm in such a way that there, under the heavens of the ideas, he does not feel alien to the earth, nor does he feel alien to the heavens here on earth. With what store of knowledge does he make this descent? With what store of knowledge does he descend to the dust or clay from which he must sculpt? Once again, and first of all, he returns with the knowledge that this very clay is the living Earth, which remains in its primordial and natural correlation to the higher and more real truths of being; that it is improper and impossible to impose upon the Earth from without any form of a higher law that it does not already contain within it either as datum or as a polarity that seeks its complementary polarity in this law. Therefore, the more fruitful the ascent, the more insightful and vital will the descent be.

> The clay formed itself in my fingers
> Into the fine visage of my sons—[39]

says Prometheus in one tragedy, in his role as the creator of the human race. This earth, mixed with the dust of the Titans who had consumed the preworldly infant Dionysus, still contained the living flame of the dismembered god:[40]

The living earth awaited my fingers,
In order to resolve the captivity of the godlike
And to return the flame of the Infant to the light of day.
I was their creator, if he can be creator
Whose name among the gods is Liberator.[41]

Thus, the highest law for one who descends must be reverence for lower reality and obedience to the will of the Earth, to which he brings the ring of betrothal to higher reality, not the tablet of suprasensible truths. Only then does creativity become good news, and matter's obedience to the artist becomes subordination to God, for He is freedom and not slavery to man's coercion. And the knowledge that we can gain from the works of truly descending art is knowledge of the true will of the Earth, of the genuine thought of its things, and of the torments and presentiments of the World Soul, which are unutterable except in the language of the Muses. Most important here is the correct determination of correlations, correspondences, and contiguities between the higher and lower realities, between height and depth, between what is usually recognized as fundamental and essential and what seems merely transient and accidental. It is in works of true art that we find the correct determination and insightful selection of these features in a reality that is depicted artistically, because their creators penetrated into the more-real to achieve an actual synthetic apprehension of the reality they depict.

Thus, the artist ascends to a certain point in the realm of higher realities, the experience of which makes intuition possible for the first time, in order then to descend to lower reality. But let us recall that on his way to this point, he had to cross a membrane of reflective mirages, which was unable to detain him since the strength of his talent enabled him to make this crossing like Odysseus, who did not allow himself to be captivated by the tempting calls of the Sirens. In his descent, the artist will again have to cross this land of illusions, but here it does not present any danger to him, for he has already surmounted it on his path of ascent as the mirror temptation of pure subjectivism. On the contrary, now he will intentionally tarry in this land in order to form its plastic mistiness into phantoms—models of his future clay molds. The incorporeal images he creates are phantasms or shadowy "idols," as the ancients would have said,[42] not having anything in common with the creations of arbitrary fantasy: they possess objective value insofar as they mark the higher realities that reveal themselves to the artist. At the same time, they are acceptable to the earth as the most accurate projection of its soul in the ideal world. These visions, summoned forth by artistic charms, are Apollonian visions, in which the Dionysian agitation of the intuitive instant is resolved. The creation of these phantoms is the properly mythopoetic moment; it is deserving of this name insofar as it reveals higher realities in a way that is both content-rich and transparent. What next? The possessor of phantom models of the imminent incarnation, the artist, shall await a new and once again Dionysian (although in a different way) agitation, about which Pushkin says: "The soul is oppressed with lyric agitation, it trembles and sounds forth, and seeks, as if in slumber, to pour out at last in a free expression." He immediately adds: "And here I am approached by an invisible swarm of guests, old acquaintances, fruits of my fantasy," i.e., those phantoms of whom we have spoken, which he molded earlier out of the malleable mistiness of Apollonian dreams. And just as on

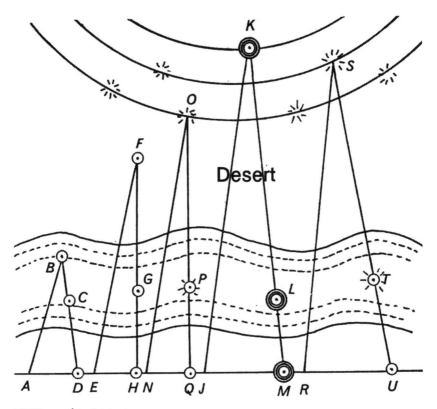

ABCD — subjectivist art.
EFGH — realist art (Flaubert).
JKLM — Dante's art.
NOPQ and RSTU — types of high Symbolism.
B — the point of subjectivist mirror reflection.
F — the point of the transcendent contemplation of the reality that is being overcome.
O, S, K — points of the intuitive comprehension of higher realities.
C, G, P, L, T — points of the Apollonian contemplation of the apogees of ascent, the artist's "dreams."
D, H, Q, M, U — points of artistic incarnation (e.g., M is *The Divine Comedy*).

that occasion the artist's Dionysian agitation was resolved in an Apollonian vision, so in Apollonian incarnation the new musical wave is resolved, forcing Pushkin's fingers to reach for a pen and paper and promising him: "A moment will pass, and verses will flow forth freely."[43]

VI

We have seen that the epistemological significance of art is conditioned by the correct ascent of the artist (whether as one who discovers or as one who is being created) and by his descent (as creator). Creativity in the proper sense (and not in the sense of the preparatory states and preliminary qualitative conditions of the personality) is descent; and it is only descent, which determines artistry as an act, that determines also the artist's efficacy. This efficacy is conditioned by matter's willingness to accept the form that is brought, or, more precisely, revealed to it as good news; consequently it is, first of all, the liberation of matter. The efficacy of art is proportionate to its symbolic character, i.e., to its conformity to the law of higher realities, which receives a seal of matter's assent to this law. The richer the content of the revelation of higher realities, the more effective it is relative to the matter it liberates (on the condition that matter assents to this revelation being made incarnate within it), and the more matter is awoken and liberatingly transfigured by its acceptance, as it were, of this seed of the Logos.[44] The poorer the content of the revelation of higher realities in the artist's creation, the less effective it is relative to the liberated matter: the matter remains slumbering and idle, and is not impregnated by the Logos. The artist's act is a sacred rite, insofar as it alters Nature and the World Soul in a liberating manner by fertilizing it with seeds of the Spirit through the mediation of artistic genius, which spreads these seeds as a bee or wasp spreads the pollen that fertilizes flowers.

But if, as has been argued above, art is one of the forms by which higher realities act upon lower ones, must we accept that in its correct realization it is already theurgic, since it transforms the world? This can be accepted only in such a limited and relative sense that I think the word "theurgy" is inapplicable to the artist's normal activity: that which is worthy of being called by this name is too solemn and holy. The efficacy of art of which we have been speaking is not yet "theurgy," i.e., an act marked with the seal of the divine Name; the sacrament of the symbol is not a sacrament of life. For, although any true symbol is a kind of incarnation of divine truth, and thus by itself reality and real life, still it is reality of a lower order, ontological only within the concatenation of symbols, but only conditionally ontological relative to lower reality, and meonic in comparison to higher reality. Consequently, the symbol is true life to an endlessly lesser degree than Man, who is truly alive and being, which he remains even when face-to-face with the First of Beings Himself, which is why it is said that he is little different from the angels.[45] On the other hand, the symbol as we know it in art is infinitely less alive than Nature, for Nature also is life itself in the eyes of God. The symbol, by contrast, is mediating and mediated life, not a form that contains reality, but a form through which reality flows. By turns, reality flares up and is extinguished in it. It is the medium of epiphanies that stream through it. And the liberation of matter that is achieved by art is only a symbolic liberation.

The artist's torment and the torment of the matter obedient to him are one and the same: both long for living, nonsymbolic life. In submission to the creative genius, Nature expresses its assent to collaborate with the human spirit in the achievement of the longed-for liberation of the world. Nature says to man: "Lead me, and I shall follow." But the human genius limits itself to good news and promises; it would want to, but it is unable to accomplish a theurgic act and accomplishes only a symbolic act. Matter, for its part, does more than the so-called creator and poet: it acts not symbolically, conditionally, and hypothetically but demonstrates directly and by deeds its will to follow spirit along its mysterious paths. There is more sanctity in marble or in the element of the word and in any flesh of any art than in the human spirit when it symbolically animates this flesh, whether visible to the eye or audible to the ear, in a work of art. The face of the earth glitters with creations of beauty, symbols of the arts, which are like precious stones of the holy diadems of the sleeping Bride. In these works, people revere icons of divine essences, idols of the gods, and at any minute, they are ready to worship them as idols, whereupon they forget that they are idols and begin to value only their abstract form. This is the beginning of aestheticism, i.e., stripping beauty of its soul, and defenders of "art for art's sake" sing the funeral dirge for art as living life, because this life was not life-creating but only alive. Then the marble of a statue yearns; the Soul of the World yearns in the godless marble and could say to the artist: "I did not obey you, believe you, and succumb to you for this, and you deceived me."

> When the stone that obeyed the chisel
> Stands forth in its clear beauty
> And the mighty flame of inspiration
> Gives life and flesh to your dream:
> At this forbidden bound
> Do not imagine that your labor is complete,
> And from the divine body
> Do not await love, Pygmalion!
> Love needs a new triumph. . . .[46]

Thus Vladimir Solovyov describes the forbidden bound of art; Nature cannot follow the artist any further, for the artist has nowhere further to lead her. But the World Soul suffers when the human spirit leaves incomplete the liberating labor it has undertaken; it demands from it efforts of another and greater kind. "Love needs a new triumph": a triumph of the spirit in its new manifestations, in new, supreme tasks. Here, according to the conception of Vladimir Solovyov, the artist's work ends and the mask of the sculptor Pygmalion falls away, revealing the former idol maker and lover to possess the archangelic might of the warrior Perseus, whose fiery mask falls in its turn to reveal the Christ image of the resurrecting god Orpheus. In the symbolics of this poem, such are the three hypostases of the human labor: the labor of the chisel, the labor of the sword, and the labor of the cross. These correspond to: the task of inspired creation, the task of social construction, and the task of divine humanity; or else: spiritual culture, the state, and the church. But we are analyzing only the first labor and scouting the "forbidden bound" in order to map out the theurgic border of art.

From the earliest times and to our own day the breast of the Muse has been agitated by dark recollections and presentiments, about which she whispers to her confidants words that are incomprehensible, unearthly, and sometimes tempting to human ears. She reminds them that once, in the golden age of the arts, there sang lyres that subdued trees and beasts, waves and cliffs, and that the sculptures of artful hands lived and did not age. Michelangelo dreamed that his creations were really animate and only pretended to be stones. The artist is alarmed and tormented by the desire to cross the border where miracle begins:

> The genius idol-maker will become sad
> At molding clay and cutting marble,
> And he will seek to robe his plan
> In the image of finer incarnations:
> And he will crave man. . . .

Such is the logic of Eros, and the artist finds it difficult to awake from his madness and assure himself that his Eros is only the Eros of form. He will sooner imagine that some fateful secret, some ancient fall and curse have smashed integral creativity, giving rise to the separate arts of which each is only art, and have broken the single unity of love and life into the multitude of love's transient obsessions, fleeting fancies, and empty mirror images. In any case, he clearly hears the plaint of matter, to which he is able to give form, but he is powerless to communicate true life. The sensation that he has failed to utilize the powers and tendencies of the very matter on which he works has a productive effect, leading the poet to reveal new possibilities of the word, leading the musician to seek hitherto unheard harmonies, and leading the painter to a new vision of things and colors. Theurgic torment can be resolved only in technical objectivizations or aesthetic madness, but it never ceases, somewhere below the depths of consciousness, "to disturb the Muse's virginal soul in prophetic dreams."[47]

It is therefore easy for the artist, this regular guest of the enchanted world, to substitute a conditionally realizable attempt at magic for the unattainable ideal of theurgic art. And it is characteristic of Alexandrian art, which had ceased to be religious and had forgotten the theurgic pathos of the Hellenic artistic tradition, that it transformed the myth (which, to be sure, was itself far from ancient) of Adonis's animation of Aphrodite into the romance of the sculptor Pygmalion animating his statue. Moreover, as it was thought on Cyprus, whence the original myth can be traced, Pygmalion's sculpted beloved bears the name of a sea nymph, one of the servants of sea-dwelling Aphrodite.[48] Indeed, even earlier there existed the story of the maiden Galatea turning into a boy; the maiden was probably christened Galatea to indicate her tendency to metamorphose, which is a general feature of sea goddesses. But it is one thing to create an icon of Aphrodite and be so pleasing to it that the icon becomes animated by miracle-working force; it is another matter entirely to breathe enchanted life into one's own sculpture by the charms of magic art. Truly a transgression is committed here: the "prohibited bound," the threshold forbidden to Pygmalion, is overstepped in the wrong direction. All quests for magism in art radically pervert the holy possession of theurgic yearning that is innate to art.

Indeed, the artist is forbidden to breathe life into matter, whether it be his own or drawn from outside; and he can desire to do this only by ceasing to be an artist, i.e., by forgetting that matter is already alive, or else by consciously intending to do violence to it, to turn its most tender, obscure life into a medium of alien animation. Thus, the theurgic "transition" of art—its "transcensus"—beyond the bound which is "forbidden" not in the sense of being devoid of grace, but in the sense of its being inconsistent with the laws of the given state of nature—such transcensus is impossible within the limits of the presently given state of the world and can be defined as the spirit providing direct aid to potentially living nature, in order that it achieve actual being. It is correct to strive for this miracle in art, and it is desirable for the artist as such that art enter this realm, outside the bounds of any art known to us heretofore, that it go beyond the enclosure of symbols, which are like towers chiseled out of ivory, erected at its outermost borderlands and revealing a view of the seas and the mountains of eternity; for here the symbol becomes flesh, the word becomes life-creating life, and music becomes the harmony of the spheres.

VII

But why should one speak of this? It is reasonable to do so because the beautiful stones of sculptures cry and moan about it,[49] because the Muse's whisperings are too often a mere temptation to the human ear of the artist, and because, finally, to contemplate this, even if it is unattainable, helps us to attain a new religious consciousness, which rests on the postulates of faith and requires, before all else, correct expectations. . . . In this light, what do we find to be the conditions of the aforementioned transcensus? I believe that this question should be answered in the following way.

Art as we know it presents the artist descending to matter with the good news of forms that he has acquired on the steps of his human ascent. This ascent, moreover, is marked with features of individual initiative and thus, to a greater or lesser degree, is limited by the individual. In contrast, theurgic art, divine art, presupposes the opposite correlation of the conditions determining the achievement of the goal. In our art, the man ascends and the artist descends; in the art that we await, the man must descend to the point at which he achieves spiritually real contact with Mother Earth and more-real intuition into her, while the artist must ascend to an unmediated encounter with the higher essences at each step of his artistic action. In other words, each stroke of his chisel or brush must be such a meeting, directed not by the artist, but by the spirits of divine hierarchies that guide his hand. His patron and archetype must be the holy carpenter Joseph, Mary's betrothed: he will be old like Joseph, in the historical succession of generations, and perhaps only at a late date will he be granted this mission. Like Joseph, he must be humble to the end and, as it were, to the point at which his outer image melts; and just like Joseph, he must be only an obedient dreamer and a vigilant, reverent guard and guide of the World Soul as it conceives directly from the Holy Spirit. . . . So severe are the demands of the holy truths addressed to the artist, so distant are they from the contemporary spirit of the personality's rebellious self-affirmation, distant right up to the transcendent nature of the call, and at the same time, so simple, right up to their seeming attainability in the labor of a holy life. Let us not deceive ourselves: beauty does not save the world. But if the prophet who promised that beauty would save the world is correct, he did not mean our beauty and our art, the art of Prometheus's children who desire to rob heaven.[50] At the same time, the coming Mysterium (in the true, i.e., theurgic, meaning of this word) will be similar to the gathering of the faithful when "they were all with one accord in one place,"[51] at the coming of the day of the first Pentecost after the Lord's Resurrection. . . .

When contemplating the bounds of art, who shall we turn to for advice and instruction if not to Goethe, the artist of the boundary kingdoms between art and nature, art and mysticism? And lo, in his "Novella" about a child taming a lion, I believe we find hints of the intellectual nature of the transcendent art whose divine and miraculous activity will be directed no longer at the idol-making of symbols but directly at the liberation of the World Soul.[52] And, as Goethe thought, the standard of this art seems to bear the inscription: "unless you are converted and become as little children, you will by no means enter the Kingdom."[53] As he descended into the lion's pit, the youth sang:

> I hear a mellifluous melody
> From Daniel's grave.
> God's force descends into the pit
> To quell the beast's wrath.
> With their meek power the songs move
> The heart of Angel and lion.
> The lion and lioness lick the wounds
> Of him who is interred in the pit.

"His father accompanied this song with the sounds of the flute; his mother intermittently joined in the melody with a second voice. Then, with force and animation, all three began":

> Almighty God rules the earth,
> He views the breadth of seas.
> The wave rushes and is frozen;
> The king of beasts becomes a lamb.
> The sword will become still in the heat of battle,
> And blood shall not be shed below.
> Perhaps everything is the miraculous love
> Of a single prayer.

The youth approaches the lion and the lion obediently follows him. A song issues from the child's mouth:

> From heaven God's Angel descends
> To counsel the good children
> He finds a path for good will,
> There is no room for evil will.
> And with an infant's holy possession,
> Faith in God and a melody,
> He tames the furious wrath
> Of the lion who was raised by the desert.

PART II

The Games of Melpomene

Presentiments and Portents

The New Organic Era and
the Theater of the Future

I

Should one see contemporary Symbolism as a return to the Romantic schism between dream and life? Or can one discern in it a prophetic message about a new life, with the Symbolist dream merely anticipating reality? Put this way, the question is misleading.[1] First of all: what does the term "Symbolism" include? We hasten to explain that by "Symbolism" we mean not only art in and of itself but, more broadly, the contemporary soul that has given rise to this art, the works of which are marked by a demonstrative gesture, like the outstretched finger that points to something beyond the border of the canvas on the paintings of Leonardo da Vinci.[2] We mean, therefore, neither the prophetic nor any other significance of individual creations of modern art, nor any particular theoretical affirmations of modern thought, but the general orientation of its emotional landscape and the characteristics of the inner and half-subconscious tendency of its creative energies. So we ask: is the soul of contemporary Symbolism Romantic or prophetic?

Further essential clarifications should be made to ground this dilemma. Why must the choice necessarily be between Romanticism or prophecy? Why not some third thing?[3] Because it is only in these two types of spiritual construction that art ceases to be tranquilly self-contained within the borders determined by its concept and seeks to step beyond the bounds of absolute beauty, now becoming the herald of the personality and its ambitions, now pronouncing judgment over life and imposing upon it, or at least opposing to it, its own law. In either case, whether it consciously prescribes the paths life should take or with all of its unconscious striving denies life in the name of another life, art affirms itself not as an isolated cultural sphere but as a part of the general cultural energy, which develops in a dynamic form, in the form of process and becoming. Therefore, art either strives for formlessness or else constantly shatters its forms since they cannot encompass its incommensurable content.

Contemporary symbolic art is distinguished by its constant concern for what lies beyond the border of immediate perception, beyond the natural sphere of the contemplated phenomenon. Our creative work is conscious of itself not only as the reflective mirror of another way of seeing things but also as the transfiguring power of new insight. Therefore, it is clear that contemporary symbolic art is one of the dynamic types of cultural energeticism, so different from self-sufficient and inwardly balanced classical art.

But why do we oppose prophecy to Romanticism? Could the historian not define as a form of Romanticism what the mystic takes to be prophecy? We feel that it is appropriate to distinguish the inner features of both concepts.

Romanticism is a yearning for what cannot come to pass, prophecy—for what has not yet come to pass. Romanticism is the evening sunset, prophecy— the morning sunrise. Romanticism is *odium fati;* prophecy is *amor fati.*[4] Romanticism is in dispute with historical necessity; prophecy is in tragic union with it. The temperament of Romanticism is melancholic, while that of prophecy is choleric. The impossible, irrational, and miraculous are postulates for prophecy, while for Romanticism they are a *pium desiderium.*[5] Romanticism is the "golden age" in the past (the concept of the Greeks); the "golden age" in the future (the concept of messianism) is prophecy.

This last contrast is merely an example. And, in order at once to calm the skeptics who will remind us that "the golden age has not yet come to pass," we would explain that by prophecy we do not necessarily mean a precise foreseeing of the future but always a certain creative energy that precedes and initiates the future, an energy that is essentially revolutionary. In contrast, Romanticism does not have and does not desire to have the power of historical progeneration; it is in conflict with any reality, especially that which is nearest historically, and it awaits something better from an impossible return of the past.[6]

II

Of course, only the future will provide an answer to the question of whether the soul of contemporary Symbolism is Romantic or prophetic. For our part, we judge by conjectural intuition and by self-observation. Our psychology is not the psychology of the Romantics. To Romantic dreaminess and Romantic languor, we oppose the willful act of mystical self-affirmation. Romanticism, if it is *only* Romanticism, is only a lack of faith; it lacks faith because its faith's center of gravity is not only outside of it, but even outside of the world, and it does not find within itself the strength to follow mysticism *ab exterioribus ad interiora,*[7] into itself away from everything external, in order that creative will might achieve self-awareness in the depths of inner experience and define itself as the dynamic principle of life.[8]

96

Schiller's short narrative poem "The Wayfarer" is typical of the relationship between Romanticism and mystical prophecy.[9] A pilgrim abandons his
native home while still a child in order to seek out at the end of his wanderings a mysterious "temple" where he once again will receive "in celestial im-
perishability" all the earthly things that he has rejected although they were
dear to his heart; he has Faith as his "guide," and Hope makes his endless
and apparently vain journey easy and alluring. The poem seems a mystical
"Pilgrim's Progress," right up to the last stanza, where the deceptive mask
is suddenly torn asunder, and we hear the final word of the Romantic:[10]

> Above me for eternity
> The radiant sky and earth
> Will never merge, just like today,
> *There* will never be *Here*. . . .

This sigh for the unattainable is resolved differently in a related poem
by Vladimir Solovyov: "until midnight with bold steps" the wayfarer will
walk to the shores of mystery and of wonder, where—as he knows—he is
awaited and will be met by a secret temple that sparkles with flames.[11]

Romanticism desires the objects of its dreams. We, in contrast, call
for something that we perhaps anticipate as tragic. Our love for what is to
come includes a sacrificial renunciation of something different, with which
we are tied by the finest organic threads, by heartfelt connections. Romanticism has only one soul; prophecy—too often!—has two souls: one resist-
ing, the other violently attracting.[12] Prophecy is tragic by nature. The
Romantic remembers only too well that his unfulfillable dream is unfulfillable; that his ideal lacks the endurance and resistance necessary for tragic
conflict. In the Romantic's worldview, it is not life, new and unknown, that
stands in opposition to living reality but rather dreams, *simulacra inania,*
that oppose life.[13] Tragedy is inwardly alien to Romanticism. This is why Romanticism so loves tragic pomp and the external disorder of passions—until it capitulates before reality (and naturalism in art). The sensitive soul of
prophecy, in contrast, is often afraid and hesitates to awake the sleeping
storms of already stirring chaos.[14]

The Romantic knows the names of the corpses whose shadows he dis-
turbs in their graves, whereas we invoke unknown spirits. Our symbols are
not names; they are our silence. And even those of us who pronounce names
resemble Columbus and his companions, who gave the name of India to the
continent that was only just emerging from beyond the distant horizon.

III

From a certain perspective, the matter of which we "prophesy" adds up to
the presentiment of a new organic era.[15] For positivism, which was recently

triumphant, it was well-nigh obvious that the alternation of "organic" and "critical" eras was finished, that humanity had finally entered a phase of criticism and cultural differentiation. Meanwhile, in the nineteenth century, an entire series of symptoms revealed a rising tendency toward the reintegration of cultural forces, toward their inner reunification and synthesis.

One of these symptoms was the entrance of Russian novelists onto the world stage. It is not surprising that it was precisely these barbarian newcomers who heralded the imminent return of an organic era (once again primitive, and in a new way); Jean-Jacques Rousseau was only half barbarian in spirit. However, one could also discern analogous strivings in the West. Thus Wagner, and then Nietzsche, appeared in the cultural sphere of the Germans, our elder brethren among the barbarians.[16] Wagner called for a fusion[17] of artistic energies in a synthetic art that would gather into its focus the nation's entire spiritual self-determination. Nietzsche appeared with the message of a new, integral soul for which (so opposed is it to the soul of the "theoretical man," the son of a critical era!) the will is already knowledge, knowledge (in the sense of affirmation) is already life, and life is already "faithfulness to the earth."[18] Independently of Nietzsche, Ibsen willed us, the "dead," to "arise":[19] he rose up against beauty that had broken down into arts and into separate, self-contained, and isolated artistic creations, prophesying that all beauty would become life, and all life—beauty.[20]

Ideas of social restructuring,[21] conditioned by new forms of class warfare, bore *implicite* within themselves the demand for an organic era and presupposed new opportunities for cultural integration. Meanwhile, the evolution of the moral consciousness was accompanied by the collapse of ethics, which had been tempered into various systems of external norms, and also by a mistrust of the very idea of obligation; instead of the former images of duty, it endorsed moral amorphism and adogmatism.

The crisis of moral imperatives revealed unbounded horizons of mysticism, understood as the free self-affirmation of suprapersonal will within the individual. Individualism sought to integrate the personality's emotions, while at the same time isolating and differentiating the personality in the social plane. But mystical supraindividualism builds a bridge from individualism to the principle of universal *sobornost'*, and in the social plane, it coincides with the formula of anarchy, which in its pure idea presents a synthesis of absolute individual freedom with the principle of collective [*sobornyi*] unity.

Various phenomena were symptoms of a nascent integration in the religious sphere: attempts at religious syncretism; at introducing into the Christian consciousness elements of a pantheism that has been uniquely refracted in its medium; and new, more spiritual revelations of the theocratic idea.[22] Finally, in the realm of philosophy, the reaction against habits and methods of thinking characteristic of a critical era is manifested in the overcoming of idealism itself and in the tendency toward primitive realism. Nietzsche is not the only one who has felt closer to Heraclitus than to Plato. And it is not unreasonable to conjecture that the near future will create types of philosophical creativity close to those of the pre-Socratic, precritical period, which Nietzsche called "the tragic age" of Hellenism.[23]

IV

In the sphere of symbolic art, the symbol is naturally revealed as a potence and embryo of myth. The organic process of development turns symbolism into mythopoesis. The inner, necessary path of symbolism is preordained and has already been proclaimed (in Wagner's art). But myth is not a free fiction: true myth is a postulate of collective self-determination,[24] and therefore it is not at all a fiction and certainly not an allegory or personification. Myth is the hypostasis of a certain essence or energy. An individual myth that is not generally binding is an impossibility, a *contradictio in adiecto*.[25] For the symbol is also supraindividual by its nature, which is why it has the power to turn the most intimate silence of an individual mystical soul into the organ of universal unanimity of mind and feeling, similar to the word but more powerful than the ordinary word. Thus art, in its tendency to mythopoesis, tends toward the type of grand, universal art.[26]

We have lived through our critical era, our era of differentiation, the cycle during which our art was "intimate." We have entered the cycle of "reclusive" art, the art of hermits, supraindividualists, who have overcome in principle the old individualism, who are outwardly isolated but inwardly united with the world, who are people not of a personal but of a universal willing and striving in the plane of personal freedom.[27] The art of recluses is already universal art, but only potentially, in the form of concealed energy. Will they become organs of mythopoesis, i.e., creators and craftsmen of universal art? The realization of this possibility would mean the arrival of an organic era in art. And if such an integration of artistic energies were fulfilled in reality, it would, according to the inner logic of its development, be expressed and concentrated in a synthetic art of universal rite and choral drama.[28]

V

But before moving to a study of the nature of choral rite, it is necessary first to take a look at the problem of architecture as it relates to the possible advent of a new organic era.

Unerring induction assures us that each organic era in history has been marked by the appearance of an essentially new architectural style. Actually, it could not be otherwise if organic eras are indeed characterized by the full integration of artistic energies: their synthetic unity is imprinted in the unified style of the era, and architecture is the preeminent art of style.

Might one, however, suppose that in the more or less distant future an independent architectural style will arise? True, if one allows for an absolutely new cultural era, one must also admit absolutely new cultural needs, the imprint of which cannot fail to cause profound changes in architectonic forms. It is enough to point to the chorus and round dance postulated by the development of myth and drama; these are musical-poetical elements that prescribe to architecture motifs of the circle and of ring-shaped borders, for example, a circular colonnade.

Nonetheless, we are inclined to believe that it is not static architecture that will characterize the incipient organic era, which is no longer capable of being primitive in the sense in which its historical predecessors truly were. Instead, this era will be marked by the dynamic and liquid architecture whose name is Music. It is for good reason that, in the round dance of arts in our dynamic and liquid culture, music is the preeminent art for our time. Just as in the primitive eras all creativity was characterized by a unified architectural style, just as all of its streams flowed into the holy receptacle of the temple, so will all creativity of the future arise "from the spirit of music" and pour into its all-encompassing womb.

Architecture was hieratic to the extent that primitive art was religious to its core. It seems that architecture fell together with the fall of the temple as a fetish. The future organic era can only be more spiritual than the preceding ones: fetishism, this eternally present and profoundly vital cultural factor, will not disappear but, in all likelihood, will arise in its most refined aspect, perhaps as a melodic fetish or a musical suggestion.

However this may be, ever since Beethoven and Wagner, music has occupied its rightful place in our aesthetic consciousness as the initiator and guide of any future synthetic rite and art. In respect to the coming organic era, music is equally preordained to dominance and hegemony in the entire sphere of art. It was important to establish this result so that we might continue our study of the choral rite.

VI

The energy whose name is Art appears to us either gathered and crystallized in the stable and ready forms of its objectivization, which we perceive aesthetically by, as it were, melting and re-creating them anew in our consciousness; or else it appears to us liquid and developing before our eyes, becoming objectified for the first time in our perception. The pole of stasis in art is represented by architecture, while that of dynamism is represented by music. Of the remaining arts, closest to these extreme points are sculpture and dance: the former is closest to static rest, the latter to dynamic motion.

But even dance is only a sequence of sculptured moments; and in music itself from the harmonic waves, there suddenly arises a palpable form of sun-lit melody that stands as an Apollonian vision above the dark-purple depths of orgiastic waves. There is stasis in music and dynamism in the plastic arts.

The Sistine Madonna walks. The folds of her clothes betray the rhythm of her steps. We accompany her in the clouds. The sphere that surrounds her is the confluence of active lives: all the air is filled with angelic images. Everything lives and bears her along; before us is the harmony of the ce-lestial powers, and within this harmony is she herself, as moving melody; and in her arms is the Infant, with his gaze cast into the world, filled with will and the decisiveness of genius—the Infant whom she surrenders to the world or, rather, who himself draws her, his flesh, into the world, also draw-ing along behind him the entire sphere where she wanders.

In every work of art, even of plastic art, there is hidden music. And this is not only because rhythm and inner motion are necessary components of art; the very soul of art is musical. The true content of an artistic depiction is always broader than its subject. A creation of a genius speaks to us of something dif-ferent, more profound, more beautiful, more tragic, more divine, than what it expresses directly. In this sense, it is always symbolic; but that which it en-compasses with its symbol remains unencompassed by the mind and inef-fable for the human word. The incomprehensibility and immeasurability of its ultimate meaning must be palpable in order for a work of art to produce its full aesthetic effect. Hence the striving for the ineffable that comprises the soul and life of aesthetic pleasure: and this will, this impulse, is music.

VII

After these prefatory remarks regarding the static and dynamic forms of artistic energy, let us turn to the paths that remain open to the theater, keep-ing in mind our assumption that the fate of modern art as a whole is being determined by the general cultural tendency toward the gathering and in-tegration of differentiated energies.

Indeed, even without this assumption, it is impossible to overlook the widespread craving for another, as yet unrevealed theater. This indetermi-nate and mute craving is accompanied by an equally indeterminate and mute dissatisfaction with the existing theater. In other kinds of art, artists anticipate the needs of society and must battle with tradition not only for their own creative work but even for the very principle of change and innova-tion. In contrast, in the realm of the scenic Muse, "the idea that experimen-tation is desirable meets with practically universal agreement, expressed sometimes directly, but sometimes only symptomatically and in silence."[29]

Just as scenic art formally belongs to the dynamic type of art (insofar as drama develops before us in time), there can also be no doubt that, by its inner nature, it is an active energy. The active energy of the stage aims not only to enrich our consciousness by inspiring in it a new image of beauty, as the object of will-less contemplations, but also to become an active factor in our emotional life, producing in it some inner event. After all, even the ancients spoke of the "cleansing" ("catharsis") of the spectators' souls as the goal pursued and achieved by true tragedy.[30]

In the meantime, the universal-historical development of the theater displays a significant deviation from this primordial self-determination of the scenic Muse toward the static pole of the plastic arts. Drama was born "out of the spirit of music," in Nietzsche's phrase, or, in more precise historical terms, out of the choral dithyramb. Everything is dynamic in this dithyramb: each participant in the liturgical circular chorus was an active molecule of the orgiastic life of the Dionysian body, of its religious community. The Dionysian art of the choral drama arose out of ecstatic sacrificial worship. The earlier real sacrifice subsequently became a fictive sacrifice: this is the protagonist, the hypostasis of the god of orgies, who within the circle depicts the suffering fate of a hero condemned to die. The round dance was originally a community of sacrificers and communicants of the sacrificial mystery.

The further destiny of Dionysian art was determined by differentiation among the parts of its primordial composition. The dithyramb was separated into the independent genre of lyric poetry. In drama, the deeds and passion of the heroic protagonist attained unequaled significance, attracting the all-consuming attention of those present, turning them from the former participants in a holy rite, from the performers of ritual, into viewers of a festive spectacle. The chorus, long ago separated from the community, also became dissociated from the hero. It was now only an auxiliary element of the central event, which reproduced the peripetias of the hero's fate. The chorus then became utterly unnecessary and even restrictive. Thus arose "theater" (*théatron*), i.e., "spectacle" (*Schauspiel*), *only* a spectacle. The "mask" of the actor thickened, so that one could no longer glimpse through it the countenance of the god of orgies, whose hypostasis the tragic hero once was: the "mask" condensed into a "character."

In the age of Shakespeare, everything was calculated to reproduce this "character." And was not French theater of the seventeenth century the apogee of the stage's closeness to the plastic arts? It was an era that confined the liquid music of nature in the motionless architectural forms of the Versailles gardens: did it not also make Melpomene's images just as static?[31] As works of plastic art, the works of that great era of drama exhilarate us. Like a statue, the hero confronts us as a living mechanism of muscles, each of which, when tensed, reveals the beauty and striving of the rest. Only fate concerns us, and its logical nature is such that everything is conditioned by everything else, and the loss of one link in this pragmatic chain would destroy the whole. Dramatic development becomes the demonstration of a mathematical theorem, while the stage becomes an arena where gladiators of passion and destiny enter the fray. The crowd disperses, satisfied by the spectacle of battle, sated by murder, but not washed with sacrificial blood.

VIII

Modern theater is once again tending toward the dynamic principle. Is this not true of Ibsen's theater, where the electricity of accumulated energies condenses in stuffy languor and several cleansing blows are struck in this demonic magnificence, without freeing the atmosphere, however, of its ominous tension? Or of Maeterlinck's theater, which leads us off to a labyrinth of mystery only to leave us before a locked iron door?[32] Or the theater of Verhaeren, where the crowd itself is the protagonist?[33] Or of the Wagnerian rite of Tristan and Isolde, where in convulsions of tragic passion, the countenances of the lovers rise out of the waves of dark chaos, of the universal Meon, only in order to descend again and melt away in it; in the words of ancient Anaximander, as individuals, they pay with their death the redemptive retribution for their very own birth,[34] so that nothing remains before the lost witness of their fate except the endless purple ocean of irrepressible world Will and inexhaustible world Suffering?

The principle of dynamism is perhaps most evident in the so-called realistic theater, which wants to be consciously *terre à terre* and therefore, by eliminating the "hero," takes as the central subject of the drama Life itself, as a liquid and unresolvable process of becoming. Those who go to contemplate these cinemas of everyday life know ahead of time that they will not witness the first confluence of a new knot of vital forces, and that they will not see any "denouement," because "life" itself is the only knot of the universal drama, a fragment of which will be performed on stage, and no denouement has yet been given by reality. They are satisfied if the dramatist presents a particular topic from this life, if he poses a question to be subjected to discussion by public opinion at a demonstration. But the dynamic principle of drama is fully affirmed here. The goal of the spectacle is not so much aesthetic as psychological: the need to intensify the inner event that everyone experiences—"life"; to be horrified at seeing and recognizing one's own double; to throw a torch into the black chasm yawning beneath everyone's feet in order to illuminate with its fleeting ray the bottomless immensity. But this is an almost Dionysian tremor and "rapture on the edge of a gloomy abyss."[35]

If modern theater is once again to be dynamic, let it be so in full. Following the example of the ancients, who used ecstatic music and the exciting rhythms of dance as a treatment for frenzy, we seek the musical intensification of the affect as a means capable of producing a healing resolution. The theater must completely reveal its dynamic essence; thus, it must stop being a "theater" in the sense of mere "spectacle." We have had enough of spectacles; we do not need *circenses*.[36] We want to gather in order to create, to "act," in a collective [*sobornyi*] manner, and not only to contemplate: "zu schaffen, nicht zu schauen."[37] We have had enough role-playing; we want a rite. The spectator must become an actor, a coparticipant in the rite. The crowd of viewers must merge into a choral body similar to the mystical community of ancient "orgies" and "mysteries."

IX

In the Dionysian orgies, the most ancient cradle of the theater, each participant had a twofold goal: to coparticipate in the orgiastic action (*sumbak-cheúein*) and in the orgiastic cleansing (*katharízesthai*), to sanctify and be sanctified, to attract the divine presence and receive the gift of grace—an active, theurgical goal (*hierourgein*) and an emotional, passive goal (*páschein*).

The individuation of the elements of the original rite limited the range of the community's inner emotions: it was allowed only to "experience" (*páschein*) the charms of Dionysus; and the ancient theoretician of drama, Aristotle, speaks therefore only of the passive emotions (*páthē*) of the spectators.[38] It is not surprising that the action itself was moved from the orchestra (the round platform for the chorus in the midst of the horseshoe of seats) to the proscenium, which rose ever higher above the level of the orchestra. This drew between the actor and the spectator that enchanted border, the elevated stage,[39] which to this very day divides the theater into two incommensurate worlds: that which only acts and that which only perceives. There are no veins that could join these two separate bodies with the common blood circulation of creative energies.

The elevated stage of the theater separated the community, which was no longer to be conscious of itself as such, from those who were only conscious of themselves as play actors. The stage must step beyond the elevated stage and take in the community, or else the community must swallow up the stage. This is a goal that some have already understood; but where are the paths to its realization?

It would be useless to try to approach this goal by predetermining the content of the new drama we desire. Whether the theater we seek will be a "theater of youth and beauty" or a spectacle "of human happiness without tears" (according to the recent demand of Maeterlinck the theoretician);[40] a theater of sacred recollections or prophetic presentiments, of sweet fragrances or holy tremors, of teachings of a cognitive or an instructive order; a theater that serves as a "platform" or one that serves as a lectern: none of these programs provides the means for breaking the spell of the theater's elevated stage.[41] One can invent tricks to make it easier for the public to interfere in the performance; one can invite comments from among the spectators

104

(which are not uncommon at performances of Italian and French melodramas); it would not be difficult, if politics are involved, to turn the hall into a public demonstration: but none of this, of course, offers an aesthetic resolution to the problem. Purely external and decorative innovations will have just as little effect: the modern theater will remain the same in spirit even if the open sky forms a blue roof over the spectators or if the volcanic outline of the shores of beautiful Lake Albano looks in from behind the stage.

Fruitless are all attempts to establish a connection between the problem of the elevated stage and the question of what should form the subject matter of the future drama. For there must be room for everything in this drama: for tragedy and comedy, mystery and popular fairy tale, myth and social concerns. It is not a matter of *what?* but of *how?*—*how* understood both in the musical and psychological sense and in the sense of developing forms that would be inwardly capable of bearing the dynamic energy of the future theater. We envision merging the stage and the viewing hall only by unleashing the concealed and constricted Dionysian element of dramatic act—in the orchestral *symphony* and in the independent, musical, and plastic life of the *chorus*.

X

Drama, on the one hand, and so-called music drama, on the other, at the present time, live their own lives, flowing in two separate channels, divided by a watershed that appears unbridgeable. The single energy that feeds the two parallel streams has been depleted and weakened in both. Fortunately, there are signs indicating that the schism will be short-lived and that the channels will reach a point of confluence.

We shall limit ourselves to one example. Is it not revealing that Maeterlinck's drama *Pelléas and Mélisande* requires musical interpretation and finds it in the music of Debussy?[42] But what is Debussy's music to "Pelléas" if not a reductio ad absurdum of Wagner's principle of "endless melody" or, if you prefer, of a recitative that seeks at any cost to prevent living speech and vivid dramatic acting from entering the enchanted circle of the musical kingdom? Only one additional step is needed for speech to triumph over the conventional necessity of singing, which has already been bled of its color to the point of a moribund recitative declamation.[43]

It is clear that music drama must become simply drama; music will preserve and affirm its hegemony in the symphony and chorus, with its mass explosions and various groupings, polyphonies, monodies, and *soli*, on the dance platform or *orchēstra* of a unified synthetic rite, the individual roles of which will be performed on the stage by dramatic actors.[44]

Indeed, drama is drawn to music. Only with the help of music is it capable of fully revealing its dynamic nature, its Dionysian element. Only

105

music will impart to it a grand style and make it the bearer of universal art. Drama must not follow after the other arts but lead them in an aspiration (that has been foreordained by our epoch) away from intimate and refined confinement toward grand lines and all-encompassing forms, from the miniature and the picture to painting al fresco. Music for its part must incorporate verbal drama because on its own it is incapable of resolving the problem of synthetic theater.

XI

In clear contradiction of the synthetic principle, Wagner excludes both the play of the dramatic actor and the real chorus with its song and orchestics from his "round dance of arts."[45] It would seem that this inner anomaly can be explained only by the cultural-historical friction that conditions the slow and gradual surmounting of deeply rooted traditions. True, as far as the chorus is concerned, Wagner's formula rests on a particular theoretical justification,[46] the critique of which has incidentally been facilitated by Wagner himself insofar as, in theory, he not only accepts the idea of the chorus, but even sees it as the true bearer of the tragedy revealed in the images of heroes.[47]

For Wagner, the chorus is the very content of the drama, or, as we would say, the very Dionysian element that creates the drama. But this chorus is hidden and voiceless: it is the orchestral symphony that signifies the dynamic basis of being. This symbolic, wordless chorus is mute Will, which with its incessant tide throws human images and voices of "endless melody" onto the spectral island of Apollonian dreams of the stage. Those who have gathered at the *Festspiel* are conceived of as molecules of the orchestra's orgiastic life;[48] they participate in the act, but only latently and symbolically. Wagner the hierophant does not give the community a choral voice and word. Why? The community has a right to this voice because it is supposed to be not a crowd of spectators but a gathering of orgiasts.

But the orchestra depicts the metaphysical chorus of universal Will; the *choreutói*,[49] even as a mystical throng, would still be the voice of a merely human consciousness. This objection falls since the song of the chorus would not replace the symphony but would simply flow into it as a component part. The symbol of the choral word, in a worthy manner, would represent in the boundless cosmic ecstasy the Dionysian soul of humanity as its conscious and active bearer, as the mythical Hippa who accepts into her snake-bordered cradle the newborn Bacchus.[50] And, apart from this, some mysterious aesthetic law demands that the artist always use anthropomorphism and avenges him for its elimination by cursing him with amorphism, aridity, and monotony.

Wagner stopped halfway and did not utter the final word. His synthesis of the arts is not harmonious and not full. With a one-sidedness incompatible with the entirety of his plan, he presents the solo singer and ignores speech and dance, manifold vocal expression, and the symbolism of the manifold. In Wagner's musical drama, "just as in Beethoven's Ninth Symphony, the mute instruments try to speak, straining to utter what is sought for and ineffable. Just as in the Ninth Symphony, the human voice alone will utter the Word. The chorus' ancient rights must be restored in full. Without the chorus there is no common rite, and the spectacle dominates."[51]

XII

Thus, our formula for synthetic drama requires, in the first place, that the scenic action arise out of the orchestral symphony and also end with it, and also that this same symphony be the dynamic basis of an action that would interrupt the music with inwardly consummate episodes of dramatic play. For the Apollonian vision of myth arises out of the Dionysian sea of orgiastic turbulence and disappears in these same emotional depths of ecstasy, having completely illuminated them with its miracle, when the cycle of musical "cleansing" is complete. In the second place, our formula demands that the real chorus become part of the symphony and part of the action. Third, it demands that the actors speak rather than sing from the stage.

It is necessary to add to the second demand, as a condition of its realization, that the *orchēstra* be restored. The floor must be cleared for choral dance and choral play so that it might be accessible from all sides, resembling the flat bed of a valley at the foot of sloping hills that are covered in front by the stage and on the remaining sides by the rising rows of seats. The orchestra must either remain unseen in the recess provided for it in Wagner's theater or else situated in other places.[52] The *coriphaeus* of the instrumental orchestra, dressed in clothes corresponding to those of the chorus, with his magical staff and with the rhythmical gestures of an all-mighty magus and mystagogue, does not offend our aesthetic sense: he might stand in view of the entire community.

We envision a double chorus: a smaller chorus, immediately connected to the action, as in the tragedies of Aeschylus, and a chorus symbolizing the entire community and capable of being increased spontaneously by new participants. The latter chorus is therefore numerous and it interferes in the action only at moments of the highest animation and full liberation of Dionysian energies; the dithyrambic chorus of Beethoven's Ninth Symphony is an example of this. The first chorus naturally adds play and orchestics to the synthetic rite; the second is limited to more important rhythms, i.e., more animated ones. It gives form to movement (processions, theories) and acts with the massive grandiosity and collective [*sobornyi*] authority of the community it represents. In the independent life of the chorus, free rein is given both to all forms of musical differentiation and to constant innovations in the program of choral *intermezzi*. The chorus can therefore serve as the receptacle for the incessant creativity of the communal orgiastic consciousness.

These changes doubtless presuppose the stage's renunciation both of vulgar realism and, to a significant degree, of its desires for theatrical "illusion." However, neither of these losses is likely to distress our contemporaries and, of course, is even less likely to distress future national masses with their innate predilection for ideal style. Both vulgar realism and scenic illusion appear to have uttered their final word, and their resources[53] have been completely exhausted by modernity. In any case, by predicting a new type of theater, we negate neither the possibility nor the desirability of other types that might coexist with it, both those that are already known and implemented or others that have not yet been developed from obsolete or aging forms.

XIII

Without a doubt, our vision of the theater of the future would be an obedient tool of the mythopoesis that inner necessity compels to arise out of truly symbolic art, as long as such art ceases to be the heritage of solitary individuals and achieves harmonic concord with the self-determination of the national soul. Therefore, divine and heroic tragedy, such as was ancient tragedy, and mysterium, more or less analogous to medieval mystery plays, most closely correspond to the forms that we expect the synthetic rite to take.

But these forms are more flexible than they might seem at first glance. Political drama is fully compatible with them and even attains through them for the first time choral (i.e., symbolically universal) resonance. We should not forget how often the mythopoetic tragedy of the Hellenes was at the same time political drama, and the community that celebrated the festival of the Great Dionysia in the theater naturally turned into a secular gathering, placing its delight or its hatred on the state scales of the national assembly or council of elders. The same influence, but to a greater degree, was exerted on the social body by the comedy of elevated style, the comedy of Aristophanes.[54]

It is only in the choral forms of the musical rite that modern comedy, which has long been tied to everyday life and concerns, will find the courage of free flight; only here—without ceasing to evoke laughter, quite the contrary, resurrecting divinely orgiastic laughter—will it carry the crowd away to the world of the most whimsical and unbridled fantasy and, at the same time, serve as an organ of social self-determination.

XIV

Among the various objections that might be raised against our theories, we foresee two whose elimination will allow us to complete our sketch of the future choral rite. One of these objections is of a formal nature and is based on an understandable aesthetic misconception. The other concerns the inner aspect of our topic and requires detailed consideration.

Music and song combined with speech usually strikes us as aesthetically unacceptable. We know it and do not like it, for example, in operettas. However, it cannot be ignored that here the unfavorable impression is caused, above all else, by particular factors that comprise the specificity of this type of theatrical performance. It is unbearable when an actor who has only just been involved in an ordinary conversation that was in no way rhythmical and that even stressed its everyday style suddenly offers a comment in the form of a song or in a ditty. It is simply unpleasant when conversation and song take place on the same stage, which, while pursuing the goal of illusion, remains unconvincing.

How differently we perceive the performance of the chorus in ancient tragedies, in those rare and fortunate cases when we hear it really singing! In the choral rite that we envision, it is not only that the realm of music and the realm of rhythmical speech are separated most of all in a topographical fashion, but the entire style of dramatic play, as it follows from the heart of the matter, is so different from the modern style that one is unable to affirm prematurely the inevitable disharmony of the musical and dramatic elements.

And if the modern elevated stage disguises the people who speak and gesticulate before it, is it at all possible to give a satisfactory account of the visual and acoustic conditions of the choral drama of the future, which would lead us out—if not under the open sky and into the light of day—then in any case out from within the walls of the contemporary theatrical hall, this expanded salon, into another architectural setting and into the perspectives of completely different types of space? Of course, all mysteries of illusion, the entire art of staging will be used to make the actors' appearance seem grandiose; all acoustic means will be used to make the sound of their speech louder and more exalted. And, above all, it will be necessary to resolve the underlying problem: to develop a style of acting and diction that corresponds to the new needs.

It is likely that, on the other hand, the new conditions of drama will make its pragmatic content less complex, the action less developed (just as we find it in the ancients), and the characters' speeches less verbose.

XV

This last remark leads us to the other anticipated objection. Modern drama wants to become inner drama. It "detaches itself from the phenomenon and turns away from discovery."[55] The mathematical boundary of this tendency toward the inner pole of the tragic is silence.[56] It may be asked whether the idea of drama's striving for silence is commensurate with the affirmation of the principle of chorus and *sobornost'*, as the bases of the future rite.

109

Our negative answer might seem a paradox. But we know that individualism is resolved in supraindividualism; and if before our very eyes a solitary hero battles and perishes, where can the current of Dionysian orgiastic communion between him and us lie if not in the potential or real choral consciousness and unity of feeling? And the more solitary the hero's silence, the more necessary is the chorus. Thus, in Aeschylus's tragedy *Niobe,* the heroine was silent until the final turn in the action, but the viewer of her destiny lived her inner life with the chorus and in the chorus.[57]

When the hero who battles Fate in Beethoven's Fifth Symphony seems defeated after his extended and violent battles with the Fate that knocks at his door, what can console us in his tragic lot—which is our own lot due to Dionysian ecstasy and suggestion—except the chorus as our collective [*sobornyi*] "I"? And we hear that an invisible throng is setting off at someone's distant call—to crown the hero and praise the triumph (which may be only ideal) as the triumph of the one who is perhaps himself defeated.

Only the aesthetic dullness of our perception allows us to bear endings of tragedies—such as Maeterlinck's: "Je crache sur toi, monstre!"[58]— without seeking healing resolution and cleansing from the torture of this harrowing dissonance in the orgiastic charms of the Liberating God.

XVI

These thoughts encourage us to analyze the mystical nature of the choral rite. But this matter requires an independent and methodologically different study. For the present consideration, we are obliged only to mention that the organization of the choral rite of the future is the organization of universal art, which itself is the organization of the national soul.

Theaters of choral tragedies, comedies, and mysteria must become the hearths of the nation's creative or prophetic self-determination. The problem of fusing the actors and spectators into a single orgiastic body will only be resolved when, with the vital and creative mediation of the chorus, the drama becomes not a spectacle offered from outside, but the inner work of the national *community* that has chosen this particular *orchēstra* as its focus. I would give it the conventional term "prophetic," in contradistinction to the other communities that are active in civil construction (communal or "royal") or ecclesiastical-religious life (based on free parishes or "sacerdotal").[59]

And we might add that real political freedom can only be achieved when the choral voice of such communities becomes a genuine referendum of the true national will.

PART III

On Cultural History

On the Joyful Craft and the Joy of the Spirit

Ennoēsas, óti tòn poiētēn déoi, eíper mélloi
poiētēs eínai, poiein mythous, àll' ou lógous.[1]

I. THE ARTIST AS CRAFTSMAN

The dispute about the calling of art—whether art is justified inwardly by its very existence, as "art for art's sake," or whether it must be justified by life, as "art for life's sake"—is now declared to be resolved, but it remains unresolved in the depths of our souls. It did not trouble minds at all in those most happy ages for artistry, when art was ultimately the combined creative work of an artist-craftsman and his patrons. These patrons could be representatives of the popular masses to whom the latter had delegated, as it were, authority in such matters (for example, the magistrates of ancient republics and the archbishops of the medieval church); or individuals who presumed to express the tastes and needs of the time (such as the Medici),[2] assertive people who, while having risen out of the crowd, remained akin to it in spirit; or rulers who, while ruling over the crowd, nevertheless retained their ties to it and firmly assured its imitative subordination to themselves (such as Louis XIV).[3]

For a true artist, insofar as he is an artist (*artifex, technitēs, dēmiourgós*),[4] is a craftsman, and his psychology is most of all that of a craftsman: he needs commissions not only in a material sense but also morally; he is proud of his commissions, and if he is liable to proclaim that he is "king," and that, as such, he "lives alone,"[5] it is only because he is angry at those who remain dissatisfied with his work, or at patrons who stay away. When he tells himself, "you are your own highest judge," he is only repeating the ancient boutades of self-confident and uncompromising masters, such as Michel-Angelo Buonarroti or the stubborn Benvenuto Cellini,[6] who also, refusing to sell his works, would at times shut himself up in his goldsmith's workshop in order "to perfect the fruits of beloved thoughts."[7]

Such self-glorification of the artist is the natural reaction of talent, which is always perspicacious and demanding of itself, to the lack of recognition by nearsighted and haughty evaluators and to the stiff inflexibility of consumers. We can find such a reaction in all artistic epochs. But it is possible that the bitter consciousness of art's practical superfluousness and the yearning for the real stimulus of a commission capable of giving flight to inspiration can first be detected at the courts of patrons, where a Torquato Tasso was valued as if on faith and therefore had no actual need to rush to complete his promising epic poem, apart from the obligation placed on him by this trust.[8]

When the religious impulse for artistic activity, so strong in the Middle Ages, disappeared, the artist was left without specific commissions and deadlines; he thus became an individualist and hurried to invent individualism. What is it that made Petrarch so exaggerate the significance of his philological erudition and Latin narrative poems, to the detriment of his immortal and national lyric poetry, if not the secret thought of the intimate and therefore superfluous nature of those love canzones and sonnets that Dante once tossed to his friends, who then gave them away to the rabble?[9]

Any kind of "playing at genius" (*genialisches Treiben*)[10] and Romanticism is the haughty idleness of an artistic bohemianism that has been forced to work only for possible future use. It immediately raises this to a principle and, in its conceited jargon, calls it "art for art's sake." If, however, people begin listening closely to these "vain idlers," these "priests only of what is beautiful,"[11] the latter take the attention they arouse as the ideal surrogate of a paid commission, seeing "life" itself or the "epoch" as their patron. They willingly agree to "create" for the promise of an indefinite future glory as mankind's leaders and liberators. Thus, they turn out not to be opposed to the formula "art for life's sake," if only they are allowed to understand life as their dream of life and to imagine themselves its organizers or even creators. Thus, Byron overthrew the tyrants, and Heine liberated Germany.[12]

Artists are especially inclined to sign a contract for "art for life's sake" if only life is understood as something very broad, cosmic, and quite vague. In this, they are greatly helped by their friends, the philosophers, for whom, ever since Plato, beauty has been a necessary precondition for the goals of theodicy and metaphysical harmony; ever since the time of Kant, the concept of "genius" has been extremely useful, even irreplaceable for the wholeness and ideal stability of those aerial edifices that we call philosophical systems (an example is Schopenhauer).[13] On this path, the artist as such becomes, in his own conception of himself, a high priest, a hierophant, a prophet, a magus, and a theurgist.

II. THE ARTIST AS CREATOR OF IDOLS

If enthusiasts find misplaced irony in these "observations of a cold mind" and "mournful notes of a heart"[14] about artists' human, all-too-human, weaknesses, this will be only because so far I have spoken about only one aspect of the integral truth about the artist, an approach dictated by the universally antinomical nature of things. The other aspect of this truth emerges

most clearly from the observation that, whatever the role of the artist in society, and whatever his theoretical self-affirmation or self-justification, he
invariably manages his task well given one condition: that he possess talent.
Thus, in odes that are incomparable in their musical energy and majesty of
imagination, odes composed on commission and for payment, Pindar glorified the free Hellenic cities and the city rulers who were true to the popular spirit.[15] Thus, the poet laureate Virgil, in his official epic, expressed the
immortal idea of imperial Rome, and Torquato Tasso did, after all, find the
time to complete *Jerusalem Emancipated* in accordance with his duke's
wish.[16] Individualism, as the conscious and vital self-determination of the
autonomous personality, was the work of the poet-humanists and the
Shakespearean pleiad.[17] Romanticism placed its stamp on the generations;
we recall Byron as one of our liberators; and continuing the work of Beethoven, who had restored to music its dithyrambic *orchēstra*,[18] and who restored to the choral *orchēstra* the countenance of its individualist hero and
his tragic myth, the mystagogue Richard Wagner sowed seeds deep into the
European consciousness,[19] seeds that have already sprung up on one part of
the field as the ideas of Friedrich Nietzsche, this "prime mover" of the
modern soul.

There exists an interaction between life and art, and—given this dynamic connection—the question of whether art serves life or is self-sufficient
has a purely methodological significance: one can analyze art in its closed
sphere, with its own inner purposefulness;[20] one can also analyze it in connection to "life," understood both in the sense of the unified aggregate of
phenomena and in the sense of present and immediately given conditions
of reality.

Within this interaction, it matters little how art defines itself as a factor of life in general, or how life outside relates to the isolated sphere of art.
In exchange for its values, life demands values from art: art invariably answers this demand by partially shifting values, by gradually revaluing them.
Commissions are almost never fulfilled according to the patron's intent; and
if the patron is stubborn, the artist for his part will also persist, refusing to
sell his works and thus committing himself with all the more energy to the
development of new values, as a true creator of idols.

The force of resistance necessary for this incessant struggle is talent.
Talent is also the condition that creates the value that life demands from
art. For in the finished product, the patron wants not to recognize his own
intent, which inspired the work; he orders for himself something unexpected and surprising. He seeks something new, unforeseen, better, and is
glad for this new thing, insofar as he can comprehend it. He demands that
the artist assert himself and assumes that the artist will be proudly independent; he imagines himself to be a horseman and desires that his steed be
wild and ardent. Just as fire will judge all, according to Heraclitus,[21] so also

the final criterion in disputes about the significance of the artist and artistry is the presence of talent. All that is talented is valuable and is sent down to life as a gift. But one must know how to receive gifts, and if givers are not always accompanied by that one of the three Graces who teaches to give smilingly and pleasantly, then the second Grace, the one who knows the art of grateful acceptance, visits us barbaric and wild people even more seldom.[22]

How often people forget, for example, that in revolutionary epochs it is unreasonable to demand revolutionary declarations or themes from works of art! If the revolution that is being lived through is a true revolution, it will take place not only on the surface of life and not only in the forms of life but in the very depths of consciousness. True talent cannot help but express the ultimate depth of its contemporary consciousness. Thus, true talent in such epochs necessarily serves revolution, even if it seems to others and even to itself to be its opponent. The smallest features of a talent's works will contain the poison of the general revaluation of outdated values.

The artist imperceptibly shifts our horizons in harmony with the entire elemental aspiration of the national soul. If he refrains from destroying institutions, he destroys everyday life, the bulwark of all institutions. If he refrains from teaching hatred and compassion, then he forces people to love differently and to suffer in a new way. At the same time, he knows by the instinct of talent the scale and character of what is open and accessible to him. Artistry avoids abstractions, which inevitably become the rallying cries of struggle. In its essence, artistry is a joyful science, the incarnation of rhythm and measure, a sensitive ear for subtle currents,[23] a prophetic voice of inspired whispers: how should the Muses dance before the Gorgon's head?

But Tyrtaeus also uses songs to inspire those going to battle.[24] The preeminently lyrical kind of art naturally responds to the calls of those engaged in battle, in those urgent and tragic moments when the rhythm of a martial step is necessary. Yet in a revolutionary epoch these impulses do not exhaust the content of art's creative life. It will be revolutionary in its own way, and dissatisfied patrons will either have to withhold their commissions or learn to find their inner calm even in a storm,[25] just as an artist is able to do thanks to the light gift and great promise granted by beneficial forces.

III. OUR DISCORD

In surveying contemporary art in Russia, we easily distinguish two types of artistic production. There is art that achieves large and dependable sales, and that, consequently, presupposes the existence of patrons; and then there is art that is not assured of sales and that works at its own risk, for possible future use. The latter is uncommissioned art.

Naturally, this latter affirms itself either as "art for art's sake"—such is our recent Decadence—or as art that creates life, in the final account and in the most profound meaning of this word, the art of people who seek a religious synthesis of life.[26]

If the Decadents took too much to heart Pushkin's words that poets are born "for sweet sounds," then these latter artists were more drawn to the end of Pushkin's phrase: "and for prayers."[27] The former happily focus their vision on their Western brethren in spirit, the latter—on Dostoevsky (whom they sometimes betray, though only through thoughtlessness) and Vladimir Solovyov. Incidentally, Dostoevsky was able both to prophesy and to satisfy the mass patrons of the Russian land simultaneously, things our artist-mystics do not always combine felicitously, if we are not wrong in our observation that the gift of prophesy is declining noticeably in direct proportion to its assurance of sales.[28]

Essentially, this group was conceived in the womb of that very same Decadence, when the latter began to celebrate its first modest victories over the widespread and ill-considered inattention toward the valuable and talented elements it bore within it. This example, therefore, confirms our previous observation about the alacrity with which "art for art's sake" can turn into "art for life's sake" with privileged status and *sub specie aeternitatis.*[29]

Thus, these former Decadents have recently begun to treat life with every possible care: they instruct and prophesy; they invent means of personal and universal salvation and paths of inner work and social action; and quite frequently, they even try to tune their lyres in harmony with the civic cacophonies of the sworn executors of corresponding commissions:[30] this latter, however, they do *bona fide* and only in obedience to an inner impulse of inspiration, for it is always somehow awkward, out of place, and slightly askew.

With respect to art that responds to popular demand, the art of the idol creators of Diana of Ephesus who raised a popular revolt against Paul and Barnabas, it is manifesting a marked tendency toward becoming somehow official, i.e., obligatory, tediously ritualized, accepted, and approved in advance.[31] Consequently, it is liable to bore everyone for good (a danger that is always inherent to commissioned artistic production: let us recall Perugino, whose great talent we value relatively little for the sole reason that he fulfilled too many commissions).[32]

On the other hand, commissioned art displays an inclination to avoid subjects and techniques thrust upon it by the patron, seeking instead to immerse itself in that peculiar playing at genius that occasionally results from being spoiled artistically. Therefore, instead of depicting external reality, which our patron most of all desires to understand and overcome, our artistic production increasingly aspires to general and abstract themes, to a foreign or conditional reality; instead of a vital word about vital life and the wrath of the living against the living, it gives us with ever-increasing frequency a philosophical scheme or two-faced symbol that has not been made fully incarnate in flesh and blood, just like the sect of Decadents and mystics, but without their love (which, incidentally, is often platonic) of the beautiful form. And this we see from those very Brutuses on whom we had placed so many hopes for liberation. Is the unique goddess Diana of Ephesus no longer great for them either?

In general, art by commission was somehow always unsuccessful in Russia, even in the sphere of literature, which was on the whole so successful. A *Sportsman's Sketches* or Nadson's poetry, Shchedrin or Uspensky are all exceptions, of course, insofar as they immediately and completely satisfied the need that called them to life.[33] But Gogol also anticipated his readers, as did Chekhov, who fulfilled the most important commission of recent times by reducing our rotten and distraught reality to the absurd, by depicting the senility and decomposition of stagnant Russia. And he fulfilled this commission despite the long-standing resistance of his customers, who at first could not understand that this writer was telling them what was most needed and most useful, in full agreement with their inner desire for something useful, suitable, and practical.[34]

A commission that is productive for artistry is tantamount to coparticipation in creative work, and therefore glory is due to Justinian for the Church of Sophia, to the Pitti family for the Pitti mansion, to Augustus for the Augustan age, and to Napoleon for the age of Empire, just as we fondly recall Pericles and Pope Julius.[35] But whom can we praise for being such a patron in modern Russia? Not the *poet* Pushkin, who commissioned *Dead Souls* from the poet Gogol?[36]

IV. CULTURE AS THE JOY OF THE NATIONAL SPIRIT

Here we touch upon something fateful in the destinies of our country. Throughout the recent period, her collective [*sobornyi*] soul has been inert and, only in the best of cases, receptive. Like a dead princess, she has been lying in her grave awaiting her knight. Russia's greatest talents have primarily shown themselves in artistic activity and, as artists, were supposed to be liberators, to anticipate the questions of the crowd, sometimes giving ready answers to questions that had not yet been posed in the social consciousness. There was no demand for the feminine side of talent: we needed manly initiative and masculine coercion.[37]

Speaking more simply and directly, a writer (and our artist was most often a writer) ended up in the role of teacher or preacher. This burdened or split his soul, distorting the purity of his artistic work, lowering the energy of the purely artistic potential (Nekrasov), killing the artist within the man (Lev Tolstoy), killing even the man himself (Gogol and so many others).[38]

Artistry was turning into a cultural mission, into a seed instead of being a blossom. And therefore, whenever one speaks of art in Russia, one must inquire about the relationship of art to culture in general, first of all asking oneself what Russian culture is and whether it is inevitable that a Russian artist necessarily be a missionary, a teacher in life, and a leader.[39]

Will art in Russia ever be a joyful craft, such as it would like to become, and not a jeremiad and satire, as it has defined itself almost from the beginning of our letters? Will art stop being instruction and even prophecy but the joy of the spirit? For man is made joyful not only by wine but by any play of his divine spirit. And will the craftsman of the joyful craft execute joyful commissions and stop mourning and fasting like John, and, like John, calling itself "a voice that cries out in the wilderness"?[40]

Of course, even we are not entirely deprived of joy, as long as it is understood as the idle joy of idle people. And justice dictates that we add that there are "idle people" who also know the joy of the spirit, these wise distributors of joyful commissions to which the craftsmen of the joyful science happily respond, since they see these commissions as legitimate and righteous before the face of their Athena-Ergana, the goddess who patronizes crafts.

Nevertheless, this joy is too often for show—moreover, there is too little of it—and the craftsman involuntarily resorts to strict, pompous, and mournful themes, because only despair is joyful at a feast at the time of the plague.[41] Joy is possible only in public. Only the nation's joy brings forth the true joy of the joyful craft.

The fate of our art is the fate of our culture; the fate of our culture is the fate of the nation's joy. This is the name of culture: the joy of the nation's spirit.

We, in contrast, imagine that culture is a seedbed of spiritual vegetables, the even rows of prosaic gardens, with everything handmade, regular, registered, and purposeful in its marked-off and closed-in space, with a full register of so-called objective values, and with an equally full inventory of their available objectivizations. In general, this is more dressing than culture, although the very word "culture" sounds quite dry, scholastic, practical, and tasteless in the German way, because it denies all that is indigenous or god-given, affirming only what has been planted, sown, tended, trimmed, grown, and grafted; because it does not include the concept of creativity, while that which we, for the lack of a better word, are obliged to call culture, is precisely creative work. We know this creative work in two main types: first, as barbarian or elemental, autarchic and spontaneous, creative work; and, second, as inherited creative work, or culture in the strict sense.

V. THE HELLENES AND THE BARBARIANS

Out of the humus of several ancient cultures, the greatest of which was the Egyptian, there arose a Mediterranean culture that would remain unified for several centuries: its name was Hellenic culture. There is no culture in

Europe apart from Hellenic culture, which subordinated to itself Latin culture and is still alive today within Latin culture, sprouting new shoots from
the branches of its thousand-year-old, decrepit, but enduring, trunk. It is
rooted in the blood and language of the Latin tribes. It was never able to
achieve dominion over the Germans and Slavs, who are foreign to it in blood;
at least it was never able to turn these peoples into imitations of itself or
change completely the organic tissues of the nation's soul, although it did
impose on the barbarians all its forms (even granting linguistic forms to
Slavdom),[42] and although it burned all its brands on the hides of these forest centaurs.

The great non-Hellenic element, barbarianism, lives its separate life
next to the world of the Hellenic element. These two worlds relate to each
other as the kingdom of form and the kingdom of content, formal harmony
and birth-giving chaos, or Apollo and Dionysus—the Thracian god of the
trans-Balkans whom the Hellenes transformed, revealed in plastic form,
tamed, and rendered harmless, but who still, in his very element, remains
our barbarian, our Slavic god.[43]

The old tale of Helen's abduction by her uncivilized lovers is repeated
eternally: eternally the barbarian Faust falls in love with the Beautiful One,[44]
eternally Chaos seeks harmony and an image, and the Scythian Anacharsis
travels to Hellas for the wisdom of form and measure.[45] Again and again,
there occurs a "renaissance," there are endless new delights for the Pythian
tradition's students of genius. And every time, this renaissance repeats the
first lessons of the people of Theodoric and Charlemagne.[46]

But in the womb of Latin culture, everything seems one continuous
"renaissance" of antiquity, for antiquity itself lives within it and the constant
influx of barbarian influences is incessantly balanced by forces that flow
from the native and inexhaustible depths. The forces of genius, with which
the untiring Earth is everywhere fertile,

> Denn der Boden zeugt sie wieder,
> Wie von je er sie gezeugt,[47]

these creative forces of genius are rarely capable of impressing us with their
blinding, novel appearance when they manifest themselves in Latin culture.
The regular nature and inner logic of their genesis deprives them of a considerable part of their novelty and excludes the irrational and immeasurable
element that we know and love in Shakespeare and Byron, Rembrandt and
Beethoven, Dostoevsky and Ibsen. In Latin culture, these geniuses feel like
the citizens of a great city—the *Polis*—whereas in barbarian culture they
feel like "unrestrained" personalities (as Goethe angrily called Beethoven),[48]
like individualists in an anarchic world.

Schiller claimed that it is not always possible for a genius to keep within
the bounds of good taste.[49] From the barbarian's point of view, among the

many obstacles and pitfalls to be overcome by a mind of genius in its triumphant ascent, the most dangerous temptations are those Sirens of higher
culture—refinement, skepticism, and good taste. The first stage of Friedrich
Nietzsche's path of sorrow was the island of these Sirens, for which he abandoned his "dear comrade," Odysseus-Wagner.[50] Truly, what to those Athe-
nians is wisdom, to barbarians is madness.[51] The fate of the former is to
preserve the heritage and traditions of their "elders"; we, as Lotophagi, feed
on the lotuses of oblivion.[52] On the other hand,

> There is a thirst within us
> For a freedom unknown to you.
> Your centuries are only years,
> Where the inclement weather washes ashore
> Nameless graves. . . .[53]

VI. HELLENIC CULTURE AND WE

Thus, each new "renaissance" comprises for us barbarians a vital need, like the
rhythm of breathing, like those crises of emotional maturity such as the fateful moments of passionate love in individual life, when our necessity and
our freedom enter into league with each other and conspire to bring the inevitable to pass, leading those of us who are willing along dangerous paths of
somnambulant daring whither the unwilling would be dragged by force.

Are we not witnessing the very same thing now in Russia? Classicism,
as a type of school and aesthetic norm, cannot catch on here; but perhaps
never before have we listened with such greediness to echoes of the Hellenic worldview and disposition. We desire to become blind and deaf to
everything that distracts us from our one sacrificial action, from our social
and universal tasks. But, it seems, "man never wanted you with such passionate craving as that with which you have captivated us, O enchantress
Beauty! . . ."[54]

We summon forth Ares: he is accompanied by Aphrodite, who loves
him. Captives in prisons philosophize about the rhythm of the heavenly
bodies, and those sentenced to death compose poems. "Descend beneath
the vault of dungeons with the melody of the stellar Muse. . . ."[55] Rainbows
hover over the cloudy furies.[56] Perhaps we are now on the eve of the cataclysms and eclipses of the spirit when "wise men and poets, keepers of the
mystery and faith, will carry away the lighted torches into the catacombs,
into the deserts, into the caves";[57] and we hurry, as it were, to sow in the nation's spirit the future shoots of refined enlightenment and distill in monastic cells or high towers the mysterious poisons that are to transfigure the
flesh and transform the blood of later generations.[58]

As we analyzed it above, the general norm of historical relations ob-
taining between the barbarian world and the single culture defines the spe-

121

cific character of the Russian soul's interaction with the spiritual life of the West. Barbarians in the purest sense, we use whatever is essentially new in the West to study not so much this novel phenomenon itself, but all culture through its prism. Thus, in the fifteenth and sixteenth centuries, the barbarians used the antiquities of late Rome to study not what was late Roman, but antiquity as such, some abstract Greco-Roman classicism that never actually existed. This is why in their minds Homer was compared to Virgil and Statius to Orpheus.[59]

Our so-called Decadence, like the new "Parnassianism" (its sensible nuance and obligatory correlate), was just such a cultural-historical misunderstanding, both enlightening and fruitful despite its false artificiality of pose and sometimes naive, although inwardly inevitable lapses of taste. It was on the whole talented;[60] but the talents of barbarians, whether they be unrestrained personalities of genius or Anacharses, experienced in the Athenian art of dialogue, who returned to Scythia to teach the youth the Hellene skills, will themselves not know who they are, nor whence and why they came (in Briusov's words: "I myself do not know what I mean, but still I am tidings for the world"),[61] while in Latin culture, each figure of intellectual life knows his historical place and keeps his "formula" at the ready.

VII. ALEXANDRIAN CULTURE AND THE BARBARIAN RENAISSANCE IN THE WEST

It is unquestionably true that the epoch we have been experiencing throughout so-called modern history is a "critical" one. The century whose border we crossed so recently can be seen in some sense as its apogee. Indeed, we have achieved a previously unknown degree of disintegration, individuation, isolation, and consequently, also of the inner deepening and enrichment of separate spheres of life, both material and intellectual, of separate areas of consciousness, both social and individual, and of certain abilities and possibilities of the human spirit.

It seemed from the end of the nineteenth century that a new "Alexandrian period" of history had appeared on the peaks of European culture.[62] It seemed that the world was once again repeating that period when "theoretical man" first appeared in humanity;[63] when the individualized branches of religious, scientific, and artistic creative work had finally and variously determined their particular tasks; when such a multitude of values and treasures had been accumulated in the past that the generations made it their most urgent task to collect, preserve, and, finally, to reproduce by imitating and repeating what had gone before in elegant and refined miniature; when people learned what a scholarly library is in the full sense of the word, and what a museum is; when that which we call general education was affected by historical perspective (which the nineteenth century was so fond of,

122

under the name of "historical sense," *historischer Sinn*);[64] when the art of dilettantes and the mysteries of "cenacles" flourished;[65] when the inner atomization of culture was combined with the universal horizons of intellectual syncretism in religion and philosophy, in aesthetics and morals.

The art that signified the waning of the last century (poignant and luxurious in France but paler in other countries) breathed on us with a truly Alexandrian fragrance of elegance and dying, of flowers and the sepulcher. It was no accident that it located its most refined poisons of the age in Paris under the highly significant slogan, proud on the lips of these citizens of ancient and noble civic feeling: *décadence.* People wanted to be known as late descendants, and the more insistently they declared themselves the last of the nonbarbarians, the more energetically did they affirm the genealogical antiquity of their clan and all their cultural atavism.

In France, Decadence, analytic in its essence, was closely tied to the movement of the Parnassians, just as true Symbolism, the first attempt at synthetic creativity in modern art and modern life, nourishes its roots in artistic realism and naturalism.[66] Insofar as Decadence does not merge with Symbolism but contrasts itself to it, it inevitably tends toward the art of the Parnassians. Here again one sees the closeness and blood kinship between the late nineteenth century and ancient Alexandria, which truly combined within itself a museumlike "Parnassus" and the elegant "decline" of fatigued lovers of refinement.

The barbarian (i.e., primarily Anglo-Germanic) renaissance of the nineteenth century defined itself in all its manifestations as a reaction against the spirit of the critical epoch (which had left its mark in the Alexandrian nature of the culture contemporary to it), as an impulse to reunite the differentiated cultural forces into a new synthetic worldview and holistic construction of life. The Englishmen William Morris and Ruskin, the American Walt Whitman, and the Norwegian Ibsen are agents of a universal liberation of unincarnated energies of new life.[67] Even the Decadent and Hellenist Oscar Wilde, obedient to the law of the barbarian soul, was obliged to betray the idea of aesthetic individualism in the name of the idea of *sobornost'*.[68]

Hellas serves the humanists of the barbarian "renaissance" as a thesaurus of values necessary for the revaluation of all values. Following the banner of Friedrich Nietzsche, they aspire to a different Hellas than that which up to now has been dear and holy to those who would evoke Helen, not the Hellas of radiant harmony and harmonious balance, but barbarian Hellas, orgiastic, mystical, primordially Dionysian Hellas.

It is not Hellenic plasticity and measure that they seek to resurrect and introduce into the contemporary consciousness, but the corybantism of Asian flutes and the music of the tragic choruses.[69] Modern Latin culture needs Alexandria and Periclean Athens; modern barbarianism needs Asia Minor of Heraclitus or the tyrants and the archaic dithyramb. Richard Wagner's art has initiated the restoration of primordial *myth* as one of the determining factors of universal consciousness.

VIII. ALEXANDRIAN CULTURE AND
THE BARBARIAN RENAISSANCE IN RUSSIA

What could Decadence become in Russia? Engendered by decrepit Latin culture, Decadence was a phenomenon of cultural complexity, saturation, and fatigue. In a primarily barbarian medium, it could only dimly reflect its own outlines, without inculcating its poisons. We could not conceive anything from the spirit of Western decline. But neither did the toxic filtrate poison us: for us it was medicinal, as a stimulus that liberates creative energies.

In Russia, Decadence was most of all an experimentalism in art and life, the adogmatism of seekers, and the pathos of perceiving things in a new way. Aestheticism, taken as an abstract principle, was to leave us the imperative of "artistry," the testament of concerning ourselves with the perfection of form, both in the sense of its artistic refinement and—it can be affirmed with respect to the best representatives of the movement—in the sense of its rigor, even if this rigor was subordinated to canons which, from the point of view of the old canons of aesthetics, were heretical. Love for form was crowned by triumphs in the area of technique and invention, and also by splendid achievements in the sphere of verbal expression, most particularly in our native language, which once again became fresh and exalted.

Within the bounds of poetry, the greatest merit of Decadence as intimate art[70] was the simple, yet endlessly complicated and subtle fact, that contemporary poets severed poetry from "literature" (mindful of Verlaine's "de la musique avant toute chose . . .")[71] and rejoined it as an equal member and sister to the round dance of arts: music, painting, sculpture, dance. Indeed, until quite recently, poetry seemed only a kind of literature and was therefore subordinated to the general principles of the verbal and logical canon. The Decadents realized that poetry has its own language and own law, that much that seemed irrational from the common literary viewpoint was rational in poetry, understood as a particular art of the word, or as a particular word. Poetry regained, as its ancient fortune, a considerable part of the domain it had lost to literature.

As far as the conceptual content of the new movement is concerned, it proclaimed individualism, understood, if it is permissible to say so, as intellectual Don Juanism, grasping everything in the fleeting nature of self-sufficient "instants," the atomized state of autotelic and autarchic moments. The individualism of Decadence was unstable, just like any purely aesthetic individualism.

From its very beginning in Russia, Decadence was originally Symbolism, on the strength of its cult of eternity and all-unity within multicolored reflections of instants ("im farbigen Abglanz haben wir das Leben," as Faust says).[72] The symbol was the principle that caused the disintegration of individualism, leaving it the autocracy of daring as its only legitimate domain. But the individualistic principle of our former daring yielded to a supraindividualistic principle.[73] The word that became a symbol was once again seen as a generally comprehensible symbol of collective [*sobornyi*] unanimity.

Universal truth was discovered in symbols, which surrounded the spirit "like a forest" (in Baudelaire's simile).[74] They were revealed as the forgotten language of the lost knowledge of God. The symbol came to life and began to speak about nonpersonal, i.e., primordial mysteries. The soul hearkened to these vital whispers and was carried away listening to them, once again gaining knowledge:

> What the Earth and forest prophesy, what the spring roars in its prattle,
> What the Sisters wove in their deep-shadowed cave by the spring . . .[75]

But this also meant hearkening to the nation's soul, to the ancient, primordial element of prophetic "somnambulant consciousness," which has been drowned out by the noise of epochs of enlightenment. The Dionysus of the barbarian renaissance returned to us—myth.

Like the first shoots of spring grasses, symbols give forth the embryos of myth, the first fruits of mythopoesis. The artist suddenly recalled that he had once been a mythopoet (*mythopoiós*), and toward the nation's soul, he timidly bore forth his own, new-old soul, which was revived with new intuitions, filled with the voices and tremors of previously unknown mysterious life, sprinkled with the dew of new-old beliefs and clairvoyant visions.[76]

IX. DREAMS OF AN ARTIST-NATION

Art is directed toward the nation's soul. Myth is born of the symbol. The symbol is the nation's ancient heritage. Old myths naturally turn out to be kin to new myths.

Painting desires frescoes, architecture desires a national assembly, music a chorus and drama, and drama desires music. The theater desires to fuse the entire crowd that collects at the festival of shared [*sobornyi*] joy into a single "rite."[77]

What does poetry want to become? Universal, infantlike, mythopoetic. Its path to universal all-humanity is through its national identity; its path to truth and infantlike simplicity is serpentine knowledge; its path to the mysterious service of religious creative work is the great freedom of the inner man, love that dares in life and spirit,[78] an ear sensitive to the beating of the world heart. Its path is antinomical,[79] leading to the feminine planetlike state of universal mythopoesis through the masculine sunlike state of an initiative that affirms the mystical personality.[80]

125

The language of poetry, our language, must grow through the thick growth of contemporary speech; it is already growing from the subterranean roots of the nation's word, in order to ring out as the loud forest of the all-Slavic word. *Poetry's* knowledge is fated to spring from the depths of the subconscious through the layers of contemporary knowledge. Its religious soul is to shoot up from the valleys of the contemporary ignorance of God through the storm clouds of theomachy to the white peaks of a face-to-face vision of the divine. When it overcomes abstract individualism and "the Euclidean mind,"[81] when it attains vision of divine countenances in the world, it shall write on its tripod the words: Chorus, Myth, and Rite.

In this way, art aspires to the sources of the nation's soul. For

> Vernunft fängt wieder an zu sprechen,
> Und Hoffnung wieder an zu blühn!
> Man sehnt sich nach des Lebens Bächen,—
> Ach, nach des Lebens Quellen hin![82]

"Because universal reason once again began to speak in individual reason, and then hope blossomed; and we began to yearn for the sources of life; we wanted to fall to the living springs."[83]

The frightened friends of culture exclaim: "A long night of moribund stagnation is nearing. Education is in decline. Vandalism is appearing. The possibility of the overthrow of the ruling classes is a mortal threat to all cultural values." . . . We do not believe these friends of culture, which they see as a tidy garden and plowed vegetable plot on land belonging to the owner. We place our hopes on the elemental, creative strength of the nation's barbarian soul, and we beg the forces that preserve us only to preserve the imprint of the eternal on temporal and human things—on the past, which may be stained with blood, but which is dear to memory and holy, like the tombs of forgotten ancestors.

We fear another danger, the danger posed by "culture." Those who organize factions and their victories are not thereby called automatically to organize the nation's soul and its inner creative life. Let them beware of violating the poetic virginity of the nation's beliefs and traditions, the vatic blindness of the mythological worldview; let them beware of uprooting the shoots of original artistic and religious initiative, of leveling shared conceptions, of teaching and scholasticizing, and, in their conflict with the state church, of fighting faith as such. The atrophy of organs of religious sensitivity and religious activity is also the atrophy of the organs of artistic sensitivity and activity. Let the cup of spiritual slavery pass by our nation![84]

And if it passes us by, our nation's soul will also be revealed in an artistry that comes from the nation and is summoned forth by the nation. Then our artist and our nation will meet. The country will be covered with *orchēstrai* and *thymelai* where a round dance will dance, where true mythopoesis will be resurrected in the action of a tragedy or comedy, a national dithyramb or a national mysterium (for true mythopoesis is collective [*sobornyi*]), where freedom itself will find hearths for its absolute, unsullied, immediate self-affirmation (for choruses will be a genuine expression and voice of the nation's will).[85] Then, for the first time, our artist will be only an artist, a craftsman of the joyful craft, the executor of the commune's creative commissions, the hand and voice of a crowd that knows its beauty, and a vatic medium of the nation-artist.[86]

On the Russian Idea

I

If one observes the dominant moods in our intellectual life of late, one cannot fail to notice that certain old words or slogans have come to life and entered our intellectual vocabulary anew, and that, consequently, the old problems linked to these words and slogans are also facing our social consciousness once again. Perhaps we sometimes hear these words in previously unheard-of combinations; perhaps these problems are being posed in a different form than that of years past. In any case, did it not seem outmoded not so very long ago to inquire about the relation of our European culture to the national element, about the estrangement of the intelligentsia from the people, about turning to the people for God, or serving the people like some god?

How can this renaissance of forgotten words and seemingly obsolete viewpoints be explained? Is it, as some claim, that writers and artists, the perpetrators of all "new words" and new ideologies, have repented of their proud rebellion against paternal tradition and have returned to the original testaments of Russian literature, which from time immemorial has devoted itself to social edification, the preaching of the good, and the exhortation to undertake spiritual labors? But to speak thus is to describe the fact in a more or less tendentious fashion, rather than to clarify its causes.

We had apparently formed such an exaggerated first estimate of the goals of the liberation movement, which seemed to break off upon completing one preliminary cycle, that it seemed the end and resolution of all the contradictions in our social conscience that had formerly seemed so urgent.[1] When an interlude occurred, we were shocked to find the former correlations unchanged and the former Sphinxes still in their old places, as if the flood waters had receded to reveal that the silt had hardly covered their unshakable foundations.

On further contemplation, we inevitably reach the conclusion that some enormous truth was always evident in the contours of these old prob-

128

lems of ours, even if these contours had been shifted by time and the mist of temporary misunderstandings. We see that however their outline might have changed at the present time, we will never escape their truth. At every turn of our historical path, we come face-to-face with our primordial and, as it were, distinctly Russian questions of individual and society, culture and element, and the intelligentsia and the people.[2] And now, just as before, each time we confront these questions, we seem to be gradually solving a single problem, that of our national self-determination, and to be giving birth in pain[3] to the permanent form of our universal[4] soul, the Russian idea.

II

Agrippa of Nettesheim[5] taught that 1900 would be one of the great historical turning points, the beginning of a new universal period. . . . It is unlikely that anyone in our society knew of these calculations by ancient practitioners of black magic; but it is beyond doubt that, precisely at the border of the new astral era, sensitive souls picked up something resembling certain new shudders and vibrations in the interpsychic atmosphere around us, perceiving them as portents of a new, unknown, and awesome epoch. Vladimir Solovyov suddenly broke off his usual tone of logicizing mysticism and, like a fool in Christ,[6] took to speaking of the beginning of the end of the world, about pan-mongolism, about the Antichrist. . . .[7] There was a ferment of ideas refracted through the prism of apocalyptic eschatology. In an unprecedented way, its rainbows colored the entire world, including epistemological problems and the demands of the moral consciousness, the spirit and the flesh, creativity and social action.

Dostoevsky and Nietzsche, the two guides of the modern spirit, had only just departed the stage, having shouted into the world's ears, the one his new and extreme *Yes*, the other his new and extreme *No*—to Christ. These were two heralds, inviting people to separate into two camps in preparation for impending battle, to gather around two warring banners. These seemed to be portents of the final schism of the world, between the friends and enemies of the Lamb. . . .

World events did not delay to follow their shadows: for, as Mommsen says, events cast their shadows before them as they approach the earth.[8] Our first Punic War with Yellow Asia began.[9] War is the touchstone of national self-consciousness and an ordeal of the spirit; it is less a test of external might and external culture than of the inner energy with which the collective [*sobornyi*] personality is able to affirm itself. Yellow Asia labored to fulfill the task prepared for it, the task of testing Europe's spirit: to determine whether Christ is still alive and vital in Europe.

We Russians were the first to be confronted by Yellow Asia, which forced us to consider the nature of our self-affirmation. But there was only discord within us. And, with painful spasms, an inner process began within us, the true meaning of which lay in our efforts to achieve self-determination. It was for self-determination that we craved freedom.

Then, within searching minds, all the elements of this self-determination, in the form of urgent needs of consciousness, arose in their primitive chaos, and we needed an equally urgent synthesis in order to overcome it. . . .[10]

This I wrote in the spring of 1905, and in 1904, I had already come to the following conclusions about our first defeats at war:

> Rus'! The spirit of martial vengeance
> Arose against you, slaying your firstborn;
> And threatened you, as you trembled,
> With a quick and final execution:
> For turning mute while standing
> At the cross of intersecting roads—
> Daring to bear neither the beast's scepter,
> Nor the easy yoke of Christ.[11]

But there was neither final execution nor, in the following years, final liberation. The denouement, which had seemed so close, was postponed. But truly, albeit mutely, Russia realized that, while the emotional body of the enemy power was in its characteristic inner harmony and in the greatest tension of all the forces available to it, our collective emotional body was in disharmony, inner discord, and extreme limpness, for it did not hear the Spirit passing over its chaotic and dark waters.[12] The Russian soul was unable to make up its mind and choose its way at the crossroads. It dared neither to mount the Beast and raise high its scepter, nor to take up wholly the easy yoke of Christ. We had no integral desire, neither for dominion over the ocean, which would be the focus of all the Earth's vital forces, nor for humble service to the Light within our borders; and we fought in no one's name.

Our revolutionary movement was marked by a weak attempt to make a final choice and decide, to find ourselves, to achieve independent self-determination, to become a cosmos and lift high a torch. We wanted to be free fully and in our own way, to decide the issues of the land and the people, and to achieve a new religious consciousness. This was the desire not only of dreamers and abstract thinkers, but also of the people. We decided nothing, and, most important, we made no final choice; and, as before, there is chaos in our emotional body, which is open to all attacks and the invasion of all our enemies (who have in no sense laid down their weapons). The only force capable of organizing the chaos of our emotional body is a free and integral acceptance of Christ as the single, all-defining principle of our spiritual and exterior life: this is the main idea of my entire essay.[13]

> Just as holy winter seed smolders
> In tempests of autumn—the spirit
> Hovers quietly over the black grave,
> And only the lightest souls are able
> To discern its untrembling murmur

> Among the inert stones:
> So my Rus' defies mute death
> By silently conceiving new being.[14]

The slow work of our self-determination did not cease, and it will not cease. The people's thought, in the person of its millions of mystics, does not tire of forging a spiritual sword that must sunder from what is Christ's all that is hostile to Christ,[15] both in spiritual consciousness and in external life. The intelligentsia is uneasy within the limits of its isolated sphere of consciousness and life. It has disturbed and perhaps partly awoken the Church.[16] Even if only platonically, even if almost always helplessly, it has not ceased to strive toward the people. Its practical groups have only devoted themselves to a material concern for the people and external activity. By contrast, the peaks of our intellectual culture, our foremost spiritual forces, have sought to overcome individualism in our consciousness, have considered how to pass from individual creative work to universal art, have striven to approach the people with an open soul. In part, they have proclaimed *universality,* having perhaps sensed correctly that nothing divides in principle the ultimate simplicity of the wise (who are wise in inherited and borrowed wisdom) from the wisdom of the simple among us. In part, they have proclaimed *new populism,* as if affirming that the elite intelligentsia is still only intelligentsia but that it must become something else lest it perish.[17]

III

But it is impossible to speak of the "intelligentsia" as a phenomenon of our "culture" without asking what natural material has been subjected to artificial development in it, what soil has been plowed over and sown in it. It is likewise impossible to analyze the people, who comprise the preeminent expression of the elemental principle of our life, without taking full account of what our element itself is. For it is beyond doubt that any culture with respect to its element is *modus* with respect to substance.

Thus, in order to understand both forms of our historical being in their interaction, in order to oppose them as thesis and antithesis, it is necessary to unite them in a characterization of the integral soul of the entire people, since even the intelligentsia, although severed from the earth, is still a phenomenon of Russian national life. Seeking to define the common basis of both forms, the national element in the true sense of the word, we must undertake an excursion into the realm of national psychology where through observation alone we will seek to abstract out our psychic substrate, the distinctive traits of our collective consciousness. On the other hand, we inevitably begin searching for synthesis, as the third and supreme form, which cancels the contradiction of the two lower forms: "the people" and "the intelligentsia."[18] Insofar as we are moving beyond the definition of the

131

substrate to the development of a synthesis, we must speak of postulates and not accomplishments, of our hopes and not of historical achievements. *Only that which is, becomes;*[19] when we reveal potential being in empirical presence, we also reveal the being of the idea that is to be fulfilled in incarnation. Therefore, it is hardly surprising that the results of a psychological observation would find their alternative expression in terms of religious thought.

But is it possible—indeed, is it proper—to speak at all about a national idea, as if it were some structure of moments characteristic of the national self-consciousness? Has not this old topic also been abolished, just as the old slogans about the people and intelligentsia also seemed to have been abolished? We think that it is both possible and proper. It is possible, because the concept "national idea" was not invented by Herder and Hegel;[20] it was not invented by philosophers hypostasizing some abstraction or metaphysical scheme; rather, history created and realized it as one of its basic facts. It is proper, insofar as the national idea is the self-determination of the collective soul of the people in its connection to the universal process and in the name of universal fulfillment. This self-determination prefigures historical achievements and, therefore, directs the energies. Any affirmation of the national idea becomes false only when it is incorrectly bound to national egoism, or when the concept of nation is confused with the concept of the state. Let us not forget that even without a state the Jews felt their national calling to be a nation of priests who would give the Messiah to the world; indeed, it was precisely without a state that they felt their calling most urgently and clearly. The Second Isaiah's universal concept of messianism arose among the Jews in the epoch of Babylonian captivity.[21]

The Roman national idea was developed through a complex process of collective mythopoesis: they needed both the legend of the Trojan Aeneas[22] and the Hellenic and oriental Sibylline prophesying[23] in order gradually to strengthen the vital sense of Rome's universal role of uniting the tribes into a single political body, which was already universal in spirit, and within the harmony of this body, which the Romans called *pax Romana.* "Let others make metal soft and marble alive, and let statues arise under their creative chisel with the breath of life; they will do this better than you, o Roman! But you must remember one thing: rule the nations powerfully, show mercy on the obedient and overthrow the proud."[24] Thus spoke Virgil to the nations and ages on behalf of and in the name of his nation; speaking thus, Virgil affirmed not national egoism, but rather the providential will and idea of imperial Rome, which was becoming the world.

True will is the intuition of necessity; an idea is being's will to reach fulfillment in historical becoming. The fact that Rome permanently severed the idea of empire (as it developed in Rome) from the national idea shows clearly that there was no national egoism in Virgil's words. History has repeatedly proved this—by the medieval Holy Roman Empire, and even by

132

Napoleon's empire: Napoleon betrayed French statehood when he became emperor, but his unsuccessful attempt was no betrayal of the universal content of the French national idea.[25] Whenever a national idea has reached full definition, it has been defined in connection to the nation's general, universal task, and it has always called the nation to universal service. From Roman times, the national idea has by its very essence been incompatible with the political ambitions of national selfishness; it is inherently religious in essence. Thus, the reason we are so disgusted by the egotistical affirmation of our statehood by the epigones of the Slavophiles is that it is not in statehood that we see our calling.[26] Even if there was a certain truth in the name "Third Rome,"[27] the very christening of our universal idea (for "Rome" is always "the universe") with the name of the "Third Rome," the "Rome of the Spirit,"[28] reveals to us: "You, Russian, must remember one thing: universal truth is your truth; and if you want to preserve your soul, do not be afraid to lose it."[29]

It is unnecessary to explain that there is nothing fatalistic in becoming aware of one's national idea. To feel light within oneself, and to break through to the voice of this light, to its secret call, is not the same as feeling an outer inevitability that destroys the freedom of individual and social action. Our times demand from us precisely free self-determination: there are various ways that our universal soul can determine itself and embody its deepest will in action. Thus, I touch upon the great and mysterious question of the mystical significance of our self-determination in the near future. Mystics of East and West alike are agreed that Slavdom, and particularly Russia, is being handed a certain torch precisely at this moment; whether our nation carries it high or lets it fall is a question of world destiny. If our nation drops the torch, the consequences will be dire not only for Slavdom, but for all; if it carries it aloft, it will benefit the entire world. We are experiencing for humanity a great crisis, and humanity is experiencing it in us. The comparison Aleksandr Blok made between the Calabrian and Sicilian catastrophes and our fate was not a mere comparison.[30] Truly, "everyone is guilty for everyone and everything";[31] and our country, which wants, but is unable to become free, is laboring and exhausting itself on behalf of everyone.

In this way, my topic is justified: the following exposition will present my understanding of those distinctive traits of our national self-awareness, the structure and synthesis of which we are accustomed to call "the national idea."

IV

If the problem of "the people and the intelligentsia" continues to disturb our social conscience, despite all the historical events that should have convinced us that the old antithesis has been eliminated by a new social arrangement and that one can no longer speak simply of the "people" and the "intelligentsia," then does it not behoove us to conclude from the vitality of this obsolete *formula* that it conceals within itself the truth of a living *symbol?*

What is signified by this symbol, which is logically and sociologically suspect and justly disputed, but which inwardly and psychologically is so easily comprehensible and close to us? What life keeps it alive in us and about which unfulfilled truth does it speak to us?

Does this vitality not testify primarily to the fact that, in our national psychology, any cultural separation and disintegration meets the subconscious resistance of integrating forces, an organic tendency toward restoring the unity of divided energies? Nowhere in other nations' history do we find an alienated social group with such a yearning for reunification with the masses, such a class-based *taedium sui*,[32] such a profound and, in its very tragic nature, lyrical schism in the heart of the nation. We Russians are alone in being able to accept our differentiated self-determination only by establishing its connection and harmony with universal self-determination.

Universality is the immediately given, outer form of the idea which seems to us the basis of all our aspirations to bring the truth of those severed from the earth into accord with the truth of the earth. But what is the source of this will to universality? Whence arises our suspicion, which remains constant despite all the changing masks of our intellectual and practical searches, that we have lost our way, having betrayed the national truth? Whence this primordial barbarian distrust for the *principle* of culture among all the geniuses who labor in the cultural sphere in Russia? Whence this frequently suicidal attraction to extinguishing in the national sea everything that has isolated and elevated itself, even if this elevation be the raising of light and a guiding beacon above the dark sea?

There are peculiarities of the national psychology, features of the national character and genius, which one must accept as a typical phenomenon and the inwardly inevitable mover of a country's destiny. However we might explain them—whether by geographic and ethnographic conditions, material facts of the historical process, or causes of a spiritual order—we must still admit their presence, their activity, and perhaps their providential role in the development of the nation. We would be mistaken in our expectations of what is to come and in our social action if we failed to take account of them as vital forces. And, on the contrary, we would discern much beneath the surface of things, in the subconscious sphere of the collective soul, where the roots of events are hidden, if we could divine their secret nature by way of synthesis and intuitive insight.

V

National ideology and Westernism, our innate national traits, and our culture (which at first was merely borrowed, but which has now attained international legitimacy), are just as mutually opposed as are the concepts of primitive culture and critical culture.[33]

Primitive culture, the culture of so-called organic epochs, is one in which a unity of fundamental ideas about the divine and the human, right and wrong, lead to the achievement of a unity of forms in lifestyle and a unity of style in arts and crafts, where conflicting forces do battle on the field of common norms. The rivals understand each other thanks to their shared awareness of the general principles that determine life, which the individual can challenge only by violating them but not by negating them. Primitive culture is where everything creative is by its very nature impersonal, and everything individual is only an accidental phenomenon whereby an individual egotistically affirms his personal will to domination and power. Such were the most ancient cultures, like that of Egypt; such was the culture of the anonymous architects of the Middle Ages.

Critical culture, in contrast, is that in which the group and individual, belief and creativity are divided and affirmed in separation from the social whole, where they display not so much communicativeness and, as it were, a spirit of conquest toward the whole, as an inclination toward concentration and perfection within their own boundaries. This causes yet further disintegration within the microcosms that have separated from the whole. The consequences of such a state are, on the one hand, an ever-increasing estrangement and ever-decreasing mutual understanding among specialized groups. On the other hand, the consequences include a tireless quest for more certain truth and more perfect form (a quest that is essentially critical, for it is conditioned by the constant comparison and reevaluation of conflicting values), an inevitable competition of one-sided truths and relative values, and the inevitable lie of an affirmation of abstract principles that have not yet been brought into the New Testament concord of complete all-unity. I say "New Testament" concord, because any anticipation of a new organic epoch in an epoch of critical culture is a sign of a new religious consciousness, insofar as it coincides with the quest for a universal synthesis and the reunification of divided principles. For example, in the critical epoch of pagan Rome we find just such a quest in Virgil's "messianic" Fourth Eclogue, which is truly and prophetically New Testament in its spirit.[34] Any anticipation of a new organic epoch is also accompanied by the constant feature of eschatological premonition, a spiritual foreboding of catastrophic revolution, of a sudden universal miracle.

Without a doubt, the historical reality of each organic epoch reveals, on closer analysis, many features of the coming differentiation. It is therefore impossible to find a purely primitive culture within the horizon of history, only perhaps beyond its bounds, in the prehistoric age. But it is also doubtless that, at least in the epoch of Anaxagoras,[35] the primitive structure of Athenian life was so powerful that the demos that expelled him was sim-

135

ply incapable of understanding him, and that the accusation of godlessness
raised against him was first and foremost an accusation of amoralism and
apoliticism, since the reigning system of divine veneration was thereby the
system of the entire life of the nation. Without a doubt, Socrates, sentenced
to death for denying the gods recognized by the people and for introducing
new gods, was also, in the eyes of the demos, "a member of the intelligentsia severed from the national element,"[36] unable to understand the people and incomprehensible to the people.

Naturally, any innovation in the area of religious worldview and religious action during an epoch of organic lifestyle is obliged to conceal itself
in mysteries. The form of mysteries, which presupposes that one abstain
from open conflict with the worldview of the people, allows religious innovations to achieve social recognition and even patronage: Pisistratus, the great
reformer of Hellenic religion, was the founder of mysteries and was remembered by the people only as a tyrant, as a power-hungry and imperial
individual, but not as a rebel against the national faith like Anaxagoras and
not as a religious innovator like Socrates.[37]

In the epoch when critical differentiation triumphed in the entire intellectual life of ancient Rome, in the epoch of confessional freedom that
went hand in hand with this differentiation, Christians were subjected to
persecutions for their faith. This was because material and social life preserved the structure of primitive culture. Not desiring to be merely one of
the multifarious phenomena of the critical epoch that had long since arisen
in the sphere of spiritual culture, Christianity rose up against the entire organic structure of ancient life in its essence, calling for the dawn of a new
epoch that would be primitive in a new way and organic in accordance with
the New Testament. Christians were executed merely for refusing to show
reverence to the emperor, i.e., Caesar, as the incarnation of all Rome, with
its traditions and cult of ancestor worship, with its land and heritage, customs and institutions. Christianity did not want to be just one of the cells
of critical culture; it did everything it could to avoid conflict, promising
"Caesar" all that did not belong to "God,"[38] organizing itself in the form of
mysteries; but these mysteries were mere superstructures over life, only
"theosophy," and the entire world turned out to belong to "God." Christianity was to penetrate all life, to transfigure the flesh and transubstantiate the
blood of the world. To the organic tradition—those old skins that could
hardly contain the new critical culture—it opposed the new skins of New
Testament expectation.[39] Thus religion, as it is regenerated in critical epochs,
when the measure of division is complete and the process of reunification
has been initiated, enters life as a unified, all-determining, supreme principle.

An organic epoch is analogous to the Edenic state of childlike being
in the womb of the Creator, not because it is paradise and the golden age
of lost happiness, of course, but because the center of consciousness is not

within the individual personality but outside of it. In contrast, a critical epoch is one of Luciferian revolt by individuals desiring to become "as gods."[40] In a critical epoch, thorns and thistles grow on the earth, which before was a joyfully generous mother and now is man's miserly and hostile stepmother.[41] Of course, this is not because the external conditions of existence have changed for the worse but because the individual has learned to dare and suffer, and because new, unheard-of labyrinths of the heart's Spirit and Golgotha have been revealed.

Critical culture is the culture of Cain's sons, the forgers of metal and the inventors of musical instruments.[42] But Luciferianism is annulled by the New Testament, which reconciles man's true theomachy with the truth of Abel, by means of dividing man into empirical personality and inner personality. The latter is home to Heaven and the Father in Heaven, so that man's true will is no longer man's own will, but rather the will of the Father who sent him, and man no longer affirms himself in his ascent to God, but God within man affirms Himself in his descent to humanity.[43]

Today, insofar as human culture is godless, it is still a merely critical, Luciferian, Cainite culture. But each time the religious principle is introduced into it, not as an abstract concession but as the supreme norm determining all life, a process is begun whereby the conflicting energies are reintegrated correctly. This prepares a revolution that will destroy all the values of critical cultural construction, in order to replace them with values of another, all-embracing consciousness in God.

VI

Russia has engendered a critical culture, but, since it preserves in its depths the remnants of another, primitive culture, it does not allow our hearts to rest easy in this division. The attempts of the intelligentsia to raise the people to its own level, to make the entire people *intelligentsia* in the sense of a critical and therefore nonreligious culture, have thus far foundered on the elemental conditions of our historical being. And even if they were fated to succeed, something unexpected might occur: the elite might overcome their own critical culture, yet the *entire* people would still not be united in the untruth of the cult of abstract principles. If the children are silent, the stones will cry out.[44] For both the intelligentsia and the people yearn for a New Testament culture: the people hope for resurrection;[45] the intelligentsia craves reunion. But reunion is only attained in resurrection; and we should not search for God among the people, for the people themselves want a new, living New Testament culture, while we should seek God in our hearts. Knowledge of the *Name* is innate to our national soul.

Critical culture frees up energies hidden in the stagnation of primitive culture. It is not surprising that our national will to universality has been so clearly manifested in our intelligentsia, which has expressed its mute yearning for organic unity in life through its profound dissatisfaction with its solitary achievements; through its clear awareness of its duty before the people; through its Romantic idealization of the people; and through all its attempts to serve them and unite with them. The intelligentsia is not conscious of the religious meaning of this yearning; it has not comprehended that it is not the people it needs but rather that which the people also need—a New Testament synthesis of all the principles that determine life and all the energies that fulfill life. The intelligentsia does not know that the organic-primitive spiritual being of the people is an Old Testament hope that its truth will be revealed in a new religious consciousness. It does not know this, but it has hoped (just as the Old Testament gentiles did) for that very New Testament. Burdened with being the ruling and educated class, the intelligentsia has revealed a historically unprecedented example of a will to poverty, simplification, self-abnegation, and descent. Everywhere, in all epochs, we observe the opposite phenomenon in the cultural process: every elevated group preserves itself, defends the position it has achieved, stands up proudly for its own values, affirming and multiplying them. Our most attractive and noble aspirations are sealed with a craving for self-destruction, as if we were secretly bound to the inescapable charms of a peculiar Dionysus who makes self-depletion the most inspiring of all passions, as if other peoples were deadly selfish, whereas we, a nation of self-immolators, represented the vital principle in life, which Goethe saw as the butterfly Psyche who yearned for a fiery death.[46]

The fundamental trait of our national character is the pathos of renunciation, the craving to renounce all our robes and clothing, to tear off every mask and every ornament from the naked truth of things. Our multifarious virtues and strengths are linked to this feature, as are many of our weaknesses, deviations, dangers, and falls. Here lie the roots of the skeptical and realistic mind-set of incorruptible Russian thought; its need always to follow everything to the end and to the edge with mercilessly clear consistency; its moral and practical structure and tendency, which hates the contradiction between consciousness and action; and its suspiciously harsh judgment and aspiration to devalue values. The Russian soul instinctually thirsts for the absolute, instinctually renouncing all that is conditional. It is barbarically noble, i.e., profligate and recklessly broad like the empty steppe, where the snowstorm covers nameless graves.[47] It unconsciously rebels against all that is artificial and all that is artificially raised to the status of value and idol, taking its tendency to devalue to the extreme of insulting the human image and humiliating the personality, which just an instant before was so proud and uncontrollable; to the extreme of distrusting everything in man that carries the divine seal, whether in the name of God or of no one. It carries this tendency to the extreme of the intoxicated soul's suicidal impulses, to all kinds of theoretical and practical nihilism. Love for descent, which is displayed in all these images of renunciation, whether positive or negative, comprises the distinguishing feature of our national psychology. It is the opposite of the ceaseless will to ascent that we observe in all pagan nations and in all nations that issued from the world-embracing womb of Roman statehood. Only among Russians can one observe a true will for organic universality, a will affirmed in our hatred for the culture of isolated peaks and achievements, in our conscious and unconscious disregard for such culture, in our need either to abandon or destroy what has been achieved, and to descend to everyone from heights that have been conquered by an individual or a group. Does not all of this mean, when put in the terms of religious thought: "leave all and follow me"?[48]

VII

In terms of religious thought, descent is an act of love and a sacrificial lowering of divine light into the gloom of the lower sphere, which seeks enlightenment.[49] For man, true descent primarily means to yield to and serve the lowest of all creation (signified by the symbol of the washing of the feet),[50] a willing subordination prescribed to the personality by its own awareness of its debt to whoever aided its glorification. "I bow down before you; I have risen higher than you because I trampled you with my feet when I was ascending; I crushed you with my heel." This voice sounds unceasingly in the soul of our intelligentsia, unceasingly calling it to a sacrificial act of self-renunciation and self-depletion for the sake of a descent to those whose voiceless sacrifice created the advantages the intelligentsia now renounces. This very fact proves that the Russian soul's religious consciousness is a kind of innate consciousness, immanent and psychological, vital and active even when the mind resists it and the mouth contradicts it. Only our nation could give rise to a sect whose banner reads: "You are more than I."[51]

But the law of descent, this creative energy of our soul, this metaphysical form-energy that irresistibly pulls us toward the New Testament entelechy of our national idea, has even more profound meaning. The divine sends down its light into dark matter so that it might be filled with light. From one plane of divine all-unity to another, from one hierarchy of creation to another, the Logos descends, and the light shines in the darkness, and the darkness cannot encompass it.[52] This is the mystery of the Second Hypostasis, the mystery of the Son. "A seed will not come to life unless it die."[53] *Vis eius integra, si versa fuerit in terram:* its strength will be preserved whole if it is turned into the earth.[54] These mysterious testaments seem to me to be written on the brow of our nation as its mystical name: "the imitation of Christ,"[55] the energy of its energies, the living soul of its life. The imperative of descent that calls our nation to the dark earth, its

139

pull toward these boulders that crave the seed of lights, determines it as a nation whose entire subconscious sphere is filled with a feeling of Christ. *Hic populus natus est christianus.*[56]

The Russian nation does not hope for the immediate descent and inspiration of the Spirit. When it is told, "the Spirit is here," it refuses to believe. It awaits a different manifestation of the spirit. Reproducing in its half-blind consciousness, in its collective [*sobornyi*] inner experience (which still remains obscure to it), the Christian mystery of Death on the cross, it awaits and is consoled only by the promise of the Comforter.[57] It waits and craves resurrection. The seed that died among the dark clods of earth must rise again. We die in Christ and are resurrected by the Holy Spirit. Hence the New Testament hope for an instant, miraculous ascension in the Spirit, which is to occur at the moment of mortal passion and burial in the earth. Thus (a characteristic feature of our religiosity), it is only in Russia that the Bright Resurrection is truly a feast of feasts and a celebration of celebrations.[58] At this moment of its religious life, our nation's collective [*sobornyi*] inner experience is essentially different from the inner experience of other nations, who consider the mystery of Nativity brighter and closer, this feast of initiations, this celebration of achievements, when man feels sublime and ennobled through the descent and incarnation of God. The Russian soul finds more content in the feast when

> . . . the bell at Paschal night,
> Like a white light, in the suffering prison of hearts
> Will illuminate New Jerusalem. . . .[59]

This is how I see our national idea in its religious expression. It reveals the most profound meaning of our aspiration to universality, of our energy of renunciation, and of our craving for descent and service. It alone provides the resolution of the enormous misunderstanding that divides the intelligentsia from the people, through which the intelligentsia always knows that it must go to the people but does not always know what it should bring them. Sometimes, yielding to the insistence of the first voice, the intelligentsia does go, yet brings the people what they do not want. For its part, the people desire to meet with the intelligentsia but not with the intelligentsia that comes to it. This misunderstanding can be resolved only by communing in a third thing—in the light of Christ, which is equally hidden from the eyes of both the intelligentsia and the people. But there will be a moment

> . . . when hearts shall be moved,
> And candles will touch in a shudder
> In the fiery communion of a god-bearing meeting;
> And the hidden will flame up on distant faces
> In the reflection of the Single Face.

VIII

There are two equally powerful and constantly active natural laws in the cosmos, the laws of self-preservation and self-destruction. The latter is clearly active in the secret mystery of descent. But the peculiarity of the Christian idea, which has expressed and ennobled the idea of humanity most fully and absolutely, is that it itself—in contrast to Buddhism, for example—serves as the basis for the correct conditions of descent. These conditions limit the suicidal pull caused by the conscious affirmation of this second law in the individual, and reconcile it with the law of self-preservation. The Christian sensibility cannot accept the legend of Buddha, who gave his flesh to a hungry tigress; at the same time, Buddha was not nailed to the cross in the flesh for the sins of the world, and tragedy, as the purely human element of religion, is profoundly foreign to Buddhism. Tragedy arises in Christianity from this very presence of the law of self-preservation. Blood does not flow from the pores of the body in Christianity; rather, Christianity preserves its blood for the final tragic denouement, for Golgotha.

In the illumination of the Christian idea, the law of self-preservation turns into the law of preserving light—not the light of the empirical personality but of its suprapersonal, divine content. Physical suffering protects the organism from destruction by leading it across the range of irritations, beginning with pleasure and enjoyment, and ending with unbearable pain, which shows that expansive energy must yield to the opposite drive for Tranquillity. Similarly, in the moral sphere, the vital sense of evil, this unthinking protest of conscience, shows when the spiritual monad, this bearer of moral consciousness and of inner spiritual light, has strayed unsustainably far from the hearth of divine light, when its light energy is ready to expire, when darkness is just about to envelop the light, when it is necessary to return, and when it is necessary to *ascend* anew.

The Russian character is not always able to stop on this threshold; this is the source of our nation's unique attitude toward sin and the criminal, to which Dostoevsky so insistently pointed.[60] On the one hand, the principle of collective responsibility and the choral principle applies also to the moral sphere, creating a living awareness of the collective [*sobornyi*] responsibility of everyone for everyone.[61] A personal transgression is in a sense removed immediately from the individual by a general, universal confession of collective guilt; the individual arouses only sympathy insofar as he refuses to affirm the proud isolation of his personal sin. Instead, he communes with the earth, committing to it his sin. The earth welcomes everyone and forgives everyone (in this we see features of a most sublime and subtle moral sanctity, which testifies to the fact that, whether the individual is conscious of it or not, Russian morality is always religion, always mysticism, but never the abstract principle of duty). On the other hand, a purely religious rehabilitation of the criminal, strong enough to create among us an entire religious movement of sinners, even conditioning, in some sects, a particular reverence for sinners (i.e., those who have accepted a part of the shared sin) can go so far as to justify sin in principle as the most radical form of renunciation and descent. This is the subject of Leonid Andreev's recent story "Darkness," where a typically Russian craving for brotherly equality culminates in the paradox that it is a betrayal of one's brothers to be the friend of a sinner without sinning, to have compassion for the fallen without joining their ranks.[62] And if Andreev reproaches Christ for not sinning with the sinners, in the speeches of Ivan Karamazov Dostoevsky already presented the idea of the aristocratic nature of Christ's teaching, which is intended for the strength of the few.[63]

The general composition of the Russian soul is such that one might say that the Christian idea comprises its nature. It expresses the central content of the Christian idea, the categorical imperative of descent and burial of the Light, and the categorical postulate of resurrection. Its typical deviations and errors are only distortions of its fundamental nature; its danger lies in a falsely precipitous relinquishing of its light and in suicidal death, at *the very time* when what is dying is still unworthy of a death that will lead to resurrection. If our nation has been called a "God-bearer," and God has been revealed to it primarily in the countenance of Christ, then our nation is precisely a "Christ-bearer," Christophorus.[64]

The legend of St. Christopher[65] depicts him as the half-wild son of the earth: huge, unwieldy, immobile, and heavy. To save his soul, the future saint settles at the dwelling of a hermit on the bank of a broad river, across which he carries pilgrims on his enormous shoulders. No burden is too heavy for him. One stormy night he is awakened from heavy sleep by the weak sobs of a child, which reach him from the opposite bank. He goes reluctantly to fulfill his usual duty and takes upon his shoulders the Divine Infant, whom he does not recognize. But this light burden turns out to be so heavy that it is as if he had to carry by himself the entire burden of the world. With great difficulty, almost despairing of success, he crosses the river and delivers to the riverbank the infant—Jesus. . . . Thus also Russia is threatened by the danger of becoming exhausted and drowning.

IX

The law of the descent of light must be realized in harmony with the law of the preservation of light. Before descending, we must strengthen the light that is within us; before turning our strength to the earth, we must preserve this strength. Three moments determine the conditions of correct descent: in the language of mystics, they are denoted by the words *cleansing* (*kátharsis*), *teaching* (*máthēsis*), and *action* (*práxis*). Cleansing is expressed in the call *metanoeite* (i.e., change inwardly, repent of what was before), with which

Christ began his preaching.[66] Here the awakening of the mystical life of the personality is the first and necessary foundation of religious work. Here one comprehends that all the values of our critical culture are relative values, and this prepares the way for the restoration of all true values in their connection with divine all-unity.

This is an "irreconcilable No," an integral, religious *nonacceptance* of a world wholly infected by sin.

> Fire will wash the world with a love that hates,
> You who hope, who see, destroy and kill the idol![67]

The second moment, the moment of *teaching,* is the discovery of the *Name.* Here mysticism becomes aware of itself as the nurse of religious truth:

> My wedding ring has sunk to the purple seabed:
> O violent storm, reveal the Face in the azure depths!

Here the visionary is blinded by the *Image* it sees; here is *acceptance* of the world in Christ.

> From native Chaos—look, look—a Star.
> From irreconcilable *No*—a blinding *Yes.*[68]

The third moment of correct descent is action—*práxis;* if the first two conditions are observed, descent here becomes not only an efficacious but also a true descent in the name of God, undoubtedly fruitful and resurrectional— a descent of light that will not be engulfed by darkness. Here any social action is light and joyful. Any abstention from social action, when this latter is incompatible with the religious imperative in the given historical conditions, becomes asceticism; it becomes asceticism because man in his private activity creates for himself an equivalent of social activity that is heavy and burdensome.

Observance of these conditions banishes all fear from the soul. The element is frightening only because it can destroy; the element is frightening to critical culture and its idols. It is with good reason that Nietzsche says: "A mistake is always cowardice. The old idols will have to learn the cost of having clay legs."[69]

In the religious consciousness of the Old Testament, fear of the element turns into the fear of God (*timor Dei*), and this is already a positive religious value; but the consciousness of the New Testament removes any fear. Love is the name of the equivalent of fear in the New Testament, and love does not know fear.

With the impatience of love, the consciousness of the New Testament awaits a trial by fire,[70] which will wash over the world with hating love. With the impatience of love, it listens closely to the apocalyptic promise of Him Who is the First and the Last: "Behold, I come soon, and My retribution is with Me. Blessed are those who have a right to the Tree of Life and the power to enter by the Gates into the City."[71]

143

Ancient Terror

On Leon Bakst's Painting *Terror Antiquus*

I

Terror Antiquus . . .

The artist tells us of ancient truth and, in sacrificing to the Muses, he worships the great and wise goddess Memory.[1] But the Muses themselves, like their nursling, Pushkin's playful maiden Rhyme, "are obedient to strict Memory."[2] Memory-Mnemosyne was one of the seven Mothers who conceived of Zeus. Memory gave birth to the nine Muses. And the mellifluous sisters struck up an eternal round dance, affirming in their rhythms the established harmony of the balanced world, pleasing the gods with holy tales, and reminding mortals of the preeternal models of incorruptible beauty and the sublime destinies of their heroic ancestors. Thus, the Muses sang that the beautiful is dear, and what is not beautiful is not dear,[3] ever obedient to "strict Memory."

Mnemosyne is Eternal Memory:[4] this is another name for the continuity of communion in both spirit and energy between the living and departed. This continuity is what we, people of a reified and dissipated age, venerate under the name of spiritual culture, without being aware ourselves of the religious roots of this veneration. Culture is the cult of the departed, and Eternal Memory is the soul of its life, which is characterized preeminently by *sobornost'* and founded on tradition.

But there is, Plato says, Preeternal Memory (*anámnēsis*): when the soul recollects its pretemporal contemplation of the divine Ideas.[5] This is the source of all individual creativity, any intuition of genius, and any prophetic initiative. For creativity occurs in the Spirit, Who is also the herald of completed being, when becoming has ceased and the words "It is finished"[6] have been pronounced. He is the culminating, reunifying fullness of original being.[7] And the prophetic gifts of the Spirit, a foreboding of final being, are revealed in the memory of original being.

When a newborn is cut from its mother, like fruit from a tree, it becomes an isolated man and resembles a new shadow, the ethereal guest of Hades who has only just drunk from the streams of the Lethe, the waters of Oblivion.[8] As a soul, according to an ancient esoteric belief, in order to ascend to the light, must first find the springs of Memory and slake its burning thirst at the lake of underground Mnemosyne, so also does Memory reunite us with the Beginning and Word, which "was in the Beginning."[9] And we know that, when Man is perfected, Adam will remember his entire self, in all his hypostases, in the reverse stream of time flowing back to the gates of Eden;[10] and primeval man will remember his Eden.

Thus also is the artist most of all a creator when he awakes in us a living sensation of our blood ties with the Mothers of What Is and restores our ancient memory of the World Soul. Any true intuition of the nature of things is the native tale of an ancient mystery: the roots extend into the past, and the rock strata speak silently of what was of old. And every true comprehension of causes is a holy verse from the chronicle of Being.[11]

Eternal Memory is the root strength and lifeblood of any constructive work that is social in spirit.[12] We serve our descendants falsely when we, forgetting about maternal causes, with youthful and blind zeal seek to pursue abstract aims that we understand one-sidedly, or when, in the name of our descendants, we dream of building anew on the unmarked, decimated tombs

145

of the past; a generation of children immediately grows up and abolishes its fathers' work. But those who engage in living communion with the departed gather strength that they will transmit to their own descendants, keeping the ancient fire alive on the native hearth of generations. Those who live for both their ancestors and descendants, for the vindication of the departed through the expected achievements of future generations raise the walls of a divinely human temple on solid rock:[13] these are the true liberators. And if they do not only preserve but also destroy, it is to destroy the tombs from which the resurrected wish to rise;[14] and if they crush the old tablets, it is to break the curses that kept bewitched life in mortal captivity, where there was no hope for resurrection.[15] For they are filled with the understanding that is granted by love, love not only for their visible family but also for their unseen neighbors.[16] Only a living sense of the immortality of the personality can make our society truly a society in the sense of the universal connection of all living people (after all, everyone is alive in God) and the voluntary acceptance of responsibility for all. Eternal Memory is unifying [*sobornyi*] and, in a mysterious sense, sacerdotal energy. He who worships and sacrifices to it performs mysterious divine service, just as an artist is the high priest of Mnemosyne and the Muses. For divine service is oriented toward the past and is commanded to preserve the tradition of sacred treasures.[17]

Antiquity knew that memory teaches wisdom; since it believed in the memory of the Earth, it also believed in the tradition of holy memory. Of modern humanity, Goethe comes closest to sharing this sensation of the ancients:

> Antiquity comprehended the truth
> And raised a commune of the wise;
> Hearken to the ancient wisdom.[18]

II

In his dialogue *Timaeus,* Plato tells of a conversation between the famous Solon and one of the Egyptian high priests, in whose temples the student-Hellene was instructed in supreme theurgic knowledge, possession of which gave the Athenian legislator the fame of one of the Seven Wise Men (i.e., the seven initiates of the Hellenic world).[19] It is fair to assume that Plato himself learned this famous tale from his religious teachers and mystagogues during his stay in Egypt, although he preferred to attribute it to the family tradition of his clan. Plato's royal clan traced its lineage back to the mythical Codrus[20] through Solon, who, according to the "divine" philosopher, intended to relate the high priest's story in an epic poem which, if only he had applied himself to this plan, would have surpassed the epic poems of Homer and Hesiod by the power of its very subject.[21] "You are still young of age, o Hellenes, and verily there is not an elder among you," the

146

high priest taught. When asked "why?" he answered: "because you do not have any tradition or instruction about ancient times, you are eternally young in soul."[22] The Egyptians were elders and the Hellenes—children. The Hellenes did not know whence they sprang and what preceded them; the Egyptians, in contrast, remembered the past both for themselves and for the Hellenes. On more than one occasion, the world has been shaken to its foundations, and it will undergo many more cleansing revolutions. Fire and water have both been known to erase all human edifices and human glories. Aeschylus says that, as a sponge erases all writing, so do the supreme forces erase all the creations of mortals.[23] The flood waters receded, and the human race grew once again. Generations were born who had forgotten all their fathers' knowledge and skills, why they had died, and what they had achieved. Without writing or the arts, "bereft of the Muses and illiterate" (ámousoi kai agrámmatoi),[24] these free people began a new life with a fresh and virginal soul, with primitive and open feelings. But in Egypt things were different: the preeternal law of the country, embodied in the divine rhythm of the Nile's overflowing and receding, preserved Egypt from both universal fire and universal flood. Thus, the holy earth became a treasury of the most ancient knowledge and the ark of humanity's ancestral memory. And all wisdom is only communion with the forgotten fullness of revelations.

According to the teaching of Plato's high priest, eight thousand years before Solon, Egypt had already recorded events that changed the face of the earth as it was at that time, while the other tribes had managed to lose the art of writing several times since then; and these records were preserved untouched in the temples.[25] Engraved in these holy writings were the actions of the peoples who had inhabited Atlantis, the great island that extended far to the West, beyond the Pillars of Hercules,[26] to an area no less than the surfaces of Asia and Lebanon put together, in places where today the water has extended its realm. Engraved in hieroglyphs was the memory of the Atlanteans' conquest of neighboring countries up to Etruria and Asia, of the crimes they committed against people and against the gods, and about their final death from cowardice and the flooding of the entire island, which in the span of one day and one night sank and was buried by the ocean's waves. Only one nation was ever triumphant in its resistance to the armaments of the Titanic Atlanteans: that was the forefathers of the Hellenes, whom their descendants forgot, forgetting their greatest glory together with their name.

Thus, Plato (in the *Timaeus* and the *Critias*)[27] evokes the universal shadow of Atlantis, whose existence has found partial confirmation in the hypotheses of geologists. For archeologists and historians of culture, however, its possible existence is tied to the distant hope of combining Plato's myth with memories of the universal flood, in order to find a missing link that would connect a multitude of similar and yet divergent phenomena, such as the monuments of ancient Egypt and Mexico, and to solve many mysteries of Mediterranean culture, such as the mystery of Crete or the Etruscans.[28]

III

As if from the depths of sepulchral crypts, we hear these hushed words about the earth's ancient tremors, about the cataclysms of the still-chaotic world, in which higher life sprang up like the seeds of the sun,[29] in conflict with the darkness, but the darkness did not eclipse it.[30] We all feel that we live at a time of the waning and taming of the world's elemental forces and humanity's elemental energies, but we still hear, somewhere below the level of conscious and superficial life, a distant, deep song of native chaos.[31] We do not believe it; we do not even believe it when beneath our cities the world suddenly begins to settle and open wide in unexpected fits of long quieted fever. Thus, it would seem that we are distant from *horror fati,* a terror of destiny.[32] But two or three Messinas would be enough for "ancient terror" to become for us the terror of today.[33] For our Tranquillity is based on everyday inductive reasoning and on the customary calculation of probabilities; yet our induction is limited by the bounds of our short historical memory, which measures by short measures; and our optimism regarding the probabilities of a cosmic order has to a significant degree been instilled by our brilliant triumphs over the nature that surrounds us and is nearest to us. This optimism is unstable and may easily pass over into its opposite, unless we attain some inner ground for looking at the shuddering world in ways other than with the madly dilated eyes of "ancient terror"; unless the Love unknown to those ancient people blossoms in us, love that does not know fear; if in spirit also we are only the degenerate descendants of a waning world, the belated children of an Earth that is exhausted by its futile efforts to give birth to children of the Sun who would be worthy of their father's light, an Earth that is exhausted by its endless *miscarriages—avortons,* in Madame Ackermann's vatic phrase.[34]

But we still stubbornly refuse to believe in anything extreme and divinely sudden. We refuse to believe due to an almost unconscious inner feeling that the denouement is premature, a feeling that issues from a deep awareness of our feeble inability to fulfill any measure (whether of good or evil) in its universal fullness, whether by labors or crimes. Besides, we fear altogether little and we almost love to take risks: thus, we have learned to live in a way that is hurried and superficial and phantomlike, insouciantly, i.e., irresponsibly. Truly, it would be easy for us to perish suddenly: for living blood is tormented when it must part with its beloved flesh, while false dreams and bloodless schemes are quickly dissipated. And it is for good reason now, with a presentiment of the final terror, *terroris futuri,* that we want only to laugh, only to laugh. There is also a laugh of horror, *risus terroris.*

To such a degree are we children of Decadence that even ancient Epicurianism is too healthy for us. Nietzsche compares Epicurianism with the evening contemplation of the smooth surface of the sea from under the melancholy foliage of a hidden garden.[35] However much Epicurianism might tire or shield itself from life, it has more love for life and less tedium of phenomena than we who throw ourselves into the giddy carnival of shadows, into the masquerade of black masks of nonbeing, while dressed up in the agitatedly lurid colors of sacrilegious rags. Epicurianism cast its gaze back at ancient terror with the same feeling of sweet security that Lucretius attributed to people who, standing on the shore, observe the sea chasm and the people perishing therein,[36] but it could still oppose to the chaos of the past the beautiful wane of the age it was experiencing and of a day that was burning its last, e.g., in such verses as these:

> Believe, the gods of heaven did not eternally drink
> The nectar of languor from sapphire cups!
> The revelry of preworldly banquets was violent
>   The blind onslaught of the first waves.
> Our suns are a quiet hangover,
> And their crystal shows scarlet at the base:
> Intoxication is easier, joy is more concordial
>   And sadness is more pensive. . . .[37]

We are no longer capable of it. Thus, in a certain sense, ancient terror is once again closer and more comprehensible to us.

But let us turn to a painting that shows us the long since tamed revelry of universal demons, "the blind onslaught of the first waves."

IV

The waves rush in and inundate a stone continent, which is destroyed and apparently sinks into the chasm. Of course, the earth shakes, and the sea rushes onto dry land from subterranean tremors, while crackling thunder argues with the roar of the waves, and lightning spear-bearers provoke a battle, so that, when they tire from the first attack, they can give the signal to armed legions of storm clouds, ready to crash in a downpour of the flood. The layers of clouds are so unusually dense and deep that day leaks through them in the deathly paleness of gloomy dusk, such as arises when the sun is exhausted by an eclipse and the lifeless face of the earth dims into the ashen shade of a corpse. This is the death of the great whore of the pagan apocalypse,[38] which shifted everything into the past just as the Christian apocalypse shifts everything into the future, which prophesied in Memory the way Christianity prophesies in Hope; this is the death of Atlantis. . . .

But where then is Terror? Why does the viewer understand it but not experience it? Why do his eyes contemplate but his heart not shudder? Why do we not join those people who, having gone mad, rushed to the idols of the gods and heroes, their crowds covering the city square? Why do we not join this triumphant, imperturbable woman, who smiles with her eternal smile, cruel and meek,[39] who modestly rests in her incomprehensible harmony,[40] in the irresistible attractiveness of female charm and voluptuous languor? Or why are we already under her spell, having already forgotten and forgiven all the despair and bitterness of death, perhaps even accepting it both for those who are perishing and for ourselves, so that we might merely look at *her*? Did the artist really fail in his task; was he really unable to instill terror? Or did he want to use the picture to say, like the elders of Ilium about Helen, "verily heroes would find it worth perishing for such a woman"? For they had her within their walls, although they forgot about her at the hour of their death, when they ran to the heroes for protection.[41] For such possession, it was only fair to pay boundless retribution to the Moirae. Yet the viewer both sees the retribution and almost does not see it, since he is enchanted by the charm of the goddess. And what on earth would not seem small and insignificant compared to the One Woman?

But however we might speculate about the artist's hidden intentions, in a simple and extraordinary way, our aesthetic attitude can only remain one of agreement and grateful satisfaction that the depiction removes these events boundlessly far from life—into a sphere where they become the subject of unalloyed, absolute contemplation—and only contemplation.

Do we then enjoy the tragic catastrophe, like the people Lucretius describes observing drowning sailors from the safe shore? Is it morally permissible for a tranquil spirit to feel such harmony before the spectacle of universal disharmonies? We involuntarily ask ourselves such questions, we who were raised on Dostoevsky's great testaments and demands.[42] But therein lies the artist's supreme right (which is also his obligation), to use purely artistic means to turn conflicts of ethical consciousness into the harmonious concord of a soul reconciled with divine law, a soul that says *yes* to divine law by means of an inner intuition of beauty, before this *yes* is wrenched from the rebellious spirit by an ultimate understanding of the truth. True artistry is always theodicy; it was for good reason that Dostoevsky himself said that beauty would save the world.[43] The egotistic pleasure of the observers of other people's death in Lucretius is the apotheosis of the individual's miserly self-preservation. The healing Tranquillity and cleansing (*kátharsis*) that tragedy achieves are the beneficial charms of Paean-Apollo; they correctly restore the personality after it has renounced itself and found within itself noble strength for pure, will-less contemplation. It is in the painting's ideal distancing of the central tragedy of ancient terror from the viewer, in its refusal to communicate affect, in its cathartic refraction and mediation, that I see the particular merit of the artist, whose spirit has become truly ancient.[44] But how is this refraction achieved, this effect of distancing to an unattainable realm?

The technical means were dictated by the artist's inner attitude toward his theme. It is easy to study these means. It is not for nothing that the artist transports the viewer to some invisible elevation, which is the only vantage point capable of presenting the panoramic view that unfurls somewhere in the depths beneath our feet. The closest object to the viewer is the hill that bears a colossal statue of the ancient Aphrodite of Cyprus. But the hill, the pedestal, and even the legs of the idol remain beyond the borders of the canvas. As if free from the fate of the earth, the goddess arises close to us, right on the gloom of the deeply set sea, which rages and fuses its wave crests to form the outline of a captivating shell, as if having espied the goddess and suddenly changed its vociferous thunderclaps for a love hymn to Anadyomene, born from the foam.[45] Whoever has stood on considerable elevations directly above the seashore will easily comprehend both the painting's perspectival conditions and the precise realism of the exquisite mapping of the shore's contours; this mapping has displeased some critics, who would apparently prefer a closer, more densely populated scenery to this authentic landscape of heights, which is the only landscape capable of communicating a feeling of the cosmic enormity of the events that are coming to pass. For before us lies not a landscape of human measures and human perceptions but rather an icon of the birth pangs of Mother Gaea; our attention is caught not so much by the cities and the death of the people as by the divine struggle of elements and their so strikingly varied image: the world of the watery element, the world of air, and the world of stone (the geological world of various rocks and strata) are painted in a manner accessible only to one who "by the proud shores of the southern land"[46] has prayed before these sarcophagi of the sun, before these bodies of petrified Niobidae,[47] which were wrapped in limestone and basalt. The cosmic scale of this idea required the artist to encompass within the frame of the painting both man and the elements, both the transient and eternal: he could accomplish this task only by distancing his subject immeasurably far into space. This is what gives us the impression of temporal distance and of the historical cosmos. To this he added a frescolike gloom, proper to the grandiosity of his subject, and also a Tranquillity of coloring that borders on frigidity. He thus used all the elements capable of producing the aesthetic effect of purely ancient, objectively harmonic detachment, the inner basis of which we find in the features of the visionary art we have correctly sanctified by the name of Apollonian art.

151

V

All ancient art was dedicated to Memory; Mnemosyne stood behind Apollo, the leader of the Muses' round dance, silently granting inspiration.[48] Since antiquity created and prophesied within the border of Memory, its creations were filled with a harmony almost incomprehensible to us. Antiquity adored tragic myth; all that is sublime in drama and lyric, painting and sculpture, was the re-creation of fatal destinies, the mask of terror. But art made it possible to behold the Gorgon's head with impunity. An Apollonian veil protected the mortals' gaze from the baneful arrows of the transcendent gaze.[49] This is Apollo, whom Nietzsche calls the god of dreams and whose essence he explains with the verses,

> Remember the single testament:
> The poet is born to be a dreamer;
> The spirit grasped all that is truth
> In an instant of somnolent reverie, an instant of vision,
> And all art of harmonious words
> Is the interpretation of vatic dreams—[50]

Apollo is *the force of visionary contemplation in memory.*

When a soul succumbs to oblivion, it is enveloped in a profound, golden silence, and on the distant horizons, it encounters images preserved in the recollection of the World Soul. For truly not an iota will be lost in the scroll of her Memory,[51] and all that has passed continues to occur eternally; Cleopatra still turns the bow of her gilded galley to flee from the watery field of battle at Actium.[52] A life unknown to us has been saved in the shadows and coverings (in Democritian *eídola*),[53] separated from things and faces which have long since decayed—a painless, widowed life, abandoned by the seeds of spirit. And while the souls of people of old have left for their resting places, their half-animate, ethereal forms continue their spectral existence in the bosom of the World Soul as an indestructible part of her. In the second part of *Faust*, Goethe grants such a spectral existence to the immortal Helen, summoned from the depths of the Mothers, and to her incorporeal companions, who half belong to nonbeing.[54]

The evocation of such forms is the work of Apollo's charms; and truly the artist followed an Apollonian visionary path by creating a work so convincing not only in its inner truth but also in its impression of an unattainably distant vision, a prophetic dream of far-off, painless Memory. It remains for us to comprehend with our reason the quiet abyss that it reveals to our inner gaze.

But first let us cast another glance at the painting, this pale magic mirror of the incorruptible world. Let us turn our attention for an instant to a mistake that, although it would seem a result of the artist's negligence, is actually an internally significant feature of his visionary art: the colossal idol of the martial god or demigod is depicted incorrectly. In his right hand, this ferocious warrior holds a shield, while his murderous sword is in his left hand. The confusion of right and left is a typical symptom of purely visionary perceptions, and the biblical expression about infants incapable of distinguishing right from left is not accidental:[55] it indicates the rational self-consciousness of a personality that has yet to achieve self-determination and that is still wholly engulfed in the sphere of somnolent consciousness, which nurtures the roots of sentient being.

But again our contemplation fastens on the image of the smiling queen of a world that shifts by turns between birth and destruction, but which is indestructible, just like the queen herself who creates, animates, and destroys it, in order to animate again what she has destroyed. For her name is immortal Love, and it is for good reason that she bears on her beautiful fingers, bent like the petals of the Egyptian lotus,[56] her holy bird: the dove of the ark will proclaim that the flood has receded, and that a love stronger than death has once again been conceived across the face of the earth.[57] While the artist performs the work of a sculptor by creating with his brush this genuinely ancient idol, dressed and decorated in clothes appropriate for female hypostases of Mystery, at the same time, as a painter, he triumphs over the task of tangibly representing stone and the soul of stone. All the charm of femininity is expressed by the lines of this body, resilient like the stem of a lotus, which breathes with the irresistible force of alluring languor. She must be beautiful, or at least seem beautiful, this Maya, illusion, this somnolent haze of a spirit undergoing incarnation.[58] Of course, she is beautiful: thus did the idol makers of ancient Hellas see her. But her beauty is only the charm of eyes and the enchantment of somnolent reverie. She does not have a human face. In her features we cannot guess her innermost mystery: like the Sphinx, she is incomprehensible, and, like the Sphinx, immobile and imperturbable. But she is alive. She is surrounded by a halo of influence, a cloud of strength that issues from her. She has been erected as a symbol and likeness. This hill and this idol will fall, but she can only abide eternally. She is stronger than those wild male gods, who are already powerless to defend the nation they once led against nations and gods. The artist accomplished the task of depicting beauty in a symbolic fashion, as Lessing teaches with an example from Homer:[59] he reveals the action of beauty but not its incomprehensible, unportrayable image.

Such are the aesthetic aspects of Bakst's creation. But, from the height of the hill where fateful ancient Aphrodite resides, other perspectives also open up—perspectives of a religious-historical nature.

VI

"Terror Antiquus": that is how the artist named his painting. By ancient terror he meant the terror of fate. *Terror antiquus* is *terror fati.* He wanted to show that the ancients viewed as relative and transient not only all that is human but also all that was revered as divine. Only Fate (*Eimarménē*), or universal necessity (*Anánke*), the inevitable "Adrasteia," the faceless countenance and hollow sound of unknown Destiny, was absolute. This was the true religion of primordial Greece, this was its true pessimism—so the artist meant to tell us. Fortunately, however, he said something more and even something entirely different.

Let the unknowable fateful force destroy all that has arisen: Love smiles its immortal smile and young life will once again celebrate its short-lived, but constantly rejuvenated, celebration.[60] The indestructible force of Life, Love the Birth-Giver, opposes the absolute law of Fate the Destroyer, Fate-Death. The artist also needed to add this, as he was a cheerful pessimist and fatalist satisfying the needs of his own consciousness with attempts at an inner intuition of distant and mysterious antiquity, which seemed to him to have gazed on the world with his eyes. Thus, he intended to give us an ancient *Trionfo della Morte* but gave most of all an ancient *Trionfo della Vita*.[61] Moreover, he clearly revealed the universal infirmity of proud, ferociously self-affirming, active, and violent male might. He showed masculine daring and warring to be powerless before the will of Destiny and transient before the implacable judgment of the goddess, the possessor of undying life. He parceled out the world between Ananke-Fate and Aphrodite-Love. Thus, he said more and something different than what he signified with the title "Ancient Terror."

In order to show that he was contemplating only a part of the truth while he made the absolute truth incarnate in his artistic act, it is necessary to understand historically what the artist was apparently unaware of: that the primordial belief did not exhibit this dualism of Fate the Destroyer and Love the Birth-Giver, but rather the smiling goddess was also Fate itself. "'Know me,'—so sang Death: 'I am passion.'"[62]

Yes, *Terror antiquus* was *terror fati*. Fate was mightier than the very gods: the fateful moment was unforeseeable and unavoidable. It is impossible to mollify Fate with sacrifices, or to defeat her with resistance; one can neither appeal to her emotions nor repel her. In the Inevitable One, there is no arbitrariness, no human likeness, as there is in other divinities. And originally there was no justice in her either. Her will is universal necessity, as was thought later on; she is Ananke. Necessity, Ananke, did this mean "the causal connection of phenomena"? They did not think of this. They knew only the absolute within her faceless essence, and they knew that she was one.

Behind the three hypostases of the Moirae, the sister-fates, was concealed The One. Three countenances signify the multiple revelation of a single essence. The nine Muses (originally the goddesses of spring water) are a potentialized triad: there are many springs but the water is one. The nine

Muses are three times three Muses, i.e., preeminently three. This is one of the female triads, such as: the Orae, the Graces, the Erinyes, the Maenads, and others. But the three Muses are nothing other than the one Mnemosyne, their mother, the sovereign of the living waters that grant memory, i.e., restore life, grant immortality (*amrta, ambrosía, l'eau de Jouvence*).[63] The one essence distinguished in three female persons is usually interpreted as the mother of the three daughters: Ananke was recognized as the mother of the three Moirae.

Thus, apart from her absolute and single nature, another feature was from time immemorial attributed to Fate: that of gender. Woman was queen over mortals and gods. The female principle was affirmed monotheistically. Whenever the idea of fate was developed, polytheism turned out to be only polydemonism, demonology.

There was a unique dualism at the basis of the religion of Fatum: the fateful female principle was opposed to everything that was subject to destiny, whether divinity or human, man or woman. Most telling, however, are the traces of what appears to be an attempt to exempt the female from the sphere where the general conditions of a fatal end hold sway: the death of women was the responsibility of the great female goddess Artemis; it was their privilege to be killed by their own goddess, to fall from her silent arrows. It is in her womb that they arise as individuals, and it is in her womb that they disappear and drown.

VII

Is it not evident that the religious conception articulated above could not be primordial and that the hypostasis of Woman-Fate was merely the differentiation of an integrally monotheistic idea of the Woman goddess, the one supreme sovereign, single and absolute? That the incomplete dualism about which we spoke was only a weakened vestige of a more ancient dualism of two principles: the female, absolute principle and the male, relative principle? That the idea of Woman-Fate contains the obvious contradiction of formlessness and gender only *because* it represents an incorporeal abstraction, an inwardly empty scheme abstracted from the all-encompassing dogma of the One World Goddess?

Is not the reason that the Moirae were thought to inhabit the depths of the earth that Fate-Ananke, the future Dike-Justice, is the Earth herself, the ancestral mother Gaea, the Gaea of Dodona with her aphrodisian doves on the prophetic oak of the Selli?[64] Is this not the reason that female objects of belief are trebled, that Fate gives birth to the three Moirae, that she is not only the Earth, but also the Moon, triune Hecate, who consistently marks the passage of time for people in the three different hypostases of the lunar period, and who subordinates to her eternal law female life and its fertility?

Is this not the reason that fate holds power over the very mountain of the gods, Olympus, that she is also Urania, the Heavenly One, the supreme mover of time and the creator of cosmic harmony? No matter under which name the many-named Goddess might be concealed—whether Artemis or Aphrodite, Athena, Astarte, or Isis—any study of the history of female divinities leads us to the traces of a primordial thelymonotheism, the belief in a single, female goddess. All female divine hypostases are varieties of the single goddess, and this goddess is the female principle of the world, one gender raised to the absolute.

Thus Fate, the object of ancient terror, Fate the Destroyer, is that very goddess of love, with her smile and dove, whom we see on the foreground of the painting celebrating some unending affirmation of life, while the masculine forces that have fallen in love with her perish. It is she who condemns to death the masculine element, and the masculine element dies, paying retribution for female love; it dies because it did not satisfy the Insatiable One and because it proved to be weak before the Invincible One. This unconscious, primordial memory of the mortally doomed nature of the masculine element and of the necessity of paying with one's life for the possession of a woman is what makes the mysteriously alluring and mystically terrifying truth of Pushkin's "Egyptian Nights" so enchanting to us.[65] All male energy together lacks the power to fulfill the measure of the many-faced goddess's immortal desires, and thus she destroys her lovers, from whom this many-breasted Cybele gives birth only to premature fetuses and miscarriages; she destroys and re-forms anew in the hope of a true marriage, but there is too little of the Sun's impoverished power in its sons, these husbands of Jocasta, and once again they perish, blinded like Oedipus, i.e., bereft of the sun. But the goddess continues to await true insemination from the Sun.[66]

This is the mystical truth about the World Soul and its expectations of a heavenly Bridegroom, a truth that had already been revealed to those ancient people who venerated the One Goddess (just as this same supreme truth is also reflected in the biological phenomenon of male animals dying after the act of insemination and in the phenomenon of triumph and domination over males, for example, among bees). And another mystical truth was revealed in ancient female monotheism: the truth of the Virgin. For the goddess, like Helen, had many husbands, but these were not legitimate husbands but violators who had taken possession only of her shadow and protective periphery, who loved her phantom and from it engendered spectral life.[67] They loved Maya as a wife and mother, but their impotent masculine aggression was unable to encroach upon the virginity and unattainability of the unwedded Bride,[68] the deepest and secret essence of the World Soul, the unapproachable reality of virginity behind the feminine appearance of one who seemed the mother of love and flesh, desire and procreation, behind the deceptive charm of her eyes, beneath the luxuriously woven veil of mysteriously and ambivalently smiling Maya. This truth was revealed in the cult of virginal Artemis, and it was also imprinted in the words carved at the base of the veiled goddess of Sais, who, according to Herodotus, was a hypostasis of the Virgin-Athena,[69] and who was called Neith in Egyptian: "I am what is, what has been, and what will be, and no mortal and no god has ever lifted my veil."[70] In depictions of the marriage of Zeus and Hera, the lord of the heavens raises the veil from the face of his new bride: the goddess of Sais was an unmarried virgin, and she was known by no man.

Female monotheism, however, naturally required a complement. One gender could not be raised to the absolute without the apotheosis of the other gender. And, at the same time, the male correlate had to have a relative character, to appear in the aspect of a principle that is subject to disappearance and experiences death. The male correlate of the absolute goddess acquired traits of the suffering god, like Dionysus and Osiris. The martyrdom and murder of the male god was the central motif of female religions (as was the religion of Dionysus), religions whose roots were nourished in the everyday life of those forgotten societies, where woman was matriarch and queen.

Recent attempts to refute the matriarchate affect only the degree of its validity. It is impossible to affirm the general and ubiquitous domination of mothers in a certain period of antiquity. But there is no doubt that Bachofen's immortal works have enriched scholarship not with a hypothesis but with a solid discovery.[71] Only their details still need verification and correction, while at the same time they continue to find confirmation in new observations. Clear traces of the matriarchate in Egypt and among the Etruscans might allow one to link the idea of the blossoming of female dominion precisely with the myth of Atlantis, insofar as the latter appears to contain lost historical truth. Whatever the case might be, the epoch of mothers' dominion and the epoch of the great conflict of the genders can be traced back to the man-slaying cults of Artemis, with her Amazonian communities and her ritual torture of boys, Dionysus with his Maenads, as well as the multifarious traces of man-slaying in other cults of female divinities: one need only recall the myth of the Egyptian Danaids[72] and of the Lemnian sin.[73]

VIII

The grandiosity and monstrosity of the forms in which the dominion of women and female monotheism were affirmed can be judged by the energy of the male reaction against female despotism and the destruction of men by women. This reaction was still vividly remembered by the author of the *Oresteia*. In Aeschylus's depiction, Orestes' emotional conflict is largely a matter of choosing between his mother and his father. The sons took the side of their murdered fathers and drew swords against their mothers: they received blessing for this from the new high priests, who affirmed patriarchal principles and the cult of heroic ancestors. This was a reaction of harmony and order against orgiasm, of solar religion against lunar religion. The symbols of this movement were the sun, the oak, and the serpent. The sun-priest Orpheus fell victim to the women and, dismembered, became similar to their Dionysus. The Druids raised high the golden bough of omele, a plant dedicated to the Sun, which curls around the boughs of the oak.[74]

Woman was tamed. The prophetesses entered into union with the high priests, the Druids with the Druidesses; the Selli united their oak with the cult of the subterranean Woman and her doves. Apollo took possession of the Delphic oracle, yielding second place to its previous occupant Dionysus as a coruler, and with the help of the prophetesses, he began the task of building a new religion and society. Theogonies were created, the hierarchies of divinities were firmly established, and the father of the gods and people was affirmed on his Olympian throne.

Ancient Ananke was not abolished but was removed to a distant sphere. It was impossible to forget about her, but there was no need to fear her anymore. Apollo was the Moiragetes;[75] he himself undertook to lead the round dance of the Moirae. The ancient terror of fate was finished. Only Zeus had anything left to do with it: but his kingdom was secure for long aeons. It was enough for man to tremble before him alone and before his immortal family. The high priests sought to replace the terror of fate with the timorousness before god and piety (*deisidaimonía, eusébeia*), the fear of god.[76] They inspired the fear of god as a principle of duty. The gods were declared the enforcers of the moral world order. Patriarchal morality was transferred to Olympus, a fatal step for the future destinies of Hellenic religion. The divinities were cosmic entities, but cosmic law had nothing in common with human virtue. Since the cosmic character of the gods was indestructible, they proved to be unvirtuous, and people renounced them.

A great injustice lay at the source of the beneficial creative work of the enslavers of woman, the restorers of male religion, and the legislators of the patriarchal and divinely obedient system. The world was turned into a sunlit and well-organized city of immortal kings and their mortal citizens. But when night fell, the gloom that set in from beyond the city preyed on souls, flowing in the lunar streams of enchanted Hecate and watching with eyes of unspeakable terror from the caves, which summoned the departed shadows to the subterranean realms. And man was ready to lose his reason from the ambivalence of the cosmos, this unresolved conflict of unreconciled powers. The greater the trust with which he submitted to the life-creating solar charms, the further he cast away from himself all that was lunar, female, unknowable, nocturnal—the more insistently did the mad

voice of another terror, solar terror, sound in his soul, contradicting everything by which he had lived and in which he had been instructed and raised.
Ancient terror is often understood as panic terror, the terror of Pan. In the
white, scorching noontime, it would attack man—at the moment of universal drowsiness, when all that was blindingly solar suddenly began to seem
not reality but an inescapable haze, when there was no moisture, nothing
female, maternal, flowing, dark, lunar; everything that blinded with its
solar power seemed to have expired and abandoned the earth, across whose
scorched mountains and empty, red-hot gorges there rolled the laughter of
the goat-legged god.

Thus, the enslavement of woman was linked to the enslavement of all
chaotic and orgiastic energies, and the organization of the world in the
name of obedience to the gods was linked to the extinguishing of all human
daring and free self-affirmation. The spirit grasps greedily at ancient tales
of the theomachy of the mighty; it once again seeks succor from images of
indomitable warriors, from the shadows of those who rebelled against the
aggressively rational system and against a divine harmony that had been
purchased at too high a price and that finally awarded immortality to the
gods and death to the mortals. And then once more the dethroned queen
arises, now not to destroy masculine daring but to support it in its rebellion
against the foreigners who have usurped the throne. The Titans find themselves women-friends, and Niobe continues to affirm the pride of her father
Tantalus.[77] The Okeanides are Prometheus's faithful companions in his passion and ultimate execution, and Aeschylus chooses as his mother Themis
herself, primordial Truth, who grants him knowledge of secrets that are fatal
to his enemy Zeus.[78] Again, subterranean Truth raises her supreme voice,
before which the heaven dwellers become mute; but this Truth is the very
same ancient Ananke, the very same One Goddess, who had bowed ancient
man under the yoke of the first terror. The prophetic Truth of Woman, superior to the relative truth affirmed by people and embodied in the Olympian
gods; the unwritten law to which Antigone appeals before her judges;[79]
inner morality, free from the power of the statutes and coercion—this truth
was discovered anew by man in the truth of Mother Earth, and she, acting
alone, saved his spiritual freedom, the energy of his willful, creative, godlike self-determination.

IX

Are not these universal problems the same ones that are currently disturb-
ing our spirit and causing disharmony in our religious consciousness? Insofar as they are worrying us, we must recognize that, much as ancient terror
is still close to us, so our consciousness remains pagan with respect to the
problem of obedience to god and theomachy, or, as we now say, sidestep-

ping the unclarified question of God, "man-godhood." Is it not the same universal necessity that appears to us as the all-determining principle, clothed in the form of causality, of the law of nature, of determinism? Does this necessity not coincide with the "will" of Schopenhauerian philosophy, with the will to being and propagation in bad eternity?[80] Is not our human self-affirmation, our recollection of the Serpent's ancient testament to "be as gods,"[81] just as insistent, and just as helpless and weak? Do we not want in the same way to combine our proud human self-affirmation with the law of some supreme truth that is unknown to us? Is it not in the name of this truth that we smash the old tablets in order to liberate the spirit from the shared guardianship of the high priests of religion, which tells us of obedience to preeternal statutes (and sometimes human statutes as well), and of the high priests of science, who attempt to prove the necessity of submitting to necessity? Thus, we founder within the walls of the old prison that paganism also foundered in, and our new despair is only the new mask of ancient terror, which already in antiquity had taken the form of *"taedium vitae"* and *"carpe diem."*[82] In this way, our risible despair makes us late epigones of pagan Decadence.

The cause of our malady is that we have forgotten Christianity. Humanity has forgotten what has already been revealed in Christianity; it not only fails to discern what is not yet revealed in Christianity but has long since ceased to understand what it had formerly understood. I shall dwell on two ideas introduced by Christianity, on two of its answers to the ancient needs of paganism: I have in mind the Christian understanding of human self-affirmation, and the Christian view of the World Soul.

Human self-affirmation is false insofar as its subject is the limited personality. It is necessary to find one's true "I" in order to affirm oneself in it. Christianity teaches that such an "I" is inwardly present in man: "The Kingdom of Heaven is within you."[83] There is a heaven within man, and the Father is in this Heaven. The exterior of man, his flesh, is his Earth. This is the Bride, the World Soul, within him. That which man usually calls his "I" holds dominion over his Earth. But the man she venerates as her husband and master is not her husband.[84] Just as the World Soul seeks the Bridegroom in the macrocosm, so in the microcosm man's Earth seeks its other "I" and hopes for the approach of the Son. Man's "I" becomes the Son only by surrendering its will to the inner light that is the Father in man's Heaven. If the will of the human "I" becomes His will, then Christ will be born in man, and he will become worthy of being called the Son of Man. Then his Earth will have found her Bridegroom, and the Son of Man his Bride, and the prayer will have been fulfilled about the will of the Father being accomplished not only in Heaven but also on Earth.

Such is the anthropological principle of Christianity: apart from this true self-affirmation, there is no efficacious and fruitful self-affirmation for man, since by any other self-affirmation, he desires to preserve his soul but actually loses it,[85] affirming a shadow and the dream of a shadow (as Pindar called man)[86] but not his personality, which is the countenance of the Son. Such is the Christian truth about man, which makes man free for the first time. Here for the first time, external obedience to God ceases and theomachy is abolished. All the vital energies of human, masculine daring only find an outlet and fruitful application in this principle of mystical energeticism.[87] In order to have masculine daring before the face of Necessity, man must exercise daring and courage not on the prompting of his own feeble intention and arbitrary will but on the force of divine being, in the name of the Father in Heaven; for only when man becomes a son is he granted the face and strength and power of the Bridegroom.

Necessity is the flesh of the world. Those ancient people who perished in cataclysms of old worshiped the Flesh, the cosmic Woman, and the goddess cast off whichever men she did not desire. For they were belligerent but infirm, and they were only her sons, knowing within themselves only *her*, the flesh taken from their mother. She, however, wants seeds of the Logos (*lógous spermatikoús*, as the Stoics said).[88] She wants men born "not in the lust of the flesh" but of God,[89] and from such men shall she conceive her new kingdom. Necessity, understood as an aspect of the World Soul, is treated by Christian consciousness as its Mother, who is exhausted by man's evil will and who is to be transfigured only by the new will of Adam, who has been redeemed by the one Man-Redeemer. Christianity imprints its transfiguring kiss on the Earth, the long-suffering Mother, the widow of Eden. This masculine kiss of love provides the Christian overcoming of natural necessity.

For natural necessity is the causal connection of phenomena; but each phenomenon and each fleeting instant is not the offspring of an unwedded mother but the offspring of a marriage between a female cause and a male seed of Logos. And the light of this seed shines in the darkness, and the darkness will not encompass it.[90]

Man's true self-affirmation in the Father, as a Son who has no will but that of his Father, grants him life in freedom. Freedom is initiative power, the possibility of a beginning. Whoever is unable to initiate, but can only continue, is not free: his actions are only consequences of causes that lie outside of him. Only by gathering the new content of our "I" from that primordial being which is He Himself in us and the Father in our Heaven do we acquire the masculine strength of initiative, which the World Soul awaits. Otherwise, all our actions are only the consequences of the World Soul's own laws, and she does not receive a seed of Logos from us.

But woman is always true to herself. The Serpent tempted Eve with the promise of divine self-knowledge. She thought to achieve it through matter and ate of the fruit and gave it to Adam, becoming the beginning of guilt.[91] And Adam fell into slavery to the flesh. Retribution for this tragic

161

guilt, which we call the fall, merely developed the content inherent to it. In her maladies, the Universal Woman began to give birth to feeble offspring. Female monotheism corresponds to Adam's subordination to woman as matter. There followed new retribution for Eve's guilt, and the male element began to dominate over the female, and a new sin was committed— the sin of Woman's enslavement. This enslavement saved nothing; it only exacerbated the extent of the calamity.

Christianity provided a resolution for the conflict of the genders. The male element as the Son, the female as the Bride, each action as a marriage of the Logos and the World Soul, the Earth like a woman standing on the Moon and clothed in the Sun when she meets her Bridegroom:[92] these are the symbols of the mystery of female and male that is revealed in Christianity. True understanding of this mystery can only be achieved through inner contemplation and experience; only this mystery is capable of saving us from ancient terror, that terror which is still our terror.

On the Crisis of Humanism

Toward a Morphology of Modern Culture and the Psychology of Modernity

I. THE SNAKE CHANGES ITS SKIN

1. "Do Not the Icy Seas Spew Fire?"[1]

Our dynamic times are like a river, crashing downward in tempestuous rapids above which, like smoke above a fire, there rises a shifting spray that looks like a cloud to the observer.

Thus does our life appear when viewed from without, as motion and the rhythm of motion, and as the illusory overcoming of stagnation and gravity.[2]

On the psychological plane, however, the life we are experiencing, filled as it is with contradictions and conflicting feelings, is exalted and cruel, impulsive and confused. It appears to the spirit as the vision of a frozen city enveloped at night in a crimson blaze, where clouds of phantom flame, licking the stalactites of overhanging icicles without melting them, spread out with a furious but vain hunger along the motionless snowdrifts.

Never before, perhaps, has man combined within himself such a readiness to renounce all and accept all, to weather any new test and new experience, with such emotional fatigue, mistrust, indifference; it would seem that man has never been so liquid and fickle, and never has he been at the same time so closed and walled-off within his selfhood, so cold of heart, as he is today. . . .

However that might be, it seems that everything around affirms the words of Heraclitus: "All is in motion, and nothing ever remains in the same place."[3]

2. The Crisis of the Phenomenon

The general shift of external (political, social, economic) relations corresponds to a possibly even deeper and earlier shift in relations of an inner order. The essence and basis of this emotional shift lies, I believe, in some

163

mysterious change in the very image of the world that looks out at us; I would dare to call this problematic change *the crisis of the phenomenon*.

Not so long ago, the phenomenal world appeared to man different than it appears to him today. Man has not yet forgotten that previous appearance, yet he no longer finds it before him and is upset at not recognizing that recent world, as if someone had made a quick switch. Where is the customary visage of things? We do not hear their familiar voice. Space and time themselves are felt in a new way, and it is for good reason that not only the adepts of philosophy but also those of the physical and mathematical sciences have begun to speak of the "relativity" of space and time.[4]

Attentive and perspicacious people could detect the features of this psychological fracture even before the historical turning point came to pass, in the war and revolution. The reordering of life's previous order began imperceptibly, and when it began, many felt a vaguely unsettling sensation as if the soil was shifting from under their feet, for which reason they naturally felt confused and despondent. They approached things with their previous trusting expectation; but things no longer gave people what from time immemorial they used to collect from them as a constant tribute, like fruits from a fertile tree. That which once had nourished, gladdened, and satisfied now brought only "boredom and anguish on a soul long dead"[5]—or, even if not dead, then seeming dead to itself.

3. Whirlwinds

This confusion and despondency became particularly intense before the war and were manifested in frequent suicides. An epidemic of suicides raged not only in Russia but also in the West, as I myself learned to my surprise while traveling to Rome in 1910 through Vienna.[6] The war broke out and the individual personality was forced to adjust to the elemental course of events, which outpaced the individual consciousness that sought to make sense of it.

People's confusion turned into a daring and courage that essentially were rooted in passivity, not spontaneity, into an inevitably sacrificial readiness for any burnt offering, even self-immolation,[7] and for a frenzied surrender to the whirlwinds of the age; despondency hid in cruelty, risk, and mischief. People were drawn into the hurricane of the suprahuman rhythm of historical demons.

The types of whirling movement change, but to this day the overriding force of suprapersonal influences remains equal to itself in its ascendancy over the activity of the individual consciousness, which tries to set goals and seeks to make sense of life. It is difficult in our day for man to preserve his inner independence; it is difficult for him, if his soul is indeed alive, to choose ways of action in life independently, in accordance with the demands of his conscience and the guidance of his thought, without being drawn along by fate like a slave, or spun about by a fateful storm, like a leaf torn from a tree.

4. The Change in the Tissues of the Phenomenon

That which I have called the crisis of the phenomenon can best be described as the disintegration of the inner form of what appears. For all that appears, as an image, engenders within us an image of its image, entering as it were into marriage with our inner essence. The inner form of an object is its interpretation and transformation within us by the active content of our emotional powers. The charm of an artistic reproduction of reality inheres precisely in the revelation of its inner form through the mediation of the artist who in his depiction reworks it emotionally, returning it to us changed and enriched.

The crisis of the phenomenon consisted of the old inner form of things becoming decrepit and moribund within us. A new form was to appear to replace it; but the complex process by which the living tissues of what appear are reborn takes place in the generations through the gradual influence of concealed historical forces. Until it is finished—until a new inner form of the world of perception has been developed in us by organic growth—the personality will be despondent and, so to speak, intoxicated, unless it is endowed with gigantic powers of autonomous spiritual growth and creation.

Humanity is molting, like a snake shedding its old skin, and therefore it is ailing.

5. The Crisis of Art

Art, which has presentiments of the inner processes of life, has also noted this change: this was the crisis of art. A skeptic might say that this so-called crisis is an empty word, and he might explain the phenomenon it denotes as mere saturation, fatigue, rejection of tradition, a vain craving for novelty, a rebellion for the sake of rebellion. I would remind such a skeptic how the ancient skeptics regarded the passive state of one who experiences something—or *pathos*, as this passive state was called, which means "suffering" in Greek: the ancient skeptics were ready to regard everything as illusion, both the cause of the suffering and the suffering person, but suffering itself was for them an authentic truth. The state of the contemporary artist presents just such authenticity: he is suffering. The crisis of art is a real crisis, i.e., a decisive minute after which current kinds of art might utterly cease to exist; here we face the real possibility of a fatal outcome of the disease— or else art will recover and, after a fashion, be reborn to new being.

The crisis in the art of the word is the widowhood of the poet who has lost the Psyche who once was alive in the word, who has lost the inner form of

165

the word;[8] it is a yearning for its renewal, vivification, transfiguration; it is the hunger of Tantalus in the fertile verbal garden,[9] which is how the shifting and deceptive phantom of abundant language appears to us. The crisis in painting consists of the impossibility of seeing the former landscape, the former face; painting loses the inner form of what is visible. The crisis in sculpture is a sensation of the forced captivity of the inner form within stagnant outer limits, or the tortuous, hideous growth of the inner form through the outer limits, an awareness of the dungeonlike quality of limits that once were self-sufficient. The crisis in architecture is the fruitlessness of the outer construction of soulless forms. And everywhere we see the same widowhood, the same orphanhood, the same feeling that the old inner form has been disincarnated and that its former veils have become lifeless.

In the sphere of music, the crisis of art has expressed itself primarily in the search for new harmony, which symbolically relates to melody as the inner form relates to the outer form. . . . But as a result of the general crisis, we find tendencies that are extreme to the point of chaos, pained to the point of suicide: such in poetry is the desire to be liberated from the word with its tradition and laws.[10]

It stands to reason that one can make only one or two steps in this direction: beyond this, one either has to stop, renouncing poetry as a verbal art altogether, or lay down one's weapons before the primordial datum of the word. Fortunately, however far the contemporary critical state of each individual art might lead its most daring practitioners, the musician will still want to remain a musician, the painter—a painter, and the poet—a poet. In other words, all keep an oath of allegiance to their native element: the musician to the element of tone, the painter—to the element of color, the poet—to that of the word.

Language is becoming vague, incorporeal, and aerial as it moves away from the tradition of the inner form of the word into the dreamy distance that teems with illusions of the possibilities of new inner forms. We are in danger of sundering ourselves from the native soil of language,[11] just as the artist is in danger of being cut off from the harmonious system of images that exists in the world of objects. Language is the earth; a poetic work grows out of the earth. It cannot raise its roots into the air. How are we, however, to strive forward in the rhythm of time, which tosses us upward and pulls us apart, to surrender ourselves to the call of universal dynamism, and at the same time remain "tied to the earth," true to our nourishing mother? This task is apparently insoluble, and it threatens poetry with death. But what is impossible for people is possible for God, and there may occur the miracle of a new recognition of the Earth by her belated offspring. If we fall lovingly to the heart of our native language, this living verbal earth and maternal flesh of ours, we might suddenly hear in it the beating of new life, the tremor of an infant. This will be a new Myth.

Mechanism has been assured a dictatorship over the worldview of the next few generations, but despite its self-satisfied confidence, I do not believe in the feasibility of a godless and soulless world. In the dim and motley skin that is falling from the world as from a live snake, we recognize the outlines of former trees and waters and celestial bodies, and it is this skin that we, people of the threshold, perceive as lifeless and merely mechanical: once so clear and vital, now these outlines are but the dead hieroglyphs of God-forsaken, paralyzed Earth. But from out of the cracks of the worn-out skin, one catches faint glimpses of the new, fresh pattern of those very trees and waters and celestial firmament, filled with the breath of the living Spirit. A new feeling of divine presence, divine fullness, and universal animation will create another worldview, which I am not afraid to call mythological in a new sense. But for this new conception, man must broaden the limits of his consciousness so far into the whole that the former measure of humanity will seem to him a tight cocoon, just as it seems to the butterfly escaping its cradle of captivity.

This is why what we now call humanism, a word that foreordains the measure of humanity, must perish. . . . And humanism is perishing.

II. THE BATTLE FOR THE HERO'S BODY[12]

1. Antiquity and Humanism

By humanism, I mean an ethical-aesthetic norm that determines man's relation to everything that is marked by, or serves as, an inner sign that shows it to belong naturally to the human race. Moreover, an abstract notion of the natural dignity of man as such forms the basis of this relation, equally independent of any religious or metaphysical premises and of concrete social conditions. Human features are attributed a positive value, and the harmonious development and equilibrium of these characteristics and capabilities, which determine human nature in a positive sense, are judged to be the measure of the human personality's proximity to perfection.

The cradle of humanism was Hellas, in particular the Ionic tribe of Hellenes, with its openness to all that "is human in man,"[13] with its receptivity to foreign influences and with its democratic social structure. The Athenian democracy became the metropolis of humanism, since here a humanistic coloring was lent both to the doctrine of the gods and to heroic myth (as witnessed in the development of the artistic forms of religious anthropomorphism, e.g., in the type of the Athenian forefather Theseus and in the image of Sophocles' Antigone);[14] where the conflict of cultural principles, represented by Asia and Hellas in the epoch of Greco-Persian wars, was interpreted according to this same tendency; where Aeschylus depicted Prometheus as a martyr of love for man ("philanthropy");[15] where the pan-

Hellenic cult of youthful beauty was justified by philosophical thought, where the ideal of supreme elegance in the innerly and outwardly beautiful man (*kalos kágathós*) was sculpted; where, finally, man was significantly and ambiguously declared "the measure of things."[16]

Alexandrian cosmopolitanism and universalism provided new nourishment for this mind-set (together with its opposite, the mystical mind-set); and Greek culture on Roman soil, especially in the person of such an interpreter and proponent of Hellenic ideas as Cicero, placed antiquity under the banner of humanism for all ages. This is how it was received by the so-called humanists of an entire series of consequent "renaissances" of classical antiquity—in the Middle Ages and in modern times, even up to our own day.[17]

2. The Objections of Matter and Spirit

It goes without saying that the historical reality of the ancient world, whose political and social traditions rested on conquests and the slave trade, was far from corresponding to humanist ideology, which relates to the life that begat it in the way that Aphrodite Anadyomene relates to the seed-bearing abyss of the sea, and which rises above life's cloudy element like a Hellenic sculpture, which in its divine clarity is withdrawn from life.

But it is noteworthy that not only history, whose passage is not predetermined by ideas, but also the abstract political thought of ancient theoreticians of the state and society such as Plato and Aristotle manifests absolutely no features of humanism. Indeed, it is in direct conflict with humanism. Barbarian and Scythian, slave and freeman, are opposed by these thinkers as different genuses; and, in the case of man, as a city-building or civic being (as a "political animal," according to Aristotle's famous definition),[18] this particular characteristic is stressed and developed with an exclusivity that radically denies personal self-determination, personal originality, even the harmonious unfolding of the integral personality in the full variety of its gifts and strengths.

Not only the primordial bases of religious consciousness, despite all the anthropomorphism of the prevailing views of the divinity, but also the mystical ideas and theories of a later age remain no less foreign to the spirit of humanism. If, in the old testament of Hellas, an impassable chasm is affirmed between the happy family of the heaven dwellers and the pitiful race of the mortals who inhabit the earth,[19] if in this case, the only common denominator of humanity is found to be equality in slavery and death, then even for the Orphics, "Olympus is the smile of God, tears are the human race":[20] man is a mix of the rebellious, chaotic, "titanic" principle, infected by the original sin inherent in matter, and of the spiritual flame of Dionysus; man is liberated from the wild Titan within himself only by way of a slow redemptive process; and these pagan ascetics' and gnostics' view of man—as he is now, as he is here—contains neither humanistic optimism nor proud, humanistic self-consciousness and self-sufficiency.

The principle of cleansing, initiation into mysteries, and rebirths from the womb of Persephone poses a dynamic problem of spiritual growth in place of the insistent humanistic self-affirmation of the human individual (*homo sum*).[21] It is as if the mysteries, this preparatory school of death, address the personality with a summons that Goethe would later repeat: "die and become" (*stirb und werde*), with the scornful reminder that, until man comprehends this truth, he will be but a despondent guest on the dark earth ("und solang du das nicht hast, dieses Stirb und Werde, bist du nur ein trüber Gast auf der dunklen Erde");[22] and finally with the prophecy that man is something within us that must be surpassed and overcome, as Nietzsche announced so recently with such solemnity as if he were proclaiming the final result of man's final freedom.[23]

3. Humanism and Christianity

Thus, there was, in this respect, no inherent contradiction between the mysticism of Hellenic paganism and Christianity. Christianity took such a pessimistic view of the human condition that it even deepened and endlessly postponed the task of humanity—to create the image of transfigured man.

True, it was Christianity that reached down like a tender mother to man in his concrete state, in his irreplaceable uniqueness, with a sympathy and good will that were previously unknown. Christianity pitied the tragic combination within him of flesh and spirit, of slavery to sin and the freedom of God's children, and raised him to the dignity of the king's prodigal son, ordering him to grow to his Father's perfection, to the fulfillment of the divine human within him. True, Christianity promised to man's corporeal makeup not the voluptuous harmony of the outer form but the integral transfiguration of his inner form on the day of universal resurrection. True, as is recognized by all, it was Christianity that for the first time blessed and divinized the personality, bringing into the world the revelation of the person.

But humanism dislikes the maximalism of transcendent hopes and has consequently been obliged to reject Christian promises as a bargain too risky and unprofitable for earthly economy,[24] for the balance of the human energy that is spent on the immediate construction and decoration of life. The position adopted toward Christianity remained unchanged from the Athenian Areopagites (who, at first, were prepared to approve of the flowers of Paul's grandiloquence, but then shrugged their shoulders and exchanged ridiculing glances) to Anatole France, and from Celsus to the Marxists.[25]

When the heroic attempt of the Middle Ages to build an earthly society according to the supposed scheme of heavenly hierarchies collapsed, humanity vividly sensed that the humanist idea was a concretely liberating force,

169

that it was first and foremost healthy. At the first decoding of a couple of lines from hitherto incomprehensible Greek manuscripts, at the first glimpse of marble idols dug up from the ground, man rejoiced that "life was returned to him with all its charm."[26] And, having rejoiced, man so firmly resolved to make full use of the life that was returned to him that historical reality itself with its feudal tradition was to bend under the yoke of humanism, at least for show, and to bear "The Declaration of Human and Civil Rights. . . ."[27]

4. Humanism and the Scythians[28]

But now it would seem that the "city-building animal's" very same historical reality is avenging itself. Explosions have upturned everything around us that had not hitherto been destroyed, and it is of no matter how many elements of the old revolutionary tradition (which stems from the eighteenth century) and of red culture affirmation this melinite contains:[29] this dough was not raised on the leaven of humanism, and one cannot use it to bake the wafers necessary for divinizing "proud man," for the heresy of "man-godhood,"[30] a temptation some of our religiously paranoid contemporaries saw in humanism. For there is in humanism a vital leaven, and its name is Adam's will, which is neither good nor bad by itself but rather both good and bad; Adam wills the realization of his unity, the same ancient impulse that showed itself in Plato's visions of an antihumanist City.[31]

The crisis of humanism is the crisis of the inner form of human self-consciousness within the personality and through the personality. When this form changed, it became eccentric with respect to the personality; left to itself, it was as if the personality had become formless. A vague but mighty sense of the all-human whole became ascendant in our souls, engendering in them an elemental impulse to unite into collective bodies. Humanism was completely based on surmounting people's individuation, separation, and isolation, their mutual foreignness, transcendence, and impenetrability, the "autarchy" of harmonious man. This inner form of consciousness has become obsolete because the personality was unable to fill it with universal content, and it became the mummy of former life or a decaying corpse. The decaying remains of inner form infect the personality with miasmas of corruption.

Heroic humanism is dead. As in Homer's tales, we are waging a battle for the body of a hero who no longer breathes, so that the wild hordes of the possessed might not take it from us and submit it to desecration, so that we might be able to embalm it, and mourn it, and bury it, and glorify it magnificently at the coming funeral repast. . . .[32] I am, though, speaking only of humanism, which is mortal, and not of the soul of Hellas, which is immortal. And it is for good reason that the soul of Hellas so recently appeared to us in a dream separate from its beautiful, but corruptible, form: Dionysus was the form it took in the dream of the inspired Nietzsche, this last and tragic humanist, who overcame humanism within himself with a crafty madness and suicidal ecstasy (just as possessed Ajax laid his own hands on himself),[33] who rejected and scorned the human norm as "human, all too human," and who proclaimed the "Superman." For Dionysus resists humanism and sets his maenads on it, as on Pentheus.[34]

5. The Testimony of Art

In any case, art, which has presentiments of the inner processes of life, no longer finds ripe pastures within the bounds of humanism. The nomads of beauty,[35] pressing forward, following their instinct, have imperceptibly left the kingdom of humanism and no one knows where they are now wandering.

Thus, Scriabin's break with the entire musical past was the break of a modern genius with humanism in music. His harmony leads beyond the limits of a humanly secure, studied, and well-formed circle, such as Bach's tempered clavier.[36] The canon, and not only the aesthetic canon but also the essentially ethical one, is based on the idea of the unity of the normative activity of the human spirit. The rejection of the canon is musical transhumanism, which must seem to every right-thinking humanist not even "native" chaos,[37] which "gives birth to a star,"[38] but "a horrible cry of insanity, that shakes the soul,"[39] a paean of frenzy and destruction.

Ancient depictive art aspired to the typical, which it understood as the idea of things. The light of this idea illuminated things with a kind of illumination that was divorced from the earth and therefore always slightly mournful. For the universal and typical bore things as if on the crest of the phenomenon, not permitting them to immerse themselves in the depths of individuation, which comprised the principle of full incarnation. But this "single in the many and through the many," as Plato and Aristotle define the idea, also affirmed each separate phenomenon in its form. The general served as a symbolic principle of the structure of the particular, now it serves as the analytical catalyst that brings on its disintegration. In order to depict a violin as such, Picasso is fated to "break it down." And, first and foremost, the artist breaks down the integral composition of his inherited worldview. He overcomes the "human, all too human" within himself by destroying its former subjective center. His creatively wise spirit flees its human home like a raven from the ark, and it wanders, pecking at the corporeal remains of the flooded world, at the rags of Isis's former veil, the dead wrappings of a destroyed phenomenon. . . .[40]

Today's painter, with his trans-subjective and mobile visual focus, is similar to the child of a new race of thousand-eyed Arguses:[41] he stares into the world with all his awakening and still-unconscious eyes and, at the same time, is attracted to the colorful spots in front of him, unable to distinguish their distance.

III. BEYOND HUMANISM[42]

1. Monanthropism

But this is not yet life, not consciousness beyond humanism, but only the first feelers of a young consciousness, which have reached beyond the boundary mark of the human as individual. As it matures, it will necessarily be determined as a religious consciousness, and, perhaps, will turn out to be religious par excellence compared to previous experience of universal connection. However, I envision this consciousness not as one of a set of correlated religious forms, which could only be affirmed in the place of the old form it supplants: on the contrary, I think that, having come with a light step,[43] it will be only the inner illumination of any of the existing religious confessions. But only that one confession will not die that will find within itself the strength to withstand this test of being conceived by the sun.

In any case, not a single iota will pass in Christianity.[44] Christianity will miraculously come to life and be comprehended in full when, for the first time, it hears and assimilates what our Christian zealots have long hinted at: Dostoevsky, who taught that everyone is guilty before everyone and for everyone and everything, and that there is no border separating man from man;[45] Fedorov, whose single thought was of the "universal task" of resurrecting our fathers, which cannot be realized without surmounting individuation;[46] and Vladimir Solovyov, who preached universal divine humanity and professed faith in the Supreme Being proclaimed by Auguste Comte.[47] For then will be understood the meaning of the Gospel words about the attraction of all into Christ and about the branches of a single vine.[48] The verbal signification of the truth that is to be revealed in men's hearts was long ago discovered and sounded forth in the desert of the world: that very same Dostoevsky discovered the word "Allman."[49]

The sages of India have also long known that Man is one; but they lack the knowledge of our Christian mystery, that this universal "I" of humanity as such is a living and concrete Person, truly and in the full sense of this word. On the contrary, Indian theorizers present it as impersonal. However that might be, I see the next generations growing up with a new comprehension of the fact that we are all a single Adam (this comprehension being "new" not in its logical or mythological form but in its experiential vitality and immediacy). I do not suppose, however, that this inner revelation, like any revelation, will avoid becoming a temptation for many, but it will certainly improve people and subdue human passions. Still, there is a great difference in the emotional experience of those who so recently saw killing an enemy as the killing of a life that was foreign to them, and of those who, while committing the same evil act, are conscious of themselves (not in delirium, but in full command of mind and memory) stabbing their own real double. I think that the inner-experiential knowledge of which I speak will become so general a law that people who are incapable of engendering it within themselves will become savages. In contrast, very many of those in whom it is revealed will abuse it terribly and will inflict on humanity unheard-of dangers, causing new and terrible diseases. . . . But, as Aeschylus's chorus sings: "good win out in the end! . . ."[50]

The single dogma of this new "revelation of things unseen,"[51] as simple as a self-evident truth, is: "man is one." And if each thought that pretends to the significance of an idea must be christened in the transparent Jordan of ideas, the Hellenic word, then we shall call in Hellenic what these lines are attempting to assert: *monanthropism* (*Mónos ó ánthrōpos*). "But why must this knowledge be religion?" our contemporaries will ask, as they cannot help but ask: for the single reason that this is not even knowledge in the usual scientific (and not inner-experiential) sense of the word but only a relation and the establishment of a connection, a "testament" of sorts. If we understand religious perception as the acceptance of a certain premise on faith, we have profoundly forgotten the essence of the religious phenomenon as it is observed in ancient epochs of unmediated religiosity. Before, it was not the objectivity of a religious fact that divided opinions but the subjective attitude toward it, the subjective attitude of the will: the Israelites did not dispute the reality of Baal or Dagon when they refused to venerate the one or the other.[52] But, at that time, ritual proofs of recognition and citizenship were the heart of the matter; today, it is the rhythm of silence and the paths of freedom.

2. The Mutual Responsibility of a Single Conscience

The living value of a religious-moral norm changes with every new stage of cultural-historical movement, and the best definition of this value at any given time is its trial in the fire of the emotional torments of man, who is caught in discord with himself, lost in the secret passages of his own labyrinth, all exits from which appear to be surrounded by flame.

In the post-Homeric epoch, criminals began to appear in need of religious cleansing. This was provided, more than at other temples, at the altars of the immaculate god Phoebus, who took so many sins from the burdened consciences of outcast pilgrims who had been rejected by the gods and by people, who took so many sins upon himself, that Aeschylus's Erinyes saw the Delphic hearth as desecrated by the miasmas of human blood that streamed from it.[53] But the matricide Orestes, the prototype of Hamlet, who was sent by his nefariously murdered father to avenge his death, did not find liberation at Apollo's home from the hunting dogs of Night, the enforcer-Erinyes, who drove him to madness. He was forced to resort to the universal court of Athenian elders, the Areopagites. Apollo appeared at the trial as his defender; the virgin Pallas-Athena, "her father's daughter," decided the conflict

173

of divided opinions by casting her vote for the "father's son." Suffering Orestes, now justified, not only ascended to the throne he inherited but also attained peace of soul, which he had desired more than the kingdom.

The times changed, the new faith brought with it new kinds of cleansing, but they also stopped healing the enlightened society of the eighteenth century, which had been isolated from the church first by Luther's reform and then by the freethinking of the age. Goethe, undertaking a poetic depiction of Orestes' passions, ended up as the juror at a new trial of the very same eternal defendant—the juror insofar as he represented the entire humanism of the epoch. In accordance with his new motives, he upheld without hesitation the ancient verdict: "not guilty." But Goethe, that apostle of so-called humanity (later, he became fundamentally different),[54] was wholly ruled by the superficial voluptuousness of aesthetic formalism. It is sufficient to recall Goethe's drama (*Iphigenie*) to see clearly that the terrible antinomy of ethical consciousness receives its magnanimous resolution through the idyllic awakening of elegant humanity, even in savage worshipers of the homicidal Scythian goddess.[55] Goethe was overly complacent in trying to say more than Shakespeare himself wanted to say, and he still stumbled. Hamlet did not need to raise his hand against his own mother, but even then what did his obedience to the will from beyond the grave cost him! Like Goethe, Shakespeare was deprived of religious help, but then he was also deprived of the poetic decisiveness necessary for action: in Hamlet, it is Shakespeare himself who is painfully inactive.

It is noteworthy that our creator of *Crime and Punishment*, in his resolution of the problem of cleansing spilled blood, coincides with the ancient Aeschylus. To take upon his own shoulders a cross offered as if by God himself, to go out into the square, to kiss the Earth, to confess everything and repent before the entire nation: is this not essentially the same as abandoning the throne one has only just ascended to and going as a humble pilgrim to pray to Phoebus, and then to affirm Phoebus's inner cleansing by the communal [*sobornyi*] decision of the holy national Areopagus? This mystical socialization of conscience; this placing of *sobornost'*, as a new energy and value not characteristic solely of man in isolation, on a rung higher than all beautiful "humanity" in each individual man; this view of the criminal as one who has rejected society and who is in need of reunification with the whole: this, of course, is not humanism.

Here ancient memory and new presentiments converge. This marks the future of those cleansings whose religious meaning consists of the acceptance of the individual will and guilt by all humanity, understood as a living universal-personal unity. . . . But, in conclusion, I readily admit that the Cassandra in me never sustains her role to the end.

PART IV

Pilot Stars

Nietzsche and Dionysus

There is an ancient myth: when the Hellenic warriors were dividing the spoils and booty of Troy, the dark lot fell to Eurypylus, the marshal of the Thessalian troops. From the threshold of the royal treasuries, which were engulfed in flames, furious Cassandra hurled to the feet of the victors the renowned ark, fashioned by Hephaestus, which had always been kept locked. Zeus himself had given it to old Dardanus, the builder of Troy, as a sign of divine patrimony. The foresight of the secret god had bestowed this hallowed relic on the Thessalian as battle tribute. Eurypylus's fellow leaders tried in vain to persuade him to beware of the snares of the frenzied prophetess: it would be better, they assured him, to cast his gift to the depths of the Skamander.[1] But Eurypylus was eager to test his mysterious lot, and he carried the ark off; opening it, he saw by the reflected light of the burning city not a bearded man in a coffin, crowned with sprawling branches, but a fig-wood idol of King Dionysus in an ancient sarcophagus. Hardly had the hero glanced at the image of the god when he went mad.

Thus appears before us the holy tale as sketched by Pausanius.[2] Our imagination is tempted to follow Eurypylus along the burning paths of his Dionysian madness. But the myth, which went unnoticed by ancient poets, is silent. We hear only that at times the king regained his senses, and in these intervals of healthy understanding, he set sail from the shores of ruined Ilium heading not for his native Thessaly, but for Cyrrha, the Delphic harbor, in order to seek healing at Apollo's tripod. Pythia promised him redemption and a new homeland on the shores where he would encounter a foreign sacrifice and set up an ark. The wind carried the seafarers to the coast of Achaia. In the borderlands of Patrae, Eurypylus stepped onto dry land and saw a youth and a maiden being led to be sacrificed at the altar of Artemis Triclaria. Thus, he recognized the final resting place that had been foretold him; and the inhabitants of that country, for their part, recognized in him the promised savior who would free them of the obligation to offer human sacrifice, the one whom the oracle had taught them to expect in the person of a foreign king bearing an ark with a god unknown to them who would cease the bloody worship of the wild goddess.[3] Eurypylus was healed of his holy ailment; he replaced the cruel sacrifices with merciful ones in the name of the god he proclaimed. Having instituted the veneration of Dionysus, he died and became the guardian hero of the liberated nation.

This ancient patronal legend seems to me a mythical reflection of the fate of Friedrich Nietzsche. Thus also, together with other people strong of spirit, did he attempt to conquer Beauty, the Helen of the Hellenes, by burning ancient strongholds; thus did he win the destined sacred object. Thus did he go mad as a result of his mysterious acquisition and insight. Thus also did he proselytize Dionysus and seek protection from Dionysus in Apollo's power. Thus did he with new divine knowledge abolish human sacrifice to the old idols of a narrowly understood and externally imposed duty, removing the yoke of despondency and despair that hung over people's hearts. Like this hero he was mad in life, and from out of the depths of the earth, he became the benefactor of the human race he liberated, a true hero of the new world.

Nietzsche returned Dionysus to the world: this was his mission and his prophetic madness. Dionysus's name sounded in his mouth like the falling of "many waters."[4] The charm of Dionysus gave him an immense influence on our epoch and made him the forger of our future. The hollow magic of a stifling illusion, the bewitched captivity of dim souls, was shaken. Meadows became verdant under the vernal breath of the god; hearts began to burn bright; the muscles of sublime will became taut. Each fleeting moment became significant and vatic; every breath became lighter and fuller; every heartbeat became stronger. Life glanced into people's souls more brightly, more deeply, more fully, and more penetratingly. The universe shuddered with echoes, as if the sighs of an unseen organ were echoing through the Gothic pillars made of pipes bundled like barrels and plaited into a sheer, arrowlike form. We felt ourselves, our earth, and our sun taken up in the eddy of a universal dance ("the Earth dancing around the Sun," as Shelley sang).[5] We have tasted of the universal divine wine and become dreamers. Our dormant potential for human divinity made us sigh over the tragic image of the Superman, over the resurrected Dionysus that was made incarnate in us.

There glistened in our souls the fulfillment of the covenant:

> Whoever breathes you, o god,
> He is not burdened
> By the mountainous masses,
> Nor by the blue glass of moisture
> Resting in the solemn noon!
> Whoever breathes by you, o god,—
> In the many-winged altar of creation

He is a wing!
In the storm of fraternal powers
Around the suns
He hurries the burning sacrifice
Of the suffering earth. . . .[6]

There are geniuses of pathos, just as there are geniuses of the good. Without revealing anything essentially new, they force us to sense the world in a new way. Such was Nietzsche. He turned the funereal yearning of pessimism into the flame of a heroic funeral repast, into the phoenix fire of universal tragedy. He gave life back its tragic god . . . *Incipit Tragoedia!*[7]

II

In order to equip Nietzsche for the labor of his life, two Moirae with differing images bestowed contrasting gifts on him at birth. This fateful dichotomy can be defined as the antithesis of spiritual sight and spiritual hearing.

Nietzsche had to possess sharp vision to distinguish the pale forms of primeval writing on the palimpsest of hidden traditions, which was covered over by a later hand. His small and elegant ears, an object of vanity for him, had to be vatic ears filled with "noise and sound," like the hearing of Pushkin's Prophet, sensitive to the inner music of the world soul.[8]

Nietzsche was a philologist, as Vladimir Solovyov defined him.[9] In order to discover Dionysus, Nietzsche had to wander through the Elysium of pagan shadows and converse with the Hellenes in their own language, as he obviously could since many of his pages seem translations from Plato (who knew, the ancients said, the speech of the gods). Following the mountaineers of scholarship, he was to ascend to the point where we now find the study of the Greek world. It was necessary that Hermann reveal to us the language,[10] Otfried Müller the spirit,[11] August Boeckh the life,[12] and Welcker the soul of the Dionysian nation.[13] It was necessary that the future author of *The Birth of Tragedy* have Ritschl as an instructor[14] and that he critically anatomize Diogenes Laertius or the poem about the contest between Homer and Hesiod.[15]

Nietzsche was an orgiast of musical raptures: this was his second soul. Not long before his death, Socrates dreamed that a divine voice was exhorting him to take up music:[16] the philosopher Nietzsche fulfilled this wondrous testament. He was to become a participant in the Wagnerian throng dedicated to the worship of the Muses and Dionysus. He was to assimilate musically what Wagner had perceived in the legacy of Beethoven: his prophetic mantle and his Promethean, fire-bearing, hollow thyrsus—in other words, his heroic and tragic pathos. It was necessary that Dionysus be revealed in music (the mute art of deaf Beethoven, the greatest proclaimer of

179

the orgiastic mysteries of the spirit) before he could be revealed in the word or in the "ecstasy and frenzy"[17] of Dostoevsky, that great mystagogue of the future Zarathustra.

And it was also necessary that the state of minds in the epoch during which Nietzsche appeared correspond to his dichotomous nature: that his critical lucidity and visual striving for classical clarity and plastic precision be tempered in the positive frigidity of his epoch's scientific spirit; that his orgiastic egress beyond the bounds of the self encounter ancient Indian philosophy (which Schopenhauer's pessimism had grafted onto contemporary thought) together with its faith in the illusoriness of individual division and its anguish at the separation that is caused by the haze of appearances.[18] To the student of the spirit of tragedy, this philosophy revealed the essence of Dionysus as a principle that destroys the charms of "individuation."

Nietzsche's genius needed the Apollonian (formative, cohesive, and centripetal) elements of personal predispositions and external influences as limits within which to circumscribe the boundlessness of the musical, dissolving, and centrifugal Dionysian element. But the dichotomy of his gifts or, as he himself would say, of his "virtues," inevitably led them into mutual conflict and conditioned his fatal inner discord.

Only on the condition of a certain inner antinomy is it possible to play at self-bifurcation, a game of which Nietzsche often speaks[19]—to play at seeking oneself, catching oneself, eluding oneself; to have a vital sense of wandering within oneself and encountering oneself, an almost palpable vision of the interminable passages and inscrutable recesses of one's emotional labyrinth.

III

Dionysus is the divine all-unity of "What Is" in its sacrificial separation and suffering transubstantiation into the many-faced nothing (mè ón)[20] of the world, which flutters spectrally between appearance and disappearance.[21] The eternal sacrifice and eternal resurrection of the suffering god—this is the religious idea of Dionysian orgiasm.

The "son of God," the inheritor of the father's throne, mutilated by the Titans in the cradle of the ages;[22] the same god in the image of a "hero," i.e., a godman, born in time from an earthly mother;[23] the "new Dionysus," whose mysterious appearance was the only possible hope of a consoling divine descent for the Hellene, who knew not Hope:[24] this is the god of ancient philosophical and theological doctrines who is so close to our religious understanding of the world. In the universal, naturalistically tinged belief, he is the god of the martyr's death, of hidden life in the pregnant depths of death, and of an exultant return from the shadow of death, of "rebirth" and "palingenesis."

The mysticism of the religious veneration of Dionysus, which is the same in both its esoteric and popular forms, is immediately accessible and universally close to us. It combines Dionysus the sacrifice, Dionysus the resurrected, and Dionysus the comforter into a single integral experience; each instant of true ecstasy reflects the entire mystery of eternity in the living mirror of an inner, suprapersonal event of the frenzied soul. Here Dionysus is the eternal miracle of the world heart in the human heart, and the world heart is irrepressible in its fiery beating,[25] in the tremors of its penetrating pain and unexpected joy,[26] in the fading of mortal anguish and in the renewed ecstasies of ultimate fulfillment.

The Dionysian principle, antinomial by its nature, can be variously described and formally defined, but it is fully revealed only in experience, and one would seek in vain to comprehend it by studying *what* forms its living composition. Dionysus accepts and simultaneously rejects any predicate; in his conception "a" is "not-a"; in his cult, the sacrificial victim and priest are united as an identity. Only the Dionysian *how* presents to inner experience its essence, which is not reducible to verbal interpretation, just like the essence of beauty or poetry. This pathos of universal reconciliation within the divine resolves the polarities of living forces in liberating storms. Here that which is spills over the edge of the phenomenon. Here the god, playing in the womb of divided being,[27] breaks the limits of this womb by growing within it.

Universal life as a whole and the life of nature are definitely Dionysian:

> Orgiastic madness in wine,
> It rocks the whole world in laughter;
> But in sobriety and peaceful quiet
> That same madness sometimes breathes.
> It's silent in the hanging branches
> And it guards the greedy cave.
> (F. Sologub)[28]

Equally Dionysian are the dances of satyrs in oak groves and the motionless silence of a maenad lost in the inner contemplation and sensation of the god. But the human soul can reach such a state only on the condition of its egress, its ecstatic transport beyond the limits of the empirical "I," on the condition that it partake of the unity of the universal "I" in its willing and suffering, fullness and schism, breathing and lamentation. Within this holy intoxication and orgiastic oblivion, one should distinguish the state of tortuously blessed oversaturation, the sense of miraculous power and a surfeit of strength, the consciousness of an impersonal and will-less elemental force, and the terror and ecstasy of the loss of the self in chaos and of the new discovery of the self in God. Even this, however, does not exhaust the innumerable rainbows that embrace and inflame the soul as a result of the refraction of the Dionysian element within it.[29]

Nietzsche's musical soul knew this *how*. But from this sea, where, in Leopardi's words, "shipwreck is sweet,"[30] his other soul sought to summon forth a clear vision, a certain visual *what*, and then to retain it, captivate it, give it logical definition and lasting stability; to petrify it, so to speak.[31]

The psychology of Dionysian ecstasy is so rich in content that he who gathers even a drop of the "moisture that encompasses worlds"[32] remains sated. Nietzsche sailed in the seas of this living moisture but did not want a "sweet shipwreck." He wished to land on a firm shore and look from this shore at the agitation of the purple depths.[33] He experienced the divine intoxication of the element and the loss of his personal "I" in this intoxication, and this experience was sufficient for him. He did not go down into the deep caves—to meet his god in the gloom. He recoiled before the religious mystery of his purely aesthetic raptures.

It is telling that in the heroic god of Tragedy Nietzsche almost failed to notice the god who experiences suffering (*Dionúsou páthē*).[34] He knew the ecstasies of orgiasm, but he knew nothing of the mourning and moaning of passionate worship that allowed the grieving women to summon from the depths of the earth the son of Zeus after his suffering and death. The Hellenes, according to Nietzsche, were "pessimists" due to the fullness of their vitality; their love for the tragic, *amor fati*,[35] was their overflowing strength; self-destruction was their way out of the blessed torment of overabundance. Dionysus is the symbol of this abundance and excess, this ecstasy caused by a sudden influx of vital energies. Thus runs Nietzsche's narrow conception. There can be no doubt that Dionysus is the god of excessive wealth, that he makes his abundance the rapture of death. But historically and philosophically, an abundance of life and dying comprises the *prius* of his religious idea and is subject to dispute. Tragedy arose from the orgies of the god who was mutilated by his frenzied worshipers. But what is the origin of this frenzy? It is closely tied to the cult of the souls and the primitive funeral repasts. The celebration of the funeral repast, this sacrificial worship of the dead, was accompanied by the unleashing of sexual passions. Was it death or life that tipped the overloaded and teetering scales? But, in the eyes of those ancient people, Dionysus was, after all, not the god of wild weddings and sexual intercourse, but the god of the dead and of the mortal shade; surrendering himself to be mutilated and carrying off into the night countless victims, he introduced death into the exultation of the living. And in death he smiled with the smile of exultant return, this divine witness of the indestructible generative force. He was the good news of joyful death,[36] which concealed in itself promises of another life there, below, and of renewed raptures of life here, on earth. The suffering god, the exultant god: these two images were from the very beginning visible in him undivided and unconfused.[37]

It is terrifying to see that it was only after the onset of his emotional disorder that Nietzsche intuited in Dionysus the suffering god, as if unconsciously and at the same time prophetically; at any event, he intuited this outside and in spite of the dogma he had completed and propagated. In one letter, he calls himself "the crucified Dionysus."[38] This belated and unanticipated admission of the kinship between Dionysianism and Christianity, which he had so severely rejected up to then, shocks the soul like the clear voice of Tiutchev's lark, unexpected and horrifying, like the laughter of madness, at an inclement and dark hour of nightfall. . . .[39]

IV

Inspired by Dionysian intoxication,[40] Nietzsche was aware that for the illumination of our earthly image (for he willed no less), our heart must change, that within us there must occur some profound transformation, the transfiguration of our entire emotional makeup, the retuning of the entire range of our feelings, a rebirth like the state denoted in the original language of the Gospels by the word "metanoia," which is what allows one to see the "kingdom of heaven" on earth.[41] And behold, he proclaimed two postulates, essentially mystical but antireligious in the arbitrary application and interpretation that Nietzsche himself, or else his anti-Dionysian double, gave to them.

In the realm of epistemology, he proclaimed that the autonomy of subjective truth, the truth of inner willing, can negate whatever is affirmed as an objectively obligatory truth. But the means by which we affirm ourselves beyond the bounds of our "I" is faith; and Nietzsche's postulate, seen from a religious point of view,[42] is the principle of faith. In the realm of ethics, he came forth with the doctrine that one must live beyond "good and evil." In the religious aspect, this coincides with the principle of sanctity and mystical freedom, as Christian ethics expressed it by transferring the moral criterion from the empirical world into the realm of intellectual willing, or as ancient Indian wisdom expressed it by the esoteric liberation of one who has "awoken" from all evaluations and norms of worldly morality. However, Nietzsche does not stop here; by inconsistently substituting the formula "in accordance with whatever augments the life of the species" (*was lebenfördernd ist*)[43] for the formulas "beyond objective truth" and "beyond good and evil," he rejects the Dionysian *how* in favor of a definite and non-Dionysian *what*, thus revealing himself to be a theomachist who has rebelled against his own god.

A votary of the god "the Liberator,"[44] Nietzsche has hardly freed the will from the chains of outer duty when he again subordinates it to the supremacy of a certain general norm: the biological imperative. This amoralist proclaims himself to be an "immoralist," i.e., again a moralist in principle. And the votary of "life," who condemned the "theoretical man" of contemporary humanity,[45] does not tire of speaking about "knowledge" and calls his

183

followers "those who know."[46] The principle of faith becomes a challenge to truth from unbelief. And, though it was not carried out in all its applications and consequences, we would consider this skepticism to be the breakdown of extreme positivism, were it not above all the instructive trick and the far-sighted calculation of a legislator: Nietzsche makes us quarrel with self-evident truths, not in order to replace them with others that are even more evident to the spiritual gaze but in order to create within us hearths of blind resistance to the powers that oppress us, a resistance that he sees as a factor conducive to the evolution of the human race. This cerebral and calculating quality radically undermines his original intuition and inspired impulse. But it would be premature, on the basis of these accusations, to call Nietzsche a false prophet: for we have before us the edifying example of the prophet Jonah.[47]

Nietzsche the scholar, "Nietzsche the philologist," remained a seeker of "knowledge" and never ceased to immerse himself in the works of Greek metaphysicians and French moralists.[48] He should have remained with Tragedy and Music. But his second soul summoned him out of the wild paradise of his god into the foreign, non-Dionysian world; this was not the soul of the orgiast and universal man but a soul enamored of the total clarity of beautiful limits, the proud perfection of the incarnation of a self-enclosed, particular idea. He was captivated by

> the Delphic idol: the young visage
> Was wrathful, full of terrible pride,
> And breathed with an unworldly power.[49]

In music, Nietzsche's development gravitated away from harmony, where the polyphonous Dionysian element celebrates its dark feast, and toward melody, circumscribed and illumined in the manner of Apollo. In his final period, Nietzsche considered melody to be the most noble and "aristocratic" principle of music. His aesthetics became more and more an aesthetics of taste, style, measure, refinement, and crystallization. Similarly, in the sphere of the moral ideal, he was irrepressibly drawn to the pathos of overcoming and of clear domination over the creatively elemental movements of spirit; to the beauty of "the star born of chaos, moving in a rhythmic dance";[50] to the mighty and haughty image of the wise ancient tyrant; to the magnificent cruelty of "Mediterranean culture"; to the idea of the "will to power."[51]

The psychological motifs of his enmity for Christianity reveal the expanses of dry, sunny deserts that Nietzsche entered in his movement away from the moist and shaded paths of his god.[52] Christianity, in the primeval image of its attitude toward life, is the love-filled orgiasm of a soul that has lost itself in order to gain itself outside of the self, splashing over into the paternal womb of the One; it is the Nysian white paradise of lilies of the field[53] and the purple vine of sacrificial grapes,[54] the ecstasy of blessed infantlike insight into the truth of the Father in heaven and into the reality of heaven on earth,[55] which presents itself to the eye in a new way. It is well known that the Dionysian religion was regarded as the most democratic religion in the Greek world: Nietzsche directed the entire force of his attack precisely at the democratic element of Christianity. Here, even the lucidity of a historian failed him: the Dionysian idea was in equal measure an inwardly liberating force and a kind of "slave morality," as was Christianity, but it was just as far as Christianity from being the leaven of social indignation and "slave rebellion."[56]

V

In the doctrine of the "Superman," propagated through the "Dionysian" Zarathustra (*der dionysische Unhold*),[57] the fateful dichotomy of Nietzsche's attitude toward Dionysus ripens to the point of crisis and is resolved by a definite turn toward the anti-Dionysian pole, a turn that is completed by the final formulation of the doctrine of the "will to power."

If we trace how the philosopher's conception of superhumanity developed, we once again witness the gradual substitution of the Dionysian *how* by the anti-Dionysian *what*. Originally Nietzsche worked under the sway of thoughts about the "death of the old God" (*der alte Gott ist todt*)[58] and about the divine inheritance of the human "I." Nietzsche hesitates to pronounce what Stirner, working from an identical premise, uttered with the self-satisfaction of a vagabond; at times, we encounter ellipses in Nietzsche's texts, right where the logic of his thought suggests: "I am a god."[59] So this position was unspoken and mystical for him: he was still possessed by Dionysus. For the religion of Dionysus is a mystical religion, and the soul of mysticism is the divinization of man, whether through the grace-bearing approach of the Divinity to the human soul, which results in their complete fusion, or through an inner insight into the true and eternal essence of the "I," into the "Itself" in the "I" (the "Atman" of Brahman philosophy).[60] Dionysian frenzy is itself the divinization of man, and he who is possessed by the god is already a Superman (to be sure, not in the sense intended by Goethe, the creator of the word *Übermensch*).[61] But Nietzsche hypostasizes the superhuman *how* into a certain *what;* he lends his fiction some arbitrarily determined features and, falling into the tone and style of messianism, he proclaims the coming of the Superman.

Endless are the levels of penetration by the divine, great are the possibilities of the spirit, and inextinguishable are the primeval hopes for the illumination of the human countenance and for the perfect man, who is the guiding star of all quests, the postulate of self-awareness, and the testament of Christianity. But in Nietzsche's thought, as his spiritual vision gradually becomes focused on the image of the Superman, this image becomes more and more alienated from the mystical roots whence it originated in the contemplations of the Dionysian thinker. Nietzsche goes still further and lowers his ecstatic and inspired vision to the level of a hope for some ideal selection that is to crown the human race in a final, culminating link of biological evolution.

Like any inspired state, the Dionysian state is unselfish and undirected; "the divine approaches with a light step,"[62] in Nietzsche's own words. This is not what he teaches in regard to the Superman. The philosopher as legislator does not tire of exhorting humanity to exert itself and to try to develop its superior type, its culminating image. The life of the human species must be constant striving for a single goal, the increasingly tightly drawn string of one titanic bow. The Dionysian state is will-less: human will, according to Nietzsche, must become an inexhaustible feat of overcoming.[63] The Dionysian state releases the soul and, accepting ascetic ecstasy, knows no ascesis: the destroyer of old tablets, demanding that man unceasingly will to surpass himself, again raises the ascetic ideal.[64] Nothing can be more opposed to the Dionysian spirit than to deduce the impulse to the superhuman from the will to power: Dionysian power is miraculous and impersonal, whereas Nietzsche's conception of power is mechanically material and egotistically aggressive. The Dionysian state knows its own single, boundless instant, which carries within it its own eternal miracle: each instant for Nietzsche is an ascending and mediating level, a step toward the great future time.

The Dionysian state is an egress from time and an immersion in the timeless. Nietzsche's spirit is turned completely toward the future; he is entirely within the dungeon of time. With tragic power, Nietzsche relates how he gained revelation of the mystery of life's cyclical nature and the eternal return of things, this dogma of ancient philosophy (*Fröhliche Wissenschaft*, sec. 341): "Would you not cast yourself down and gnash your teeth and curse the demon who had whispered this knowledge to you?"[65] His powerful soul was almost crushed by the burden of the realization that there would never be anything new in the countless repetitions of the selfsame world and the selfsame individual, nothing new, "even this spiderweb and this moonlight between the trees";[66] but, rearing up with a superhuman effort of will, which he has summoned for its final self-affirmation, his soul finishes with a hymn and thanksgiving to irrevocable fate. This ecstasy of happiness is clearly the strain of his spirit; this knowledge is clearly a logical conclusion; this conception of the world is clearly a mechanical conception. And the ethical application of the dogma of cyclical return—this imperative of the utmost effort and the utmost achievement—is a final self-defense, made necessary through the force of circumstances and the fateful threat of an avenging repetition. The ecstasy of eternal rebirth, profoundly Dionysian in its nature, is clouded by the first despair and is deadened by disbelief in the

Dionysian miracle, which abolishes old and new, making everything at every instant simultaneously eternal and newly revealed. A tragic perception of the idea of eternal return seems to have marked a final and pained flash of Dionysian frenzy in Nietzsche's soul. This flash blinded his long-suffering soul with its terrible light and, burning up, cast it into a deaf and dumb night with no dawn.

VI

"This happens," says Faust, blinded by the sunrise, "when a longing hope, having achieved the goal of its highest striving, sees the gate of fulfillment wide open: the flaming abundance bursts from the eternal depths, and we stand in shock. . . . We wished to ignite the enlivening torch and we ourselves are engulfed in a sea of flame! Is it love or hatred that embraces us with its burning, equally monstrous in its periods of pain and joy? So that we again lower our eyes to the earth, seeking to conceal ourselves under its veil of infancy."[67] Nietzsche saw Dionysus—and reeled away from Dionysus, as Faust recoils from the luminous orb in order to admire its reflections in the rainbows of the waterfall.

Nietzsche's tragic guilt lies in his not having believed in the god whom he himself revealed to the world.

He understood the Dionysian principle as an aesthetic principle, and life as an "aesthetic phenomenon."[68] But it is first and foremost a religious principle, and the rainbows of life's waterfall, toward which Nietzsche turns his face, are refractions of the divine Sun. If the Dionysian intoxication of life is only an aesthetic phenomenon, humanity is a throng of "Dionysus's craftsmen," as actors were called in antiquity.[69] It was with good reason that the psychological mystery of playacting always fascinated the Dionysian philosopher. And, of course, life is divinely inspired and transparent, and the deep spirit is true to its eternal "I," if we keep alive the consciousness that we only wear our temporary masks for play, having clothed ourselves in the incidental forms of our individuation (*upadhi* in Hindu doctrine). Originally, however, "Dionysus's craftsmen" were his clergy and priests; moreover, they were his hypostases and "Bacchae"; and a truly Dionysian understanding of the world requires that in our consciousness our mask be the countenance of the many-faced god himself and that our playacting at his cosmic altar be a holy rite and sacrificial worship.

Like Eurypylus the Thessalian, Nietzsche wanted to see the god with his own eyes, and having accepted him as a visual perception of beauty, he fell into the snares deployed by providential powers.[70] Eurypylus should have accepted the ark as a sanctuary, and he should have accepted the mission of a god-bearer as his fate; he should have begun with a prayer at the prophetic tripod and fulfilled what had been entrusted to him without tempting the secret god, and he would not have fallen into fatal madness. But he recklessly glanced at the mysterious idol, and a divine force made him the bearer of good news. His attitude toward Dionysus was the resistance of unbelief and not the obedience of faith. Nietzsche's fate was determined by the very same features of insight into the divine and resistance to it.

Like the mythical Lycurgus, "who raised his hand against the heaven-dwelling gods" (*Iliad* VI.131), and who was punished with madness and a martyr's death for persecuting "furious Dionysus," Nietzsche was both a theomachist and the victim of theomachy.[71]

But the peculiar feature of Dionysian religion is that it identifies the sacrificial victim with the god and the priest with the god. Theomachist types in the cycle of Dionysian myths themselves take on Dionysus's image. Suffering, they mystically reproduce the sufferings of those who suffer at their hands. And, just as Jacob the theomachist elicited a blessing,[72] so also did Nietzsche take on the suffering imprint of the suffering god, whom he both proclaimed and rejected. Prophet and foe of Dionysus in his passions and torments, in his guilt and his death, he displays the tragic features of the god whom the Hellenes believed to have himself experienced universal martyrdom repeatedly beneath the heroic masks of mortals.

The Religious Task of Vladimir Solovyov

I

"The Lord's work is hard." Such were Vladimir Solovyov's last words, according to the testimony of Prince Sergei Trubetskoi.[1] It was a sigh of exhaustion, but what enviable exhaustion! This was the blessed exhaustion of a faithful laborer in the garden of the Father. He was happy to receive his daily wage from the Lord of the garden. But *our* gratitude has yet to be woven into an unwilting wreath. Its fragrant spring flowers blossom in only a few souls. And even if they have blossomed, we still are unable to gather and weave them together. Could we really weave a single wreath, we who are scattered and divided, we who have squandered the old mystery and know not the new mystery of universal [*sobornyi*] communion? But without the inner experience of *sobornost'*, we are powerless even to understand what Vladimir Solovyov taught us. He is still fated to remain uncomprehended; we cannot yet measure his significance.

It is rare that we find in ourselves the courage to glance within ourselves or to survey what surrounds us attentively without flattering ourselves by forgetting what is within us and around us. Whenever we do, it is only our confusion and our despondence, bordering on hopelessness, that force us to look back at one who knew the meaning of life and who did not take fright at its visage, and who was not afraid of the countenance of death. Only our confusion and our despondence cause us to recall this faithful witness and to hope that his testimony is true, to recall this rigorous instructor and dependable leader with the orphan's feeling of being abandoned in the misty bounds of spiritual hunger and aimless wanderings. But let this hunger not be sated by unworthy food! Let the constancy of those who seek and knock not be exhausted! As long as one seeks one shall find.[2]

II

Dostoevsky and Vladimir Solovyov majestically directed our society's thought to questions of faith. Their initiative is like two mountain glaciers feeding

189

the narrow, yet constant and undwindling, current that we have come to denote as "the quest for a new religious consciousness."[3] Lev Tolstoy's turn toward a labor of the inner personality, coinciding in time with Dostoevsky's passing, marked a third defining moment in our religious awakening.

Dostoevsky's prophetic fever and delirium first shook us with a tremor that was kindred to our soul's most profound and elemental nature. This was the tremor of those irrational feelings that Dostoevsky himself called "ecstasy and frenzy."[4] It was a sermon on touching other worlds; on the guilt of all before everyone and everything; on the living Earth and man's ability to achieve union with her by singing her hymn and venerating her; and on the living Christ, resurrected and recognized by the soul of the god-bearing nation. A wave of Dionysian force, which serves as the primordial basis of any mysticism, splashed from this mystic's ecstasies into the stream of generations.

Lev Tolstoy demanded an absolute value and conceived of an absolute principle, and these he placed like the Gorgon's head in face-to-face opposition to all the principles and values of the culture we assimilated and cultivated (although we remained incapable of revealing their relative nature until culture itself proclaimed it).[5] To the law of life, conditioned by necessity, Tolstoy opposed the law of the freely self-determining inner personality, which discovers itself only by overcoming the outer personality, which is subordinate to the law of life. By becoming the *devaluer* of values, he appealed to our elemental national tendency to expose all that is relative, to renounce all coverings and masks, to flee from the charm of eyes and mind, to descend from all heights of worldly pride, to bare the truth in its final, severe, and destitute simplicity. This sermon was a Socratic, universal verification of all the fundamental tenets that find affirmation in the law of life and in this law's self-interest, of all the consolations and comforting illusions of a cheaply and hypocritically tranquil spirit, and all the "sublime deceits," the presence of which the Russian character is stubbornly inclined to suspect in the temptations of the beautiful and sublime, and for which it will not sacrifice even the lowest of its "low truths."[6]

Both artists of genius were powerless to overcome the formlessness and incoherence of their religious synthesis: Tolstoy, insofar as he was an anarchist; Dostoevsky, as an orgiastic and tragic genius. Both found in society timid and faltering responses, but nonetheless, both swayed the elemental foundation of our spiritual-moral consciousness. They provided, as it were, a musical basis for our intellectual struggle for a religious worldview. The true *composer* [*obrazovatel'*] of our religious aspirations, our lyre-playing Orpheus, who bore the principle of constructive harmony, was Vladimir Solovyov, the singer of Divine Sophia.[7] But he was heard by fewer thinking people than the other two, and, we dare to aver, was also less understood than they. This observation, incidentally, becomes self-evident if we are not mistaken in another observation: that ten years after his death, we have turned out to be less the continuers and completers of his task than, once again, mere seekers. He himself was also a seeker but in another meaning of the word. The object of his seeking was but the study of what remained uncertain in the specific conclusions and applications of his general theory, while the fundamental tenets of the theory itself were Solovyov's indisputable discovery.

III

Unlike those two great amorphists, Vladimir Solovyov was an artist of the inner forms of Christian consciousness. Russian thought, still almost in its infancy, staggered in confusion from this multifariously composed and compartmentalized unity, which, despite all its crystal clarity, was coordinated in so complicated a manner, so variously balanced, so cosmically organized. The very harmony of the worldview Solovyov articulated was frightening in its proportionality and completeness. The chaotic nature of the other two writers was nearer to us than this icon of heavenly Aphrodite.[8]

From another point of view, one might say that Tolstoy was understood better than the other two, though it may be that this only resulted in all the more vigorous dissent. He was in a certain sense simple and lagged behind the others in respect to the fullness of his spiritual understanding. He turned us toward God on an individual basis, outside the Church; we were childishly grateful to him for this freedom without suspecting that such individualism made all that was positively affirmed in his teaching insufficiently grounded and even downright untenable. The most difficult thing for the Russian intelligentsia to attain (and herein must lie the tragic guilt for its so-called alienation from the national soul) is a clear understanding of the idea of the Church. I mean the concept or idea of the Church as a mystical entity and not the outer, nominally *ecclesiastical* organization, not of the social forms of the confessional collective.

Dostoevsky, in contrast to Tolstoy, was profoundly ecclesiastic in spirit.[9] He analyzed the crisis of the isolated personality with a profundity that will last the ages, imprinting it in his creations; he saw the only salvation of the individual personality and of humanity in living, mystical *sobornost'*; he awaited the transubstantiation of statehood into the theocracy of Christ in holy Rus'.[10] By affirming the integrity of the nation as the bearer of God, he affirmed in it the potential being of the growing Church. But once and for all, society decided not to accept this writer fully. The abundance of genius grants the artist the privilege of satisfying various people with various gifts; in Goethe's saying, anyone can find something for himself in one who brings much.[11] Dostoevsky's integral intuition marks a new age in our spiritual life.

191

As far as Vladimir Solovyov is concerned, we argued with him com-
paratively little, at least over the foundations of his teaching; even less were
we angered by his being a mystic. But then those who listened to him were
primarily people who needed to deepen and cleanse their own, already existing faith. It was necessary to accept or reject his teaching *in toto;* to such
a degree was his entire teaching inwardly mediated and connected, archi-
tectonically fused, almost organically indivisible. This, by the way, is not
true for his applied ethics and all that is so carefully analyzed and stipulated
in *The Justification of the Good,* a work I would compare in a certain sense
only with Plato's *Laws,* which bear the imprint of that ancient thinker's attempts to reconcile an ideal with a practically realizable reality, to combine
minimalism in the former realm with maximalism within the bounds of the
latter.[12] This, however, was of little significance. The essence of Solovyov's
worldview lay in the concept of the Church, and this explains his inaccessi-
bility as a thinker. And still, Solovyov the educator[13] managed to sow in our
religious consciousness the thought that we are wholly dependent on the
degree to which we assimilate the truth of the Church.

Moreover, sometimes society felt that Solovyov wanted only to be an
apologetic theologian, that his fervent defense of Church tradition hin-
dered him from responding vitally to the religious needs of the changed
structure of the modern soul. Indeed, is it not he himself who, in the tract
on the *Future of Theocracy,* views his task as purely apologetic?[14] "To justify the faith of our fathers . . ." But let us see how he conceives of this
justification. In the words immediately following these, he defines his intention more precisely: "by raising it (the faith of our fathers) to a new level
of rational consciousness."[15] Thus, the very concept of the "new religious
consciousness" stems from Vladimir Solovyov, just as he was also the source
of other formulas and definitions in our current religious searchings.

IV

The "new level of rational consciousness," according to Solovyov, is an actual apprehension and active assimilation of the idea of positive unity. This
level is reached when one acknowledges the relative truth of all the heterogeneous principles developed by human thought in the realm of cognition, moral consciousness, artistic creation, and social organization (by the
acknowledgment of the relative truth of these principles, I mean insofar as
they are parts of a single truth and are therefore determined relative to the
whole); likewise, when one acknowledges the demonic falsehood of these
very principles, insofar as each one is affirmed in self-sufficient exclusivity,
in separation from the whole and in conflict with the whole, which results in
their being principles alienated from the complete all-unity, or, in Solov-

yov's terminology, "abstract principles."[16] And do they indeed not turn into empty abstractions without a living connection to the living reality of absolute being? It is in these ways that Solovyov is most of all the restorer of cultural values, as opposed to Tolstoy, who is their devaluer. If the universal verification undertaken by Tolstoy stops at suspicion or negation, then Solovyov defines the preconditions for the universal *justification* of all aspects of truth. In their historical succession, Solovyov sees landmarks of the path humanity has passed in divine education and natural revelation, landmarks of all forms of creative energy that conceal within themselves the spark of Promethean fire:

> And not in vain was Hellas granted
> The heavenly gift of Prometheus.[17]

Solovyov sought to reveal the absolute within the relative; and wherever he failed to find a true correlation of the relative to the absolute, he mercilessly rejected the relative. Thus, an attempt at universal justification became in turn a universal judgment of abstract principles. And this elevation of the second commandment of the law[18] was not an abstract judgment of the world of abstractions, as we can see from Solovyov's vital and practical protest (when he predictably and consistently became a social commentator) against exhibitions of the base, god-resisting self-affirmation of separate and self-enclosed spheres of legality, statehood, ecclesiastical formalism, and so on, such as capital punishment, the untruth and cruelty of egotistical nationalism, the violation of religious tolerance, servitude to the fact, and the idolatrous worship of the idea of state majesty and might, which identifies the nation and the state power with the absolute principle and subordinates to them even the Church.[19] Solovyov's preeminent virtue was truly that of fairness, both as public figure and as thinker. But this fairness was not the legal justice of the Old Testament, barren of grace; it was not the Roman juridical *suum cuique;*[20] it was rather a Christian, joyful appreciation of all and reverent attention to everything that in manifold and various images shows forth the single God-human Image that glorifies the Father of many mansions with his multifarious gifts and powers:[21] Solovyov's fairness was his living icon-veneration.

But if rational consciousness means to be conscious of positive unity, or, by the same token, to contemplate divine all-unity, its new level signifies only a revelation of the truth about the Church in a new image that corresponds to the complicated and differentiated visage of modern culture. His doctrine about the true correlation of abstract principles, or their universal justification, is not only an epistemological but also a mystagogical introduction to his doctrine of godmanhood, or, by the same token, to his doctrine of the restoration of humanity and nature in their divinity by means of the free reunification of all the world's moving forces in the living sum of Christ's Body.[22]

V

The Church has no body, except in the sacraments (*Ecclesia non habet corpus, nisi in mysterio*).[23] Although these words do not belong to Vladimir Solovyov, I do not think that he would dispute the essence of this formulation if he heard it. I, for my part, pronounce it inasmuch as, if I became convinced of Solovyov's disagreement with it, I would not be able to speak of his teaching from the standpoint of one who shares his views.

The invisible union of souls comprises the developing, divine-human body. God alone sees who, in this sense, does and does not belong to the Church. For membership in the Church is an essential membership, not a phenomenal one, and external proofs do not have decisive significance here. True, there are negative criteria that bear witness to a lack of full consciousness, or its lack of truth, such as would seem incompatible with the activity of the Spirit, which bestows grace and vivifies all the members of the divine body. Thus, the inability to confess Christ is an indication to the faithful that warns them against communing in prayer and sacrament with those who reject the Word. But this indication serves only to guide the faithful in their earthly being, so that they might avoid the temptations of the world and preserve undesecrated the vessels of the Spirit that have been entrusted to them. The Church is the mystery of universal love and free unity in Christ.

It was not the study of Church history that led Vladimir Solovyov to his pure catholicity,[24] in which there is no separation between East and West; it was rather his full apprehension of the mystical truth about the Church. The history of the external events that condition the visible separation served only to confirm the universal feeling that was given in the inner experience of his personality; and it was only concern for the correct paths of collective [*sobornyi*] national life, the mysterious call to "fulfill all righteousness,"[25] and not at all the need to escape his personal emotional conflicts, that compelled the author of *Theocracy* and the book on *Russia and the Universal Church* to act toward the formal reunification of the churches.[26] But it is clear that this historical, concrete aspect of the problem gradually lost for him the urgency of its original formulations, and "The Short Tale of the Antichrist" shows that in the depths of his soul, Solovyov valued the historical features of the confessional types of Christian consciousness, the separation of which will continue, according to the "Tale," until the completion of the fullness of time.[27]

On the other hand, analyzing history as the process of achieving divine humanity, a process that unites God's children on the Earth and the Earth itself into the single divine Body of the Woman clothed in the Sun,[28] Vladimir Solovyov could not fail to attribute positive value to all the moments of this development in which he saw consistent realizations of the uniting and organizing principle; hence his doctrine about the triad of energies (the sacerdotal, regal, and prophetic) in the historical formation of free theocracy, and also, in accordance with this triad, the affirmation of the earthly ecclesiastical hierarchy, state authority, and theurgic activity.[29] This provides a profound and harmonious scheme that is reduced (once again through a concern for the true paths of *sobornost'*, a concern that this time seems to me excessive) to the justification in principle of historically given states that are infinitely far from the ideal goal charted by the philosopher, and even to such an idealized picture of the state in which it appears as nothing other than "organized pity."[30] What is more, the subject of this pity, apparently the sum of citizens, inevitably coincides with its object, and the state appears as a collective that is called to pity itself. But these apologetic excurses à la Hegel into the realm of historical reality (which here are a less than successful application of Schopenhauerian ethics, based on the solidarity of compassion,[31] to the philosophy of law) do not obscure his crystal-clear conception of the Church. However Solovyov might have imagined the links in the chain of theocratic evolution, he was capable of distinguishing preparatory steps from real mystical realizations of the coming theocracy. Otherwise, the teacher would bear responsibility for the fatal confusion of the awaited kingdom with this world, which lies in evil.[32]

VI

Vladimir Solovyov's ecclesiastical consciousness was so vital and active that he drew from it the entire content of his philosophizing. It also served him as an epistemological principle, although initially he was not fully aware of this new and as yet inchoate epistemology. It was present from the first as a kind of unconscious foundation for his entire thought. Vladimir Solovyov himself hardly seemed to know what to do with epistemology; only at the end of his life did he undertake studies in this realm, studies that were to remain unfinished.[33] Meanwhile, the answer was present from the outset.

Allow me to use a comparison. Man, as creature, is conscious of his cognitive dependence on some external reality, and he seems to himself to be similar to a living mirror.[34] All that he cognizes is a mirror reflection subject to the law of the refraction of light, and, consequently, it is an unfaithful reflection. In this reflection, the right side becomes the left, and the left becomes the right. The connection and proportionality of the parts remain the same, but the parts switch places. The projection of the reflected body onto a surface does not match the original figure, even though the lines are combined in the same order. How can truth be restored to the reflection? Through its secondary reflection in a mirror pointed at the mirror. For man as cognizer, this *speculum speculi* (the second mirror that corrects the first)

195

is another man. Truth is justified only when contemplated in another. Where two or three are gathered in the name of Christ, there, among them, is Christ Himself.[35] Thus, faithful cognition of the mystery of being is possible only in mystical communion, i.e., in the Church.

Contemporary philosophy, with its desire to be rigorous and scientific,[36] seeks to limit itself to the realm of the theory of knowledge. This is its obligation even more than its right. As a result of neo-Kantian research, the subject of cognition (which is what the personality has been reduced to) sees itself as locked in a continuous circle. All that is within the magic circle is relative; all that is beyond the circle is undefined datum. But woe if the enchanted ring be broken in an arbitrary fashion: transferred into life, epistemological relativism turns into ontological meonism.[37] It is to be desired that this process of settling final accounts with the nature of the abstract personal consciousness might end as soon as possible. In this way, the study of the authenticity of isolated cognition, enclosed in the empirical "I," the study of the objectivity of the norms it posits and the values it affirms, might achieve extreme acuteness and arrive at last at its final, negative conclusion, which will most likely coincide with the hypothesis of the Hellenic Sophist Gorgias: "there is no being; even if there were, it would be beyond cognition; even if it were subject to cognition, it would be inexpressible and incommunicable."[38] It is impossible to live according to such an epistemology; the ring of the isolated consciousness cannot be broken except through an act of our suprapersonal will.

In practical life, this act is accomplished each time my love utters to another "thou art," dissolving my own being in the being of this "thou." An act of love, of love alone, positing the other not as an object but as a second subject, is an act of faith and will, an act of life, an act of salvation, a return to the Mother who bore both of us (my "I" and my "thou") in her womb, and participation in the mystery working of the World Soul that weaves the single living fabric of the universal body. Only here does another, higher consciousness awake within us, in comparison to which my former consciousness, imprisoned within the small "I," begins to seem a nasty and false dream. Here begins the Church and her comprehension in the personality. Only when philosophy completes this path, when it exhausts the entire content of abstract individuality and exposes the irreality and irrationality of its *ratio,* will humanity mature to knowledge in the Church. Only then will people understand the philosophical significance of Vladimir Solovyov, who, as if naturally imbued with the power of universal Logos, knew no other kind of knowledge.

VII

Armed with the logical energy of the Church, Vladimir Solovyov did not limit himself to an immediate revelation of the meaning of life but also turned with unprecedented daring to the final problems of the individualistic pathos.

He exposed the untruth of an individualistic formulation that turns the postulates of these final problems into abstract principles, and he restored the
radiant truth of these problems in the illumination of positive all-unity, as
the truth of the Church. I have in mind the problem of superhumanity, the
truth of which Solovyov not only acknowledged, in the aforementioned sense,
but even affirmed, as a true presentiment of the coming fulfillment in the
divine-human universal kingdom.[39] Moreover, insofar as Vladimir Solovyov
saw the criterion of true superhumanity as victory over death, this problem
serves as the focus of all his theories. According to Solovyov, individual fear
of death is cowardice and madness, but irreconcilability to the fact of the
death of our fathers, our loved ones, and our future descendants is a noble
and morally obligatory stimulus for all our life action.[40] "Call death out to a
fatal battle,"[41] this is a call to the greatest labor. But only a banner carrying
the inscription "in this shall you conquer" assures victory in this unequal
battle.[42] Closely tied to the question of man's victory over death, as the reverse side of a single mystery, is the question of the meaning of love. Perhaps no one after Plato has offered such profound and vital words on love
and sex as Vladimir Solovyov, who crowned the former and restored the human dignity and divine-human purpose of the latter,[43] who glorified the
"roses that rise above the black earth" and blessed the "roots thrust deep
into the dark womb."[44] For love also—O, for love most of all!—the final task
and third mysterious and greatest labor, is the overcoming of death. . . .[45]

But let us not dwell on these elevated theories and prophetic intuitions, just as the theurgist himself, whose sublime shadow abides among
us, summoned by the tremor of our love and the yearning of our mortal
separation, refused to dwell for long on distant matters that did not seem to
him to be immediately, essentially necessary for the education of contemporary generations. Truly, he was a toiler and he toiled at the Lord's work.
Inspired toil is not perceived by the toiler as work. And, if Solovyov spoke
of work, he, of course, meant above all that ascetic and tragic labor in which
one abstains from freely giving in to contemplative inspirations. In this labor,
we see the greatest sacrifice of Vladimir Solovyov the man to the historico-
universal principle. Despite the beauty of his transparent and harmonious
word, despite the abundance of the purely poetic and artistic element
sprinkled throughout his works, despite the wealth of hints that allow a
glimpse of the supreme mysteries to those who have been given the gift of
perceiving and guessing these significations, I still see the sum of his works
as a compendium of didactic arguments and instructions that above all pursue an edifying purpose and achieve their relative accessibility at the cost of
leaving unsaid highly significant things that, if revealed, would present their
creator's power of genius in resplendent magnificence.

And this is precisely why Vladimir Solovyov's poetry has acquired an
invaluable significance. His sonorous poems were mere drafts, sometimes

left without final artistic polish, but they were always exquisitely profound, true, intimate, and, at the same time, essentially new. The hints of which I spoke are wrapped in even thicker veils but veils that are woven as if from the transparent fabric of moonlight. They are distributed more generously, and they speak with truly prophetic daring in their own symbolic language about hidden Isis.[46] These poems are models of pure realistic Symbolism, which, as Solovyov's muse shows, has essentially nothing in common with the solemn pose of a hierophant.

I am not speaking of the external techniques of verbal depiction that are also called Symbolism, such as the verse: "a gray fog hung over the precipices of aimless wandering."[47] This verse, while depicting a mountainous locale that surrounds the untiring traveler, simultaneously and involuntarily casts a vivid representation of the poet's own image, with his introverted gaze, gaunt cheeks, and prematurely graying locks of luxurious curls, overhanging a high, clear forehead. But Solovyov is a Symbolist in another sense: he sketches what he sees and experiences, be it a fleeting landscape that once glimmered in the distance like the shore of Troy, or a meeting with white spring flowers that grew out of the graves, or the suddenly intuited presence of the shadows of departed loved ones that is brought by the west wind, or the shudder that marks the desired arrival of the mysterious Lady.[48] Solovyov is a realist who invents nothing, and at the same time a Symbolist, for everything in nature and in his soul trembles with the hidden life that breathes close to him, giving notice of that which is, which is half-concealed by the veils of the divine symbolics of the visible world.

Solovyov's significance as poet of heavenly Sophia, the Idea of Ideas, and of the World Soul that reflects Sophia like a mirror, is also determined by the fruits of his poetical works: in his poetry, he initiated an entire movement, perhaps even an epoch in Russian poetry. When the Eternal Feminine is summoned, a certain god leaps like a child in the womb of the World Soul;[49] and then the singers begin to sing. Thus, it was after Dante, thus, in the person of Novalis, was it after the poet who uttered: "Das Ewig-Weibliche zieht uns hinan."[50] Moreover, as a teacher, Vladimir Solovyov found words that opened the eyes of poets and artists to their true and supreme calling: Solovyov defined art as theurgical service.[51]

But more significant and more holy than all his other deeds was the self-determination of our national soul that spoke through him. While he is usually seen as abolishing Slavophilism, he only cleansed our old tradition of belief in our national calling, rooting out the falsehood of nationalist tendencies, since nationalism is an abstract principle, i.e., alienated from universal Truth. But he preserved faith in the national soul as a living reality, and in our special providential calling, and he lost nothing of this heritage. Through Dostoevsky, the Russian nation became conscious of its idea in a psychic way (that is, in the activity of the World Soul), as the idea of all-humanity. Through Solovyov, the Russian nation became conscious of its calling in a logical way (that is, through the activity of the Logos), the calling to serve the principle of the universal Church even if this entails the loss of its national soul. When the awaited kingdom nears, when the dawn of God's City begins to break, the chosen and faithful of the City will recall Solovyov as one of their prophets.

Lev Tolstoy and Culture

I

Lev Tolstoy's departure from home and, soon thereafter, from life,[1] was the double, step-by-step emancipation of his completed personality, a double liberation that elicited a reverent tremor in millions of hearts. "Whoever strove untiringly we are able to free": thus sang the heavenly spirits over Faust's remains.[2] It seemed that this last cry of unflagging human aspiration was followed by an exclamation of someone offering a greeting in response, as if from beyond the world's bounds. These two sounds—the earthly and tortuous, and the transcendent and triumphal—gave a vague echo in myriad emotional labyrinths that created an event of the instant contact and concord of countless souls in a single "amen."

Of course, the essence of this universal event remains obscure. What was it? Was it the delight of the world's spectators at witnessing the last sigh of a tragic protagonist who has played his role well? *Lusi, plaudite. . . .*[3] Or, like the toll of a solemn bell, was it the momentary sound of a single word in a nonhuman language, perhaps the only word of his part that the hero's immortal personality does not renounce even at his final emancipation— the word "good"? For it is only when the word is heard from beyond the bounds of relative being that it does not seem to us to be a "spoken lie."[4] . . . "Why do you call Me good? No one is good, only God."[5]

Is the meaning of this universal event, therefore, that an instant plebiscite of humanity suddenly affirmed the concept of absolute value—and, of course, only for an instant; that the misty shrouds of our limited, isolated consciousness were suddenly pierced by the ray of another consciousness, which in the future will be disclosed as the consciousness of the universal Church, and that a certain "yes" or "amen" automatically broke from all lips in response? Or is this only the voice of "the blind hopes sown in our hearts,"[6] Prometheus's guiding deceit? . . . Whatever the case may be, the delight the spectators felt at the fifth act was authentic, i.e., "cathartic" delight.[7] And, despite all the doubts of our skepticism, does tragic "cleansing" itself not express that very same unconscious "yes," that same willful affirmation of absolute value?

In any case, this was the meaning of Tolstoy's entire "sermon," as it was called. He set the Gorgon's head of a single value or the single name of "the good" (which was for him also the name of God) in opposition to all the values that we recognize both in theory and in practice, in order to expose their relativity and thus devalue them.

If we exclude from consideration immediate disciples of their mentor's letter, who are few in number and weak with the infirmity of the dead letter, hardly a single one of Tolstoy's instructional tenets is accepted in our day or will subsequently be accepted by a significant number of people.[8] Even if one allows that the doctrine of nonresistance and nonaction contains a ferment of great destructive power and may become the slogan of a worldwide neoanarchist movement, it is difficult to imagine that this testament could be assimilated in the same logical and psychological connection in which Tolstoy perceived it, as the result of his religious and moral searchings.[9] But throughout this thinker's intellectual work, there is a "stable pole of circulating phenomena":[10] the dogmatic and pragmatic affirmation of a single and absolute norm. As such, this will be silently accepted by everything that is not "underground" in man.

And even if we dare to acknowledge that Tolstoy said nothing else and was unable to determine this absolute value but only confessed it with the entire life of his word and the entire breath of his life, we will perhaps have acknowledged the one thing that best corresponds to his profoundest truth and was most desirable to his immortal will.

II

In truth, he most of all desired and even demanded from himself and from those who listened to him untiring efforts of liberation, which he knew only in its negative form as baring, exposing, and simplifying, as the stripping of all veils and coverings, the removal of all relative and incidental accretions and features.[11] An artist of the word, he constantly emancipated himself from the power of this very word, just as he was a visionary of the human soul and the soul of nature yet sought independence from psychology.[12] He was fated to undergo an ascetic labor of slowly killing the living membranes and coverings of breathing flesh and, moreover, exhausting in an almost suicidal way the dark Psyche drawn to his dear flesh.

Thus, like Odysseus sailing past the island of those singing enchantresses, the Sirens, he rejected art. And soon the tempting melodies began to dissipate in the empty spaces far beyond the rudder's wake. They became indiscernible, losing their charm and almost fading entirely. "The Kreuzer Sonata," this logical consequence of *Anna Karenina*, shows how he tore himself from the charms of sex and, at the same time, from the element of music;[13] it shows him killing a sacred possession—that of love and femininity, violently liberating himself from tender binds, and failing to bestow a blessing as he parted from and blasphemously abandoned the murdered body of a life that had hardly stopped breathing.

From the very beginning, Tolstoy bore within himself sacerdotal murder and fanatical suicide, revolt, division, and the desert. The desert grew within him, according to Nietzsche's image;[14] but he still heard God in the desert. He was a lion of the desert and tortures of the flesh were unable to satisfy his spiritual hunger.[15] When he turned his face toward life, he found only words of prohibition. Like an angry lion, he forbade others to satisfy their cravings with their natural prey.

Man ascends to God by various paths, and man's mental image and sign differ from his visible appearance. Tolstoy's outward meekness and infantlike simplicity concealed the great wrath of a proud spirit. His inability to act issued less from timidity than from a leonine inertia in initiative and slowness in rising. And where could he even go from his earthly cage? He was left to measure his cage back and forth with leonine steps, counting the iron barbs of life (as a monk counts his prayer beads), each of which was cursed with a meek prohibition: "do not drink," "do not smoke," "reject sensuality," "do not curse," "do not make war," "do not resist evil," and so on.

The goal was to liberate the personality from the law of life; the psychological basis of this aspiration was *taedium phaenomeni*,[16] an indistinct yearning, and, most of all, a squeamish disgust aroused by phenomena, especially the phenomena of human, nonnatural life. This disgust was not aroused by the static nature of the phenomenon, its constant and faithful composition, which has an unfailing rhythm but no forward motion. Rather its source was the phenomenon's dynamism and efforts to produce something new, the creative fertility of the phenomenon, this inexhaustible and always unforeseen productivity of the many-headed Hydra, these indomitable conceptions of passionate will, this indefatigable idol making of a spirit seeking to be made incarnate.

Tolstoy's inability to celebrate the multiplicity of incarnations corresponded to his hypertrophied normative sense, for his willful affirmation of the very basis of being remained powerfully alive. He wanted only to extinguish life with life "in accordance with God's will," "in good," by the morality of simplification, i.e., by decomposing complex forms into their simple elements: then the profound feeling of vital being truly turned into the feeling of a desert hearkening to God.[17] This could have given rise to a powerful contemplative mysticism, but the extraordinary, elementary vitality of his emotional and bodily organism directed this energy toward practical, incidental matters, *parerga*, which he mistook for work, *ergon*;[18] toward the external path of Martha instead of the internal path of Mary.[19] Thus, his vitality elicited only the monotonous, undifferentiated growth of an inward personality that had pushed up powerfully and blindly, like the exposed trunk of a palm tree. Above all else, "to live according to God's will" meant for Tolstoy to live the paradoxical life of a man who has turned from the countenance of life, to live upward, baring oneself and stripping the veils, higher than the law of life, into the realm of empty freedom, into the realm of a pure "Yes" to absolute being.

III

The primal basis of Tolstoy's personality contained *odium generationis,* which is the resistance to the principle of life that engenders forms, the nonacceptance of Dionysus, or rather the nonacceptance of the world in Dionysus. This gave rise to a peculiarly dichotomous self-consciousness, most of all in Tolstoy the artist, who was closely followed by his double, Tolstoy the judge.

Homer's every epithet and verb is a naive "yes" to things and actions, however they may be and simply because they are; in contrast, each image of Tolstoy the epic poet casts a shadow of negation onto the blank walls of his inner, unapproachable fortress, where his hungry and fierce spirit had shut itself up. After each word of this rhapsody, one hears the echo of a pessimistic "no," like the murmur of distant strings. In his similes, Homer's admiration of things sometimes condenses to create extensive pauses in the narration, thereby allowing for a full admiration of both phenomenon and the other object of the simile; so also the force of Tolstoy's criticism and protest demands digressions of an abstractly rational and generalized form (which conflicts with the very principle of living variety) in order to underscore and expose the futility, falsehood, and sad illusoriness of phenomena.

The pathos of Tolstoy the artist is primarily that of disclosing and exposing; inwardly it is therefore an antinomical and an essentially antiartistic principle. For an artistic genius is called to reveal the noumenal in the clothing of the phenomenon. Moreover, the energy of artistic symbolism does not wish to leave intellectual essences of the spiritual world only incompletely incarnated, nor to push them beyond the limits of incarnation; instead, it wishes to present them in a transfigured incarnation, as if in resurrected flesh that is at the same time the most real flesh and the actual essence itself. Tolstoy, the antipode of Dostoevsky, was not an artist who *manifests the truth,* which is the natural state of an integral and happy artist, a creator of masks that are transfigured instead of "decaying." Neither was he a Symbolist artist, who knows that God wants life and that life can encompass God, despite the declaration of one of our contemporary poets: "God does not want life, and life does not want God. . . ."[20]

But Tolstoy was also free of the tragedy that develops on this basis for the symbolic worldview: the tragedy of a conflict between the countenance of Aldonza and the countenance of Dulcinea.[21] He was utterly ignorant of the latter, and he only wanted to instruct Aldonza, to correct her and make her a good and virtuous woman, notwithstanding all her simplicity and lack of intelligence: the moralist within the poet simply sought to enslave the artist.

IV

Though it distracted the artist from his natural task—the noumenology of phenomena—Tolstoy's critique of world phenomenology formed the basis of his religiosity, which could be defined in its root as a negative religiosity.[22] It also created his "faith," which many consider to have displayed Buddhist tendencies but which Tolstoy himself seems to have considered to be correct and healthily conceived Christianity. Yet it is hardly fair to ignore the profound ontologism of Tolstoy's faith, if Buddhism is understood (as it often is) as an aspiration to liberate the personality and the world not only from the fetters of incarnation, but even from being itself. On the other hand, the Christian, New Testament self-determination of religious will (and its progress with respect to the Old Testament principle of ascent from the world)[23] is distinguished by its will to a graced and transfiguring descent from God into the world; to the restoration and justification of the earth in God; to the resurrection of the flesh; and to the mystical marriage of the heavenly Bridegroom with the earthly Bride. Insofar as this will is the distinctive feature of Christianity, Tolstoy's worldview seems infinitely far from Christianity and the Christian Church, understood not as a confessional community, but as a sacramentally realized gathering of souls in Christ into a single, divine-human Body.

These same emotional and intellectual traits distance Tolstoy from the pole of our national self-determination that represents the thesis or affirmation of our national soul as a mystical essence. They draw him toward the pole of antithesis, of unbelief in the supraempirical reality of national being. The antagonism of these opposing tendencies is signified by the old slogans of Slavophilism and Westernism, which we understand in such a way that Vladimir Solovyov, for example, would be counted as a Slavophile, insofar as Russia existed for him as a living soul and fate, and the call he addressed to Russia to lose her soul is a condition and testament of its rediscovery.[24] Historically, Tolstoy seems not to fit into this antagonism, but essentially he stands among the ranks of the Westernizers.[25] However, Tolstoy's Westernism did not seek to merge with Europe, as earlier Westernizers had before him; rather, in Tolstoy, the Russian national genius extended a hand to America. Tolstoy's spiritual teaching shares features with Anglo-Saxon preaching. America's wide expanses recognize as their own such an affirmer of life and, at the same time, devaluer of old values as Whitman; they would also recognize as their own the negator and devaluer

Tolstoy: he needs virgin, fertile soil that is open to all on equal terms, free from historical tradition and old, ancestral culture and all "unnecessary memories," in the words of Goethe, who praised America since "it was not disturbed in living time by futile memory and vain battle."[26]

Tolstoy is not a direct expression of our national element; he is more a product of our cosmopolitan culture, of our social elite, than our national depths. This explains his attraction to simplification; for the original simplicity of the national worldview strives to develop its content into a certain complexity by way of religious, artistic, or practical creativity, if only it does not first sacrifice its own content for another, more complex content, borrowed from without. At the same time, Tolstoy's individualistic fortress of personal self-determination led him along the boundary of populism, without permitting him to cross this boundary. He wanted to grow close to the people only in order to develop an independent type of life according to the proddings of his conscience and the aesthetic preferences of his pure, exacting, even partially satiated taste. But if this is so, it is necessary to analyze Tolstoy's significance as a question of culture, not as an elemental force.

V

The humanists considered Greco-Latin antiquity to be the ideal type of a culture that is comprehensive and internally complete within its own bounds, and they thought that it anticipated and predetermined many phenomena of modernity in simple and perfect forms. If this view is just, is it not permissible to see the problem of moral consciousness that is signified for us by the name of Lev Tolstoy as the Socratic moment of modern culture?[27]

Although the analogy between Tolstoy and Socrates is untenable in some respects and is especially unsuited for measuring the historical significance of our artist, we believe that it is fruitful in one sense: it helps us to understand this phenomenon in the context of the needs of the epoch we are experiencing.

The latter half of the fifth century B.C. was a time in the Hellenic world when the suddenly enfeebled forms of religious life suffered necrosis, and when the recent, synthetic faith broke down into elements of morality, aesthetics, theoretical thought, mysticism, and the traditions of state and custom. This was a time when the cultural composition disintegrated, when the entire heritage of the organic epoch was rationalized, and spiritual values underwent a general, critical review; it was a time of incipient rootlessness and philosophical relativism.[28]

Hence arose Socrates' "I know that I know nothing";[29] hence he undertook the epistemological and ethical verification of all aspects of the culture of his day and of all the available theoretical points of view that provided the bases for both the general and personal worldview and for cultural activity.

His goal was to expose universal blindness and unawareness, which were combined with the illusion of seeing and understanding. This presupposed an original allowance that knowledge held primacy over creativity; but doubts about knowledge subsequently caused a turn toward life.

By separating the sphere of pure cognition from the sphere of ignorance concerning that which truly is—and in which life moves—the Eleatics safeguarded, so to speak, the self-regulation of human creativity. But with the splitting of the connection between absolute and illusory being, between truth and the world of "opinion" (*dóxa*), thought could not but take fright in the labyrinth of its own freedom, where everything had become arbitrary, illusory, and false. The god of the holy rite had departed, but his universal role-playing continued: this was already madness and devilishness. It was necessary to revolt against instinct and save knowledge for life by sacrificing knowledge in its essence. If there was not a more real divinity outside of life's natural creative instinct, which had created the divinity's obscured images in people's "opinions," it was necessary to seek the divine within the norms of rational consciousness, to divinize logical capacities and elicit objective moral norms from human self-determination. Morality was to serve as a means for taming the chaos of a life abandoned by the gods.[30] Man's craving for real knowledge made him a moralist. It was necessary to choose between wealth and madness, or poverty and reason: Socrates chose poverty and reason. For whoever says "know good and evil" cuts the roots out from under the tree of life.[31]

Tolstoy's worldview is distinguished by the same conviction in the futility of scientific, metaphysical, and even mystical intuition into the essence of things and into the essence of divine being; by the same disavowal of the creative and instinctual principle of life; by the same faith in the rationality of good, in its coincidence with the only knowable truth, and therefore by the same belief that it is possible to teach the good and that it is incomplete and vague knowledge that causes people to deviate from the paths of the good; by the same view that morality and religion are identical; and by the same choice between creativity and morality, a choice decided in favor of the moral organization and, therefore, the impoverishment of life. The circumstances of a primarily analytical epoch gave rise to Tolstoy's worldview as a partial reaction (in contrast to Socrates' fundamental reaction) against the relativity of any cognition and against the objectively religious rootlessness of moral values that was proclaimed by the leading minds of the nineteenth century.

VI

Both Socrates' and Tolstoy's personalities shone forth in forms that present a striking, yet elusive peculiarity or paradoxicality: this is the Socratic "incommensurability" or eccentric "absurdity" (*atopía*), which so delighted those who were enamored of the mysteriously ironic debunker of ancient riddles from Athens, the "demonic" righteous man of his disciples. Moreover, Socrates' admirers did not mean by this the substance of the Socratic teaching, which at first glance seemed crystal clear. We who analyze the phenomenon from our customary points of view are immediately struck by the fundamental irrationality of this rationalistic morality.

Most incomprehensible in Tolstoy's sermon is his neglect and, as it were, misunderstanding of all the factors that determine the personality, such as heredity, psychophysical idiosyncracies, peculiarities and anomalies, the influence of the social environment, upbringing, and so on. How could this abstract and generalized moral doctrine, especially this belief in the coincidence of the good with correct knowledge, coexist with the poetic insight of a man who described humanity and chronicled life, who made a special study of the soul and its affects? Could Tolstoy really think that one has only to take proper account of what the good is in order to become not only a morally conscious personality but even a personality that is morally consistent in its actions? . . . But Socrates thought the same way, and he was, according to Pythia, "the wisest of men."[32] . . . This is the *credo quia absurdum*[33] of rationalism as a moral pathos.

Of course, a moralist naturally resorts to the pedagogical technique of allowing or, if you will, insisting that the personality possesses the immediate fullness of its free self-determination, whether or not he himself essentially believes in the real tenability of this premise. But Tolstoy, like Socrates, presents us not with a pedagogical technique but with a profound belief in the integral freedom of the personality, moreover, not only in its metaphysical but also in its empirical freedom. Perhaps both thought that the cognitive process is, as it were, an act of dividing or separating the inner core of the human personality, of man's genuine self, away from the crust of his empirical being. Perhaps they thought that as soon as this spiritual trunk acquires the freedom of self-sufficient growth, the outer coverings would become powerless to restrain this growth, that they would fall from it as the skin shed by a snake, that they would change by themselves as they enveloped the changed emotional body. Man grows into the freedom of God from the law of life, just as a water lily raises its calyx above the dark waters. Thus does a personality become complete. This is the equivalent of positive religion in the pure morality of the Socratic type: this morality contains an affirmation of the noumenal reality of the inner self, or, as it is usually put, an affirmation of faith in the soul's immortality.

In the person of the Sophists, Greek society of Socrates' day taught, just as modern epistemologists teach today, that "even if there were pure being, it would be beyond cognition; even if it were subject to cognition, it would be beyond expression and communication,"[34] and that "man is the

measure of all things."[35] Then the Socratic apologetics of the absolute neu-
tralized the poison of these views by opposing to them something like their
own reflection in an altered form: "absolute being is both expressed by virtuous acts and cognizable through the sense of being free from the law of
life; the measure of things is not the human, only human, but the human
personality itself, removed from the law of life."

The progression of culture has led man to a consciousness of the relativity of all its values and of its own rootlessness. The Socratic moment of
culture is defined as an attempt to place the mirror of the inner personality
before the mirror of culture and life:

> The winged steed jumps to the abyss,
> The shield is raised up like a mirror,
> Seeing itself, the dragon is overthrown and
> And disappears forth into the chasm.
> (Vl. Solovyov, "The Three Labors")[36]

VII

The power of Tolstoy's sermon lies in the fact that he undertook a universal
trial of the values affirmed by people as such, which are therefore transitory
and dispensable, and of the values hypocritically affirmed in the name of
God, but which are actually only human and temporary. He demanded
commensurability to the absolute norm from all that he apprehended with
his gaze, which was perplexed wherever people had reached mutual understanding and was skeptical wherever people had agreed not to doubt.
Tolstoy also demanded wholeness from all who claimed to know the real
name of their idols, since Tolstoy supposed that the falsehood of any idol
could be exposed if one tried to affirm it in spiritual wholeness.

This universal verification of values was necessary in an age that worshiped the relative under the symbol of culture, which was understood as a
system of relative values. If Tolstoy's word did not affect us and was, so to
speak, wholly unheard by us; if we refused Tolstoy's challenge to take part
in this juridical competition, failing to recognize the very challenge as a profession of the absolute truth that Tolstoy was unable to call by its real name
but in whose name he imagined he was conducting a just trial; then we ourselves would place the seal of total nihilism on ourselves and on all our
work. Tolstoy was not a revaluer of values—his attempts at revaluation were
fruitless and his rules were without effect; but he was, however, a devaluer
of the relative, i.e., the godless. Speaking in a language that was equally
comprehensible to all, he said that it is impossible to live without God, that
one must and therefore can live in accordance with God's will.

From the religious-moral point of view, we distinguish three types of
conscious attitudes toward culture: the relativist, the ascetic, and the sym-

bolic. The first signifies the rejection of any religious foundation of culture (understood as a system of relative values). The second type (to which Tolstoy belongs) lays bare the moral and religious bases of cultural activity and contains a rejection of all cultural values of an artificial, relative, or irrational nature. This type inevitably leads to an attempt to subordinate the instinct, the play and arbitrariness of creativity to moral utilitarianism. It rests on a profound mistrust of the natural principle, on a lack of belief in the world soul, on a mechanistic understanding of nature, although it is inclined to point out the advantages of living "in accordance with nature" (*homologouménōs tēi fúsei zēn*), seeking to affirm in this way the identity of the "necessary" with the "useful" (*ōphélimon*) and the morally correct.

The third type of attitude toward culture is, in our opinion, the only healthy and correct one. However, the path it predetermines is one of difficulty and temptation, due to the constant accretions that the chaotic tide of life adds to the foundation of the temple that is being built, as well as to the constant danger of distortion and falsehood on the part of the builders themselves. This is the heroic and tragic path of emancipating the world soul. Those who know this path have sworn fidelity to the banner that signifies a decision to transform human culture through the continual efforts of generations into a coordinated symbolics of spiritual values, which is correlated to the hierarchics of the divine world; it signifies a decision to justify all humanly relative creativity by its symbolic correspondences to the absolute. In other words, this task is defined as the transfiguration of all culture, and of all nature together with it, into the mystical Church. Moreover, the principle of this work coincides with the theurgical principle. If the second type exhibits a natural inclination to iconoclasm (insofar as it overlooks the difference between idol and icon), the third type wholly affirms icon-veneration: for it, culture is being wrought as an icon of the Sophianic world of eternal archetypes.[37]

Tolstoy was not a Symbolist, and—in contrast to Socrates—was not a theurgist. Socrates was a theurgist insofar as he spiritually gave birth to Plato, antiquity's greatest representative of the symbolic justification of culture. Truly, Socrates paid heed to the voice he heard shortly before his death that ordered him to devote himself to music. This occurred in the last dialogues, which Plato took upon himself to reveal. In Plato, Socrates devoted himself to music.[38] This was achievable insofar as Socrates' teaching contained positive content and erotic inspiration. Socrates' sober establishment of concepts created the divinely intoxicated music of the world of Platonic ideas.

The Socratic moment of culture also marks a Socratic danger. In Hellas, we find a hint of it in Cynicism. True Socratism postulates Platonism. Lev Tolstoy is a *memento mori*[39] to modern culture, and a *memento vivere*[40] to the Symbolism that, exhorting the artist to ascend from the real to the most real (*a realibus ad realiora*), contains the force of faith to turn its face to worldly reality and, sending into this reality a doer and creator of life, bringing him down to the real after his wanderings in the world of higher realities (*ad realia per realiora*), to bid farewell with the reminder: let the lower be as the higher, and the real as the most real (*realia sicut realiora*).

Scriabin's View of Art

Not only in Russia but also in foreign lands, enlightened minds are gradually being convinced and confirmed in the view that, in the person of
Alexander Scriabin, who departed from us so prematurely, Music mourns
one of its main architects, and that the entire round dance of the Muses
mourns one of those artists whose ideas have marked an epoch in the history of art. Some people are able to discern even more: in their eyes, Scriabin's appearance is direct evidence of a turning point that is coming to pass
in the consciousness of humanity. I also feel that Scriabin's creative achievements and, to no less degree, his unfulfilled plans constitute a significant
event in the universal life of the spirit.

In what sense and within what limits do I affirm the importance of
this event? This is the question that circumspect people will ask before
agreeing with me; and they will do wisely, for full agreement with the answer I will sketch (and only sketch) below is possible only if our worldviews
share their most profound bases. On the other hand, those who have already
uttered in their souls a sympathetic "yes" to my assertion are also correct:
after all, if one accepts the first assertion—regarding the unique nature of
Scriabin's artistic labor—it is not at all difficult to admit, at least in part, the
justice of ascribing to Scriabin's task important meaning for universal culture.

Indeed, is it conceivable that one of the separate arts (which even in
their separation still remain facets of a single creative process) could witness a real shift without the other realms of creativity experiencing a corresponding and correlated displacement? If Music, this unmediated herald of
the heart's depths, begins to speak of something new and unprecedented in
a new and mighty tongue, is this not a sign that the very soul of the age is
giving birth to a new word out of the depths of its concealed will?[1] Is it
possible to deny such a mutual responsibility among all spheres of spiritual
activity, whereby any absolutely new discovery in one is necessarily accompanied, whether openly or covertly, by related changes in the others?

Scriabin himself not only knew this law, he was even inclined to extend the breadth and depth of its validity in a unique manner.[2] He believed that any outwardly manifested event is an expression of some inner act in the life of the world spirit. This act is realized in the spiritual activity of a few people. Their insights and decisions, their constructive work, which is invisible to the world at large, determine not only the general tendency of thought but all the destinies of the earth. In the final analysis, wars, civil turmoil, and even the elemental movements of natural forces depend on the suprapersonal vision and strength of will of nameless great ones, who might with equal justice be called either the chosen of universal will or—the doomed.

Scriabin had definite *presentiments* of himself as marked and, as it were, anointed for a great, universal task. Such a presentiment, which I would call the magnetism of his profound will, is essentially incapable of deceiving its bearer, even if, more often than not, it engenders deceptive ideas about the forms and paths of the expected action. This secret voice and this inner experience were, of course, not a proud invention; still less were they premeditated intention. The ambition of hungry pride and lustful arrogance clouds the soul and is unable to coexist with the childlike clarity, the joyful trust in life and people, that I observed in Scriabin and that I recognize as the distinctive and captivating mark of all true genius, of a spirit that is divinely abundant and consoled by its own plenitude. As a thinker has written concerning the consciousness of genius, a tall man cannot help but know that he is taller than others.[3] Scriabin's self-consciousness was just as unmediated; only in the soul of this born mystic, it was tempered by the sense of mystery, by the expectation of a calling that has not yet been fully comprehended. When such inner enlightenment and plenitude are revealed indiscreetly, when such faith is revealed ingenuously, they are not forgiven: the crowd will shout of the egotism, megalomania, and satanic pride of the chosen one:

> Look, here is an example for you!
> He was proud, could not live with us;
> The blind one wanted to assure us
> That God spoke through his mouth. . . .[4]

But we would be cruelly mistaken if we supposed Scriabin to have harbored the slightest arrogance or smugness. On the contrary, although the underlying harmony of his being was always preserved intact, his mood was constantly one of dissatisfaction and discontent with himself, a mood that was nourished precisely by his craving for the supreme accomplishments whose earthly tool he felt himself preordained to become; by his zealous drive to serve with all his will and understanding the goals of the suprapersonal, all-human principle, risking thereby the final annulment of his personality; and

212

by the passion of his faith and impulse and by his inability to stop short and reconcile himself to something relatively insignificant, a passion that can justly be numbered among his firm achievements and ultimate triumphs. Hence, in his emotional life, there arose the combination of inner majesty and humility (a combination that is contradictory yet so understandable to the living heart), and in the life of his spirit, there arose the combination of abundance and poverty, which Plato held to be the parents of Eros, who fused in himself the traits of both.[5] The sharper the experience of this discontent became, the more guarded was his expectation of decisive inner events, which, after annihilating his small "I," were to turn Scriabin into a living torch that was needed by an unseen hand in order to ignite the Phoenix fire of humanity. Humanity would be consumed by the flame and reborn as a new race of people, for a new consciousness and action.

What can one say about achievements if one observes the flight of an arrow that has been shot right over the visible horizon and disappears so far away that we are powerless either to encompass or to measure with our eye the distance that has buried it? Did those other great initiators, the architects of unfinished churches, achieve their goal? Did Fate really cut short the "Preliminary Act" of the coming *Mysterium*,[6] which Scriabin was creating when the Parcae cut the thread of his life?[7] In this case, we would be left only with the unfinished poetic text of the holy drama,[8] as well as with numerous sketches of musical themes for the drama that have been discovered, which are as incoherent as the mutterings of the dying Pythia as she was drowned out by the jealous god.[9] Is it true that all the rest, which was already hovering before the artist as a misty vision, was stolen away to the realm of visions, where, in the words of Pushkin, the fragrant shadows of dead flowers bloom above Lethe's waves? . . .[10] Or is all of this a mere illusion of our vision and understanding, while all the magic music of the second half of Scriabin's creative work is itself the "preliminary act," which leads us right up to the threshold of some *Mysterium*?[11] After all, the mystagogue's own plan held that the *Mysterium* should be neither his personal creation nor even a work of art but an inner event in the soul of the world, sealing both the fullness of the time that has come to pass and the birth of a new man.

Instead of measuring expanses transcendent to us, let us admire the powerful muscles of a giant archer who was able to pull so taut the string of his bow. And let us recognize that the very appearance of such an archer among us, and his penetrating eye's discovery of a distant goal that is invisible and perhaps incomprehensible to us, are sufficient testimony that within him there flared up a vision different than our own, a craving that is still foreign to us. This vision and craving, like any discovery of new truth or even like the correct formulation of a new problem, could not help but lend unique color to the entire sum of our searchings, could not fail to encounter unexpected and, perhaps, elusive correspondences and interrelated effects in all realms of spiritual life. This is true regardless of whether we consider the particular phenomenon of our study to be the cause of some general shift or merely one of the auxiliary manifestations of some general and supra-personal motive force.

II

This is why it is important to understand Scriabin's view of the meaning and significance of art. He did not want to be the votary of only one Muse, although it was precisely to her that he elevated his service to a most subtle spiritual labor and most pure consummate sanctity. But by this he merely affirmed the center from which, as if with a compass of fire, he charted his theurgic spheres, which gradually embraced first the entire expansive kingdom of the separated, but for him inseparable, arts, then the entire realm of the human spirit and then, ranging even further, as he desired and believed, embraced even our entire cosmic environment. As it was for the mythical Orpheus, Music was, for Scriabin, a first principle, moving and organizing the world. It was to blossom in the word and evoke images of varied and perfect beauty. It was to draw nature into its charmed circle and flow into the harmony of the spheres as a new chord. For if the World Soul exists—and it does exist; and if living Nature is alive—and it is alive, how could it fail to respond with a full-voiced "Amen" to humanity, which, having for the first time remembered, gathered, and become aware of itself, issued forth a collective [*sobornyi*] call, in accordance with the World Soul's will and in harmony with its torment? . . . Such was Scriabin's holy madness, the very madness that gives birth to everything that lives. For everything that is alive is born of ecstasy and madness! Such was the radiating energy of this solar artist, who forgot that he was only an artist, just as the sun, melting and flowing forth with its life-creating force, seems to forget that it is a celestial body and not a flood of liquid fire.

If Orpheus had been asked what he considered the calling of his art or of art as such, he would not have replied: "the inner, self-enclosed, self-sufficient perfection of my hymn, insofar as it has sounded forth and fallen silent, and of any plastic creation, insofar as it is frozen within and, as the poet said of a beautiful woman, 'rests delicately in her triumphant beauty.'"[12] He would have replied that his calling is: "the perfection of the whole that will be born of my hymn, if it is perfect." And if Orpheus's hymn failed to make the whole perfect, as an "exacting artist"[13] not in a human but in a divine sense, he would not be satisfied, he would not have been filled with the perfection of his hymn.

I have not mentioned the name of Orpheus in vain: Orpheus is a symbol not only of free art but of liberating art, which is free insofar as it liberates the captive world. For whoever is alive vivifies, and whoever is truly free liberates. Similarly, true art is not only free but liberating. The nature of any creation worthy to be called a work of art is mysterious. It is simultaneously creation—with respect to its creator, the artist—and self-creating, *natura naturata* and *natura naturans*.[14] It is not a stagnant product and not the stillborn offspring of freedom; rather, it multiplies the life that lies within it and, having multiplied life, radiates it into the world as an active force. Art is liberating but not always to the same extent and depth. There is more salvation for the artist in being ignorant like a child than in intuiting the essence and meaning of his labor: if Orpheus had not known that he was leading Eurydice from the kingdom of darkness, he would not have looked back at the shadow of his beloved and, having looked back, would not have lost her. But Orpheus's art was liberating to such a profound degree that he was no longer able to remain ignorant of himself and his task. When artists ascended to a considerable height on the way to the summits of theurgy (i.e., art that achieves the transfiguration and transformation of life), the secret of their path was unveiled before their eyes: then they were pierced by the suddenly resurrected memory of the One Woman, whom Orpheus called Eurydice: with tremor and enamored torment they turned their gaze back, toward the abyss of nonbeing, whence there arose behind them the Life-bearing Beauty that they were leading out of the darkness. Thereupon, their magic power abandoned them, and they remained on this side of the theurgic threshold. . . . Such has been the fate of the noble artist up to now.

III

The religious veneration of the singer and demigod Orpheus was tied to the earliest recognition of the supreme tasks of the art that the Hellenes called (after the Muses) "musical," by which they meant the indivisible couple, Poetry and Music, together with their mentor, Dance, who though apparently their younger sister was actually their elder. This primordial sense of the world-constructing power of art was inextricably linked to the entire mythological worldview of antiquity. In the earliest speculations, it corresponded to a belief in the musical basis of the universe.[15] We are not speaking here of art's transfiguring effect on the world, in the sense of the final hopes for an all-reconciling harmony that developed on the soil of the Christian experience of the ages: after all, the world is still only being formed, and the cosmogonic and anthropogonic age of maturity had not yet been achieved. But the world is formed by the singing of the heavenly Muses. This is why the God who is the chorus leader of the Muses was also the leader of the Fates (Musagetes was Moiragetes).[16] This was the dawn of humanity, and prophetic calls sounded from afar like the morning horns of hunters who were disappearing beyond the rose-colored border of the for-

215

est. Now, by contrast, prophetic calls are like antiphonal horns sounding at dusk across the oak groves, announcing the time to gather and return home.

The heavenly Muses themselves directed the movement of the spheres and accomplished, in the correlations of universal forces, the victory of the "new gods" over the "ancient" ones, the victory of the light-bearing cosmos over blind chaos. At the same time, the art of the mortals they inspired addressed the most immediate theurgic task: to overcome chaos by creating order within man. This art established an intimate, free, and correct connection between man and the multiform living forces of other worlds; it gathered people into well-wrought cities where the eternal charter of subterraneous Truth was blessed by the dances of the rose-crowned Graces; it used rhythm and melody to heal the infirmities of the body and soul. It enchantingly subordinated everything around it to the measure of divine rhythms, which sounded in the transcendent golden temple, at the invisible hearth of the universe. According to Plato's comparison, when people succumbed to its mellifluous coercion, they became luminous and moved along the dark earth as majestically and harmoniously as the celestial lights in the expanses of the night sky.[17]

If we were to ask ourselves how this archaic ideal of art was realized in life, we would have to admit that in its holy language of myth and symbol, it correctly described not only the psychology of national being but even the very forms of historical reality. Religion filled all of life; it was life itself, not a realm of "regulative ideas" lying outside of life (Kant's barbarism fully corresponds to the prosaic nature of the concept he defined!).[18] For its part, art was an essential part of religion itself. Perhaps it was only in legend that the walls of seven-gated Thebes formed themselves out of stone blocks, obedient to the magic lyre of Amphion;[19] perhaps it was only in legend that internecine conflict suddenly subsided in Lacedaemon at the first sounds of Terpander's seven-stringed cithara.[20] However, it was not in legend but in real life that there appeared musical-ritual civic construction and legislation, musical-prophetic possession and rapture, healing by means of music and dance (an almost daily occurrence), the evolution of verse out of incantation, which was capable of binding the will of the gods through its form and rhythm, and, finally, the "syncretic rite" of time immemorial, in which religious-practical goals dictated the need to present simultaneously all the musical arts and other artistic skills (such as acting and the first achievements in the forms and colors of representational arts) that later separated and in separation lost the fullness of their active force.

True, for a long time already each art had sought to perfect itself and refine itself according to its inner laws and within its isolated sphere, distancing and liberating itself from service to the religious whole, becoming secularized. And, on the whole, the entire cultural history of Hellenism presents a spectacle of the gradual dismemberment and secularization of the unified, integral composition of theurgic religion. Individual secular schools of philosophy owe their origin to this very phenomenon. The Ionic bards of the national epos, who began, in their first generation, with national-religious tasks, finished with a quest for pure depictive artistry. But early on, as a counterbalance to the Homerides, there arose the theurgic school of Hesiod. Hesiod was initiated into the bards by the Heliconian Muses in order to proclaim to people only the truth concerning the mysteries of the gods to-gether with the charters of eternal Truth, in contrast to the "other singers," i.e., the Homerides, who "lied much" and merely amused the people with their beautiful deceptions.[21]

Notwithstanding the partial defection from religion of certain artistic movements, one can say that until the final decades of the fifth century B.C., Hellenic art, on the whole, was immersed in religion. Religion flowed in art like blood, and it lived like the soul in the body, tirelessly developing new forms that it itself needed, such as it were, to a great extent, the sacred drama and the heroic tragedy.

As concerns a theoretical view of the goals of art, until the age of the Sophists, no one thought to cast doubt on the foundations of the time-honored, collective [sobornyi] consciousness that we have described above. Plato, while meticulously distinguishing the positive and negative elements in art, based his justification of positive art wholly on the belief in miraculous "inspiration" or "madness," which is sent down on people by the gods and which makes them into tools of the tirelessly life-creating revelation of di-vine essences.[22] Aristotle was the first to undertake an independent, extra-religious grounding of aesthetics, but he also insisted on the healing and cleansing energies inherent in art, defining the goal of tragedy as the cura-tive cleansing of the soul, as a certain concretely understood medicine for the soul.[23] Ancient culture, which so frequently, especially in the Alexan-drian era, was, in a practical sense, inclined to superficial aestheticism, ul-timately failed to develop an ideology of pure, self-sufficient, and autotelic art. On the contrary, first pseudo-Longinus and then the Neoplatonists re-turned to the Platonic and theurgic theory of art.

IV

Throughout the Middle Ages, the dominant force was religion, which was understood narrowly in the kingdom of scholastics but more broadly and freely in the realm of art. To the limited extent that the Middle Ages pon-dered aesthetic theory, it was said that in the work of art matter breathes, is made transparent, and reveals to the gaze its divine nature.[24] Otherwise, in the words of Dante, who sought through his poem to lead humanity to a state of blessedness, the Middle Ages spoke of how divine "Love, which moves the sun and other stars,"[25] forces the artist to serve it and to reveal to people its secrets. In the eyes of Dante, Virgil was a theurgist, and the poet of *Paradise* himself is one of the heralds of the mystical Rose.

The Renaissance marked the complete secularization of art, the final sundering of the general cultural consciousness from the religious consciousness. True, here also theory lagged behind practice, and first it was necessary that the Platonism that had long reigned over thought fall into profound oblivion before art could feel that, within its own limits, it was finally free from all connections to the universal whole and from all obligations to it. But freedom from obligations also entailed a rejection of ancient rights and hereditary titles. By a wise irony of fate, the blossoming of the new psychology of individualism coincided with the theoretical dethroning of Man. When the personality first tried to affirm itself in autarchy, for the first time ever its excessive ambitions turned out to be ontologically groundless. The ancients concluded eternal pacts with the divinity as free and rightful beings before the face of Ever-Living God. Copernicus's discovery was taken to mean the utter destruction of an old anthropocentric prejudice, the view of man as the focus and goal of the universe. Yet the theurgic ideal is inevitably anthropocentric: how can Man continue the work of the creative All-Mother if he is not the son and heir of Nature's own Creator?

In the eighteenth century, after the rationalism of the Enlightenment era had cut all the living threads connecting tradition to artistic creation, there finally appeared a philosophical grounding of art, which was understood as being locked in a charmed and illusory circle. Art began to be seen as the most curious and captivating of phenomena, as a kind of phenomenon of phenomena. Kant discovered the "purposeless purposefulness" of art;[26] Mephistopheles, parodying Kant in the character of Faust, could cite here his image of a cat playing with its tail.[27] Following Kant, Schiller spoke of the "free play of living forces" as the universal meaning of art.[28] The theory of play struck a chord and was developed by the positivists and Spencer in a series of variations.[29] But in Kant's conception, this play was no light matter: it was important for him that, when left to itself, the isolated consciousness would illumine and crown its autonomous, but also self-enclosed, cut-off, dungeonlike, kingdom with the play of purposeless purposefulness, which was—it would seem—so similar to divine creativity. If the world is only representation; if the law of a personality immersed in this "datum" of phenomena is its moral self-determination; then art naturally remains *intra muros,* within the walls of human emotion, whence neither interaction nor even any communication with what earlier people knew as other worlds and suprasensible essences is possible.[30] In respect to its effect on life, when art was banished from the paradise of its regal dreams through the ivory gates of false dreams,[31] it received as its lot the noble task of "aesthetic education," which was a worthy decoration for its destitute state, and which Schiller, with his beautiful soul, zealously set out to proselytize.[32]

The thought of the overwhelming majority of our contemporaries still follows the channel we have described. Moreover, from time to time a well-meaning impulse encourages fanatics (whose fanaticism has made them barbarians, as often happens) to attempt to pull the Muses' winged steed to earth by the neck and subordinate art to personal or social morality, or even worse, to mere quotidian utility. This is always met by a just counteraction: art proudly declares its regional self-government or policy of nonintervention, and then it proclaims the other consequences of its legally recognized provincial liberty. Well-intentioned arbiters explain to the barbarians in intelligent and enlightened terms that they have misunderstood in their own barbaric fashion the fine task of "aesthetic education" that has been bestowed on art. When the defenders of "free art" reiterate their truism, they utterly fail to see that they are taking the concept of freedom in a purely negative sense and thereby demeaning their idol, devaluing their value. The positive affirmation of the freedom of art is an affirmation of its free efficacy, of one's faith in it as a liberating force. And this faith was alive even in Kant's age, in the soul of Goethe, in the soul of Schelling and the first Romantics of the Jena circle, and especially in the divinely inspired soul of the mystic Novalis, who brilliantly, but only intuitively, charted the doctrine of art's theurgic calling as the doctrine of restoring the long-dormant charms of the forefather of lyrists—Orpheus.[33]

It is noteworthy that Scriabin's worldview (as becomes clear, incidentally, from the notations that have recently been published as "philosophical fragments") in many respects converges with the system of "magical idealism" of Novalis, which was unknown to Scriabin.[34] Both mystics have the following tenets in common: the identification of the personal consciousness of genius with universal thought; the harmony of nature and awakened human consciousness; the merging of the transcendent and immanent in the act of theurgical creativity; the close reunion of the divided and conflicting principles in accordance with the plea of man who has resurrected within himself synthetic memory; and collective [*sobornyi*] and universal ecstasy as a path to universal transfiguration.

V

The unbelief of artists took refuge from the world within the walls of "free" art; faith affirmed liberating and world-transfiguring art, even if this was expressed as a future and hoped-for art. In Scriabin, this ancient faith flared up as both a recollection and a blinding insight. He planned to make art the flesh of mystery. Thus did Hiram, the architect of Solomon's temple, create flesh for mystery. And according to the legend, Hiram also died prematurely, without completing his task. He decorated the courtyard of the temple and placed in the courtyard the Brass Sea that he cast.[35]

Scriabin, who was anointed for theurgy, had no concern for whether the flame of mystery might consume the flesh of any art that is prepared to receive it nor for whether it might consume the theurgist himself. Death, for him, meant the completion of the personality: it was the reunification of the male hypostasis of the divine spirit with its female hypostasis, its sister and beloved, the passionate attraction to which (as the "Preliminary Act" teaches) causes the seeking spirit to fill all of the starry expanses that divide the couple; these expanses are the many-colored garments in which the female hypostasis has clothed itself in order for the amorous impulse to blossom in an epiphany of worlds. In Scriabin's personal life, this mysterious reunification came to pass: this was his death.[36] . . . He was one of those who call out, "Come!"[37] and who are unable to beseech Heaven to reduce the term of worldly torments.

In Scriabin's death, I see a clear sign of the spiritual authenticity of his impulse and labor, no matter how vaguely he may have consciously understood the ultimate meaning of what he so ardently called forth. He presented Fate with the bold demand: "Either the cleansing renewal of the world will occur right now or else there is no place for me in the world." To which Fate responded: "Die and renew yourself." With unusual, superhuman logic, he was suddenly stolen from among us, as if by the sudden force of an inexplicably fateful accident; he was struck by a Harpy right in the midst of the task which, according to his plan, was, with its outer half, to belong to the old order of things and be encompassed by the limits of art as we know it, but which, with its inner half, was to exceed art's bounds and initiate the *Mysterium* itself.[38] I revere his death, mindful that the seed will not come to life unless it dies. "Vis ejus integra, si versa fuerit in terram. . . ."[39]

How can I compress and gather into one brief word all that I have said thus far?—

> He was one of those singers (such also was Novalis),
> Who know that they are the heirs of the lyre
> Which, at the dawn of the ages, were obeyed
> By spirit, stone, wood, beast, water, air, and fire.
>
> But while the descendants all admitted
> That they arrived late at the bridal feast—
> He, he alone seemed to recognize
> The ancient curses that shook the world.
>
> So! We all remembered—but he willed and acted.
> Like Hiram, the architect of secrets, he sowed mystery,
> And cast the Brass Sea amidst the courtyard.
>
> "Tarry not!" he called to Fate; and Fate answered his call.
> "Appear!" he begged the Sister, and lo, the Sister came.
> With this sign the Spirit marked its prophet.[40]

VI

"So, we all remembered, but he willed and acted." The theurgic torment of the celestial Muse's earthly captivity was once again and with full intensity understood and experienced by modern Russian Symbolism, by those of its representatives who, following Dostoevsky and Vladimir Solovyov, sought to found it on the basis of mystical realism. Russian Symbolism understood that, no matter how prophetic the inspired symbols might be (these simulacra and significations of higher realities, which form the living tissue of any true art), they are still only icons—o, if only wonder-working icons!—but not the life-creating forces themselves. The pilgrims knew that it was only at the end of some indefinitely long path, beyond some universal pass, that the snow-covered peaks of theurgy would sparkle. Vladimir Solovyov was the first to herald this promise in Russia; in 1890, he wrote: "Perfect art has as its final task to make incarnate the absolute ideal not only in the imagination, but in actual fact; it must spiritualize and transubstantiate our real life. If it is said that this task exceeds the bounds of art, then one might ask: 'who established these bounds?'"[41] In his early speeches on Dostoevsky, he already defined the future agents of life's transubstantiation through art as "theurgists," establishing the following distinction between them and religious artists of the past: the latter were possessed by the religious idea, while the former will themselves possess it and consciously guide its earthly incarnations.[42] Even earlier, Dostoevsky, from whose works grows everything that is best in our spirit, prophetically exclaimed: "Beauty will save the world," enclosing everything in a single vatic word.[43]

If I may be permitted to introduce into my considerations several notes of personal experience and recollection, something of my intimate emotions, I confess that, after the disputes over the meaning of Symbolism, when Aleksandr Blok and I defended the theurgic testament on the pages of the impartial and seemingly disinterested journal *Apollo,* I was deeply troubled by the consciousness of our loneliness, despite the appearance of the modest journal *Works and Days,* under the guidance of Andrei Bely, which set itself the task of lending philosophical development to the content of our shared hopes.[44] Held captive by irresponsible and ineffectual freedom, as if in a sealed garden, we yearned for liberating action, but we were accused of wanting to turn the virginal queen of the garden, the Muse, into the handmaiden of some religion. No one heard us or fathomed us. Kind fate brought me to Moscow, and two years of residence in the same city as Scriabin allowed me to deepen my hitherto superficial acquaintance with him.

Until then I had not known him at all as a person and thinker, and our incidental conversations, where he touched upon matters of great concern to me—*sobornost'* in art and the choral rite—seemed to me to have no greater import than the simple attentiveness of an intelligent and courteous interlocutor. I thought that the bases of our mutual interest in these topics were, in essence, completely different for each; that Dionysian ecstasy was for him merely a psychological moment;[45] and that he himself was merely a re- fined aesthete and a demonically inclined individualist. These suspicions turned into joyful wonder when our first more relaxed meetings revealed that he found the very words "aestheticism" and "individualism" to be neg- ative, while the mind-sets they denote were capable of driving him to an- noyance. It transpired that his theoretical postulates concerning *sobornost'*, the choral rite, and the calling of art grew organically out of basic intuitions similar to my own: we found a common language.[46] I recall with reverent gratitude the intensification of our friendship, which became one of the sig- nificant facets of my life.

> The bud of our friendship opened up
> From a seed that had long lived in the depths,
> When the hand of the Gardener suddenly
> Plucked the tender flower and replanted it
> (As I hope with my shattered heart)
> Onto the best pasture of another world:
> Fate gave us a term of two years.
> I often dropped in on him "on an impulse":
> He visited my home. A high reward
> Awaited the poet for a new hymn:
> And my family piano still recalls
> The magical touch of his fingers.
> He led me into his world by the hand,
> Step by step, as a high priest leads a neophyte,
> Unveiling the eternal holy things
> Of the life-creating glories he created.
> Insistently, humbly, patiently
> The initiator taught the newcomer
> The harmonious concord of newly created spheres.
> And then, in a long conversation after midnight
> In his working temple, under a palm,
> By his faithful desk, with a gentle Chinaman
> Of eastern marble—where a new marriage
> Was taking place between Poetry and Music—
> He spoke with daring of the mysteries,
> As one who clearly saw what I foresaw
> Long ago, as if through a dark glass.
> And what we both saw seemed
> Affirmed by our mutual testimony;
> And I believe that the source of our disagreements
> Will be the cause of concord when we meet again.
> But it seemed that what we had was but the start

Of what was soon to be completed.
God judged differently, and the miracle
I hoped for did not happen—at the hour
When his final caress fell silent, and he fell
Into oblivion; I then kissed
His holy hand, which was falling cold—
And I went out into the night. . . .[47]

VII

Scriabin's tragedy is that his artistic will was heroic and that his heroism affirmed itself in the artist: he was an artist-hero. One person can be both artist and hero: an artist in certain actions and a hero in others. But Scriabin desired or rather had to be a hero as an artist and an artist as a hero. He could not reject either of these two natures, nor divide them in his actions: his will was his knowledge, and his knowledge was his will, but he could know and will only while creating beauty. Hence his untiring overcoming of himself in art and through art, as the content of a heroic labor. And this heroic labor filled life, which naturally ended in a tragic catastrophe. Tragic burials of heroes inevitably occur at the closest approaches to the threshold of the theurgic kingdom.

The Rose glorifies the sword with crimson glory;
The Rose blossoms in just battle.
In the distant, invisible kingdom
A thick grove imprisons the Rose
In fierce wilds, under a strong curse
A thousand-headed snake has a Rose.
Emblazon your armor, o you martyrs:
The Rose calls the lion to a bloody feast.[48]

The foregoing makes evident that Scriabin's artistic path was bound to pass through those stages which, according to the teaching of the mysteries, the initiate passes through on his path of spiritual growth. The ancient tradition, preserved by teachers of inner experience, instructs us that the first step of apprehending other worlds is "imagination," the second "inspiration." After this, there follows the highest and final step of touching other worlds, which in the esoteric sense (different from the usual meaning of the word) is called "intuition." At the imaginative stage, man contemplates suprasensible realities in the symbolics of the images that usually present themselves to his soul. At the stage of inspiration, he experiences these realities as living presences that approach him invisibly and act upon him. At the third stage, almost unattainably high, the initiate himself merges with the living and active forces of other worlds, becoming their worldly tool.

223

> And he cleft my breast with a sword,
> And pulled out my trembling heart,
> And placed into my open breast
> A coal burning in flame . . .
> Like a corpse, I lay in the desert. . . .[49]

"Like a corpse" because his previous small "I" has been sundered from him, after all he "is filled" with a new will that is not his own; "like a corpse" because the transition to the third stage is mysteriously linked to an essential change in the flesh itself and because it subjects the initiate's body to an experience tantamount to death and sometimes to death itself. The prophet lies "in the desert" as a corpse, not only because he had already departed into the "gloomy desert," where he met the seraphim, but also because henceforth all of his previous connections to the world are severed. Scriabin craved precisely this terrible communion with a mystery that devours man, for, according to his conception, the mystery could not be achieved in any other way. Once it is realized, it would no longer be *his* creation, a creation of the former man and artist, but would become a matter of the universal spirit. He prepared a precious vessel for the descent of the fire, which, falling into the vessel, would melt it and spread over the earth. It was for good reason that he compared himself to a "chalice," as those who were nearest to him recall. . . . But he also prepared his vessel as an artist, and he wanted the entire man within him to became wholly an artist, without remainder. For to be an artist meant for him only one thing: to be both the bringer of sacrifice and the sacrifice itself. Thus, as a hero of the spirit, he made his artistic path into a mystical one, and on the path he traveled as an artist, one clearly distinguishes landmarks of the mystical path.

According to those closest to him, ever since adolescence, Scriabin envisioned his future as a great musician as an act that would gladden or liberate everyone. Even at this early stage, his individual psychology, which comprised the main content of his works of the period (when he was mostly continuing the work of Chopin), constantly sheds light on the cosmic and universal. His *Divine Poem* seems to me to be the fruit of the artist's mystical imagination.[50] The period of initial imagination is most characteristically distinguished by the attempt to create a music drama, the protagonist of which would be a musician-creator who nurtures an artistic plan vaguely similar to the future idea of the *Mysterium*. Scriabin abandoned this plan, but only after he had come to believe fully in the dream of his hero, appropriating it as his goal in life. For a long time—perhaps forever—this vision, "incomprehensible to the mind,"[51] appeared to be initially external (transcendent) to his soul; he saw it hovering before the spiritual gaze of some imagined double of his. But gradually he himself merged with it. The motive will, having shown the vision, sought to become incarnate within him, and his will was drawn to it as if experiencing a kind of conjugal desire.

Here begins the period of inspirations: suprasensible forces approach man with their sacramental intimations, and he senses them as near presences. I see *The Poem of Ecstasy* and *Prometheus* as "inspired" in this sense. I shall cite one representative detail: by Scriabin's own admission, it was against his will that he wrote his Tenth Sonata, which is tempered by a profound insight into the World Soul. It was as if he had submitted to suggestion and coercion that entered from without. After finishing the sonata, he did not immediately like it, but later he became extremely fond of it. The creation of the *Mysterium* could only be achieved at the stage of complete fusion with higher essences, only after his individual "I," which remained separate from them, was completely extinguished, insofar as this depended on the conditions of the creative personality and not on the general state of contemporary humanity. This is why Scriabin (who incidentally did not know the scheme of the inner law I have expounded) awaited with such torment the ultimate realization of the spiritual events he anticipated, why he awaited his second birth, which was tantamount to the death of the old man. It brought death in the body: the flesh of the genius proved too infirm to contain the supreme gifts of the Spirit.

VIII

Just as one who has tasted something sweet no longer desires anything bitter, so Scriabin no longer desired human, merely human, art after he had drunk of divine wine from the ethereal cups of Olympus. As he musically re-created the movements of will, the first timid tremblings and ecstatic delights of celestial spirits' bathing in the universal expanses, he stopped loving other, more captive and caressing, panoramas. One might almost say that, tirelessly seeking to overcome himself, he stopped loving art itself, as we understand it.

But not beauty! On the contrary, all of his worldview was an affirmation of beauty alone. The cosmos was in his eyes "an aesthetic phenomenon,"[52] but not in the human sense. He thought that matter had arisen in order to accept the imprint of beautiful form from the one Spirit and then, having accepted it, matter would have completed its task. He seems to have halted for a long time at this stage of comprehending matter (almost like the Hindu concept of "Maya") in his slow progression to more penetrating and profound understanding.[53] The imprint of beauty is achieved by the sacrificial descent of The One.[54] But the Infinite One desires this sacrifice: he "wills to recognize Himself in the finite,"[55] and this recognition, at all of its stages, is beauty; and this desire is passionate love, Eros. By a primordial act of love, in the very womb of the Preeternal One, being becomes bipolar and divides into two principles, the masculine and feminine, whose reciprocal cravings give rise to all creative production. The divinely aesthetic phenomenon is, in its real basis, a divinely erotic process.

But the time of division nears completion. Matter has reached its maximal distance from its first source, the Spirit. The paths of "involution," i.e., of immersion into the depths of matter, have been traveled. The "evolution" of humanity and the world, its ascent to God, has begun, and the theurgic task is henceforth universal reunification. Thus, *sobornost'* becomes the basis of theurgic activity. All of Scriabin's creative work became a general integration, the gathering of dispersed components into the single whole, and pure and exclusive syntheticism. Synthetic was the principle of his harmony, the enclosing of a melodic series of sounds into a single harmony. He marked the top of each page of the music to *Prometheus* with a line of color to show the melody of light. He sought to master—and at times he succeeded wonderfully—the exquisite nuances of poetic technique in order to create a rigorously structured polyrhythmic dithyramb in the dramatic genre, as in the verbal part of the "Preliminary Act," where he took pains to coordinate perfectly the verbal and orchestral instrumentation. Orchestics, colors, and lines were to be worked out specially, in order to facilitate the integral artistic effect of the synthetic creation. In the coming *Mysterium,* the very peculiarities of the locality chosen for its accomplishment were to enter the greater whole as organic parts, thereby eliminating the schism between art and nature. Everything was to be borne by the chorus, which was to divide up and merge together in manifold ways, which was to be now deaf-mute, now clear in speech. It was to be a many-faced chorus but filled with a single collective [*sobornyi*] consciousness and inspiration. It was not a chorus of performers but the sacramental chorus of those who perform liturgical service. Already for the "Preliminary Act," Scriabin had firmly decided that there would be no mere listeners present, but that all who were admitted would be participants, if not of the audible chorus, then of the throng of solemn processions that would be united with it inwardly.

Thus, Scriabin resolved the problem of "synthetic art," so dear to him, by subordinating all the arts to a single goal that was set outside and above any single art: to a liturgical and sacramental goal. This artist of genius was not afraid of enslaving or degrading his own or other arts, for which he had equal reverence and which he approached in the most exacting fashion and with a purely ascetic severity. He determined that they were auxiliary forces that weave multicolored veils for the miracle Child who was to be born in the choral *sobornost'* of the *Mysterium* and was to become the soul of a new, better age. The chorus was to be gathered for the "Preliminary Act" from neophytes, and it was to receive mystagogic instruction from the work's ritual and be led by the revelations granted within this ritual. The chorus was to serve as the seed of a holy multitude capable of worthily representing in the future *Mysterium* spiritual humanity in spirit.[56] In the collectively [*soborno*] unified consciousness of these chosen ones, focused like a lens that gathers light, the memory of the entire universal epoch lived by the present human race would be resurrected. In the final fullness of understanding and overcoming, memory would find a path into new expanses of being with the unmediated wonder-working help of the heavenly "Shaft of Light," which would be called forth by love being ignited within the chosen. . . .[57]

Thus, this Russian artist and allman burned with prophetic agitation.[58] He gave his superhumanity to *sobornost'*, and for himself, he prayed only for a single gift: the fiery tongue of a new Pentecost, which would burn up the old man in him.

> Music has been orphaned. And with her
> Poetry, her sister, has been orphaned.
> The magic flower was extinguished at the border
> Of their contiguous kingdoms—and night fell darker
>
> Onto the shore where the mysterious ark
> Of new-created days flamed up. The robe of the body
> Has smoldered from the spirit's fine lightning,
> Giving up its fire to the Source of fires.
>
> Did Fate, hovering as a vigilant eagle, seize
> The holy possession from audacious Prometheus?
> Or was the earth inflamed by the tongue of heaven?
>
> Who can say: conqueror or conquered
> Is he for whom—mute with the graveyard of wonders—
> The palace of the Muses mourns with the whisper of laurels.[59]

IX

"Who can say: conqueror or conquered?" Is he conquered insofar as the miracle, as he expected it, did not come to pass? Or is he the conqueror, insofar as he prepared the ground for an accomplishment that he himself did not anticipate?

In any case, the first and antinomial condition of accomplishment was met, no matter how bitterly ironic the fateful dialectics of higher forces might seem with respect to human striving: the empirical personality has been eliminated in accordance with its final will; the earthly mortal is no longer among us; the individual principle of the initiator no longer affirms itself negatively, opposing its will to an alien will and imposing it on the latter, but in a positive fashion, by dissolving its will in the collective [*sobornyi*] principle and universal will.

Only an authority can say: "he conquered." To say "he is conquered" is fitting for the devil as he celebrates on Faust's grave. At the same time, the final answer to the question we posed above depends on the resolution of this dilemma: in what sense and within what parameters do we affirm the spiritual significance of Scriabin's labor?

The sun of this genius has suddenly been obscured by the cloudy veil of impenetrable mystery; and the final meaning of his art and the deepest meaning of his fate remain mysterious. I shall limit myself to a reminder of what should be clear and comprehensible to all. The genius walks in front and looks ahead: what, then, did he catch sight of in the distance?

The last artist-genius of our day was he who announced to the world that art would no longer play with reflections of life as it is experienced; that reflective art, which began with the experience of phenomena and ended with those very experiences, has been exhausted; that there will either be no more art at all or else it will be born from the roots of being itself and give birth to being, thereby becoming the most important and most real of all actions; that the time of *works* of art has passed and that from now on, one can conceive only of *events* of art.

The present era is experiencing a *crisis of the phenomenon.*[60] Art has become disappointed in the former wholeness of the phenomenon and breaks it down into the fibers and refuse of forms, turning the world into atomistic dust or into Empedoclean Chaos. Art thereby succumbs to even worse "psychologism," since it does not believe in being and does not seek that which truly is. The last artist-genius of our day was he who desired to gather together into a single whole all the being that glimmers in phenomena and all the spirit from all the souls of the divided world.

The last artist-genius of our day was he who believed in the divine being of man, who also knew (together with Nietzsche) that man is something that must be overcome;[61] but by this he demonstrated his faith in God (in contrast to Nietzsche, who was still the captive of the phenomenon and was unable to profess true being in man). For whoever has known true being in himself, and has at the same time known that it is also overcome by something higher, he has known God.

Thus, he caught sight of being itself as some unspoken silence of Light and as a tender mystery, and then the Sister came. . . . But there are no words for mystery and silence; there is only communion with it.

> I know not the Tender Mystery of clear images and omens:
> Does the poet dream the signs? Or is the sign itself the poet?
> I know only: no song is new to the world unless it be prophetic.[62]

Truly, Scriabin himself was such a sign. He left to the world the testament that from now on, there will be no art unless it be prophetic, i.e., unless it reunites us with being itself.

Autumn 1915

Notes

The notes to Ivanov's essays serve several purposes: to identify sources, to explain references, and to show the most important revisions made in successive drafts of each essay. The first task may seem folly or pedantry insofar as Ivanov's essays are patchworks of historical and literary reminiscences, the immediate meaning of which can be quite far from their meaning in the original sources. The essays, however, lose much of their richness if deprived of this tapestry of Ivanov's erudition. It seemed to serve little purpose to limit the notes to what we judged to be especially important or obscure.

Several limits have been observed. When Ivanov gives a Russian rendering of a non-Russian-language text, we have translated Ivanov's Russian and supplied references to the original, mostly without comment on the accuracy of his rendering. Also, we have refrained from explaining our translation choices in the notes, except in isolated cases. The only Russian word retained without English translation is *sobornost'*, which traditionally denotes the quality that distinguishes the Orthodox community of faith due to its conciliar form of government and worship (*sobornost'* is sometimes translated as "conciliarity"). The adjective on which the noun is based (*sobornyi*) has been rendered variously according to context (with the Russian word in brackets).

In other cases of untranslatable Russian terms, we have chosen a corresponding English term, attempting to minimize the English word's occurrence as a translation of other Russian words. The difficult term *podvig* (a spiritual labor or feat, sometimes a heroic deed or achievement) has been translated as "labor." The philosophical term *dannost'* (literally, something that is given) is translated as "datum." The archaic *deistvo* (dramatic act, rite), which Ivanov sometimes contrasts to *deistvie* (action, effect), has been rendered (at the risk of overstressing its religious connotations) as "rite." It might also be noted that the word "pathos" (translating Russian "pafos") is to be taken without its frequently negative associations; in Ivanov's Russian usage, it denotes the spirit or inspiration that lies behind actions.

Another circumstance to be kept in mind while reading the translations is that Ivanov used Russian grammatical gender in a way that cannot be preserved in English translation. It is well worth noting, however, that earth (*zemlia*), soul (*dusha*), flesh (*plot'*), beauty (*krasota*) are feminine, while world (*mir*), spirit (*dukh*), Logos (*logos*) are masculine. Ivanov's constant references to the spirit impregnating the soul or betrothed to the world soul therefore combine their spiritual meaning with quite literal sexual connotations. The ubiquity of such formulations in Ivanov's essays makes it redundant to explain each individual case. Ivanov also underscores the spiritual denotation of some words by the liberal, albeit inconsistent, uses of capitalization and other graphic means of emphasis, which we have strived to preserve in the translation.

We would like to express our sincere gratitude to everyone who has assisted us, especially: Mikhail Gasparov, Kenneth Hunt, Dimitri Ivanov, Boris Jakim, Kseniia Kumpan, Constance Meinwald, Margarita Pavlova, and Vasily Rudich.

EDITOR'S INTRODUCTION

1. From Ivanov's "Autobiographical Letter," written in 1917 at the request of the literary historian S. A. Vengerov. In V. I. Ivanov, *Sobranie sochinenii* (Brussels: Foyer Chrétien Oriental, 1974), 2:13. Hereafter cited as *Collected Works,* followed by volume and page number.

2. For an English translation of one of her works, see Lydia Zinovieva-Annibal, *The Tragic Menagerie,* trans. Jane Costlow (Evanston, Ill.: Northwestern University Press, 1999).

3. *Collected Works,* 1:20.

4. Ivanov's decision against an academic career should not be construed as a rejection of the methods and aims of scholarly inquiry. For him, the worlds of poetry and scholarship enjoyed a reciprocal relationship. In subsequent years, Ivanov continued to study Dionysian religion, and this work inspired two scholarly treatises as well as numerous poems.

5. See the final paragraph of Briusov's review (first published in 1903, revised and expanded in 1911). Valery Briusov, *Sobranie sochinenii v semi tomakh* (Moscow: Khudozhestvennaia literatura, 1975), 6:299.

6. Osip Mandel'shtam, *Kamen'.* (Leningrad: Nauka, 1990), p. 206. The letter is dated 13/26 August 1909.

7. From Ivanov's letter to Fedor Stepun of 22 March 1925. (Cited according to the draft in the Ivanov Archive, Rome, since the final version was destroyed in the Second World War.)

8. From "Thoughts on Symbolism" in this volume, p. 56.

9. Ivanov had far less interest in the Berlin Romantics (e.g., E. T. A. Hoffmann) than in the more speculative and mystical Jena Romantics (particularly Novalis). The rather dismissive comments on German Romanticism found in "Presentiments and Portents" (see p. 96 in this volume)

predate his discovery of Novalis, in whom he found an alter ego and powerful precursor.

10. From "On the Joyful Craft and the Joy of the Spirit" in this volume, p. 125.

11. In his analysis of a poem by Gorodetsky ("Two Elements in Contemporary Symbolism" in this volume, p. 31), Ivanov emphasizes how myth that is unrecognized can still be vibrant.

12. Ivanov sidesteps the slippery question of whether national characteristics are to be explained by "geographic and ethnographic conditions, material facts of the historical process, or causes of a spiritual order" ("On the Russian Idea" in this volume, p. 134).

13. From Ivanov's most detailed discussion of Slavophilism (1915), "Zhivoe predanie" ("Living Tradition"), in *Collected Works*, 3:341.

14. Ivanov saw a special provenance in the fact that this word was "almost impossible to convey in foreign languages," yet sounded to a Russian so "eternally and directly understandable." See the final section of the 1916 essay "Legion i sobornost'" ("Legion and Sobornost'"), in *Collected Works*, 3:260.

15. From "Scriabin's View of Art" in this volume, p. 215.

16. For more on this subject, see Irina Paperno and Joan Delaney Grossman, eds., *Creating Life: The Aesthetic Utopia of Russian Modernism* (Stanford: Stanford University Press, 1994).

17. See "Symbolism and Religious Art," part 1 of "Two Elements in Contemporary Symbolism" in this volume, p. 14.

18. From "On the Limits of Art" in this volume, p. 75.

19. Ibid., p. 84.

20. See Sergei Averintsev, "The Poetry of Vyacheslav Ivanov," in *Vyacheslav Ivanov: Poet, Critic and Philosopher,* ed. Robert Louis Jackson and Lowry Nelson Jr. (New Haven, Conn.: Yale Center for International and Area Studies, 1986), p. 43.

21. From "Manner, Persona, Style" in this volume, p. 63.

22. Ivanov wrote several essays on Dostoevsky before emigrating. In Italy, he reworked (and, to a significant extent, rewrote) them for a German translation, which appeared in 1932. This German text is authoritative insofar as the Russian, never published, appears to have been lost. The German book was translated into English by Norman Cameron (under the title *Freedom and the Tragic Life: A Study in Dostoevsky*) and has been reissued several times. We have opted to omit Ivanov's work on Dostoevsky, largely because it is already accessible in English. Another work that has been extremely well served in translation (and has been excluded from this volume primarily for that reason) is the *Correspondence between Two Corners,* an epistolary debate between Ivanov and Mikhail Gershenzon concerning the fate of culture, written in 1920—and published a year later—in the Soviet

Union. First translated into German in 1926 for Martin Buber's journal *Die Kreatur*, then into French in 1930 for Charles Du Bos's journal *Vigile* (and then into numerous other languages), this somewhat atypical work became Ivanov's "signature piece" to many Western readers. The most recent English translation is by Lisa Sergio: V. I. Ivanov and M. O. Gershenzon, *Correspondence across a Room* (Marlboro, Vt.: Marlboro Press, 1984).

THE SYMBOLICS OF AESTHETIC PRINCIPLES

"The Symbolics of Aesthetic Principles" was originally published in *Libra* (no. 5 [1905]: 26–36) under the title "On Descent: The Sublime, the Beautiful, and the Chaotic—the Triad of Aesthetic Principles," with a dedication to Andrei Bely. It was reprinted in the present form and under the present title in *By the Stars* (pp. 21–32) and included in the *Collected Works* (1:823–30).

The first publication differed from all subsequent ones in several significant ways. On republication, Ivanov omitted a paragraph on Bely and two long poetical quotations, adjusted other quotes and formulations, and added several entire sentences. The most substantial of these changes have been indicated in the notes. In the original version, the three sections bore the subtitles "Excelsior," "The Mercy [or Grace] of Peace," and "Chaos."

"The Symbolics of Aesthetic Principles" owes a significant debt to Kant, who placed the categories of the sublime and the beautiful at the center of his aesthetics in the *Critique of Judgment*. However, Ivanov considered Kant's epistemology and aesthetics to be incapable of explicating the religious significance of art. Therefore, he goes beyond Kant, incorporating many of the ideas and much of the terminology of Schopenhauer and Nietzsche. Like Schopenhauer, Ivanov posits a chaotic metaphysical basis of the earth, hidden by its phenomenal representation, the world. Only the artist comes into contact with the primeval chaos in his creative act, thus surmounting, to a limited extent, the principle of individuation and initiating a reunification of the world with the earth at a metaphysical level. In fact, the three principles of ascent/sublimity, descent/beauty, and chaos all resolve into a single chaotic substratum, with the two former pairs of categories denoting steps on the path to a liberating chaos.

Images and quotations from Nietzsche abound in Ivanov's article, from the very ideas of ascent and descent to the Apollonian/Dionysian polarity. Ivanov's heroic artist seems explicitly modeled on Nietzsche's Zarathustra. There is, however, an implicit polemic, especially with the later, anti-Wagnerian Nietzsche. As Sir C. M. Bowra noted in another connection, Ivanov "turns the tables on Nietzsche," accepting and developing what he considers to be Nietzsche's better self while reprimanding his failings. One should be wary of attributing all Nietzschean passages to direct influence. For instance, the idea of Dionysian thirst and Apollonian plenitude can be found at least as far back as Plutarch (*On the E at Delphi* 388E–389C), with whose works Ivanov was intimately acquainted.

Beyond the purely philosophical level, Ivanov is attempting to place his ideas in a Christian context. Nietzsche shares attention with Augustine, the dualistic Tiutchev with Dostoevsky. Ivanov refers to Kant for his epistemology, Schopenhauer and Nietzsche for his psychology of art, and patristic Christianity for his metaphysics. This admittedly makes for "an aesthetic poised uneasily between metaphysics and psychology" (James West, *Russian Symbolism: A Study of Vyacheslav Ivanov and the Russian Symbolist Aesthetic* [London: Methuen, 1970], p. 93), yet the conflict of these seemingly incompatible sources is resolved in the very concept of symbolics. Ivanov allows for varying apprehensions of a single, united truth and revels in the symbols these antagonistic writers actually share in their limited representations of this truth.

"Symbolics" is the aggregate of symbols given in a symbolic system. It corresponds to the adjective "symbolic," just as the noun "symbolism" (a conscious attempt to achieve symbolic art) corresponds to the adjective "symbolist." In 1913, Ivanov wrote: "By symbolics I mean the store of static and, so to speak, crystallized symbols, historically tied to certain values in a particular dogmatic system. Such, for example, are the wings of Divine Wisdom, the fish, the boat, etc., in Christian symbolics" (G. V. Obatnin and K. Iu. Postoutenko, eds., "Otvet na stat'iu [N. Bryzgalova] 'Simvolizm i fal'sifikatsiia," *Novoe literaturnoe obozrenie* 10 [1994]: 168). See also "Two Elements in Contemporary Symbolism" in this volume, p. 13.

1. "You stir and touch [within me] a powerful decision—to strive unceasingly to the highest Being. . . ." (*Faust,* II.4684–85).

2. Literally "hearts upward," "lift up our hearts," from the Latin liturgy. The phrase is also part of the Anaphora or Eucharistic Canon of the Divine Liturgy of St. John Chrysostom (see also note 8): "Let us lift up our hearts. We lift them up to the Lord."

3. This final image is taken from Ivanov's poem "Rupture" ("Razryv"), in *Pilot Stars,* which runs: "Flight of earth away from the worldly, / Immovable and petrified, / Is robed in virginal snow, / As in the linen of a priest, as in white byssos."

4. Jn 11:43. Also the title of a distich from *Pilot Stars:* "Call yourself, and constantly call, until you hear the distant answer from your own deepest depths: 'Here I am.'"

5. The phrase is from St. Augustine of Hippo's sermon "On the Holy Sabbath" (*Patrologia Latina,* vol. 46 [Paris, 1865], col. 823): "Quidquid enim Deus est, immutabile bonum est, incorruptibile Bonum est. Etsi invisibilis Deus, invisibilis anima, sed tamen mutabilis anima, immutabilis Deus. Transcende ergo non solum, quod cernitur in te, sed etiam illud, quod mutatur in te. Totum transcende, te ipsum transcende" (God is the immutable

Good, the unperishing Good. God is invisible, the soul is invisible, but the soul is mutable whereas God is immutable. Therefore transcend not only what is always in you, but also what changes in you. Transcend this, transcend yourself). In Ivanov's collection *Transparency* (1904), there is a poem "Transcende te ipsum," based on a contrast of Jacob's two wives, Rachel and Leah.

6. From Nikolai Iazykov's poem "Genius" ("Genii," 1825).

7. A paraphrase of the second line of an 1883 poem by Vladimir Solovyov ("Beskrylyi dukh, zemleiu polonennyi"). The first stanza reads: "A wingless spirit, imprisoned by the earth, / A self-forgetting and forgotten god . . . / But a single dream, and you, regaining wings, / Rush up away from vain concerns."

8. The term "transubstantiation" refers to the changing of the bread and wine into the body and blood of Christ at the liturgy. The eucharistic imagery of the article was more explicit in the first publication, where the original title of the second section, "The Mercy [or Grace] of Peace," is taken from the beginning of the Anaphora or Eucharistic Canon in the Divine Liturgy of St. John Chrysostom, as is the *sursum corda* above (see note 2).

9. From Tiutchev's "How suddenly and brightly" ("Kak neozhidanno i iarko," 1865; Ivanov's italics).

10. From Tiutchev's "The northerly wind is quiet. . . . The azure throng breathes more lightly" ("Utikhla biza. . . . Legche dyshit," 1864; Ivanov's italics).

11. The Russian *bogoborchestvo* translates as "theomachy," which literally means "battling with God."

12. In the 1905 version, this read: "Some gifts demand a divine initiative [*bogopochin*]" (p. 27).

13. See Gn 32:24–30. Ivanov associates this passage on Jacob-Israel's battle with God with a previous passage concerning Jacob's vision of a ladder stretched up to heaven, by which angels ascend and descend (Gn 28:11–22). On this latter passage, cf. "Thoughts on Symbolism" in this volume, p. 51. In 1865, the same year he penned "How suddenly and brightly," Tiutchev wrote a poem for the centenary of Lomonosov's death, "When dying he doubted" ("On, umiraia, somnevalsia"), the last stanza of which bears citation here: "Like that Old Testament fighter, / With an unearthly power, / Who fought until the star of dawn / And held out in the night battle." Tiutchev calls Lomonosov a "Russian Mind" celebrated by "Native Speech," and declares that "his grateful grandsons" sing his "memory eternal," all of which phrases are significant in Ivanov's work (cf. his poems "Russian Mind," "Memory Eternal," "Language").

14. The second and last stanza of Ivanov's "Rupture" ("Razryv"); added in the 1909 version.

15. Individuation, the *principium individuationis*, is a term inherited by Nietzsche from Schopenhauer to account for the divide between the illusory multiplicity and underlying unity of all that exists.

16. See Jn 12:24. Dostoevsky used this Gospel passage as an epigraph to *The Brothers Karamazov*. It is to the words of the Elder Zosima (later echoed by Dmitry) in Dostoevsky's novel that Ivanov alludes by "universal collective responsibility" (pt. 2, bk. 6, chap. 2a; pt. 4, bk. 11, chap. 4); on this, see Ivanov's poem "Mortal Dust" ("Perst'," a reference to Ps 104:29) from *Pilot Stars*.

17. Cf. Goethe, *Faust* II.4727; Ivanov's poem "Rainbows" ("Radugi," 1904); Konstantin Bal'mont's *Only Love. A Seven-Colored Collection* (*Tol'ko liubov'. Semitsvetnik*, 1903). Ivanov's phrase also recalls the rainbow with which God sealed his covenant with Noah (Gn 9:12–17).

18. "The tragedy begins"; Ivanov probably borrows this phrase from Friedrich Nietzsche's *The Gay Science*, bk. 4, sec. 342.

19. From Tiutchev's "Snowy Mountains" ("Snezhnye gory"; Ivanov's italics).

20. Theognis, *Elegies* I.15–18 (see also *Elegy and Iambus,* ed. J. M. Edmonds [Cambridge, Mass.: Harvard University Press, 1968], 1:230–31). Theognis of Megara (late sixth century B.C.) was an elegiac poet.

Harmony bore Cadmus three daughters, one of whom, Semele (or Thyone), became the mother of Zeus's child Dionysus. Cf. Pindar's *Pythian Odes* III.88–94. Ivanov's *Transparency* contains a triptych of sonnets entitled "The Beautiful Is Dear" ("Prekrasnoe—milo"). This passage is built on an untranslatable parallelism of three words with the same root: *milost'* (grace), *milo* (dear, pleasing), and *milostivyi* (merciful). See also "Ancient Terror" in this volume, p. 145.

21. In the 1905 version, this passage was followed by a paragraph: "In Andrei Bely's second Symphony, the scarlet Dawn laughs as it looks from the heavens at the world, which awaits in truth and is yet deceived. Lovingly cruel Dawn laughs with cunning and goodness, as if the higher powers were conducting amongst themselves a celebratory, joyful council on the dear, suspecting, and yet still mistaken world" (p. 29; for the relevant passage, see Andrey Bely, *The Dramatic Symphony,* trans. Roger Keys and Angela Keys [Edinburgh: Polygon, 1986], p. 129). This was followed by a passage from Ivanov's poem "Sphinx" from *Pilot Stars:* "Shall we not go, brothers, / To moisten the throat of the world,—to pour rain / On the drought of the ancient curse? / But just as those who hide their joy are wont to lengthen / The yearning of their friends and to tarry with the radiant news, / So that they might satisfy the hungry even more abundantly,— / It was decided: oppressing the waiting world with brotherly revenge, / To remain together there until the morning, / Although their hearts rushed to announce the good news" (*Collected Works,* 2:651).

22. *Ivanov's note:* Wenn die Macht gnädig wird und herabkommt ins Sichtbare, Schönheit heisse ich dieses Herabkommen.—Von den Erhabenen. [Quotation from Friedrich Nietzsche's "On Those Who Are Sublime," sec. 13 of pt. 2 of *Thus Spake Zarathustra.*]

23. "Many-eyed" is the particular epithet of cherubim (see Ez 10:12).

24. The "good news" (*blagaia vest'* or *blagovestie*) refers both to the Annunciation (*Blagoveshchenie*), which is related in Lk 1:26–38, and to the Greek word *euangélion,* which is translated into English as "gospel," "good news," or "good tidings" (cf. Ps 96:2).

25. The front and back faces of Greek temples were customarily topped by triangular gables, often decorated by sculptures. They were the standard or "eagle" of the Greek temple.

26. See, for example, Raphael's *Madonna in the Meadow.*

27. The Italian word "scherzo" literally means a joke; in classical music, it is a fast movement, for example, the third movement of a symphony or sonata, following the adagio. A good example of an adagio followed by a scherzo is in Beethoven's Third Symphony.

28. From Tiutchev's "Fountain" ("Fontan," 1836).

29. A *stola* is a garment or robe. In Roman times, it was a robe with slits on the sides for the arms, held under the breast by a girdle, that was worn primarily by women. References to ancient clothing abound in Ivanov's articles, reflecting an early interest in "combining my antiquarian studies with a systematic use of artistic monuments," which at one time caused him to contemplate a history of the *trabea,* a cloak worn by Roman equestrians and priests (see Michael Wachtel, "Viacheslav Ivanov—student Berlinskogo universiteta," *Cahiers du monde russe* 35, nos. 1–2 [1994]: 353–76: 368).

30. Source unknown; cf. Lidia Zinov'eva-Annibal's story "The Bear Cubs" ("Medvezhata"): "[I]t's not worth living for this earth. It's worth living for heaven's gift, my child, only for that gift" (in Lydia Zinov'eva-Annibal, *The Tragic Menagerie,* trans. Jane Costlow [Evanston, Ill.: Northwestern University Press, 1999], p. 10). See also the close of the Divine Liturgy of St. John Chrysostom: "For every good gift [*dósis, daianie*] and every perfect gift is from above, and cometh down from Thee, the Father of lights."

31. Lk 2:14. On the "good news," see note 24 above.

32. The final line of Ivanov's poem "Beauty" ("Krasota"); this use of "no" and "yes" is possibly derived from Nietzsche; see, for example, the latter's "Before Sunrise," sec. 4 in pt. 3 of *Thus Spake Zarathustra; The Antichrist,* sec. 1, 24, and 61. Cf. also Schiller's *The Robbers,* act 5, scene 1, where Pastor Moser tells Franz Moor, "And this No will then become a screaming Yes. . . ." ("Auch dieses Nein wird dann zu einem heulenden Ja. . . ."); cf. the classic Russian translation by M. M. Dostoevsky (F. Shiller, *Sobranie sochinenii* [St. Petersburg: Brokgauz i Èfron, 1901], 1:250).

33. From Friedrich Nietzsche's "Zarathustra's Prologue" in pt. 1 of *Thus Spake Zarathustra;* cf. "On the Gift-Giving Virtue" in sec. 22 of pt. 1.

34. "Das Göttliche kommt auf leichten Füssen"; from Nietzsche's *Case of Wagner* 1, where Nietzsche calls this image "the principle of my aesthetics." In notations dating from the 1880s (later published under the title *The Will to Power*), Nietzsche wrote: "Light feet might themselves belong to the concept of God." In the 1905 version, this line was followed by two lines from Ivanov's tragedy *Tantalus,* slightly different from the published version (*Collected Works,* 2:64): "Thus hard is the Sun's path to sacrificial bounds, but easy the labor of royal descents" (p. 31).

35. From "In the Alps" ("V al'pakh," 1886) by Vladimir Solovyov. "Earth" is not capitalized in the original.

36. The final lines of Ivanov's poem "Beauty" ("Krasota") from *Pilot Stars.*

37. Lk 24:1–11; Mk 16:1. Traditionally, the tears of the myrrh-bearing women turned to joy at the revelation of the resurrection. When applied to Christ, Ivanov's developed sense of the suffering god sometimes borders on the heretical stance of Patropassianism, according to which it was Christ's divine nature that suffered on the cross, not just his human nature.

38. *Faust* I.449–50.

39. A paraphrase of a line from Walsingham's hymn in Pushkin's *Feast at the Time of the Plague (Pir vo vremia chumy,* 1830): "There is rapture in battle, / And on the edge of a gloomy abyss"; see also Gavriil Derzhavin's ode "God" ("Bog," 1784).

40. The slightly altered beginning of Ivanov's poem "To Thy Name" ("Imeni Tvoemu") from *Pilot Stars.*

41. From Ivanov's "Forgive!" ("Prosti!") from *Pilot Stars.*

42. Briusov's "A Vision of Wings" ("Videnie kryl'ev") was written in 1904. In the 1905 version of this essay, Briusov's poem was quoted in full (pp. 33–34).

43. Cf. Euripides, *Bacchae* 701ff.

44. See Pushkin's "Objection to Kiukhel'beker's Articles in *Mnemosine*" (1825–26). Cf. Pushkin's 1828 "Poet and the Crowd" ("Poet i tolpa"): "Not for worldly concern, / Not for self-gain, not for battles, / We are born for inspiration, / For sweet sounds and prayers"; cf. "The Testaments of Symbolism" in this volume, pp. 41–42.

45. In the 1905 version, the last three sentences read: "Descent, as a principle of the purest beauty and, at the same time, of the good, turns the spirit toward what lies outside the personal. The chaotic is impersonal. It completely abolishes all limits" (p. 34).

46. Cf. Hesiod, *Theogony* 185–200.

47. One of Nietzsche's key phrases and the title of one of his books. Ivanov interpreted "beyond good and evil" in a supramoralistic, not amoral-

istic, vein. He considered, for instance, that being "beyond good and evil" was a criterion of sanctity (see "Nietzsche and Dionysus" in this volume, p. 183).

48. From Ivanov's "Orpheus Dismembered" ("Orfei rasterzannyi") from *Transparency.*

49. Cf. Nietzsche, "Zarathustra's Prologue," in pt. 1 of *Thus Spake Zarathustra.*

50. The giant son of Poseidon and Gaea. Antaeus was invincible on earth, but Heracles tore him from the earth and was thus able to crush him.

51. From Tiutchev's poem "What are you howling about, night wind?" ("O chem ty voesh' vetr nochnoi?" 1836).

52. From Ivanov's "Two Loves" ("Dve liubvi"), in *Transparency* (1904).

53. The slightly altered first line of Konstantin Bal'mont's poem "Midnight and light know their hour" ("Polnoch' i svet znaiut svoi chas," 1899).

54. From Ivanov's "The Scythian Dances" ("Skif pliashet") from the 1891 cycle "Parisian Epigrams" in *Pilot Stars.*

55. "Higher," "upward" (Latin). This is an echo of the "glory in the highest" from Lk 2:14 quoted above (see note 31), which in Latin reads "gloria in excelsis."

56. From Ivanov's "Orpheus Dismembered" ("Orfei rasterzannyi").

57. The information in this paragraph is based on popular etymologies of the names of Aphrodite, which Ivanov classifies in three groups corresponding to the levels of chaos, ascent, and descent. The various Aphrodites are discussed by Pausanius in Plato's *Symposium* (180C–185C; cf. 187DE).

TWO ELEMENTS IN CONTEMPORARY SYMBOLISM

This article was first published in *The Golden Fleece* in 1908 (nos. 3–4, pp. 86–94; no. 5, pp. 44–50 [entitled "Two Currents of Contemporary Symbolism"]). It was included without major changes in *By the Stars* (pp. 247–90) and *Collected Works* (2:537–61). In the two later publications, Ivanov appended two "excurses": "On Verlaine and Huysmans" (2:563–65), comprising reworked book reviews, and "Aesthetics and Confession" (2:567–72), a rejoinder to Andrei Bely's criticisms; our translation omits both excurses.

Of all Ivanov's essays, "Two Elements" made the greatest impression on contemporaries and subsequent critics. It was Ivanov's first systematic investigation of Symbolism and the first attempt to differentiate among different currents or "elements" (in the sense of elemental forces) in Russian modernism. In the context of Russian literary debates in the 1900s, Ivanov's distinction between Idealistic and Realistic Symbolism drew a clear line between the movement's first and second generations, what might be called the Decadents and the Symbolists proper, while building bridges between the younger Symbolists and the more socially minded realists, such as Gorky and Leonid Andreev. More broadly, the elucidation of a symbolic or mystical realism gave a powerful impetus to philosophical aesthetics and has been developed by thinkers ranging from Nikolai Berdiaev to Georges Florovsky. It was here that Ivanov coined his oft-quoted phrase: "*a realibus ad realiora*" (from the real to the more real).

Still, it cannot be said that Ivanov immediately succeeded in establishing a coherent theory of aesthetics. One of the elements of Symbolism, the principle of signification, owes much to Neoplatonic conceptions of art and Romantic theories of the symbol (particularly Schelling, Karl Solger, and perhaps Coleridge). This artistic aspect of Symbolism is balanced by another element, that of the transformation of reality in accordance with the symbol's revelation; this task belongs to the person (as opposed to the artist) and might be seen as the functional aspect of the symbol (as opposed to its ontological aspect, its status as *realiora*). But Ivanov quickly dispenses with the functional, personalistic element, affirming a higher kind of transformation, called transfiguration, in which the human consciousness merely accepts the higher reality instead of the lower. This banishes the human personality from the creation and perception of art, reducing art to a conjuring of higher realities. Of subsequent articles, this "theurgical" strain in Ivanov's aesthetics is most pronounced in "The Testaments of Symbolism," but it would eventually have to yield to a more integrated, personalistic account of art, presented most fully in "On the Limits of Art."

1. *Sēmeion antilegómenon* is from Lk 2:34. Ivanov's two definitions correspond roughly to the Vulgate and Slavonic translations, respectively.

2. *Ivanov's note:* Solovyov's "First Speech on Dostoevsky" (*Collected Works,* 3:175). [See Vladimir Solovyov, "Three Speeches in Memory of Dostoevsky," in *Sochineniia v dvukh tomakh* (Moscow: Mysl', 1990), 2:293.]

3. From Ivanov's poem "Creation" ("Tvorchestvo"), published in *Pilot Stars.*

4. From Is 42:3; cited also in Mt 12:20.

5. Cf. Plato, *Symposium* 206–9.

6. In the original publication, this phrase read: "He will sharpen his vision, disclosing the supraphenomenal life of phenomena" (p. 87).

7. This formulation is found later in Ivanov's tragedy *Prometheus* (*Collected Works,* 3:112).

8. An idea attributed to Schopenhauer that recurs in Ivanov's verse and prose.

9. See *Iliad* II.494–877; André Gide, *Fruits of the Earth* (1897). Ivanov contemplated including L. D. Zinov'eva-Annibal's essay on Gide (*Libra,* no. 10 [1904]) in his book *By the Stars* (1909); RGB 109.10.3, p. 60.

10. Pheidias (born c. 500 B.C.)—Greek sculptor and architect who created an enormous sculpture of Zeus for the temple at Olympus; cf. Cicero, *Orator* II.8–9, Plotinus, *Enneads* V.8.1.

11. The ancient Greek Mysteries of Eleusis ended with the worshipers being shown some secret visions in flashes of light.

12. Cimabue (real name Cenno di Pepo or Peppi; died c. 1302)—a Florentine painter whose work typifies the transition from the Byzantine iconography of the Middle Ages to the freer style exemplified by Giotto, who may have been Cimabue's student. Ivanov probably has in mind Cimabue's *Madonna Enthroned.*

13. A reference to Pushkin's "The Hero" ("Geroi," 1830): "I value a thousand low truths / Less than a sublime deception."

14. See *Republic* X.597BC.

15. Ivanov could have in mind both Hegel (especially his *Logic*) and the neo-Kantians.

16. Agathon (died c. 400 B.C.)—the best-known successor of the three great tragedians, was satirized in Aristophanes' comedy *Thesmophoriazusae,* or *The Women at the Thesmophoria.*

17. The distortion of the dithyramb and Wagner's "endless melody" are discussed in more detail in "Presentiments and Portents" in this volume, pp. 102, 106–7.

18. In Plato's *Phaedrus* (230D), Socrates says that "the countryside and the trees can't teach me anything, while the city people can."

19. "The Banquet of Trimalchio" is the main section of Petronius's *Satyricon* (first century A.D.); *The Golden Ass,* otherwise known as *The Metamorphoses,* by Apuleius (second century A.D.), is a fantastic romance of late antiquity.

20. Pan, the god of forests and fields and the patron of shepherds, represented a natural, impersonal principle, which was abolished by Christianity (according to Plutarch, the Emperor Tiberius heard a loud voice proclaiming the death of Pan; *De defecto oraculorum* 27). Pausanius wrote that the inhabitants of Arcadia could hear Pan's music wafting over Mt. Maenalus (*Description of Greece* VIII.36.8).

21. From Baudelaire's poem "Correspondances."

22. Cf. Lk 1:41.

23. Dante presents his four-part hermeneutic in his *Convivio.*

24. *Faust* II.6173–6306.

25. In the original publication, this phrase read: "the bounds of an intellect that determines itself and its world" (nos. 3–4, p. 91).

26. Raphael (1483–1520)—painter and architect, initiator of the cinquecento style. Bramante (1414–1514)—Italian painter and architect, the original planner of Saint Peter's Basilica in the Vatican.

27. Such thoughts occur repeatedly in Leonardo da Vinci's unfinished treatise "On Painting." See, for example, *Leonardo on Painting,* trans. Martin Kemp and Margaret Walker, ed. Martin Kemp (New Haven, Conn.: Yale University Press, 1989), pp. 20–21 (on the sense of vision), pp. 119–20

(on proportions), p. 202 (on the universality of the painter), pp. 224–25 (on fictional animals).

28. "A general consensus over common matters."

29. Ivanov makes reference to the two major elements of Schopenhauer's metaphysics, will and representation. Schopenhauer regarded art as an expression of the universal will that underlies all discrete representations. He regarded music generally as the most unmediated expression of will.

30. On 19 April 1910 (the Monday following Easter), Ivanov's apartment "The Tower" hosted a performance of Calderón's drama *Devotion to the Cross*, directed by Vsevolod Meyerhold, based on Konstantin Bal'mont's translation, and featuring a number of prominent cultural figures of the time.

31. Baudelaire's poem "Beauty" ("La Beauté," from *Les fleurs du mal*, 1857).

32. The "blue flower" is the elusive goal of the eponymous hero's quest in Novalis's novel *Heinrich von Ofterdingen*.

33. Gn 2:2–3.

34. "The walls of Rome."

35. One version of the myth of the founding of Rome holds that Remus and Romulus, the twin children of Rhea Silvia and the god Mars, were thrown into the Tiber by King Amulius. Having been washed ashore, they were suckled by a she-wolf and eventually overthrew Amulius. Following omens, they founded Rome in 753 B.C. and made Romulus king on the Palatine Hill. Remus revolted by jumping over the city wall and was then killed by Romulus, who remained the first Roman king. The notion that Romulus was triumphant due to his virtue of self-limitation, symbolized by his construction of a wall, may originate with Ivanov.

36. *Ivanov's note:*

> La Nature est un temple où de vivants pillers
> Laissent parfois sortir de confuses paroles;
> L'homme y passe à travers des forêts de symboles
> Qui l'observent avec des regards familiers.
> Comme de longs échos qui de loin se confondent
> Dans une ténébreuse et profonde unité,
> Vaste comme la nuit et comme la clarté,
> Les couleurs, les parfums et les sons se répondent.

37. "Louis Lambert" (sec. 6 of chapter titled "A Fragment"). Our renderings of Ivanov's translations have been made as closely as possible to the text in: H. de Balzac, *Seraphita and Other Stories*, trans. Clara Bell (Philadelphia: Gebbie Publishing Co., 1898), pp. 266–67.

38. Balzac, "Louis Lambert" (from the title character's "Treatise on the Will"), in *Seraphita*, p. 206).

39. Balzac, "Seraphita," chap. 7 in *Seraphita*, p. 150.

40. Source unknown.

41. Balzac, "Seraphita," chap. 7 in *Seraphita,* p. 91.

42. Jakob Boehme (1575–1624) was a German cobbler, mystic, and theosophist whose works include *Aurora* (1612). Emmanuel Swedenborg (1688–1772) was a Swedish scientist and theosophist who laid the doctrinal basis for the Church of the New Jerusalem. Both thinkers exhibited esoteric and even gnostic tendencies, and both had a strong influence on Romantic thought.

43. "More real things."

44. See, for example, the fourteenth letter of Schiller's *Letters on the Aesthetic Education of Man* (1795). Kant discusses beauty "as a symbol of morality" in his *Critique of Judgment* (1790; sec. 59).

45. Apart from the line "Alles Vergängliche ist nur ein Gleichnis" (All transitory things are merely a symbol, as Ivanov's translation usually ran) from the closing scene of *Faust,* one can cite several of Goethe's "Maxims and Reflexions" (nos. 279, 314, 1112, 1113), his essay "Symbolism," and the concept of the *Urphänomen* (archetypal phenomenon) as it appeared in "The Theory of Color" and other scientific works.

46. From Goethe's "Zueignung" ("Dedication," 1784). It was originally written as the introduction to the long poem "Die Geheimnisse" ("The Mysteries") and was subsequently used as the programmatic introduction to collections by Goethe.

47. *Inferno* 9.62–63.

48. *Ivanov's note:* The mystic Novalis was also convinced that poetry was "das absolut Reelle; je poetischer, je wahrer" [the absolute Real; the more poetic, the more true]. [Cf. Novalis's "On Goethe," sec. 24 (in *Novalis: Philosophical Writings,* trans. and ed. Margaret Mahony Stoljar [Albany: State University of New York Press, 1997], p. 117).]

49. *Ivanov's note:*

> Wie Natur im Vielgebilde
> Einen Gott nur offenbart,
> So im weiten Kunstgefilde
> Webt ein Sinn der ewigen Art.
> Dieses ist der Sinn der Wahrheit,
> Die sich nur mit Schönem schmuckt,
> Und getrost der höchsten Klarheit
> Hellsten Tags entgegenblickt.

[Here and further Ivanov quotes from *Wilhelm Meisters Wanderjahre,* bk. 2, chap. 8.]

50. *Ivanov's note:*

> Dass sie von geheimem Leben
> Offenbaren Sinn erregt.

51. *Faust* II.12104–45.

52. *Ivanov's note:*

> Il est des parfums frais comme des chairs d'enfants,
> Doux comme les hautbois, verts comme les prairies,
> Et d'autres, corrompus, riches et triomphants,
> Ayant l'expansion des choses infinies,
> Comme l'ambre, le musc, le benjoin et l'encens,
> Qui chantent les transports de l'esprit et des sens.

53. Here and below, "open mystery" is Ivanov's translation of Goethe's term "das offenbar Geheimnis"; see the quotation above from *Wilhelm Meisters Wanderjahre* and also Goethe's poems "Offenbar Geheimnis" and the "Epirrhema" from his 1820 "Parabase."

54. After Hiram built the temple for Solomon and it was dedicated in a triumphal service (2 Chr 2–7), Solomon became obsessed with his glory and succumbed to the temptations of wealth and luxury, indulging in wine and his harem of a thousand wives. Ivanov associates the book "Song of Songs," traditionally attributed to Solomon, with this period; the addressee of the hymns of love is usually identified as his wife Shulamite (or Sulamith), the daughter of the Pharaoh, and not Solomon's sister ("sister" is a term of address used in the book, Sg 4:9ff.).

55. In the original publication, this read: "his aphoristic terseness" (no. 5, p. 44).

56. In the original publication, this phrase read: "of faithfulness to the spirit of music and to the atmosphere of song in the artificial lyric" (no. 5, p. 44).

57. "Music before all things; / and for this prefer unevenness / more vague and soluble than air, / without anything weighty and listless"; from Paul Verlaine's "L'art poétique" (written in 1874, published in 1884).

58. "Take eloquence and wring its neck"; from Paul Verlaine's "L'art poétique."

59. See note 31 above.

60. The original publication read: "the cult of the rare and exotic" (no. 5, p. 44).

61. Francis Viélé-Griffin (1864–1937) was a French poet of American extraction, associated with the later French Symbolists. Ivanov refers to Viélé-Griffin's "Avec un peu de soleil et du sable blond" from the 1907 collection *Poèmes et Poésies*, which Briusov had used as a model for his 1899 poem "Gold" ("Zoloto").

62. A group of English poets and painters, founded in 1848 and associated with the names of Dante Gabriel Rossetti, Christina Rossetti, Algernon Charles Swinburne, William Morris, and Edward Burne-Jones.

63. *Ivanov's note:* Die Geisterwelt ist nicht verschlossen: dein Sinn ist zu, dein Herz ist tot; the words of Faust in Goethe's work [*Faust* II.443–44].

64. *Néant,* or nonbeing, and "chimera" appear in the poetry of Mallarmé, Viélé-Griffin, Louise Ackermann, and other French poets discussed by Ivanov here and elsewhere in his essays. Among Russian poets, Bal'mont's 1903 *Let Us Be as the Sun* (*Budem kak solntse*) included a pantheistic diptych entitled "The Grand Nothing" ("Velikoe nichto"), a phrase Bal'mont attributes there to Chinese Daoism. Ivanov may have coined the phrase *le Grand Néant* by analogy with Auguste Comte's concept of *le Grand Étre,* on which see note 47 to "On the Crisis of Humanism" in this volume. On the significance of the Isis myth in symbolism, see Michael Wachtel, "The Veil of Isis as a Paradigm of Russian Symbolist Mythopoesis," in *The European Foundations of Russian Modernism,* ed. Peter I. Barta (Lewiston: Edwin Mellen Press, 1991), pp. 25–47.

65. Originally this phrase read: "sociology and psychology" (no. 5, p. 46).

66. Cenacles are literally dining rooms, but in the Vulgate, the word is used for the room of the Last Supper, in which sense it is most often used. It was also a key concept in French Symbolism. Ivanov apparently means exalted literary salons.

67. "Transcende te ipsum" means "transcend yourself"; see note 5 to "The Symbolics of Aesthetic Principles" in this volume.

68. "Reclusive art" translates *keleinoe iskusstvo,* literally "art of the monastic cell," "cenobitic art," or else "cloistered art" (in a derogatory sense). Cenobiticism denotes the communal organization of monastic life, where each monk lives in an individual cell but shares property and tasks with the other members of the community. It is contrasted to eremitic monasticism, in which the individual hermit has much more independence. In "The Spear of Athena" (1904), Ivanov used "intimate" and "reclusive" to denote two types of individualistic art, corresponding to two communal kinds—"demotic" and "universal" (*vsenarodnoe iskusstvo*).

69. In the original publication, this phrase read: "like a tree from a seed" (no. 5, p. 46).

70. *Republic* 379A. Here, Plato uses the words "mythopoesis" and "mythopoetes."

71. "The reality of things."

72. Cf. Acts 17:23.

73. In Aeschylus's frag. 102 (*The Danaids*).

74. Sergei Gorodetsky (1884–1967)—originally a Symbolist poet under Ivanov's wing. *Iar'* (1906; possible translations include *Spring Grain* and *Ire*) was Gorodetsky's first book of poems, full of life-affirming energy and mythological images. Ivanov reviewed *Iar'* (*Kriticheskoe obozrenie,* no. 2 [1907]).

75. Heb 11:1.

76. Images derived from poems by Tiutchev; cf. "The Testaments of Symbolism" in this volume, pp. 36–39.

77. Aristotle identified surprise or wonder as the beginning of all philosophical thinking (*Metaphysics* 982B).

78. "Tikhoi noch'iu, pozdnim letom" by Fedor Tiutchev (1849).

79. In "Three Meetings" ("Tri svidaniia," 1898), Solovyov describes his three visions of Sophia–Divine Wisdom.

80. From "Three Meetings."

81. This image is possibly derived from Vladimir Solovyov's 1892 poem "We Met for a Reason" ("My soshlis' s toboi nedarom"), which is also quoted in "The Religious Task of Vladimir Solovyov" in this volume, p. 197.

82. The concept of *sobornost'* was a major theme of Russian philosophy beginning with Aleksei Khomiakov. *Sobornost'* is the freedom achieved by a community of believers in ecclesiastical life; it was seen as a basic condition for cognitive and ontological "integrity."

83. Cf., for example, "Presentiments and Portents" in this volume, pp. 107–10.

84. "Protiv muzyki," *Vesy,* no. 3 (1907): 57–60, esp. 59. Bely's tirade against music had raised the ire of Emilii Metner (pseudonym: Vol'fing), who answered in an article published in *The Golden Fleece,* with which Ivanov was nominally allied (see "Boris Bugaev protiv muzyki," *Zolotoe runo,* no. 5 [1907]: 56–62).

85. Mt 24:33; cf. Mt 3:2; Phil 4:5; Jas 5:8.

86. Mt 25:1–13.

87. Georg Friedrich Creuzer (1771–1858)—German philologist, author of *Symbolik und Mythologie der alten Völker, besonders der Griechen* (1810–12), where he attempted to reconstruct the mystical basis of Greek mythology.

88. A *thiasus* was a band of bacchants who sang and danced to Dionysus.

89. The Essenes were a sectarian group within Judaism, mentioned in Josephus Flavius and possibly connected to the Dead Sea Scrolls.

THE TESTAMENTS OF SYMBOLISM

"The Testaments of Symbolism" was first read as two papers in the Moscow Society for Free Aesthetics (on 17 March 1910) and the Petersburg Society of Lovers of the Artistic Word (on 26 March). It was published in 1910 in the May–June issue of the journal *Apollo* (no. 8, pp. 5–20). Upon republication in *Furrows and Boundaries* (pp. 122–44), Ivanov made several small changes, the most important of which are indicated in the notes. The later version was included in the *Collected Works* (2:589–603). It has previously been published in English as "The Precepts of Symbolism" in Peterson, *The Russian Symbolists*, pp. 143–56.

The article arose out of the so-called Crisis of Symbolism, a discussion of the paths of Russian literature that spilled onto the pages of *Apollo* in 1910 after Mikhail Kuzmin's essay "On Beautiful Clarity" was published in the January issue. Nikolai Gumilev published an essay, "The Life of Verse," in April, and Ivanov's defense of Symbolism appeared together with Blok's "On the Contemporary State of Symbolism" in May. The discussion continued, and by 1912, it had resulted in the rise of a new grouping, the Acmeists, in opposition to the Symbolists. For an analysis of "The Testaments of Symbolism" within the context of these polemics, see O. A. Kuznetsova, "Diskussiia o sostoianii russkogo simvolizma," *Russkaia literatura,* no. 1 (1990): 200–7 (cited below as Kuznetsova).

In his defense of Symbolism, Ivanov sets himself the double task of asserting the supratemporal character of Symbolism, which is less a prescriptive than a descriptive (i.e., objective) poetics, and, at the same time, affirming the rights of the contemporary Symbolist movement to the heritage of Russian metaphysical poetry. The latter goal is pursued mainly by identifying similarities in the philosophical views of Symbolism and its precursors.

The philosophical underpinnings of the article are a mix of neo-Kantian epistemology and Platonic ontology. Ivanov accepts a neo-Kantian division of knowledge into science and art, carefully delimiting the autonomous sphere of the latter as the intuition of essences. This intuition, moreover, is achieved through the very structure of language, which, as Heinrich Rickert had postulated, implicitly entails an assertion of truth as value. Naming a thing asserts that the thing truly exists and can be fathomed in its essence.

Ivanov proceeds to platonize this theory in a way that owes a great debt to Vladimir Solovyov. Ivanov identifies truth with being: since the copula "is" necessarily asserts the existence of "Is-ness" or "being in truth" (*sushchee*), any grammatical sentence is both an affirmation of relative being and of "being in truth," or God.

A distinct parallel can also be observed with the Platonic dialogues *Theaetetus* and *The Sophist*. In the latter dialogue, the Stranger shows that to say that nonbeing *is,* is to have it partake of being; he defines nonbeing as the "other" of being, or potential being (258DE). Thus, even nonbeing serves as an affirmation of absolute being. Like Ivanov, the Stranger proceeds to consider predication, which he sees as a means of asserting the true being of things (262AC), what Ivanov calls the myth of the thing. Further, the distinction between being and nonbeing leads to the identification of two kinds of imitative art: true "image-making," and false, fantastic, "likeness-making" (264CE). Ivanov follows this line of reasoning by asserting a true, iconic art, which replicates and partakes in the being of the object but he differs from Plato in affirming its divinely creative or theurgic nature. The restoration of the "language of the gods" in art is tantamount to the restoration of nature's divine being, as each relative "is" approximates its source in divine being ("is-ness"). In Solovyov's terminology, this is the theurgical task of perfecting the world soul into Sophia–Divine Wisdom and Flesh of the World. Traceable to prerational Greece and its ancestors (Egypt), according to Ivanov, this work is now being conducted in the practice and theory of the Russian Symbolists.

1. A line from Fedor Tiutchev's poem "Silentium!" (1830, 1854).

2. Ibid.

3. Literally "a fourhood of terms"; the failure to provide a common middle term between the major and minor premises of a syllogism.

4. Ivanov's usage of the word "suprasensible" (*sverkhchuvstvennyi*) reflects the Russian equivalent of the Kantian *Übersinnliche*; see James West, "Ivanov's Theory of Knowledge: Kant and Neo-Kantianism," in *Vyacheslav Ivanov: Poet, Critic, Philosopher,* ed. Robert L. Jackson and Lowry Nelson (New Haven, Conn.: Yale Center for International and Area Studies, 1986), pp. 313–25.

5. The first two stanzas of Tiutchev's "O, wise soul of mine" ("O, veshchaia dusha moia," 1855).

6. Quotations from Tiutchev's "December Morning" ("Dekabr'skoe utro," 1859).

7. Quotations from Tiutchev's "Holy night ascended to the heavens" ("Sviataia noch' na nebosklon vzoshla," 1849–50).

8. Quotations from Tiutchev's "How sweetly sleeps the dark-green garden" ("Kak sladko dremlet sad temno-zelenyi," 1836).

9. Ivanov refers to Novalis's "Hymns to the Night" ("Hymnen an die Nacht"), which he translated in 1909 and 1910.

10. From Tiutchev's "Spring" ("Vesna," 1838).

11. A reference to Tiutchev's "There is a songfulness in ocean waves" ("Pevuchest' est' v morskikh volnakh," 1865).

12. From Tiutchev's "Look how the West has lit up" ("Smotri, kak zapad razgorelsia," 1838).

13. Ivanov compares Dionysus and Apollo to the divine and human natures of Christ, which coexist "without division and without confusion"; for the roots of this formula, see Ivanov's "Excursus" to "Thoughts on Symbolism." The terms "biunity" and "biune" (*dvuedinstvo, dvuedinyi*) are formed by analogy with the Trinitarian "triunity" and "triune" (*triedinstvo, triedinyi*) and refer to the presence of two natures in the one person of Christ; here, as elsewhere, Ivanov sees Christological dogma as a universal law capable of explaining aesthetic phenomena; cf. pp. 57–58 in this volume.

14. From Tiutchev's "What are you howling about, night wind?" ("O chem ty voesh', vetr nochnoi?" 1836).

15. Quotations from Tiutchev's "The blue-gray shadows are confused" ("Teni sizye smesilis'," 1836).

16. Quotations from Tiutchev's "Day and Night" ("Den' i noch'," 1839).

17. The first stanza of Tiutchev's "A Vision" ("Videnie," 1829).

18. The final lines of Tiutchev's "A Vision."

19. Here and above, quotations from Tiutchev's "Just as the ocean surrounds the earthly sphere" ("Kak okean ob"emlet shar zemnoi," 1830).

20. A quotation from Tiutchev's "The nighttime sky is so gloomy" ("Nochnoe nebo tak ugriumo," 1865).

21. This thought, which appears in the "Tabula Smaragdina," attributed to Hermes Trismegistus, became one of the key phrases in Russian Decadence; for the Hermetic text, see Wayne Shumaker, *The Occult Sciences in the Renaissance: A Study in Intellectual Patterns* (Berkeley: University of California Press, 1972), p. 179; cf. Heraclitus's "The path up and down is one and the same" (frag. B 60). In 1907, Ivanov wrote a poem entitled "Sky above, sky below" ("Nebo—vverkhu, nebo—vnizu"), which refers to a similar thought attributed to the Gnostic Basilides: "Sky above, sky below . . . Blessed is he who understands." Cf. Dostoevsky's *The Brothers Karamazov*, pt. 4, bk. 12, chap. 6.

22. From Tiutchev's "Just as the ocean surrounds the earthly sphere" (see note 19).

23. The final stanza of Tiutchev's "The Swan" ("Lebed'," c. 1830).

24. From Tiutchev's "Silentium!" (c. 1830).

25. The last stanza of Tiutchev's "Spring" ("Vesna"); Ivanov changes Tiutchev's punctuation, which has been restored in the translation.

26. From Evgeny Baratynsky's "Songs heal the ailing spirit" ("Boliashchii dukh vrachuet pesnopen'e," 1835).

27. "On Beautiful Clarity" was the article by Mikhail Kuzmin that set new criteria for Russian prose and initiated the "Crisis of Symbolism" in 1910; see discussion in introductory note above.

28. Ivanov's list of correspondences refers mostly to mythical metamorphoses recorded in classical literature. The Furies, or Erinyes, the terrifying goddesses of revenge, were transformed into good goddesses in Aeschylus's *Eumenides*. In the *Fifth Homeric Hymn,* Hades is called "generous" (404), "hospitable" (436), and "rich" (489), since no one can avoid becoming his welcome guest and thus contributing to his wealth (cf. *Cratylus*). Asteria was the sister of Leto, both born to the Titans Coeus and Phoebe, mother of Hecate (see Hesiod's *Theogony* 404f.–410). Delos is an island in the Aegean Sea where Leto gave birth to Apollo (*Homeric Hymn III*). Astyanax or Skamandrios is the son of Hector and Andromache (cf. *Cratylus* 392B–93B).

29. Many of Heraclitus's fragments express similar paradoxes, for example, B20, B62, B88.

30. Gn 3:5: "Your eyes shall be opened and ye shall be as gods."

31. Ivanov summarized his epistemology, and later his ontological theorizing, by the phrase "Thou art" (first in an article of the same name

dated 1907). For a development of this theme, see "The Religious Task of Vladimir Solovyov" in this volume, pp. 195–96.

32. Plato explicates the notion of nonbeing (*mè ón*) as potential being in *The Sophist* (258DE and passim); the link between common or false opinion (*dóxa*) and nonbeing is also explored in *Theaetetus* (188D).

33. In the 1910 version, Ivanov specifically named Heinrich Rickert (p. 10). The phrase "our general outlook is wholly alien to these philosophers" was absent in this version.

34. "The father is good." Cf. Mt 19:17.

35. On the Cyclops's boulders, see *Odyssey* IX.

36. Plato discusses the absolute and relative nature of being, showing how all predication refers to a single, transcendent source; see *The Sophist* (252ff., 255D).

37. Cf. Schiller's "The Allotment of the Earth" ("Die Teilung der Erde").

38. Cf. Plato's *Sophist* 262ABC.

39. The last lines of Pushkin's "Poet and the Crowd" ("Poèt i tolpa," 1828). Ivanov continues to refer to this poem in the following paragraph.

40. Quote is from the first lines of Pushkin's "Poet and the Crowd."

41. "Be quiet, you senseless people, / Day laborers, slaves of need and worry! / I cannot stand your insolent grumbling, / You're worms of the earth, not sons of heaven; / You want utility in all, you value / The Belvedere idol by the pound. / You see no use, no use in it. / And yet this marble is a god! . . . So what? / You value more a cooking pot: / You can cook some food in it"; the words of the Poet to the crowd in Pushkin's poem.

42. Ivanov refers generally to the mythical figure of Orpheus. He also refers to King Amphion of Thebes, whose artful playing on the lyre caused the stones to form themselves into a wall around the city (Homer, *Odyssey* XI.260–65; Horace, *Ars Poetica* 394–96).

43. On "symbolics" see our introductory note to "The Symbolics of Aesthetic Principles" in this volume.

44. "Orchestic"—pertaining to dancing.

45. *Evening Fires* is the general title of four poetry collections by the poet Afanasy Fet (1883–91).

46. Quotations from Lermontov's poem "The Angel" ("Angel," 1830).

47. Ivanov here refers to Lermontov's poem "How often, all alone amidst a lurid crowd" ("Kak chasto pestroiu tolpoiu okruzhen," 1840), which he considered to be addressed to Sophia–Divine Wisdom (*Collected Works*, 4:363–64, 379–80).

48. From Goethe's *Faust* II.12104–5.

49. In "On the Russian Idea" in this volume (p. 129), Ivanov attributes a similar idea to Theodor Mommsen.

50. The distinction between letters and hieroglyphs, as the respective signifiers of discursive (outer) and intelligent (inner) speech, was made by Plotinus (*Enneads* V.8.6).

51. The name of Konstanin Bal'mont's famous poem from his eponymous collection is *Let Us Be as the Sun* (*Budem kak solntse,* 1902).

52. A reference to Baudelaire's poem "Correspondances"; cf. "Two Elements in Contemporary Symbolism" in this volume, pp. 22–25.

53. *Faust* II.4685.

54. "Magical idealism" is the general term given to the views expressed in Novalis's "Fragments." Novalis himself used the term rarely.

55. Mikhail Vrubel' (1856–1910)—a painter of the World of Art circle, went insane in 1905. Ivanov's paean recalls lines from Tiutchev's poem on the death of Pushkin "January 29, 1837" ("29-e ianvaria 1837"): "Peace, peace to you, O poet's shadow, Peace to your radiant dust!"

56. A reference to 1 Cor 13:1: "Though I speak with the tongues of men and of angels, but have not love, I have become sounding brass or a clanging cymbal."

57. References to the Russo-Japanese War (1904–5) and the 1905 revolution. Ivanov wrote a cycle of poems, "The Hour of Wrath" (or "Dies irae"; "Godina gneva"), on the 1905 revolution, in which he joined most of his Symbolist contemporaries in sympathizing with the democratic aims of the revolutionary opposition.

58. Golconda is a place in India, also called Hyderabad, known for its diamonds; figuratively, "a mine of wealth." In a 1910 review, Ivanov tied the image of a "conquistador of the 'refined' Golcondas of transcendental geography and illusory 'marquisates'" to Nikolai Gumilev and, by extension, to Gumilev's mentor Valery Briusov (*Apollo,* no. 7 [1910]: 40).

59. "Ashes" is a reference to Andrei Bely's book of poems from 1908, *Ash* (*Pepel*), which marked a turn toward socially engaged realism, evoking comparison to Nikolai Nekrasov.

60. Leading Symbolist poets.

61. Cf. the lines from Pushkin's "Poet and the Crowd" cited in note 41.

62. A quotation from one of the final lines of Aleksandr Blok's 1906 play *The Fair Show Booth* (*Balaganchik*). This work, along with Blok's poem "The Unknown Woman" ("Neznakomka," 1906), signaled Blok's move away from religious idealism to a gritty irony of depravity and despair. Here and further, Ivanov interprets Blok's changing attitude toward the "Eternal Feminine" with images from Revelation (see Rv 12:1, 17:1–5).

63. A reference to Ivanov's own article "On the Non-Acceptance of the World," published first as an introduction to Georgy Chulkov's book *On Mystical Anarchism* (1906). The phrase "nonacceptance of the world" orig-

inated in the words of Ivan in Dostoevsky's *The Brothers Karamazov* (see "Rebellion," pt. 2, bk. 5, chap. 4).

64. Another formulation that appeared in Ivanov's "On the Non-Acceptance of the World" and other articles; cf. note 32 to "The Symbolics of Aesthetic Principles" in this volume.

65. Aleksandr Dobroliubov (1876–1945?), an early Symbolist poet, became a religious sectarian and wanderer. Dmitry Merezhkovsky (1866–1941), who was also one of the first Symbolist poets, became heavily involved with radical politics after the 1905 revolution.

66. Elsewhere, Ivanov is particularly scornful of Heinrich Heine's "neo-Romantic" humor or irony, which he calls "a profound inner renunciation of the religious idea and a blasphemous ridiculing of the original testaments of the [Jena Romantic] school" (*Collected Works*, 4:255). In a 1908 article entitled "Irony," Blok had called Heine's "provocational irony" "an illness" (Aleksandr Blok, *Sobranie sochinenii* [Moscow and Leningrad: Gosudarstvennoe izdatel'stvo khudozhestvennoi literatury, 1960–63], 5:272), although Blok himself was quite fond of Heine and translated many of his poems into Russian.

67. Leonid Andreev (1871–1919) was a writer and dramatist close to the Symbolist movement. His works were notorious for their angst and pessimism.

68. The last two paragraphs are directed in particular against Mikhail Kuzmin and Nikolai Gumilev, respectively (Kuznetsova, p. 207).

69. A peplos is a peplum or long robe.

70. In the 1910 version: "Fiat."

71. For the image of the cosmic rose, see the latter cantos of Dante's *Paradise.*

72. Mk 8:24.

73. From Fet's poem "Tormented by life and the treachery of hope" ("Izmuchen zhizn'iu, kovarstvom nadezhdy," 1864); the quotations Ivanov adduces in his text are adjusted to fit the grammatical context. "Sun of the world" is not capitalized in the original.

74. Kuznetsova identifies this comment as pertaining to Sergei Gorodetsky, Ivanov's protégé in years previous, but it could as well be a reference to Ivanov's own formulation of Mystical Anarchism, or Mystical Energeticism as he preferred to call it, in "On the Non-Acceptance of the World."

75. Cf. Euripides' *Bacchae* l.1203ff.

76. In the 1910 version, this read: "*Veniat! Fiat!*"

77. An imprecise autocitation from Ivanov's poem "Maenad" ("Menada," 1906) in *Cor Ardens.*

78. From Ivanov's dithyramb "Fire-bearers" ("Ognenostsy," 1906) in *Cor Ardens.*

79. The final lines of Ivanov's poem "Beauty" ("Krasota"); cf. note 36 to "The Symbolics of Aesthetic Principles" in this volume.

80. *Ivanov's note:* "In contemporary literature, the lyric element seems to be the most powerful. . . . The most that lyric poetry can do is to complicate emotions, filling the soul with unimaginable chaos and complexity." A. Blok, introduction to "Lyric Dramas."

81. Cf. sec. 4 of Nietzsche's "Richard Wagner in Bayreuth," pt. 4 of *Untimely Meditations.*

82. In 1906, Ivanov wrote: "*Religio* is often interpreted as 'connection' only on the strength of an etymological error, which was admittedly common already in the time of the Christian apologetes, who sought the symbolic meaning of '*sobornost'*' in this word. At the same time I can only welcome Sergei Bulgakov's idea that the principle of inner religiosity is itself the principle of inner *sobornost'* in man" (*Collected Works,* 3:734–35); cf. also "On Law and Connection" in Ivanov's "Sporades" ("Sporady"; *Collected Works,* 3:126–31).

83. Dt 5:11.

84. See note 39 above.

THOUGHTS ON SYMBOLISM

"Thoughts on Symbolism" was based on a lecture at the Petersburg Society of Lovers of the Artistic Word on 18 February 1912, where Andrei Bely read his lecture "Symbolism." It was soon published as the lead article in the first issue of the journal *Works and Days* ([1912]: 3–10), which was initiated by Ivanov, Bely, and Blok as the unified organ of a revitalized Symbolist movement. It was republished with minor changes in *Furrows and Boundaries* (pp. 148–59), and then in the second volume of *Collected Works* (pp. 605–12). The "Excursus on Sect and Dogma" originated in a speech Ivanov gave on 20 January 1914, at a "Disputation on Contemporary Literature," a stenogram of which was then published in the non-Symbolist journal *Testaments* (*Zavety* [1914], bk. 2, pt. 2, pp. 80–84). Ivanov practically rewrote the entire speech and appended it to "Thoughts on Symbolism" in *Furrows and Boundaries* (pp. 160–63; *Collected Works,* 2:613–14). Only the most important variants to the original text of "Thoughts on Symbolism" are noted below. The essay has been published in English twice before: Peterson, *The Russian Symbolists,* pp. 181–88; trans. Samuel D. Cioran, in *Russian Literature Triquarterly,* no. 4 (1972): 151–58 (reprinted in *The Silver Age in Russian Culture: An Anthology,* ed. Carl Proffer and Ellendea Proffer [Ann Arbor, Mich.: Ardis, 1975], pp. 32–39).

In the table of contents for an unrealized German edition of his essays (in Ivanov's Rome archive), Ivanov changed the title of the current essay to "What Is True Symbolism?" As implied by this title, the essay presents Ivanov's defense of Realistic Symbolism against its contemporary detractors, some of whom had formed the proto-Acmeist Guild of Poets in November

1911 in opposition to Ivanov's Academy of Verse (on their conflict, see V. Blinov, "Viacheslav Ivanov and Acmeism: Literary Polemics of 1912–14," *Russian Literature* 44 no. 3 [1998]: 331–45). Ivanov claims for Symbolism the heritage of classical and European poetics, from Simonides to Dante and Goethe. He reiterates the erotic, and thus essentially Platonic, nature of artistic cognition, now increasing the emphasis on the interpersonal aspects of the artistic process for all of its participants. Compared to his previous statements on Symbolism, Ivanov's focus has now shifted to its ontological and personalistic nature, as he attempts to turn a limited literary polemic into yet another affirmation of the Symbolist worldview. In this, he is helped by the terminological muddle of his Acmeist opponents, which allows him to co-opt their own words to fit his meaning.

Ivanov's language, especially in the "Excursus," is particularly sacramental and Christological, although he continues to describe art in neo-Kantian terms as an autonomous faculty of knowledge. This is also evident in the note "Orpheus," published in the same issue of *Works and Days* (pp. 60–63), where Ivanov defends the integrity of mystical or artistic cognition. But Ivanov's explication of artistic cognition is clearly based on the eucharistic liturgy, and his concept of aesthetic canon is modeled on Christian dogma. Ivanov's step beyond the framework of neo-Kantian epistemology into the connections between art and being, creation and becoming, is clarified by his extensive use of imagery from Dante's *Paradise*.

Some of these connections are made explicit in "On Sect and Dogma," which contains a more direct polemic with Dmitry Merezhkovsky, whose socially engaged aesthetic Ivanov obviously found a more dangerous threat to Symbolism than Acmeist theorizing (see Blinov, "Viacheslav Ivanov and Acmeism"). It is Ivanov's clearest exposition of the Christian basis of Symbolism and presages the more directly metaphysical and less narrowly Symbolist works of the 1910s, such as the essays on Dostoevsky (collected in *Freedom and the Tragic Life*).

1. This poem, under the title "The Alpine Horn," was published in Ivanov's first collection of verse, *Pilot Stars*. It is closely tied to Pushkin's "The Echo" ("Èkho," 1831).

2. Horace, *Ars Poetica* (or "Epistle to Pisos [or Pisones]") l.361. Simonides (c. 556–c. 468 B.C.) was an ancient Greek poet, noted, among other things, for his dithyrambs; Plutarch writes that "Simonides . . . calls painting inarticulate poetry and poetry inarticulate painting" (*De gloria Atheniensium* 3 [346F]; also *De audiendis poetis* 3 [17F]).

3. Horace, *Ars Poetica* l.99–100.

4. Cf. Gn 9:9–17.

5. The structure of this opening section bears a resemblance to the chapter "The Seven Seals (The Yes and Amen-Song)," sec. 16 in pt. 3 of Nietzsche's *Thus Spake Zarathustra*.

6. Jacob's ladder is from Gn 42:24–30.

7. See Plato's *Symposium* 206D, 210A–212A.

8. Dante, *Paradise* XXXIII.145. The stars, sun, and love correspond to the three levels of divinity in the Empyrean sphere, represented by the saints (including the Virgin), Christ, and the Trinity. To stress this point, Ivanov capitalizes the words "Love," "Sun," and, in the translation only, "Stars," none of which is capitalized in modern editions of Dante and were variously printed in editions of Ivanov's own day. Ivanov had previously used Dante's line as an epigraph to his poem "Spirit" ("Dukh") from *Pilot Stars*. The entire section 3 is closely modeled on imagery from Dante's progression through the celestial spheres in *Paradise,* including Beatrice, the Divine Mover, and the poet's crown (canto 25).

9. "Undivided and unconfused" is a formula decided upon at the Council of Chalcedon (A.D. 451) given in the Athanasian Creed to describe the relationship between the two natures of Christ within his single hypostasis.

10. The priest who officiated at the greater mysteries.

11. "Wisdom" (in Greek, *Sophia*) is proclaimed in the Orthodox liturgy before readings from scripture.

12. Cf. note 21 to "The Testaments of Symbolism" in this volume.

13. Cf. "The Testaments of Symbolism" in this volume, p. 41.

14. From Lermontov's poem "The Angel" (1830); "it" refers to "the soul."

15. Cf. Jn 14:2: "In My Father's house are many mansions."

16. Jn 3:8: "The wind bloweth where it listeth, and thou hearest the sound thereof, but canst not tell whence it cometh, and whither it goeth: so is every one that is born of the Spirit."

17. "Integral personality" (*tsel'naia lichnost'*) was a central concept in the philosophical writings of Ivan Kireevsky, a founder of the Slavophile movement in Russian thought.

18. Ivanov here is polemicizing with the Acmeists but also clarifying his own earlier statements in "On the Joyful Craft and the Joy of the Spirit" in this volume, p. 113ff.

19. "Poets are born [not made]"; a paraphrase of Cicero, *Pro Archia poeta oratio* 18.

20. "Unto painting" and "let them be sweet" are phrases from Horace's poetic theory, given in their context in sec. 1.

21. The first lines of an untitled poem by Lermontov ("Iz-pod tainstvennoi, kholodnoi polumaski," 1842).

22. From Lermontov's "There are kinds of speech whose meaning" ("Est' rechi—znachenie," 1839).

23. See Jn 1:5.

24. Cf. Ivanov's note "Orpheus" in the same issue of *Works and Days* (pp. 60–63): "The typical man of today experiences a polar opposition between

his seamless and chaotic *I*, on the one hand, and, on the other, the seamless and chaotic datum of the outer world, this *other,* which frightens him with its decaying and hostile mass. The correct distribution of polar forces turns man into a vital and mighty magnet; opens up to him paths of a cognition that is simultaneously solar and lunar, rational and irrational, in the distinct separation and harmony of both independent spheres; returns him to his creative instinct in reason and not in madness; and reinforces his religious will in coincidence with his spiritual freedom. This correct distribution of polar forces is a vital feeling of the opposition of the outer *ego* and the inner *I,* a marriage between the spirit that finds self-determination in the category of divine adoption, and the soul (Psyche), or the 'emotional body,' the 'Lord's hand-maiden' and emancipated bride" (p. 62).

25. Hesiod, *Theogony* 1–35. The reference to Hesiod is particularly significant considering that the new Symbolist journal had taken its name from his *Works and Days.*

26. Ivanov elsewhere discusses such "idealistic" or "associative" Symbolism apropos of Innokenty Annensky (1856–1909), who wrote in his poem "Ideal," from his *Quiet Songs* (*Tikhie pesni,* 1904): "To solve on faded pages / The tiring puzzle [*rebus*] of being!" The Acmeists considered Annensky their mentor.

27. Cf. "The Testaments of Symbolism" in this volume, p. 43.

28. The words *dentelle* (lace) and *jeu supreme* (supreme play) are from the beginning of Mallarmé's "Sonnets" III (1887). The lines containing these words were used as an epigraph to the first volume of Briusov's *Russian Symbolists* (1894), where they attracted the particular ire of Vladimir Solovyov, who met the three issues of *Russian Symbolists* with three sarcastic reviews. Ivanov is thus joining with Solovyov against a perceived Briusov-Mallarmé alliance.

29. "From the real to the more real; Through the real toward the more real." On Ivanov's aesthetic maxims, see "Two Elements in Contemporary Symbolism" in this volume. Here and in the following examples, Ivanov answers Acmeist accusations that Symbolism ignored concrete reality in favor of idealistic schemes.

30. Ivanov links the "heavenly rose" of the final cantos of Dante's *Paradise* to Mother Earth, since both are representative of the Mother of God or Divine Sophia.

31. A slightly changed citation from Tiutchev's 1836 poem "Bright snow shone in the valley" ("Iarkii sneg siial v doline").

32. See note 45 to "Two Elements in Contemporary Symbolism" in this volume.

33. Although the common expression, both in English and Russian, would require "catholic" here, Ivanov markedly implies the Slavic equivalent, and Slavophile concept, of *sobornost'.* Similarly, below Ivanov uses

"Orthodoxy" (*pravoslavie*) instead of the confessionally neutral "orthodoxy" (*ortodoksiia*).

34. At the First Ecumenical Council, held in Nicea in A.D. 325, *homoousia* (of one essence) was chosen over its counterpart *homoiousia* (of similar essence) to describe the relationship between the members of the Trinity—the Father, Son, and Holy Spirit. This formula was included in the Symbol of Faith, known as the Nicene Creed. Ivanov's citation of *homoousia* is undoubtedly related to the use of this concept in Pavel Florensky's *The Pillar and Ground of the Truth* (1914; English translation by Boris Jakim [Princeton, N.J.: Princeton University Press, 1997]).

35. Merezhkovsky turned from Symbolist poetry to socially engaged criticism and commentary. He came to see Tiutchev's pantheistic mysticism as a breed of Russian complacency and as a refusal to recognize the primacy of social questions. The term "Oblomovism" (*oblomovshchina*) was introduced in 1859 by radical critic Nikolai Dobroliubov (1836–61), who saw in the title character of Ivan Goncharov's novel *Oblomov* a symbol of Russian indolence.

36. Cf. Mt 9:17. Vissarion Belinsky (1811–48) was an influential Russian critic and social commentator, hero and martyr, of the Russian radical intelligentsia. The 1860s saw the rise of a mature radical movement, inspired in part by Nikolai Nekrasov (1821–77), Nikolai Chernyshevsky (1828–89), and Nikolai Dobroliubov.

MANNER, PERSONA, STYLE

"Manner, Persona, Style" was originally published in the journal *Works and Days* (4–5 [1913]: 1–12). With minor changes and the deletion of the final paragraph, it was included in *Furrows and Boundaries* (pp. 167–85) and in the *Collected Works* (2:616–26).

Ivanov inherited the terms "manner" and "style" from the German idealist tradition, e.g., from Goethe's 1789 essay "The Simple Imitation of Nature, Manner, Style." They refer to stages in the dialectical synthesis of artistic method and material, which Ivanov calls the datum (*dannost'*). These stages also correspond to particular literary genres. However, the two terms introduced by Ivanov—persona (*litso*, literally "face" or "person") and grand style (*bol'shoi stil'*)—remain somewhat outside this dialectical process, having more to do with the artist's personal maturity and the general accessibility of his works. A similar linkage is found in Schleiermacher: "As man is always located in a multiplicity of ideas everything arose via adoption and exclusion. But if this or anything else did not emerge from personal individuality, but was instead superficially learned or habituated or done for effect, then this is mannered, and what is mannered is always bad style" (Friedrich Schleiermacher, *Hermeneutics and Criticism and Other Writ-*

ings, trans. and ed. Andrew Bowie [Cambridge and New York: Cambridge University Press, 1998], p. 91). While foreshadowing the distinction between the artist and the man that would be drawn sharply in "On the Limits of Art," the four-part scheme of "Manner, Persona, Style" appears to conflate the elements of artistic method and aesthetic reception into a single process.

The article is remarkable precisely as an indication of Ivanov's turn away from an aesthetization of the person and toward the personalization of art. The shift from manner to style is facilitated by the achievement of an integral personality (*tsel'naia lichnost'*, a term introduced by the Slavophile thinkers Khomiakov and Kireevsky), while the achievement of grand style indicates the poet's integration with national and universal values. The privileging of the artist's personality is in marked contrast to Ivanov's early aesthetics of ecstasy and theurgy. It returns the center of value to humanity in a way that might be termed personalist. This personalistic streak in Ivanov's mature aesthetics was developed only in "On the Limits of Art" and has attracted little attention, but it provides an important link between his aesthetics and his ruminations on culture and history. Milovoje Jovanović has claimed that Ivanov's theory of style had an important influence on Bakhtin's concept of the author ("Viacheslav Ivanov i Bakhtin," in *Vjačeslav Ivanov: russischer Dichter, europäischer Kulturphilosoph,* ed. Wilfried Potthoff [Heidelberg: Universitätsverlag C. Winter, 1993], pp. 223–39).

1. A reference to Pushkin's famous poem "The Poet" ("Poèt," 1827).

2. "The tragedy begins"; see note 18 to "The Symbolics of Aesthetic Principles" in this volume.

3. On Mikhail Vrubel', see note 55 to "The Testaments of Symbolism" in this volume.

4. Mastery is proven first in limitation; from Goethe's sonnet "Natur und Kunst" (1802).

5. The style is the man; from Comte de Georges-Louis Leclerc Buffon's *Discours prononcé à l'Academie française par M. de Buffon le jour de sa réception* (1753).

6. Cf. Nietzsche's use of the term "grand style" in sec. 11 of "Skirmishes of an Untimely Man" in *Twilight of the Idols.*

7. Cf. Dostoevsky's "Pushkin Speech" (*A Writer's Diary,* trans. Kenneth Lantz [Evanston, Ill.: Northwestern University Press, 1994], pp. 1271–93).

8. A term used by Nietzsche beginning with *Untimely Meditations,* pt. 2 ("On the Use and Abuse of History for Life"), foreword, sec. 3, 7, 8; cf. also *Beyond Good and Evil,* sec. 224.

9. Nicholas Boileau (1636–1711)—French poet and literary theoretician, author of "L'art poétique" (1674), a manifesto of neoclassical poetics. Pierre de Ronsard (1524–85)—French poet, author of civil odes, love poems, sonnets, and an epic.

10. Paul Verlaine (1844–96)—French poet associated with both the Parnassian and Symbolist movements; see "Two Elements in Contemporary Symbolism," pp. 25–26, in this volume.

11. In Richard Lattimore's translation, this is the refrain from the first strophe (lines 121, 139, 159) of Aeschylus's *Agamemnon,* paraphrased in line 349 by Clytemnestra.

12. From shortness of breath.

13. Ivanov uses quotations because he is rendering the German "Zeitgeist."

14. The Russian Futurists included Velimir Khlebnikov, Aleksei Kruchenykh, and Vladimir Mayakovsky. Their poetry in this period was characterized by the hypertrophy of the individual, alogism, and disregard for tradition. Ego-Futurism is mainly associated with Igor Severianin (1887–1941), who added a particularly Decadent note to the Futurist ethos.

15. Such are the desperate ones.

16. Plato, *Phaedrus* 244E.

17. Cf. Heb 10:31.

18. Cf. "With fear of God draw near," the call to the Eucharist in the Divine Liturgy of St. John Chrysostom.

19. Old Believers or, more accurately, Old Ritualists are Russian Orthodox who rejected the liturgical reforms of Patriarch Nikon in the 1660s.

20. Such are the flatterers of times past.

21. See Mt 16:25–26: "For whoever desires to save his life will lose it, but whoever loses his life for My sake will find it. For what is profit to a man if he gains the whole world, and loses his own soul?" See also Lk 17:33, Jn 12:25.

22. A reference to Nietzsche's *The Birth of Tragedy from the Spirit of Music.*

23. *Republic* X (597BC); see "Two Elements in Contemporary Symbolism," p. 17, in this volume.

24. Aristotle, *Poetics* 1462b.

25. *Le néant* (the nothing); *le Grand Néant* (the Big Nothing); see note 64 to "Two Elements in Contemporary Symbolism" in this volume.

26. Sophia (literally "Wisdom"), together with her daughters Faith, Hope, and Charity, were martyred in Rome in A.D. 137 (according to Orthodox tradition). Wisdom (Sophia) was also the name of the feminine cosmos in the Solovyovian philosophical tradition.

27. On Ivanov's interpretation of the word "religion," see note 82 to "The Testaments of Symbolism" in this volume.

28. Mk 5:9; Lk 8:30.

29. In the original publication, the last two sentences read: "We can demonstrate this with the example of lyric poetry: based on the foregoing considerations of the nature of style, we shall try to find the criterion of lyric

'perfection' as it might appear to the modern consciousness, which is attempting to overcome the deviations it comprehends and does not wish to submit to the formulas of ancient or modern fashion, neither the fashion of Horace or Boileau, nor the fashions of the recent Parnassus, Decadence, or modern eclecticism" (p. 9).

30. "That is why he simulates it in this way: Friends, we have *experienced it*"; from Goethe's "Venetian Epigrams" ("Venezianische Epigramme"), 33.

31. Ivanov echoes Solovyov's words at the end of "The General Meaning of Art": "If it be said that this task exceeds the bounds of art, we reply: who established these bounds?" (*Sochineniia* [Moscow: Mysl', 1990], 2:404).

32. "Genialisch Treiben" ("The Genius Game") is the title of a poem by Goethe.

33. The original publication contained an extra paragraph:

> There are some who flee life, who have an affection for the greenhouses of idle dreaming, who, like people suffering from paranoia, fear and avoid "Symbolism" as if it were some obligation and betrothal to actual reality, who think that they thus affirm "art for art's sake." (O, if only they would find the time to gain insight into the artistic practice and theory of Goethe, after which it would be impossible to argue about Symbolism in the way that those who pretend to the title of "the youth" argue with us, for we are talking about elements that culture has assimilated for good!) As far as such fugitives from life are concerned, they can be left to their delights at their own successes (O, if only in the sciences as well). Experience alone can cure us of this fateful misconception, that what they take for poetry is genuinely a great and divinely beautiful, awesome, and living force: the first stormy rain to sprinkle our spiritual draught will wash away all the paints from their canvases, which are beautiful like peacocks' feathers. (p. 12)

ON THE LIMITS OF ART

"On the Limits of Art" was originally read at the Moscow Religious-Philosophical Society in December 1913 and then in Petersburg at a public venue on 22 January 1914. It was first printed in *Works and Days* in 1914 (no. 7, pp. 81–106), and was included with a few minor changes in *Furrows and Boundaries* (pp. 187–229) and *Collected Works* (2:627–51).

Ivanov's final statement on Symbolism until the 1930s, "On the Limits of Art" provides a subtle and synthetic restatement of most of his previous thoughts on aesthetics. In particular, the ecstatic psychology of art presented in "The Symbolics of Aesthetic Principles" is applied to the universal spiritual realm. The distinguishing feature of the artist's creative persona is expressed in the Apollonian process of granting form to the spiritual intuition and communicating it in the common language of mankind. Here, the ideas of the inner canon, communication, and style (developed in the essays of 1910–13) find their most developed exposition. Most striking is the rejection of theurgy as the immediate task of Symbolism and its relegation to an indefinite, almost eschatological, future: symbols are not higher reality itself but rather revelations of it to people, who are left to employ these revelations in real life. Thus also the significative and transformative principles of Symbolism, which Ivanov opposed quite sternly in "Two Elements in Contemporary Symbolism," are reintegrated in a general theory of Symbolism.

The title of the essay echoes several important works by other authors. The full title of Lessing's famous treatise is *Laocoön: An Essay on the Limits of Art.* Friedrich Schlegel has a 1794 essay "On the Limits of the Beautiful," which contains the assertion that the beauty of art must crown, but not replace, a measured appreciation of nature and love for one's fellow men: "From nature the intellect derives richness, comprehensiveness, and living energy; love gives it an inward depth and harmonious unity, meet for the soul of that rich life, while art frames harmonious regulations, and points out the laws of the beautiful. . . . This new-found harmony is not gained by his deserts, but is his act" (*Aesthetic and Miscellaneous Works,* trans. E. J. Millington [London: George Ballard Sons, 1875], pp. 423–44). André Gide's reformulation of this in an article "The Limits of Art" is also relevant: "'Man proposes and God disposes,' we have been told; this is true in nature; but . . . in the work of art, on the contrary, *God proposes and man disposes*" (*Pretexts* [New York: Meridian Books, 1959], p. 46). Other references to Goethe and Solovyov's poem "The Three Labors" reinforce the personalistic and even moralistic interpretation of theurgy, which is now seen less as a magical incantation than the labor of "integral personalities."

1. Ivanov quoted this passage from his unfinished translation of Dante's *New Life,* which he began in 1913 (Pamela Davidson, *The Poetic Imagination of Vyacheslav Ivanov: A Russian Symbolist's Perception of Dante* [Cambridge and New York: Cambridge University Press, 1989], pp. 234–44).

2. Cf. Mt 20:16; Plato, *Phaedo* 69CD (a favorite passage of Ivanov's): "As is said in the mysteries: 'many are the thyrsus-bearers, but few are the mystics.' The latter, in my opinion, are those whose occupation is philosophy in the strict sense of the term."

3. This and the following quotations are from the final stanzas of Pushkin's "Autumn: A Fragment" ("Osen': fragment," 1833).

4. Cf. "Ancient Terror" in this volume, p. 152.

5. Petrarch's "Levommi il mio penser in parte ov' era," poem 302 in the contemporary numbering of *Rime sparse.* Ivanov's translations of twenty-seven sonnets by Petrarch were published in 1915 together with M. Gershenzon's translations of selected prose works.

6. The final stanza of Ivanov's "Poets of the Spirit" ("Poety dukha," 1904) from *Transparency*.

7. *Faust* II.4684–85; cf. "The Symbolics of Aesthetic Principles" in this volume, p. 5.

8. *Faust* I.1699–1700; II.11580–81.

9. From the "Epirrhema" in Goethe's 1820 "Parabase."

10. The preceding argument is close to Solovyov's "Beauty in Nature" (1889).

11. Ivanov subsequently made a poetic translation of this sonnet dated 9 August 1925, published in his *Stikhotvoreniia i poemy* (Leningrad: Sovetskii pisatel', 1986), p. 389.

12. "On those who are sublime," pt. 2 of *Thus Spake Zarathustra;* cf. "The Symbolics of Aesthetic Principles" in this volume, p. 7.

13. Cf. "The Symbolics of Aesthetic Principles" in this volume, pp. 5–7.

14. Cf. Mt 6:3.

15. Sandro Botticelli (1447–1510), a renowned Florentine painter of the Renaissance, became a follower of Girolamo Savonarola; after Savonarola's execution, Botticelli's art became imbued with apocalyptic foreboding. Both Gogol and Tolstoy experienced spiritual conversions that caused them to reject some of their greatest works. On Tolstoy, see also "Lev Tolstoy and Culture" in this volume, pp. 200–10.

16. Ivanov merges two lines from Pushkin's "little tragedy" "Mozart and Salieri" (1830).

17. From Pushkin's "The Poet" ("Poèt," 1827).

18. From Pushkin's "The Prophet" ("Prorok," 1826).

19. The *Collected Works* gives two additional sentences here: "In any case, one must already be at a height in order to descend. And there is no great work of art that did not have as its precondition some major events in its creator's spiritual life, even if the events have remained an eternal mystery for his biographer" (2:636).

20. Ivanov's phrase echoes Tiutchev's "O wise soul of mine" ("O veshchaia dusha moia"); cf. "The Testaments of Symbolism" in this volume, p. 37.

21. From Blok's 1910 speech "On the Contemporary State of Russian Symbolism" (*Apollo,* no. 5 [1910]), a companion piece to Ivanov's "The Testaments of Symbolism"; see translation in Peterson, *The Russian Symbolists*, pp. 157–65.

22. From Briusov's 1902 poem "To K. D. Bal'mont" ("K. D. Bal'montu").

23. Cf. Briusov's line "I myself do not know what kind, but still I am tidings for the world," quoted in "On the Joyful Craft and the Joy of the Spirit" (see p. 122 in this volume), with its allusion to being "The Good News"—the Gospel.

24. The term *ápeiron* is a concept of infinity traditionally associated with Anaximander (early sixth century B.C.); see note 34.

25. From Goethe's sonnet "Natur und Kunst" (1802).

26. The quotation is from Briusov's 1902 poem "The Temptation" ("Iskushenie," in the part subtitled "Hymn" ["Gimn"]). Bely used this quotation in the title of his essay "A Wreath or a Crown" ("Venok ili venets," *Apollo*, no. 11 [1910]; see translation in Peterson, *The Russian Symbolists*, pp. 170–74), in which he responded to Briusov's "On Servile Speech" ("O rechi rabskoi," *Apollo*, no. 9 [1910]), where Briusov had objected to the theurgic ideal ("the crown") proclaimed by Ivanov in "The Testaments of Symbolism" (see pp. 39–43 in this volume) and by Blok in "On the Contemporary State of Russian Symbolism" (see note 21). Briusov, like the Acmeists who appeared beginning in 1912, defended the independent craft of the poet, symbolized by the "wreath," but Bely, by recalling Briusov's line "Woe to him who exchanges his crown for a wreath," demonstrates the latter's inconsistency.

27. Capua was a city in Campania that deserted to Hannibal's side in the Second Punic War (218–201 B.C.) only to be besieged and recaptured by Rome in 211 B.C. and subjected to severe punishment. Hannibal's failure in the war was later blamed on the deceptive ease with which he won Capua.

28. Cf. Mt 19:12.

29. "From the real to the more real"; see "Two Elements in Contemporary Symbolism" in this volume, p. 28.

30. Shortly before writing this essay, Ivanov edited Aleksandra Chebotarevskaia's Russian translation of Flaubert's 1856 novel; in 1917, however, Ivanov insisted that his name be removed from a new edition of Chebotarevskaia's translation since he had been prevented from making all the changes he desired (IRLI 189.92, pp. 14–15).

31. "Demonic" is used here in the sense of expressing someone's inner self or daimon.

32. Ivanov lists the protagonists of Shakespeare's *Hamlet,* Goethe's *The Sorrows of Young Werther,* Pushkin's *The Bronze Horseman,* and Gogol's *Dead Souls.*

33. In the sixteenth and seventeenth centuries, French tragedy mostly followed the neoclassicist stipulation of the "three unities" (time, place, action), according to which a single main action was to be shown taking place in a single setting in the span of no more than a single day. Shakespeare's tragedies dispensed with these unities.

34. Cf. Pushkin's "The Poet" ("Poèt," 1827); cf. Valery Briusov's 1905 article "Holy Sacrifice," which takes issue with Pushkin's separation of the poet from the man.

35. *Symposium* 203BE.

36. Zeus's fiery nature made it difficult for him to consummate his love for the mortal women he was frequently attracted to. Danae, a daugh-

ter of the king of Argos, gave birth to Perseus. Semele perished from Zeus's thunder, but Zeus rescued the child they conceived—Dionysus.

37. The words of Zosima in Dostoevsky's *The Brothers Karamazov* (bk. 6, chap. 3, pt. g, "On Prayer, Love and Touching Other Worlds").

38. Cf. 1 Cor 13:12.

39. From Ivanov's 1915 tragedy *Prometheus* (*Collected Works*, 2:112); the first publication of the tragedy in 1915 (under the title *The Sons of Prometheus*) read "Into the resurrected visages of people" (*Russkaia mysl'*, no. 1 [1915]: 4), although both the 1914 (where *Prometheus* is called "a certain unpublished tragedy") and 1916 versions of "On the Limits of Art" read the same as the 1919 publication of the tragedy. See also "Two Elements in Contemporary Symbolism" in this volume, p. 14.

40. Ivanov cites an Orphic cosmology. Zeus re-created Dionysus from the dust of the Titans; for another account of Dionysus's origins, see note 36 above.

41. From Ivanov's *Prometheus* (*Collected Works*, 2:112–13). Liberator (*Luos*) is an epithet of Dionysus.

42. Ivanov probably has in mind Democritus; see "Ancient Terror" in this volume, p. 152.

43. Pushkin, "Autumn: A Fragment" (see note 3 above).

44. Ivanov here refers to the *logos spermatikos* (the seminal Logos) of the Stoics.

45. Cf. Ps 8:5; Heb 2:5–9. In the 1914 publication, this read: "which is why it is said that God placed him higher than the angels" (p. 100).

46. The beginning of Vladimir Solovyov's 1883 poem "Three Labors" ("Tri podviga"), which was originally entitled "Orpheus." This poem is cited again in this essay below.

47. This is a quotation from Tiutchev's "A Vision" ("Videnie," 1829), which Ivanov adjusted to fit the context; cf. "The Testaments of Symbolism" in this volume, p. 38.

48. According to Ovid, Adonis was a beautiful youth loved by Aphrodite, who had to share him with Persephone, goddess of the underworld. When he was killed (by Apollo, Ares, or Artemis), Aphrodite turned his blood into a rose, while her tears became anemones. Adonis thus symbolized spring and fertility in general. Pygmalion, king of Cyprus and another lover of Aphrodite, is traditionally linked to Adonis. He created a statue of a beautiful woman that Aphrodite brought to life. Her name, Galatea, was also the name of a sea goddess or nereid, beings which, like their father Nereus, were nimble and protean in character.

49. Cf. Lk 19:40.

50. "Beauty will save the world" are the words of Prince Myshkin, as reported by Ippolit Terent'ev, in Dostoevsky's *The Idiot* (pt. 3, chap. 5).

51. Acts 2:1.

52. Goethe's "Novella" was written in 1826 and published in 1828.
53. An altered citation of Mt 18:3.

PRESENTIMENTS AND PORTENTS

First published in *The Golden Fleece* in 1906 (no. 4, pp. 68–73; no. 6, pp. 53–63; with facing French translation), "Presentiments and Portents" was included with some changes in *By the Stars* (pp. 189–219) and *Collected Works* (2:86–103). A recent republication contains commentaries that have been consulted in the preparation of our notes (*Predchuvstviia i predvestiia: sbornik*, ed. S. V. Stakhorskii [Moscow: Gosudarstvennyi institut teatral'nogo iskusstva, 1991], pp. 22–39, 105–9); below cited as Stakhorskii.

The essay consists of two main parts. First, Ivanov defines Symbolism as prophetic art (as opposed to Romanticism) that leads to mythopoesis and a new organic age. These ideas are developed in "On the Joyful Craft and the Joy of the Spirit." Then Ivanov applies this Symbolist program to the theater, essentially calling for a return to primitive Greek amphitheaters with no elevation separating the audience from the stage. Ivanov expresses his general approbation of Wagner, Maeterlinck, and Ibsen, while opening a polemic with subsequent playwrights and theater critics. Ivanov draws on his own writings on theatrical topics to crystallize his dramatic theory, which he develops without significant changes in later articles. Ivanov's writings on the theater had an immediate impact on such outstanding Russian directors as Vsevolod Meyerhold and Nikolai Evreinov and continue to attract interest to this day, both as a radical critique of modern drama and as an avenue for theatrical reform.

There remains a strong tension in Ivanov's argument between the demand that modern drama seek an *aesthetic* resolution of its dilemma and the clearly *extra-aesthetic* consequences he expects from the rise of a new drama. Ivanov's aesthetic goal of shared catharsis merges with a social goal of spontaneous democracy. The convergence of both goals would inaugurate a new organic era of mythopoesis, an aesthetic golden age. Reactions to Ivanov's construct were mostly based on a rejection of such a direct link between aesthetics and politics (the latter understood in a broad sense). In the wake of the 1905 revolution, the failure of which nonetheless resulted in unprecedented civil freedoms and the election of a representative assembly (the Duma), Ivanov's call to achieve social construction through art was heavily criticized and even ridiculed. Ivanov's attempt, together with Georgy Chulkov, to articulate a social philosophy of "mystical anarchism" or "mystical energeticism" (Ivanov's preferred term) was consequently a short-lived debacle.

Still, the attempt to reunite aesthetic and moral-social realms remained fundamental to Ivanov's thought. Here, the Aristotelian concept of

catharsis (cleansing) plays the dominant role: as the fundamental characteristic of art, catharsis opens individuals up to a shared reality (whether metaphysical, social, or psychological) and is therefore the basis of interpersonal
communication and coexistence.

1. The opening originally read: "Is contemporary Symbolism Romanticism or prophecy?—Put this way, the question naturally arouses objections"
(p. 68).

2. See, for example, Leonardo's *John the Baptist* (c. 1509–15).

3. The following passage, down to "But why do we oppose . . . ," originally read:

> Because only in these two types of spiritual construction does art stop being
> self-contained tranquilly within itself and in this sense static, but becomes
> preeminently dynamic and affirms itself as but one of the factors of the gen-
> eral cultural energy that develops in a liquid form, in the form of process and
> becoming, and that therefore strives to formlessness or else constantly shat-
> ters its forms, not being able to fit in them its incommensurate content. If the
> constant concern for what lies beyond the limit of immediate perception, be-
> yond the natural sphere of the contemplated phenomenon, is distinctive of
> contemporary Symbolist art, and if our art is conscious of itself not only as
> creation (*poiēsis*) but also as searching or a prayer, or a fore-vision and supra-
> vision of the transcendent, then it is clear that our art is as it were a species
> of liquid energy, one of the types of cultural dynamism, so different from self-
> sufficient and inwardly balanced classical art. (no. 4, pp. 68–69)

4. *Odium fati* (a hatred of fate) and *amor fati* (a love of fate); Nietzsche, who first used the phrase in *The Gay Science,* sec. 276, called *amor
fati* "my innermost nature" and "my formula for what is great in man" (*Ecce
Homo,* "Why I Am So Clever," sec. 10; *The Case of Wagner,* sec. 4).

5. "A pious hope," i.e., something desirable but unlikely.

6. The final sentence of this paragraph originally continued the previous one, reading: "—while Romanticism appears to us as only a mediating factor of historical evolution and therefore doubly reactionary, both
with respect to the epoch in opposition to which it arose, and with respect
to the epoch it indirectly prepared" (no. 4, p. 69).

7. "From exterior things to interior ones"; a mystical formula found
in St. Augustine (*Patrologia latina* [Paris: J. P. Migne, 1844–64]), vol. 33,
col. 208; vol. 37, col. 1887; vol. 42, col. 201, 1038); the model of Ivanov's
"From the real to the more real" (see "Two Elements in Contemporary
Symbolism" in this volume, p. 28).

8. The final part of this sentence, from "in order that," was absent in
the original; other minor changes to this paragraph have not been noted
(no. 4, p. 69).

9. In 1809, Zhukovsky translated Schiller's 1803 ballad "Der Pilgrim"
as "The Traveler" ("Puteshestvennik"); in the 1906 version, Ivanov cites it

in German as "Der Wanderer," and in 1909 as "The Wayfarer" ("Putnik"). The words in quotation marks in this paragraph are taken faithfully from Zhukovsky's translation, with the exception of the word "Here" in the final line of the poem, which Zhukovsky did not capitalize. Schiller did, in fact, use John Bunyan's *The Pilgrim's Progress* as a model. In Zhukovsky's original stanza, the ellipsis ends the third line, not the fourth.

10. In the original, this phrase reads: "We hear the *peroratio* of the Romantic" (no. 4, p. 69).

11. Cf. Solovyov's 1884 poem "In the morning mist with timid steps" ("V tumane utrennem nevernymi shagami"); in the original, Ivanov calls the poem "analogous" to Zhukovsky's translation of Schiller (no. 4, p. 70).

12. Cf. Goethe, *Faust* I.1112.

13. *Simulacra inania* means hollow (or dead) semblances.

14. From Tiutchev's "What are you howling about, night wind" ("O chem ty voesh' vetr nochnoi," 1836).

15. The concept of alternating critical and organic eras was characteristic of Saint-Simonianism, named after the French philosopher Claude-Henri de Rouvroy, Comte de Saint Simon (1760–1825).

16. By "barbarians," Ivanov means the non-Latin peoples of Europe.

17. "Integration" in the original version (no. 4, p. 70).

18. On the "theoretical man," see Nietzsche's *Birth of Tragedy,* sec. 1, 15, 17, and "Richard Wagner in Bayreuth," sec. 9 in *Untimely Meditations;* for "faithfulness to the earth," see Nietzsche, sec. 3 of "Zarathustra's Prologue," in pt. 1 of *Thus Spake Zarathustra;* see also sec. 2 of "On the Gift-Giving Virtue" in the same work.

19. Cf. Ibsen's 1899 play *When the Dead Awaken.*

20. Source unknown.

21. "Ideas of collectivism" in the original version (no. 4, p. 71).

22. Ivanov probably has in mind the religious, philosophical, and theocratic ideas of Vladimir Solovyov, along with those of related thinkers grouped around the Religious-Philosophical Societies: Nikolai Berdiaev, Dmitry Merezhkovsky, Vasily Rozanov, and others.

23. See repeated use of this formula in Nietzsche's *Birth of Tragedy.*

24. The original reads: "True myth is a postulate of collective self-determination in the realm of imagination [*fantaziia*]" (no. 4, p. 71).

25. Contradiction in terms.

26. As in other articles, Ivanov's word *vsenarodnyi* (literally, "all-national") has been translated as "universal," in the sense of "of all nations." In certain contexts, it would also be possible to understand it as "of all the nation"—something specific to a certain nation and shared by all its members. Since Ivanov's point is that the national idea of the Russian nation coincides with the "universal idea" or "universality," the difference between the two possible meanings of *vsenarodnyi* becomes moot.

27. On intimate and reclusive art, see note 68 to "Two Elements in Contemporary Symbolism" in this volume.

28. The original posited "universal rite or choral drama" (no. 4, p. 72).

29. A citation from Ivanov's 1904 essay "New Masks," first published as an introduction to his wife L. D. Zinov'eva-Annibal's drama *Rings* (*Kol'tsa*), then in *Libra* (no. 7 [1904]), *By the Stars* (54–64), and *Collected Works* (2:76–82). In the original version, the quotation was followed by:

> True, there is no hope of achieving full unanimity regarding the underlying principle of this experimentation. But is such unanimity even desirable? Would not a certain fatalism in our view of the destiny of creation be more normal? Will not necessity triumph? And is a genius really unable to draw everyone after him when he suddenly achieves what has been sought for in inevitable and tyrannical creations of the spirit, which blows where it will [Jn 3:9]? Nonetheless, *est ratio in rebus* [there is reason in things], and let those who believe they distinguish the logos of things warn us of the impending *fata* [fates] or, at the very least, help us to orient ourselves at the crossroads. Such help can be supplied by the knowledge of expected consequences that emerge from premises such as, on the one hand, the inner nature of drama, and, on the other, the series of data that historically determine its forward progression. (no. 6, p. 54)

30. Aristotle, *Poetics* 1449:b.28 (sec. 6).

31. Ivanov alludes to such neoclassical dramatists as Corneille and Racine.

32. Maurice Maeterlinck (1862–1949)—Belgian poet and playwright of the Symbolist movement.

33. Émile Verhaeren (1855–1916)—Belgian Symbolist poet and playwright, popular in Russia between 1900 and 1920.

34. Anaximander of Miletus was a pre-Socratic philosopher of the sixth century B.C.; Ivanov paraphrases one of the few remaining fragments from the philosopher's works (frag. 12 B 1), the first recorded quotation of a Western philosopher, where Anaximander appears to expound a theory of cosmic compensation of death for life.

35. See note 39 to "The Symbolics of Aesthetic Principles" in this volume.

36. Circuses.

37. To create and not to watch; in the original version, the phrase is continued: "as Wagner already recognized and demanded" (p. 55). The line is spoken by the Wanderer to Alberich in act 2 of *Siegfried*. Ivanov is continuing his polemic with Max Hochschüler, who in *Libra* (no. 9 [1904], pp. 39–46) had disagreed with Ivanov's "Nietzsche and Dionysus" and had attacked Wagner from a Nietzschean viewpoint. In his article, Hochschüler cited the lines "Zu *schauen* kam ich, nicht zu *schaffen*" to characterize both his own and Nietzsche's reactions to Wagner's operas.

38. *Poetics* 1449:b.28 (sec. 6).

39. The Russian word *rampa* means the elevation of the stage and its consequent separation from the audience. It is commonly, but anachronistically, translated as "footlights."

40. See Maurice Maeterlinck, "Modern Drama," *Double Garden* (New York: Dodd, Mead and Co., 1904), pp. 115–35. In a 1904 review (*Libra*, no. 8, pp. 58–59), Ivanov subjected this book to severe criticism (Stakhorskii, p. 108). On "the theater of youth and beauty" see the following note.

41. In the original version, this phrase read: "Whether the sought-for theater will be the 'theater of youth and beauty' that Bal'mont promises us, or a reproduction of the possibility of human happiness without tears, according to the recent demand of Maeterlinck the theoretician, a theater of 'the past, present and future' such as is preached by Anton Krainy, or a theater of 'Mystery,' 'Sanctuary,' 'Night,' of universal questions and lofty soaring, none of these programs provides the means for removing the charms of the elevated stage of the theater" (no. 6, p. 57). "The theater of youth and beauty" was the subtitle of Konstantin Bal'mont's 1907 play *Three Blossoms* (*Tri rastsveta*); Ivanov learned of Bal'mont's formulation from mutual acquaintances while he was at work on the article (*Collected Works*, 2:745). Zinaida Gippius, who wrote criticism under the pseudonym Anton Krainy, supported "plays of the present" in her article "What and How" ("Chto i kak"), part 2 of "Triptych," included in her 1908 book *Literaturnyi dnevnik* (*1899–1907*).

42. *Pelléas and Mélisande* (1893–95, 1901–2) is an opera by Claude Debussy based on Maeterlinck's 1892 play. Valery Briusov's Russian translation was published in 1907 and directed by Vera Komissarzhevskaia.

43. Cf. Nietzsche's *Birth of Tragedy,* sec. 19.

44. Here, in order to denote the rounded floor of ancient amphitheaters, Ivanov uses the Greek-sounding form *orkhestra* instead of the usual *orkestr,* which denotes the musical or "instrumental" ensemble. We have differentiated the two spellings and meanings in the translation by italicizing the former (*orchēstra*).

45. "Orchestics" is the art of dance.

46. The preceding passage originally read: "It is only with respect to the chorus that Wagner's formula rests on a certain theoretical justification, to the critique of which we must presently turn, for it is precisely the chorus that comprises the focus of the synthetic drama we postulate. This critique, which I have already indicated in 'Wagner and the Dionysian Rite,' has been made easier by Wagner himself . . ." (no. 6, p. 58); cf. note 51.

47. See Wagner's "Opera and Drama."

48. *Festspiel* (performance festival) was how Wagner designated his festival at Bayreuth.

49. *Choreutói* is a Greek word for choral dancers.

50. Hippa is a goddess, identified with the world soul, who appears in Orphic and Neoplatonic cosmogonies.

51. Ivanov quotes his article (with some changes) "Wagner and the Dionysian Rite," first published in *Libra* (no. 2 [1905]), then in *By the Stars* (65–69) and *Collected Works* (2:83–85). This article was also part of Ivanov's polemic with Max Hochschüler (see note 37).

52. Ivanov refers to Wagner's theater at Bayreuth, where the orchestra is not visible to the audience.

53. "Charms" (*chary*) in the first publication (no. 6, p. 60).

54. See Ivanov's article "Gogol's *Inspector General* and the Comedy of Aristophanes," in *Gogol from the Twentieth Century: Eleven Essays,* trans. and ed. Robert A. Maguire (Princeton, N.J.: Princeton University Press, 1974), pp. 199–214.

55. Ivanov again quotes his own words from the 1904 essay "New Masks" (*Collected Works,* 2:78); see note 29 above.

56. *Ivanov's note:* Instead of developing this hypothesis, I shall cite the following lines from my book *Pilot Stars:*

Together with the tragic mask we are accustomed to think of
    A storm of passionate speeches, blood on the iron of swords . . .
Melpomene's ancient cathedral! Grant newcomers a step
    At the thymele! The heroes arise; they glance comprehending;
They purse their eloquent lips in silent suffering;
    Mysterious fate is meted out in the sealed hearts.
The Titans in furious battle poured out their cramped breasts' burden,
    This heavy force: now their descendants bear it within.

[Ivanov quotes from his poem "The Quiet Thiasos" ("Tikhii fias").]

57. Aeschylus's *Niobe* survives only in fragments. At about the time of this essay, Ivanov was working on his own tragedy about Niobe (which he never completed).

58. "I spit on you, monster!"; from the finale of Maeterlinck's play *The Death of Tintagiles* (1894), which Vsevolod Meyerhold rehearsed in 1905 in Moscow.

59. In the original, the parenthetic phrase reads: "I would give it the conventional term 'prophetic,' in contradistinction to political communities and ecclesiastical communities" (no. 6, p. 63).

ON THE JOYFUL CRAFT AND THE JOY OF THE SPIRIT

"On the Joyful Craft and the Joy of the Spirit" originated in a lecture "The Paths and Goals of Contemporary Art," read on 14 April 1907. It was subsequently published in *The Golden Fleece* (no. 5 [1907]: 47–55) and, in edited form, in *By the Stars* (pp. 220–46; reprinted in *Collected Works,* 3:61–77). In compiling our notes, we had the advantage of consulting Kseniia Kumpan's commentary to the article, prepared in conjunction with a projected *Complete Collected Works* of Viacheslav Ivanov.

"On the Joyful Craft and the Joy of the Spirit" represents one of Ivanov's efforts to relate the aesthetic program of Symbolism (or, as he termed it in the first publication, Decadence) to Russian social processes. The artist is said to be a craftsman, whose "artistry" is called upon by "commissions" that issue from the people or their legitimate representatives. Art fulfills these social commissions in such a way that it alters the very values upon which society is based. Ivanov implies, however, that such reciprocal action between society and art is absent in contemporary Russia.

Ivanov addresses the particular situation of his day by seeking to define a healthy current in contemporary art that is capable of reuniting the artist and nation. Symbolism, in his view, has transplanted the spirit of Western (mainly French) Decadence to the fresh soil of Russian culture. Here, it has raised the technical level of art while gaining access to the hidden treasures of national tradition. Thus, the artist's craft will be united with the nation's joy and its barbarian mysticism, creating a culture of "the nation's joy of the spirit."

Ivanov's argument is actually less down-to-earth than it may seem. In his view (common to many artists at the time), Russian society was undergoing revolution, and artists were to shape that revolution by their works. This is a leadership of the spirit, not of the sword, and it was to change the very nature of human existence by reinstating mythical art and thereby achieving a new organic epoch. The solemn finale of the essay presents Ivanov's socio-aesthetic utopia of theaters and *orchēstrai* covering the land with artists serving as the "hand and voice" of the crowd. This ecstatic vision, which seemed to confirm the escapist tendencies of "Mystical Anarchism," raised many eyebrows among Ivanov's contemporaries and contributed to the dissolution of the united Symbolist movement. Andrei Bely commented: "While I give this serious thinker his due, I cannot help but take into account the danger presented by a hurried popularization of his views" ("Teatr i sovremennaia drama," in *Teatr. Kniga o novom teatre. Sbornik statei* [St. Petersburg: Shipovnik, 1908], p. 271). Ten years later, in the aftermath of the 1917 revolution, Bely is reported to have exclaimed to Ivanov: "Do you recognize it? These are your *orchēstrai!*" (*Collected Works,* 1:161).

The "joyful craft" of Ivanov's title refers to Nietzsche's 1887 work *Die fröhliche Wissenschaft,* which in turn refers to *gai saber,* a Provençal expression denoting poetry. The discussion of art "as a craft" and references to leading figures of the English Arts and Crafts Movement indicate that Ivanov is applying Nietzsche's term quite broadly. "Joy of the spirit" translates the Russian *umnoe veselie*, in which the adjective *úmnyi* (sometimes stressed *umnói*) means not "intelligent" but "of the mind and/or spirit" (cf. *umnaia molitva, umnoe delanie*—terms used in the Hesychast tradition of Orthodox spirituality to denote silent "prayer of the heart"). It might be added that in the article Ivanov uses both possible spellings of the word "joy," *veselie* and *vesel'e,* but we were unable to discern any meaningful pattern in this usage.

 1. "Considering that a poet, if he is really to be a poet, must compose myths and not 'speeches' [or 'rational discourses']" (Plato, *Phaedo* 61B; Fowler translation). The epigraph was absent in the first publication.

 2. The Medici were a powerful clan of bankers and merchants in Renaissance Italy, the rulers of Florence from 1389 to 1494 and celebrated patrons of the arts. The nickname "Viacheslav the Magnificent," given to Ivanov by Lev Shestov in 1916, is modeled on the appellation of one of the Medici, the poet Lorenzo the Magnificent (1449–92), who was Michelangelo's first patron.

 3. Louis XIV of France (reigned 1643–1715) sponsored extensive and sumptuous architectural projects, most notably the palace of Versailles. His imperial style had a great influence on European architecture, interior design, and landscaping.

 4. *Artifex* is the Latin term for artist or craftsman. *Technitēs* and *dēmiourgós* are the Greek terms for craftsman and creator, respectively. In order to stress the technical or craftsmanlike aspects of art, Ivanov uses the word *khudozhestvo,* which in our translation of this article has been rendered "artistry."

 5. These and the following quotations are from Pushkin's sonnet "To the Poet" ("Poetu," 1830).

 6. Michel-Angelo (usually Michelangelo) Buonarroti (1475–1564)—Renaissance painter, architect, sculptor, and poet. Leading motifs of Michelangelo's poetry are the opposition of the poet to the crowd and the importance of technical mastery; cf. "On the Limits of Art" in this volume, p. 81. Benvenuto Cellini (1500–71)—goldsmith, sculptor, and author of the well-known *Autobiography of Benvenuto Cellini.*

 7. From Pushkin's "To the Poet"; see note 5 above.

 8. Torquato Tasso (1544–95)—Italian poet best known for his epic *Jerusalem Emancipated* (1575), written for his patron Duke Alfons II d'Este (1533–97). In the final years of his life, Tasso rewrote the epic to please his patron, who had confined the poet to an insane asylum; posterity has largely favored the earlier edition. Goethe's drama *Torquato Tasso* is based on a legend that Tasso and his patron enjoyed an ideal relationship.

 9. In his autobiographical "Letter to My Descendants," Francesco Petrarch (1304–74) gives short shrift to his famous lyrical poems in Italian (collected into a single volume as the *Canzionere* or *Rime Sparse*) while accen-

tuating the significance of his scholarly tracts and Latin epic "Africa." Dante Alighieri (1265–1321) was the first major Italian poet to use the vernacular.

10. "Genialisch Treiben" ("The Genius Game") is a poem by Goethe; see "Manner, Persona, Style" in this volume, p. 68.

11. From Pushkin's "little tragedy" "Mozart and Salieri" (1830); cf. "On the Limits of Art" in this volume, p. 77.

12. Byron was active in revolutionary movements in both Italy and Greece. Heinrich Heine (1797–1856), the German lyric poet, espoused radical and revolutionary causes from Left Hegelianism to Saint-Simonianism throughout his life, although his actual participation in revolutionary movements was minimal.

13. Cf. the concept of genius in Kant's *Critique of Judgment* (sec. 46–50). Ivanov devoted one series of aphorisms, published collectively under the title "Sporades" ("Sporady"), to the concept of genius; see "O genii," in *Collected Works,* 3:112–14.

14. From the "Dedication" to Pushkin's *Eugene Onegin* (1823–31).

15. Pindar's Olympian and Pythian odes were composed for royal and noble patrons in commemoration of sporting and civic events. Ivanov's debut as a translator was his translation of Pindar's first Pythian Ode, published in 1899.

16. *The Aeneid* of Virgil (70–19 B.C.) narrates the founding of Rome by the Trojan Aeneas.

17. Ivanov apparently means such contemporaries of Shakespeare as Christopher Marlowe (1564–93) and Ben Jonson (1573–1637).

18. On Ivanov's usage of *orchēstra,* see note 44 to "Presentiments and Portents" in this volume.

19. Originally: "continuing Beethoven's work, truly made incarnate in music the 'collective individualism' that has just been discovered by our youth, and sowed seeds deep into the European consciousness . . ." (p. 48). "Collective individualism" (*sobornyi individualizm*) was the title of a 1907 book by Ivanov's protégé Modest Gofman (also spelled Hoffman). Ivanov has in mind Beethoven's Ninth Symphony, which introduced a chorus (singing Schiller's "Ode to Joy") and thus, in Ivanov's view, paved the way for Wagner's operas.

20. Originally: "regularity and purposefulness" (p. 48). Ivanov refers to Kant's idea of art in the *Critique of Judgment* as "purposeless purposefulness."

21. Frag. B66 of Heraclitus, who believed fire to be the primal element to which everything will return.

22. The Grace of giving and the Grace of receiving figure in Goethe's *Faust* II ("Mascarade"), where they are called, respectively, Aglaia and Hermogena.

23. Ivanov alludes to the description of the voice of God in 1 Kgs 19:12, which in the Slavonic reads "the blowing of fine cold [*veianie khlada*

tonka]" (the King James translation renders it as "still small voice"). Ivanov regularly cited this image of divine communication.

24. Tyrtaeus (seventh century B.C.) was a Spartan poet known for his martial songs.

25. Possibly a reference to Lermontov's "The Sail" ("Parus," 1832).

26. Originally: "the art of mystics and theurgists who dream of the mysterious influence their creative work has on human destinies, which are to draw nearer to their apocalyptic end through the efforts of providential geniuses" (p. 49).

27. Originally: "Then these transformers of the world were touched most by the end of the phrase: 'and for prayers'" (p. 49). Ivanov quotes Pushkin's "Poet and the Crowd" ("Poet i tolpa," 1828).

28. Originally: "is declining especially among those who seek to resurrect the religious and Byzantine style of art, in direct proportion to their assurance of sales" (p. 49). Ivanov's formulation most likely refers to such religious artists as Viktor Vasnetsov (1848–1926) and Mikhail Nesterov (1862–1942), who developed a modernistic and somewhat sentimental synthesis of old and new religious styles in their works.

29. Attributed to Spinoza, this Latin phrase means "from the point of view of eternity."

30. Originally, this sentence read: "Thus, these decadents have recently begun to treat life with every possible care: they pray and prophesy, they invent means of personal and universal salvation, paths of inner work and social action, and quite frequently they even try to tune their lyres in harmony with the civil cacophonies of the sworn executors of revolutionary commissions" (p. 49). Ivanov may have in mind Dmitry Merezhkovsky, Zinaida Gippius, and Dmitry Filosofov, whose search for a "new religious consciousness" led them to conduct their own religious services at home and who, after leaving Petersburg for Paris in 1905, became close friends of the Socialist revolutionary terrorist Boris Savinkov (literary pseudonym Ropshin; 1879–1925).

31. Acts 19:23–41. The Temple of Diana (Artemis) at Ephesus was a center of her cult.

32. Pietro Vannucci Perugino (c. 1450–1523)—a prolific Italian Renaissance painter. Perugino has historically been overshadowed by his pupil Raphael, but he was idealized by the English Pre-Raphaelites in the late nineteenth century.

33. Turgenev's *A Sportsman's Sketches* (*Zapiski okhotnika*, 1856) has been widely credited with raising Russian consciousness of the evils of serfdom and contributing to the emancipation of the serfs in 1861. The melodramatic, civic-minded poetry of Semën Nadson (1862–87) enjoyed unrivaled popularity at the end of the century. The satirical novels of Mikhail Saltykov-Shchedrin (1826–89) and the populist prose of Gleb Uspensky (1843–1902) were also widely read by contemporaries.

273

34. On Nikolai Gogol (1809–52), see note 36. Anton Chekhov (1860–1904) was not generally held in high regard by the Symbolists, who tended to view his works, however brilliant, as characteristic of spiritual decay in fin de siècle Russia.

35. Justinian (reigned from 527 to 565) ruled over the first golden age of Byzantine art, commissioning St. Sophia's in Constantinople, among other things. The large Pitti mansion (Palazzo Pitti) in Florence was built by Luca di Bonaccorso Pitti (1395–1472) and was later inhabited by the Medici dukes of Florence; now a museum. Augustus (63 B.C.–A.D. 14; also called Gaius Octavius, Octavian, Caesar Augustus)—Roman emperor, namesake of the Augustan age in the arts. Napoleon Bonaparte (1769–1821, reigned 1804–14) commissioned many paintings, sculptures, and buildings in a style later known as Empire. Pericles (fifth century B.C.)—Athenian statesman who oversaw the building of many world-famous structures, from the Parthenon to the long walls surrounding Athens. Pope Julius II (1443–1513, elected 1503) was the great patron of Renaissance architecture and painting; among other things, he commissioned Bramante to build St. Peter's and Michelangelo to paint the Sistine Chapel.

36. In his "Confession of an Author" (in *Selected Passages from Correspondence with My Friends*, 1847), Nikolai Gogol credited Pushkin with the original idea at the heart of his novel *Dead Souls,* which Gogol called an "epic poem" (*poèma*); this is why Ivanov can call the prose writer Gogol a "poet." Ivanov's despair over the lack of artistic commissions in Silver Age Russia is actually quite disingenuous. Among the many wealthy patrons of modern art active at the time of this essay were Nikolai Riabushinsky, the publisher of the journal in which Ivanov's essay was first published, and Sergei Poliakov, copublisher of the other leading Symbolist journal *Libra.*

37. The Russian word for "manly" (*muzhestvennyi*) can also mean "courageous."

38. Nikolai Nekrasov, the leading poet of the 1850s and 1860s, concentrated on civic themes. Gogol underwent a religious conversion, adopted the tone of a preacher, and burned most of the second part of *Dead Souls.* See note 15 to "On the Limits of Art" in this volume. See also "Lev Tolstoy and Culture" in this volume, pp. 201–4.

39. Originally: "whether it is inevitable that a Russian artist necessarily be an affirmer of culture [*Kulturträger*], teacher, and a leader" (p. 50).

40. Mt 3:3–4 (quoting Is 40:3).

41. A reference to Pushkin's "little tragedy" "Feast at the Time of the Plague" ("Pir vo vremia chumy," 1830).

42. Old Church Slavonic, the liturgical language codified in the ninth century by Saints Constantine and Methodius for ecclesiastical use in the Slavic lands, was closely modeled on Greek syntax and word formation.

43. The mysterious, non-Greek origins of Dionysus fascinated Ivanov throughout his creative life, but this claim especially shows that his scholarly judgment was often subordinated to ideological concerns. In his *Hellenic Religion* (1903–5), Ivanov rejected the theory that Dionysus originated in Thrace, while in his later *Dionysus and Predionysianism,* he advanced the view that the worship of this god had its origins in cults native to the Greek peninsula and Crete.

44. *Faust* II.6173–6306; cf. "Two Elements in Contemporary Symbolism" in this volume, p. 19.

45. Anacharsis (sixth century B.C.) was a sage from Scythia who traveled widely to study the customs of other nations. Upon returning to Scythia, he decided to copy a religious rite he had observed elsewhere, whereupon he was killed by a suspicious countryman (Herodotus IV.75ff.).

46. Theodoric (c. 454–526)—king of the Ostrogoths, reigned over Italy for thirty-three years, during which time the social and economic infrastructure was greatly improved. Charlemagne (742–814, reigned 768–814)—Frankish emperor, set about restoring the Roman Empire, taking as his model the culture of Constantine the Great. His patronage resulted in a flowering of liturgical art and church architecture, as well as imperial residences.

47. For the earth creates them again, / as it has from time immemorial; *Faust* II.9937.

48. See Goethe's letter to K. F. Zelter from 2 September 1812.

49. In the tenth of his *Letters on the Aesthetic Education of Man,* Schiller wrote that genius "is close to wildness" and "testifies more against the taste of its age than for it."

50. Nietzsche's path of sorrow, i.e., his "via dolorosa," the road to crucifixion; cf. "Nietzsche and Dionysus" in this volume, pp. 182–83. On Odysseus and the Sirens, see *Odyssey* XII. Nietzsche's first philosophical work, *The Birth of Tragedy,* was largely inspired by Wagner's music and thought; by 1878, however, Nietzsche had come to see Wagner as an embodiment of bad taste.

51. 1 Cor 1:18ff. Cf. Tertullian's "What has Athens to do with Jerusalem?" (*Praescrip.* 7.9; *Patrologia Latina,* vol. 1, col. 19, 31).

52. The Lotophagi or Lotophagoi ("Lotus-eaters") live exclusively on the fruit of the lotus, which causes oblivion; see *Odyssey* IX.83–104.

53. From "The Scythian Dances" ("Skif pliashet") in the cycle "Parisian Epigrammes" (1891) in Ivanov's *Pilot Stars.*

54. From the first part of Ivanov's triptych "The Beautiful Is Dear" ("Prekrasnoe—milo," 1904); cf. "The Symbolics of Aesthetic Principles" in this volume, p. 7.

55. From the second part of Ivanov's "The Beautiful Is Dear" (see note 54).

56. Ivanov at one time planned to name his third book of poems *Iris in iris,* Latin for "rainbow in furies." He later settled on *Cor Ardens (The Flaming Heart).*

57. From Valery Briusov's 1905 poem "The Coming Huns" ("Griadushchie gunny," in *Stephanos*).

58. The reference to "high towers" is conceivably an autobiographical reference; Ivanov's own apartment in St. Petersburg from 1905 to 1912, a meeting place for much of the artistic elite, was called the "Tower."

59. Publius Papinius Statius (c. A.D. 40–c. A.D. 90) is best known for his epic *Thebaid* and the unfinished epic *Achilleid.* In the Middle Ages, Statius was considered to have been a Christian (see Dante's *Purgatory* XXII).

60. The preceding section of this paragraph originally read: "Bal'mont is a singer, marvelous in his 'melodious force,' and Valery Briusov's *Stephanos* is a book that resurrects the best traditions of the artistic perfection of poetic form . . ." (p. 52).

61. From Briusov's poem "In hac lacrimarum vale" (1902, *Urbi et orbi*); the word "tidings" (*vest'*) is an allusion to "the Good News"—the Gospel.

62. "Alexandrian culture" is a term used by Nietzsche in *The Birth of Tragedy,* sec. 18, 19. Alexandria in Greece was the center of Hellenistic learning from the third century B.C. to the late first century B.C. A great age of scholarship and synthesis, its poetry and other arts are often viewed as derivative and sterile. On Ivanov's use of the terms "critical" and "organic" to denote historical epochs, see note 15 to "Presentiments and Portents" in this volume.

63. Nietzsche introduced the term "theoretical man" to characterize the Socratic mind-set that he found dominant in modernity (see *The Birth of Tragedy*).

64. Cf. note 8 to "Manner, Persona, Style" in this volume.

65. On cenacles, see note 66 to "Two Elements in Contemporary Symbolism" in this volume.

66. The Parnassians, an aestheticist movement in French poetry that took its name from three poetic collections entitled *La Parnasse Contemporain* (1866, 1871, 1876), included such poets as Théophile Gautier (1811–72), Charles-Marie-René Leconte-de-Lile (1818–94), Charles Baudelaire (1821–67), and René-François-Armand Sully-Prudhomme (1839–1907).

67. William Morris (1834–96) and John Ruskin (1819–1900) were versatile cultural figures aligned with the Arts and Crafts movement, as well as with socialist causes. Walt Whitman (1819–92)—the American poet, first translated into Russian by Konstantin Bal'mont. On Ivanov's view of Norwegian playwright Henrik Ibsen (1844–1900), see "Presentiments and Portents" in this volume, p. 103.

68. Ivanov apparently means Wilde's "Socialism and Man's Soul" and the confessional *De Profundis.* In a 1904 review of Verlaine and Huysmans,

Ivanov wrote of Wilde: "This man did not take shelter in the enclosure of positive doctrine; but the entire life of the noble singer and humble martyr of 'Reading Gaol' turned into the religion of universal Golgotha" (*Collected Works*, 2:564–65).

69. A corybant was a priest of Cybele whose worship involved ecstatic music and dance.

70. On intimate and reclusive art, see note 68 to "Two Elements in Contemporary Symbolism" in this volume.

71. From Paul Verlaine's "L'art poétique"; cf. note 57 to "Two Elements in Contemporary Symbolism" in this volume.

72. Goethe, *Faust* II.4727. In the original version, this sentence continued: "on the strength of its dynamism and musical ferment" (p. 54).

73. In the original version, this read: "the supraindividual, universal principle" (p. 54).

74. Baudelaire's "Correspondances"; cf. "Two Elements in Contemporary Symbolism" in this volume, pp. 22–23, 25.

75. From Ivanov's "The Garden of Roses" ("Sad roz," 1906), included in *Eros* and *Cor Ardens.*

76. Originally the end of this section read:

he meekly bore forth his new-old soul, which was revived with new intuitions, filled with the voices and tremors of previously unknown mysterious life, watered with the dews of new-old beliefs and clairvoyant visions, toward the dormant soul of the nation: will the face of the sleeping beauty tremble at the whisper of ancient prophetic curses? . . .

Is it not this charmed world that is inhabited by those who have placed their ear to the mother-damp earth: Sergei Gorodetsky and Aleksei Remizov; by him who has been caught up in the intoxication and living snowstorm of a myth made incarnate in his most intimate experiences: Aleksandr Blok; by Vrubel', who came too soon over the abandoned paths of the great Aleksandr Ivanov and who has already departed from our midst? Did not Ivan Konevskoi, whom the smitten sister Water Sprites tempted to eternal rest, live by these same premonitions? . . . Mikhail Kuzmin is an aesthete and Parnassian, a genuine scion of Alexandrian culture, a living anachronism among us, a stylist who unintentionally makes charming Gallicisms without thinking in French, retaining the seal of true Latino-French classicism in his most carefree works; yet even he feels at home in the world of Old Belief, and is composing the first drafts of sincere Mysteria.

All of these artists were born "from the spirit of music," under the sign of the musically orgiastic, barbarian Dionysus. (p. 54)

Sergei Gorodetsky (1884–1967), Aleksei Remizov (1877–1957), Aleksandr Blok (1880–1921), and Mikhail Kuzmin (1875–1936) were writers to a greater or lesser degree affiliated with the Symbolist movement. Ivanov dedicated a poem to Kuzmin entitled "Anachronism" (1909). Ivan Konevskoi (pseudonym of Ivan Oreus, 1877–1901) was an early Symbolist who drowned accidentally soon after the publication of his first book, *Dreams and Thoughts* (*Mechty i dumy*, 1900). Aleksandr Ivanov (1806–58) and Mikhail Vrubel' (1856–1910) were artists; on the latter, see note 55 to "The Testaments of Symbolism" in this volume.

77. This paragraph originally read: "Painting desires frescoes, architecture desires a national assembly, music a chorus and drama, and drama desires music. Our innermost hope for the theater is that it become a simulacrum of the ancient *orchestra*, with its dance and choral introduction and accompaniment of the rite. Theater is attempting to resolve the problem of the curtain, which separates the actors from the spectators, by merging the entire crowd that collects at the festival of *sobornost'* into a unified 'rite'" (p. 55).

78. One of the sections of Ivanov's "Sporades" is entitled "On Daring Love" ("O liubvi derzaiushchei," in *Collected Works*, 3:131–35).

79. In the original version, Ivanov added: "from the 'irreconcilable No' to the 'blinding Yes'" (p. 55), a phrase from Ivanov's own 1906 poem "The Fire-Bearers: A Dithyramb" ("Ognenostsy: difiramb"). On the source of the phrase, see note 32 to "The Symbolics of Aesthetic Principles" in this volume.

80. This phrase originally read: "the masculine sunlike state of mystical daring and initiative, which affirms the mystical personality" (p. 54).

81. Cf. Ivan Karamazov's discourse on the inability of his "Euclidean mind" to accept God's world (F. Dostoevsky, *The Brothers Karamazov*, pt. 2, bk. 5, chap. 3, "The Brothers Get Acquainted").

82. *Faust* I.1198–1201. Ivanov's translation is quite free.

83. In the original version, this was followed by an additional paragraph:

"But life consists of its inert immobility and threatens, with all its nihilism . . .
And brandishing negation,
And swinging the gloom, there arises *Nothing*." (p. 55)

Ivanov quotes his own poem "The Road to Emmaus" ("Put' v Emmaus," *Cor Ardens*); on the concept of "Nothing," see "The Testaments of Symbolism" in this volume, p. 40. The two following paragraphs were also worded slightly differently, although the general sense remained the same.

84. Cf. Mt 26:39, 42.

85. A *thymele* was a sacrificial altar and an altar-shaped platform in the orchestra of the Athenian theater. On *orchestra*, see note 44 to "Presentiments and Portents" in this volume.

86. The final paragraph originally read somewhat differently (p. 55).

ON THE RUSSIAN IDEA

Ivanov first read "On the Russian Idea" as a lecture on 30 December 1908 at the same session of the Petersburg Religious-Philosophical Society at which Aleksandr Blok read the essay "Element and Culture." Ivanov's speech was published in *The Golden Fleece* in the first two issues for 1909 (pp. 85–93 and 87–94, respectively). Later in 1909, it was republished with some significant changes in *By the Stars* (pp. 309–37), and then in the *Collected Works* (3:321–38). The final version, a German translation thoroughly reworked and expanded by Ivanov, was published in 1930 (Wiatscheslaw Iwanow, *Die russische Idee,* trans. J. Schor [Tübingen: J. C. B. Mohr, 1930]). Our translation is based on the revised Russian text included in *By the Stars* and *Collected Works.*

The journal publication included a long section (pp. 88–90 in *Golden Fleece,* no. 1 [1909]), coming between sections 2 and 3 in the revised version included in *By the Stars,* devoted to "several revealing facts of our recent literary life" (p. 88), which due to its length we will summarize here. Ivanov expresses his hope that a "universal" art might evolve from literature of a neopopulist or ethnographic bent: "These attempts, taken by themselves, might be developing a kind of channel for mythopoesis of the future, but the content of this latter is, of course, neither prefigured nor even anticipated by this trend in our poetry, insofar as it does not issue from a genuinely religious consciousness of the true and central realities of the nation's spiritual life" (p. 88). Ivanov then moves on to an appraisal of the latest works of Aleksandr Blok and Andrei Bely (representing the "populist" trend), and then of Maksim Gorky's *Confession,* which propagated the idea of "nation-worship" (*narodobozhie*) or "god-building" (*bogostroitel'stvo*). He delineates two clear problems with all of these populist sentiments. First, they confuse the god-bearing nation with the divinity. Second, they leave no role for the intelligentsia (p. 90). Then followed section 3 of the book version, which seeks to define the positive role of the intelligentsia in Russian life.

The excised section actually considered a mere fraction of the contemporary literature concerning the "people and intelligentsia" and the "Russian idea." The year 1908 had seen the publication of *Landmarks (Vekhi),* a collection of essays by Russian idealists and religious thinkers, mostly devoted to these issues, which had provoked a broad discussion among intellectuals. The Petersburg Religious-Philosophical Society's previous meetings on the subject of Russian social divisions had spilled onto the pages of the local newspapers. Ivanov, as was his custom, entered the fray quite late and avoided choosing sides, preferring to indicate a synthetic resolution.

Ivanov picks a quite Hegelian point of view, envisioning a future synthesis between the "people," who remain in their undefined "inertness," and the "intelligentsia," which, even if alienated from the people, seeks to understand itself through the people. This structure is also linked to the idea, current at that time, of the "new religious consciousness," which Dmitry Merezhkovsky and Nikolai Berdiaev had tied to a "Third Testament" or "Testament of the Spirit," appealing both to Hegelian logic and the millenarianism of Joachim de Fiore, a Spanish mystic (c. 1135–1202). Ivanov seems quite close to these contemporaries, identifying the "Russian idea" precisely with the achievement of this "new aeon"; one can note how the citations from St. John's Gospel and Revelation intensify throughout the article. The various references to Eastern and occult beliefs and practices make this essay one of Ivanov's most *esoteric* works, although it is ostensibly addressed to the entire nation.

Yet even this degree of esotericism can be seen as a nod to the language of the day and not an obligatory feature of Ivanov's interpretation of the coming "organic epoch" (a truly religious culture, heralded by the mythopoesis of modern art and thought, centered on a reunited and rejuvenated Russian society). Although he changed much while preparing the German translation, the Ivanov of 1930 found himself content with the main ideas of the essay. The end of the essay is especially important for an appreciation of Ivanov's later views of Dostoevsky, who more than anyone else represents for Ivanov the potential future religious synthesis, both within Russian culture and throughout the world (see Viacheslav Ivanov, *Freedom and the Tragic Life: A Study in Dostoevsky* [New York: Noonday Press, 1952]).

1. The "liberation movement" was the accepted term for radical political thought and activity in Russia; Ivanov here speaks of the 1905 revolution, which led to limited political reforms and effectively quelled the radical threat for a few years.

2. These words feature prominently in the titles of Aleksandr Blok's essays of the period: "The People and the Intelligentsia" (November 1908) and "Element and Culture" (December 1908).

3. Cf. Gn 3:16.

4. On the translation of the word *vsenarodnyi* (literally, "all-national") as "universal," see note 26 to "Presentiments and Portents" in this volume.

5. Henry Cornelius Agrippa of Nettesheim (1486–1535) was a knight, doctor, and alleged magician who propagated the Hermetic tradition of esoteric knowledge. In his work "Esoteric Philosophy," Agrippa wrote that the cosmos is ruled by seven demons for four hundred years each. The sixth demon, Ophiel, rules from 1900 to 2300. Cf. Ivanov's lyric cycle "Carmen Saeculare" (*Cor Ardens*) dedicated to Valery Briusov, from whom Ivanov learned of Agrippa's teaching (*Literaturnoe nasledstvo* [Moscow: Nauka, 1976], 85:454–55). Agrippa figures prominently in Valery Briusov's novel *The Fiery Angel* (1907–8).

6. 1 Cor 4:10; the "fool in Christ" or "fool for Christ's sake" (*iurodivyi*) is one of the distinct kinds of Russian (and Byzantine) sanctity.

7. A reference to Solovyov's 1894 poem "Panmongolism" and 1899 work *Three Conversations, Including a Short Story of the Antichrist.*

8. Source unknown.

9. Ivanov refers to the Russo-Japanese War (1904–5). Among its parallels with the First Punic War between Rome and Carthage (264–241 B.C.): it was seen as a symbolic conflict between East and West, it was Russia's first (and only) mainly naval conflict, and Russia lost a great part of its fleet in the war. Most important, perhaps, is the Rome-Carthage rivalry in Virgil's *Aeneid*, which becomes a more direct frame of reference below.

10. The preceding paragraphs are quoted from "From the Realm of Contemporary Moods. 1. Apocalypse and Society," *Vesy* [*Libra*], no. 6 (1905): 35–38.

11. Ivanov's 1904 poem "The Vengeance of the Sword" ("Mest' mechnaia") from the cycle "Days of Wrath" (or "Dies irae," "Godina gneva") utilizes imagery from the Oedipus myth and from the New Testament (see especially Mt 11:30; Rv 13). A direct subtext is Vladimir Solovyov's 1890 poem "Ex Oriente Lux":

> O Rus'! in profound foresight
> You are burdened by a proud thought;
> What kind of East do you want to be:
> The East of Xerxes or of Christ?

12. Cf. Gn 1:1. Cf. Ivanov's 1904 poem "Winter Seed," quoted below; see also note 14.

13. In the first publication (p. 87), this was followed by a quotation from Dostoevsky's *Brothers Karamazov* (the title of pt. 1, bk. 2, chap. 5): "And let it be, let it be."

14. Ivanov's 1904 poem "Winter Seed" ("Ozim'") from the cycle "Days of Wrath" ("Godina gneva") in *Cor Ardens*.

15. Cf. Mt 5:29–30; Eph 6:19.

16. Beginning with Vladimir Solovyov, Russian thinkers returned to the Church without, however, relinquishing Western ideas and modes of thinking. In 1901, the first Religious-Philosophical meetings took place in St. Petersburg. They were an open intellectual forum for the discussion of religious and ecclesiastical issues. Founded by Dmitry Merezhkovsky, Zinaida Gippius, Vasily Rozanov, and others, the society attracted some participation by Church figures. Closed in 1903, it reformed in 1907 as the Religious-Philosophical Society, and Ivanov played a central role in it until he left Petersburg in 1912. Later, he was active in the Moscow Religious-Philosophical Society in Memory of Vladimir Solovyov (1905–17). Around 1905, the movement for reform within the Church first took definite form, and it was well represented at the Church Council that began meeting in 1917, but the degree to which the intelligentsia's extraecclesiastical activities influenced these reforms is a matter of some dispute.

17. See the introductory note to this chapter for a summary of the section Ivanov omitted here after the first publication.

18. Ivanov uses the structure and terminology of Hegelian logic.

19. In the first publication, this read: "Only that *becomes,* which already *is*" (p. 90). This formula stems from Ivanov's mystical experience in the Crimea in the summer of 1908, which he described in a 1939 article "Ein Echo" (*Collected Works,* 3:646–49); cf. note 5 to "Ancient Terror" in this volume.

20. Johann Gottfried Herder (1744–1803) based his *Ideas toward a Philosophy of Human History* (1784–91) on the view that each culture and epoch has a unique character. Georg Wilhelm Friedrich Hegel (1770–1831) also believed in the unique value of each historical epoch and culture, which he discussed most notably in *Lectures on the Philosophy of History* (published posthumously in 1837).

21. Second Isaiah is the scholarly designation for the latter portion of the Book of Isaiah, which contains many messianic prophecies echoed in the Gospels (e.g., Mt 3:3, 12:18–21). The distinction between First and Second Isaiah is not recognized by the Orthodox Church.

22. The hero of Virgil's *Aeneid,* who escaped Troy to become the founding father of Rome. Ivanov later devoted an entire article to the messianic nature of Virgil's poetry ("Virgils Historiosophie," *Corona,* Heft 6 [1931]: 761–74).

23. Hellenic and Sibylline prophesying refers primarily to the oracles of Dodona and Delphi in Greece and Sibyl's cave at Cumae and the temple of Fortune at Praeneste in Italy. The Sibylline prophecies, written in Greek hexameters, were collected in books that were guarded closely in the Roman state until they perished in the first century B.C. In Virgil's epic (book VI), Aeneas visits the Cumaean Sibyl, who conducts him through the underworld, where Aeneas sees the souls of illustrious Romans. The lines quoted follow immediately upon his leaving the underworld.

24. *Aeneid* VI.847–53.

25. Napoleon gained power by assuming leadership of the revolutionary regime. On 2 December 1804, he crowned himself emperor.

26. The "Classical Slavophilism" of Aleksei Khomiakov (1804–60), Ivan Kireevsky (1806–56), Konstantin Aksakov (1817–60), and a few others largely passed by 1860; it was followed by a series of thinkers who, while laying claim to the Slavophile heritage, tended to divorce its quasi-nationalistic politics from the religious doctrine on which it was based, attracting accusations of chauvinism and obscurantism. Those accused of being epigones of Slavophilism range from Ivan Aksakov (1823–86), a respected publicist, to Nikolai Danilevsky (1822–85), a Pan-Slav cultural typologist, the nationalists of the 1900s, and even Ivanov himself.

27. A title that has been vaguely associated with Moscow since the Pskovian monk Philotheus formulated it in the sixteenth century, after the

fall of Constantinople. It appears not to have played a significant role in Russian religious or intellectual life before the nineteenth century.

28. "Rome of the Spirit" is reminiscent of Dmitry Merezhkovsky's idea of the "Third Testament," which was to usher in the millennial epoch of the spirit, and mystical, Johannite Christianity on earth. On the influence of Hegel and Joachim of Fiore on Merezhkovsky, see the introductory note above.

29. Cf. Mt 16:26; Lk 17:33.

30. On 15 December 1908, a massive earthquake struck southern Italy and Sicily, especially the region of Messina. In his lecture "Element and Culture," Blok tied this elemental vengeance to the achievements of culture in the nineteenth century: "Before the face of the tempestuous element the haughty flag of culture has been lowered to half-mast." See also "Ancient Terror," p. 148 in this volume.

31. See note 16 to "The Symbolics of Aesthetic Principles" in this volume.

32. Latin phrase meaning "discontent with itself."

33. On the concepts of critical and organic culture, see note 15 to "Presentiments and Portents" in this volume.

34. Virgil's Fourth Eclogue is a paean to the Roman consul Asinius Pollio (40 B.C.), during whose reign a child was to be born and a golden age inaugurated. Early Christians often interpreted this as a prophecy of Christ.

35. Anaxagoras (fifth century B.C.)—Greek philosopher, father of metaphysical dualism. A friend of the Athenian ruler Pericles, he was nonetheless expelled during the Persian Wars for atheism. These events prefigured Socrates' condemnation half a century later.

36. Ivanov's formulation is most likely derived from Dostoevsky's "Pushkin Speech," in which the latter repeatedly speaks of the intelligentsia as "severed from the people" and from the "national force"; see *A Writer's Diary*, 2:1271–95.

37. Pisistratus (sixth century B.C.)—Athenian ruler who encouraged the mystery cults of Dionysus and Demeter; Ivanov saw him as the codifier of the Dionysian religion.

38. Cf. Mt 22:17–21.

39. Cf. Mt 9:17.

40. Gn 3:5.

41. Gn 3:17–20.

42. Gn 4:22.

43. Cf. the Lord's Prayer, Mt 6:9–13; Ivanov here gives a purely "immanentist" interpretation of Christianity, whereby God is seen as inherent within humanity; he develops this more in his 1907 article "Thou art" (which he later deemed excessively immanentist in expression).

44. Lk 19:40.

45. A paraphrase of the end of the Nicene Creed, the main dogmatic exposition of the Christian faith.

46. Cf. Goethe's poem "Blessed Yearning" ("Selige Sehnsucht").

47. Cf. Ivanov's "The Scythian Dances," cited on p. 121 in this volume.

48. Cf. the Parable of the Rich Man: Mt 19:21; Mk 10:21; Lk 18:22.

49. Cf. Jn 1:4–5, 9–10, 14.

50. Jn 13:1–17.

51. In the first publication, Ivanov inserted a note here: "For references to facts concerning our sects I am obliged to M. M. Prishvin, who has published his research in *Russkaia mysl'*" (p. 91). M. M. Prishvin (1873–1954) was an ethnologist and fiction writer. The slogan cited by Ivanov apparently belonged to the rather questionable sect of the "Chemreki," founded by Aleksei Shchetinin (see A. Etkind, "Russkie sekty i sovetskii kommunizm," in *Minuvshee: istoricheskii al'manakh* [Moscow and St. Petersburg: Atheneum, Feniks, 1996], 19:275–319).

52. Jn 1:5. The usual English translation runs: "The darkness did not comprehend it."

53. Cf. Jn 12:24; cf. note 16 to "The Symbolics of Aesthetic Principles" in this volume.

54. This thought, which first appears in the "Tabula Smaragdina," attributed to Hermes Trismegistus, became one of the key phrases in Russian Decadence; for the Hermetic text, see Wayne Shumaker, *The Occult Sciences in the Renaissance: A Study in Intellectual Patterns* (Berkeley: University of California Press, 1972), p. 179; see note 21 to "The Testaments of Symbolism" in this volume. The Latin phrase was also used as the title of an 1883 poem by Vladimir Solovyov, which was Ivanov's most immediate source (see his letter to E. R. Curtius in *Vjačeslav Ivanov: Dichtung und Briefwechsel aus dem deutschsprachigen Nachlass*, ed. Michael Wachtel [Mainz: Liber Verlag, 1995], p. 58).

55. The name of a famous spiritual work attributed to Thomas à Kempis.

56. "This people was born Christian." Source unknown, but cf. Tertullian, *De Testimonio Animae* 1: "anima naturaliter Christiana" (the soul is naturally Christian); *Patrologia Latina*, vol. 1, col. 377. This saying was often applied to Virgil (see note 34 above).

57. The Paraclete, i.e., the Holy Spirit.

58. "Bright Resurrection" is a standard Orthodox term for Easter. Ivanov repeated the foregoing passage in his 1916 article "The Two Voices of the Russian Soul" ("Dva lada russkoi dushi"), where he called Easter the source of the tragic "voice" in Orthodoxy in contrast to its usually epic voice.

59. This and the following quotation are from Ivanov's "Paschal Candles" ("Paskhal'nye svechi") from *Cor Ardens*.

60. In his *Notes from the Dead House* (1860), Dostoevsky stressed that criminals were often called "unfortunates" (*neschastnye*). Later, Dostoevsky's interest in the courts found particular expression in *Crime and Punishment, A Writer's Diary* (e.g., the entries for May 1876), and *The Brothers Karamazov*.

61. See note 16 to "The Symbolics of Aesthetic Principles" in this volume.

62. Leonid Andreev (1871–1919) was known for his dark, even nihilistic stories. "Darkness" ("T'ma," 1907) portrays a revolutionary who goes to a bordello to elude the police. His sympathy for the prostitute causes him to abandon his cause and join the debauchery, which then leads to his arrest. Ivanov was present at Andreev's first reading of the story (L. Andreev, *Sobranie sochinenii* [Moscow: Khudozhestvennaia literatura, 1990], 2:536).

63. Cf. Ivan Karamazov's conversation with Alesha and his tale of the "Grand Inquisitor" in *The Brothers Karamazov* (pt. 2, bk. 5, chap. 3–5).

64. See the words of Shatov in Dostoevsky's novel *The Demons* (pt. 2, chap. 1, sec. vii); cf. "The Symbolics of Aesthetic Principles" in this volume, p. 6.

65. Cf. Vladimir Solovyov's "Secret of Progress" (1898).

66. Mt 3:17; Lk 1:15.

67. This and the two following poetic quotations are the lines of "Pythia" in Ivanov's dithyramb "The Fire-Bearers" ("Ognenostsy," 1906; *Cor Ardens*). In the original, these couplets formed quatrains; cf. "The Testaments of Symbolism" in this volume, p. 39.

68. In the first publication, this quotation was followed by the sentence: "When one Hindu was asked how long it takes to be cleansed, he said: 77 incarnations or 77 years, or 7 years, but sometimes only 7 hours" (no. 2, p. 94).

69. The first part of this quotation appears in notations Nietzsche made in the 1880s (later published under the title *The Will to Power*): "Der Irrtum ist eine Feigheit. . . ." The source of the second part has not been identified.

70. Cf. Heraclitus's frag. B66.

71. Rv 21:12, 14.

ANCIENT TERROR

"Ancient Terror: On Leon Bakst's Painting *Terror Antiquus*" was first published in the fourth issue of *The Golden Fleece* for 1909 (pp. 51–65). It was included without significant changes in *By the Stars* (pp. 393–424) and *Collected Works* (3:92–110). A slightly different version, edited by Ivanov, was published in German translation by Nicolai von Bubnoff (*Corona*, Jahr V, Heft 2 [January 1935]: 133–64; reprinted in *Das alte Wahre*, pp. 31–76).

Ivanov's article is ostensibly devoted to a 1908 painting by Leon Bakst, now at the Russian Museum in St. Petersburg, which was inspired by the painter's trip to Greece. Ivanov gives a detailed description and analysis of the painting. It is possible that Bakst made his pilgrimage under the influence of his friend Ivanov, or at least that Ivanov helped to prepare him for what he would find. In any case, Ivanov clearly uses Bakst's work as an occasion to revisit Greek religion and give the fullest account of his own cosmology.

"Ancient Terror" is perhaps Ivanov's densest article, and it is worth-while citing in full the author's own unpublished summary of its themes:

Ancient Terror

Leon Bakst's painting *Terror Antiquus:* a religious-historical and philosophi-cal interpretation and development of its ideas.
  I. The three ideas revealed in the painting *Terror Antiquus:*
      a) The idea of cosmic catastrophe.
      b) The idea of fate.
      c) The idea of immortal Femininity.
  II. Astarte-Aphrodite and the male principle. The masculine is fated to death, while the feminine is immortal. The cosmic Woman as Fate and Destroyer.
  III. The connection between the most ancient terror of femininity and the matriarchate.
  IV. The reaction of the male principle against female despotism. The patri-archate. Druids. Orpheus. Apollo's religion. The female principle as the cause of cosmic guilt. The moralization of religious concepts. *Terror fati* and *Timor Dei.*
  V. Masculine theomachy in league with the earliest idea of immortal fem-ininity. Fate as primordial Truth. Human energeticism as a result of joining the theomachic [idea] to the idea of a moral order.
  VI. The Christian harmonization of masculine energy, and the religious rev-elation of femininity.
  VII. The World Soul and Christian energeticism. Causality and typology. The anthropological principle in the modern religious consciousness and the prospects [*sud'by*] for its correct affirmation in the future.
4 March 1909
Viacheslav Ivanov
(RGB 109.4.35)

Ivanov portrays the world in starkly pantheistic tones, with the cos-mos appearing as a supreme female goddess, with whom individuals achieve union by renouncing selfhood, through the mediation of Eros and suffer-ing. A cosmic fall separated the female cosmos from masculine humanity, making the feminine element appear as flesh and necessity. In developing this conception, Ivanov enters into dialogue with ancient writers (Plato, Aeschy-lus, Pindar, among others) and, in a more polemical mode, with modern historians of Greek religion (Johann Jakob Bachofen, Erwin Rohde, Nietzsche). He addresses himself most directly, however, to modern culture, which has become content with the illusory being of individuation. Even Christianity is called upon for the answers it provides "to the ancient needs of paganism" and not for its traditional, monotheistic content. God must be rediscovered through the divinity of the cosmos (the Earth) and an individual acceptance of divine will, which together are constitutive of what Ivanov calls "the new religious consciousness."

In many respects, "Ancient Terror" is a metaphysics of tragedy, painting a cosmos in which tragedy must play a vital role. Tragedy presents individuals facing necessity as something beautiful and fascinating, leading them to renounce illusory individuation and accept primordial unity. It is possible that "Ancient Terror" was even written in connection with his tragedy *Prometheus*, which, according to a notice in *The Golden Fleece* (nos. 11–12 [1908]: 89), Ivanov was completing at this time, although it was published only in 1915. Compared to Ivanov's earlier, Nietzschean writings on tragedy, "Ancient Terror" manifests a move toward a more Romantic understanding of tragedy as a dramatization of the sublime gulf between reality and the ideal. The Romantic context of Ivanov's thoughts is supported by an allusion to Schiller's writings on tragedy, and also by his 1919 commentary on *Prometheus*, where Ivanov develops some of the ideas of "Ancient Terror."

1. Mnemosyne, the mother by Zeus of the nine Muses, in ancient Greek means literally "memory."

2. From Pushkin's "Rhyme" ("Rifma," 1830); cf. also "Rhyme, songful friend" ("Rifma, zvuchnaia podruga," 1828).

3. Theognis, *Elegies* I.15–18; see note 20 to "The Symbolics of Aesthetic Principles" in this volume.

4. The title of a hymn from the Orthodox service for the departed. Cf. note 13 to "The Symbolics of Aesthetic Principles" in this volume.

5. Plato expounds this idea in his *Phaedo* (72E–76A, passim) and *Phaedrus* (249E–250C); see also an intimation of it in *Timaeus* (41DE). In a draft of the essay, Ivanov refers here to a formula revealed to him (in Latin) in a mystical experience in 1908: *Fieri debet quod est* (What is must come to be); RNB f. 304 ed. khr. 17; cf. Ivanov's account of the experience in "Ein Echo," in *Collected Works*, 3:646–49, and "On the Russian Idea" in this volume, p. 132.

6. Jn 19:30. In the first publication, this phrase originally specified "the words of Golgotha" (p. 51).

7. Ivanov owes his formulation to Vladimir Solovyov, *Russia and the Universal Church*, trans. Herbert Rees (London: Geoffrey Bles, the Centenary Press, 1949).

8. Here and in subsequent allusions to the shadows of Hades, Ivanov may be referring to the experiences of Odysseus (Homer, *Odyssey* XI.204–24) and Aeneas (Virgil, *Aeneid* VI.700–51).

9. Jn 1:1.

10. Ivanov devoted the long poem "The Dream of Melampus" ("Son Melampa," 1907) to the theme of the reverse flow of time, from effects to causes, a phenomenon he called "antirrhoia."

11. Here, "Being" (*Bytie*) could also denote the Book of Genesis.

12. This passage recalls the ideas of Nikolai Fedorov, who wrote a philosophy of the "common task," the ultimate aim of which was the "resurrection of our fathers"; cf. note 46 to "On the Crisis of Humanism" in this volume.

13. Cf. Mt 7:24–25, 16:18; Eph 2:20–22.

14. Cf. Jn 2:19–21.

15. Cf. Rom 7:7–12.

16. Cf. Lv 19:18; Mt 5:43, 19:19; Gal 5:14; Jas 2:8.

17. This was the role assigned to the priestly caste in Vladimir Solovyov's tripartite theocratic vision; see "The Religious Task of Vladimir Solovyov," p. 195, in this volume.

18. *Ivanov's note:* "Das Wahre ist schon längst gefunden / Hat edle Geisterschaft verbunden: Das alte Wahre, fass' es an" ("Vermächtnis" [1829] in *Gott und Welt*).

19. Solon (c. 640–c. 558 B.C.)—Athenian statesman and poet, archon (ruler) of Athens from c. 594 B.C., and the first poet to use the Attic dialect. The passage referred to is *Timaeus* 21A–25D. The following passage shares its phraseology with the third of Ivanov's "Imitations of Plato" ("Podrazhaniia Platonu") from *Transparency*.

20. The last legendary king of Athens; Plato intimates his kinship with Solon in *Timaeus* 20E.

21. *Timaeus* 21D.

22. *Timaeus* 22B. Ivanov continues to paraphrase *Timaeus* 22C–23D.

23. Aeschylus, *Agamemnon* 1328–30 (words of Cassandra).

24. *Timaeus* 23AB; cf. also *Phaedrus* 274–275B.

25. *Timaeus* 23D–24A.

26. Refers to the Rock of Gibraltar.

27. *Timaeus* 25D; *Critias* 113C–21C.

28. In 1895, A. le Plonjeon published his (erroneous) translation of the Mayan Troano Codex, according to which the land of Mu had perished in 9654 B.C.; Sir Arthur Evans excavated Minoan civilization on Crete, and in 1900 discovered King Minos's palace; little is known about the Etruscan civilization of northern Italy. In 1905, Konstantin Bal'mont traveled widely in Mexico and California, sending home travelogues and versions of Native American cosmogonies which served to raise interest in the area. See also Ivanov, *Hellenic Religion,* pp. 39, 167.

29. Cf. *Aeneid* VI.724–30.

30. Jn 1:5.

31. An allusion to Fedor Tiutchev's "Why are you howling, night wind" ("O chem ty voesh', vetr nochnoi," 1836).

32. Cf. Nietzsche's phrase *amor fati,* on which see note 4 to "Presentiments and Portents" in this volume.

33. On this 15 December 1908 earthquake, see note 30 to "On the Russian Idea" in this volume.

34. Louise Ackermann (real name Louise-Victorine Choquet, 1813–90), a French poetess. The source of Ivanov's quotation has not been located, but Ackermann used the almost synonymous word *avortements* in her 1871 poem "L'homme à la Nature." Vladimir Solovyov has a remarkably similar passage in *Lectures on Divine Humanity,* revised and edited by Boris Jakim (Hudson, N.Y.: Lindisfarne Press, 1996), p. 138. This might be explained by Ackermann's and Solovyov's common interest in Schopenhauer (see Marc Citoleux, *La Poésie philosophique au XIXe siècle. Mme Ackermann* [Paris: Plon-Nourrit, 1906], pp. 92–100).

35. See Nietzsche's *Gay Science,* sec. 45; cf. Nietzsche's poem "The Sun Sinks" ("Die Sonne sinkt").

36. Lucretius, *The Nature of Things* II.1–4; cf. also VI.535–607 on natural disasters. Schiller cites this passage from Lucretius in his essay "On the Tragic Art." Like Ivanov, Schiller defends the positive aesthetic value of the pity evoked by others' suffering. On the other hand, Ivanov appears to be engaging in subtle polemic with Schiller's somewhat emotional theory of tragedy.

37. From Ivanov's poem "Intoxication" ("Khmel'") from *Transparency.*

38. Rv 17.

39. "Cruel" and "meek" are words characteristic of Dostoevsky (whom Nikolai Mikhailovsky called "a cruel talent," and who wrote "The Meek One" ["Krotkaia"]), and Ivanov's depiction of the goddess thereby hints at Dostoevsky's female characters, who embody both "Madonna and Sodom" (cf. *The Brothers Karamazov,* bk. 1, pt. 3, chap. 3, "The Confession of an Ardent Heart. In Verse").

40. Cf. "She rests modestly in her solemn beauty" from Pushkin's "The Beauty" ("Krasavitsa," 1832).

41. Cf. *Iliad* III.156–60.

42. See the chapter "Rebellion" (pt. 2, bk. 5, chap. 4) in Dostoevsky's *The Brothers Karamazov,* where Ivan Karamazov expresses his outrage that God allows suffering in his world.

43. In *The Idiot* (pt. 3, chap. 5); cf. "On the Limits of Art" in this volume, p. 43.

44. A phrase from Livy (*History of Rome* 43.13.12) which Ivanov often cited (imprecisely) in the form "animus fit antiquior" (cf. *Hellenic Religion,* p. 44).

45. Anadyomene means literally "she who arose on the surface of the sea"; on the different aspects of Aphrodite, see "The Symbolics of Aesthetic Principles" in this volume, p. 12.

46. The opening line of Ivanov's sonnet "Stella Maris" from *Pilot Stars*.

47. Niobe had seven sons and seven daughters; all were killed (and, in some versions of the myth, petrified) by Apollo and Artemis after Niobe boasted of her abundant progeny to the less endowed Leto. Niobe herself was turned to stone by the intensity of her mourning.

48. One of Apollo's epithets was Musagetes, the leader of the Muses.

49. The word for veil (*pokrov*) is closely associated to the protection of the Virgin Mother, an object of religious veneration in Eastern Orthodoxy; cf. Ivanov's poem "The Veil" ("Pokrov," 1908) from *Cor Ardens*. In Nietzsche's *Birth of Tragedy* (sec. 2), it is Apollo who holds out the Gorgon's head to repel Dionysus.

50. A passage from Wagner's *Die Meistersinger von Nürnberg* that Nietzsche applies to poetic creativity in general (see Nietzsche's *Birth of Tragedy*, sec. 1). Cf. "On the Limits of Art" in this volume, p. 73.

51. Mt 5:18.

52. Cleopatra and Mark Antony were defeated by Octavian at Actium in 31 B.C., marking the passage of the Roman republic into an empire.

53. See Lucretius, *The Nature of Things* III; *Odyssey* XI.213. Ivanov's view of Democritus's concept of *eídola* is more positive in *Hellenic Religion*, p. 166.

54. *Faust* II.6173–306, 6377–565.

55. It is not clear what Ivanov has in mind; cf. Jon 4:11 (regarding the residents of Ninevah), Mt 6:3, 18:3ff.

56. The lotus was venerated in many religious traditions as a symbol of life and fertility. The shape of its petals and inner center represented the interaction of the female and male principles. In Hindu belief, Brahma, the creative god, is born of a lotus that appears from the navel of Vishnu, the preserving god; the creative process culminates in the ascendancy of Shiva, the destructive god. The three members of this divine triad correspond quite closely to the alternate roles of the goddess in Ivanov's scheme.

57. Gn 8:8–12; cf. Mt 3:16.

58. In Vedic mythology, Maya is the power of reincarnation, which turns into the force of illusion if possessed by enemies of the gods. In Hindu thought, Maya represents the illusoriness of worldly being, understood as a game or dream of the gods.

59. See Lessing's *Laocoön*.

60. Cf. Pushkin's "Whether I'm wandering along noisy streets" ("Brozhu li ia vdol' ulits shumnykh," 1829): "And at the entrance to my grave, let young life play, and indifferent nature will shine with eternal beauty."

61. *Trionfo della Morte* (Triumph of Death); *Trionfo della Vita* (Triumph of Life). These phrases are common titles for literary works, ever since Petrarch's "Trionfi," a cycle of six allegorical poems, one of which con-

cerns death's triumph over the beloved Laura; the cycle ends with eternity triumphant over time. The most relevant examples of artworks contemporary to Ivanov are Gustave Doré's *Triumph of Death*, Fedor Sologub's 1906 tragedy *Triumph of Death*, and Gabriele D'Annunzio's dark, impassioned novel of the same title (1894), which bears some similarities to "Ancient Terror" (e.g., mention of the "Wise Mother of the Earth").

62. From the fourth poem in Ivanov's cycle of nine sonnets "The Dispute" ("Spor," 1908) from *Cor Ardens*.

63. The word for the drink of everlasting life in Sanskrit, ancient Greek, and French, respectively.

64. A reference to the oracle of Zeus at Dodona in Epirus which issued its cryptic answers to questions through the rustling of the leaves of an oak tree or the sound of water flowing from its roots.

65. "Egyptian Nights" is an unfinished prose work of Pushkin (1835) that incorporates a poetic improvisation (written in 1828) on the legend of Cleopatra.

66. The "Great Mother," an Asiatic goddess.

67. Cf. Jn 4:5–26.

68. An epithet from the *Akathist* hymn to the Mother of God.

69. Herodotus II.174–75; Plato, *Timaeus* 21E; Proclus, *In Platonis Timaeon* I.30; cf. also Plutarch, *De Iside et Osiride* IX.354BC. Actually, Plato is the one to identify Neith explicitly with Athena, which explains why the Athenian Solon was well received at Sais; Plutarch identifies her as Isis.

70. On the myth of Isis at Sais, see note 64 to "Two Elements in Contemporary Symbolism" in this volume.

71. Johann Jakob Bachofen (1815–87)—historian of ancient law and religion, known primarily for his theory of a period of female dominance in antiquity, known as Mother Right; see his *Myth, Religion, and Mother Right*, trans. Ralph Manheim (Princeton: Princeton University Press, 1967); this passage corresponds closely to *Hellenic Religion*, p. 161.

72. Daughters of Danaus, who quarreled with his brother Aegyptus and fled to Argos with his fifty daughters. The fifty sons of Aegyptus followed them and married them, but Danaus forced his daughters to massacre them all.

73. Herodotus tells how the Pelasgians occupied Lemnos and kidnapped Athenian women; later, they murdered the women and their children. "Lemnian deeds" became proverbial for atrocious crimes.

74. The preceding paragraph is heavily dependent on Bachofen (*Myth, Religion, and Mother Right*, pp. 109–15); cf. *Hellenic Religion*, p. 200.

75. "Leader of the Fates."

76. Here, Ivanov reveals a polemical attitude toward Bachofen, who had associated these qualities precisely with the matriarchate (Bachofen, *Myth, Religion, and Mother Right*, p. 85); Ivanov indicates that he favors

the more primitive state of hetaerism or Amazonianism, associated with Dionysus, which Bachofen found cruel and unbalanced.

77. Cf. *Iliad* XIV.206–7. Ivanov left an unfinished tragedy *Niobe,* in which he apparently intended to show her stubborn defense of Tantalus (on whom he wrote a separate tragedy in 1905).

78. The secret was that the son of Thetis was fated to overthrow Zeus; see Aeschylus, *Prometheus Bound* 169–70, 915–27; Ivanov refers to lines 209–10 regarding Themis: "She is one though her names are many."

79. Sophocles, *Antigone* 455–56.

80. The concept of "bad eternity" originates in Hegel's notion of "bad infinity" (*schlechte Unendlichkeit*), which denotes a process that does not lead to qualitative improvement.

81. Gn 3:5.

82. These phrases mean "weariness of life" and "seize the day," respectively (Horace, *Odes* I.xi.8).

83. Cf. Lk 17:27. The following passage contains multiple references to the Lord's Prayer (Mt 6:9–13) and the Apostles' Creed. Ivanov's interpretation of the Lord's Prayer, although unusually anthropocentric, has parallels in patristic literature, e.g., Maximus the Confessor's "Exposition of the Lord's Prayer." Ivanov developed it in more detail in his 1907 article "Thou art."

84. Jn 4:5–26; cf. p. 156 and note 67 to this essay.

85. Mt 16:25–26; cf. Lk 17:33.

86. Pindar, *Pythian Odes* VIII.96–97; cf. *Odyssey* X.495; Aeschylus, *Prometheus Bound* 448. Ivanov cites this line by Pindar in *Hellenic Religion* (p. 58), where he attributes it to Pindar's knowledge of Orphism.

87. Mystical energeticism is Ivanov's preferred term for the idea of mystical anarchism propagated by Ivanov and Georgy Chulkov in the years 1906–8, on which see the introductory note to "Presentiments and Portents" in this volume.

88. "Seminal logoi"; see "On the Limits of Art," p. 86, in this volume.

89. Cf. 1 Jn 2:16: "For all that is in the world—the lust of the flesh, the lust of the eyes, and the pride of life—is not of the Father but is of the world."

90. Jn 1:5.

91. Gn 3:6.

92. Rv 12:1; cf. Mt 25:1–13.

ON THE CRISIS OF HUMANISM

"On the Crisis of Humanism" was printed as the "first meditation" in a projected series of articles, under the general title "Steep Slopes," in the first issue of the last Symbolist journal *Notes of Dreamers* (*Zapiski mechtatelei,* 1919, pp. 104–18). It was prefaced by a short introduction (pp. 103–4), and preceded by several of Ivanov's poems, thematically tied to ideas presented in the article (pp. 97–102). It was reprinted in *Collected Works* (3:367–82) and was translated into German as *Klüfte. Über die Krise des Humanismus* by W. E. Groeger (Berlin: Skythen, 1922).

Ivanov's Rome archive contains a handwritten program for Ivanov's lecture "The Crisis of Humanism," dated 24 January 1919:

I. The Snake Changes Its Skin
"Do not the icy seas spew fire." Lomonosov.—The crisis of the phenomenon.—Whirlwinds.—Changing the tissues of phenomena.—The crisis of art.

II. The Battle for the Hero's Body
The definition of humanism. Its cradle. Antiquity and humanism. The physicians of ancient humanism. The state and social structure of the ancient world, the ancient political mask. Ancient mysticism. Christianity. Medieval humanism and the humanism of modern history. Humanism and antihumanism as leading revolutionary ideas and forces. Its portent in art. Nietzsche's two-facedness.—Scriabin.—The disincarnation of the modern artist.—Art vs. humanism.

III. Beyond Humanism
The religious consciousness of the future under the banner of man.—Collectivism and man-godhood, *sobornost'* and the image of the Son of Man.

One of Ivanov's most impassioned essays, "On the Crisis of Humanism" palpably presents a basic tension in his attitude toward humanism. By education and taste, Ivanov himself was the consummate humanist, in the sense of one who studies the humanistic sciences with particular reference to ancient languages and texts. On the other hand, his intellectual aspirations (i.e., Dionysianism, theurgy, *sobornost'*, a new organic epoch) seem to contradict what is usually meant by humanism: the privileging of individual rights and preferences. Thus, in his essay, Ivanov now praises humanism, now celebrates its demise, but his precise prediction for what can surmount and surpass humanism remains muted (as he admits in the final sentence).

It may be illuminating to link Ivanov's nascent "transhumanism" to the personal aesthetic developed in "Manner, Persona, Style" and "On the Limits of Art." Here, art and human activity, in general, are redirected toward the moral and ontological regeneration of humanity itself. Key to this, however, is the recognition that humanity is distinguished by spiritual freedom and inherent spiritual value, and cannot be subordinated to some externally imposed ideal. Thus, while indicating the limits of humanism, Ivanov is reluctant to chart out humanity's future paths, which will issue only from man's free creative activity. Ivanov insists on two things: first, that this creative activity remain open to religious knowledge; second, that it seek to define itself in respect to its memory of previous human creations and conceptions. Thus, it is possible to view "On the Crisis of Humanism," together with Ivanov's mature aesthetic essays, as part of a nascent hermeneutic philosophy that shifts the emphasis from metaphysics to the concrete reception and application of truths culled from previous human expressions.

1. The quotation "Do not the icy seas spew fire?" is from Mikhail Lomonosov's "Evening Meditation on God's Majesty" ("Vechernee razmyshlenie o Bozhiem velichestve," 1743). The entire stanza reads: "But where, o nature, is your law? / The dawn now breaks from northern lands! / Does not the sun there set its throne? / Do not the icy seas spew fire? / Behold cold flame has covered us! / Behold at night day steps to earth!"

2. See Blok, "Collapse of Humanism" ("Krushenie gumanizma," 1919).

3. Cf. Heraclitus's frag. B12 and B49a.

4. Einstein published his theory of general relativity in 1915.

5. Pushkin, *Eugene Onegin* VII.2.

6. In this unusual personal note, Ivanov mentions a subject he had discussed in detail in answer to a newspaper survey ("Anketa o samoubiistvakh," *Birzhevye vedomosti* [evening issue], 30 April 1912, no. 12913). The high rate of suicide in prewar Vienna has been linked to the influence of Otto Weininger, whose 1903 book *Sex and Character* espoused suicide and who himself committed suicide in October 1903.

7. Cf. Ps 51:19 (50:19 in Eastern Orthodox numbering).

8. In "Thou art" (1907), Ivanov talked of Psyche (literally, "the soul") as the feminine substratum of the personality that seeks impregnation by the male spirit or Logos. Ivanov's concept of "inner form" owes a significant debt to Wilhelm von Humboldt and to his Russian-Ukrainian follower Aleksandr Potebnia (1835–91). Potebnia identified the inner form of a word with its basic etymological meaning, understood as a semantically rich image which was also the source of the word's poetic power.

9. In Greek mythology, Tantalus offended the Olympian gods (by feeding them his son's flesh, stealing their nectar, or revealing their secrets) and was duly punished by being set before water that receded as he approached, and under fruit trees that he could not reach. Ivanov's 1905 tragedy *Tantalus* combined all these motifs as expressions of theomachy and redemptive suffering; cf. "The Symbolics of Aesthetic Principles" in this volume, which was written in conjunction with the tragedy.

10. Ivanov alludes to Russian Cubo-Futurists (especially Aleksei Kruchenykh), who sought a "transrational" language and a "self-sufficient" word while professing hostility toward literary classics.

11. For a development of these ideas, see Ivanov's 1918 essay "Our Language" (*Out of the Depths* [*De Profundis*]: *A Collection of Articles on the Russian Revolution*, trans. and ed. William F. Woehrlin [Irvine, Calif.: Charles Schlacks Jr., Publisher, 1986], pp. 119–24) and his 1927 poem "Language" ("Iazyk").

12. In the *Collected Works* (3:373), the title of this section reads "Battles for the Hero's Body," but this is probably a misprint.

13. Source unknown.

14. Theseus was the mythical founder of Athens. In Sophocles' *Antigone,* the heroine fights Creon for the body of her brother Polynices, appealing to eternal and "unwritten" law for justification.

15. See Aeschylus, *Prometheus Bound* 11.

16. From the tract "On Non-Being" of the Sophist Gorgias (c. 485–375 B.C.); see also "The Religious Task of Vladimir Solovyov" in this volume, p. 196; "Lev Tolstoy and Culture" in this volume, p. 207.

17. Cf. "On the Joyful Craft and the Joy of the Spirit" in this volume, p. 120.

18. Aristotle, *Politics* 1253a.

19. Hesiod, *Theogony* 535.

20. Frag. 354 (Proclus in *Plat. Remp.* I. 127, 29).

21. The beginning of "homo sum: humani nil a me alienum puto" (I am a man, and nothing human is alien to me); Terence, *The Self-Tormentor* 77.

22. A reference to Goethe's "Blessed Yearning" ("Selige Sehnsucht," 1814).

23. From Nietzsche, sec. 3 of "Zarathustra's Prologue," pt. 1 of *Thus Spake Zarathustra.*

24. "Economy" is understood here as the arrangement of human affairs in general.

25. On Paul, see Acts 17:18–34. The Areopagus, which is mentioned again at the end of Ivanov's essay, was a hill where the central Athenian courts were located; it served as a central meeting place. Anatole France (pseudonym of Anatole François Thibault, 1844–1924)—French writer with a pronounced anticlerical and anti-Christian viewpoint. Celsus was a late-second-century Platonist who wrote a detailed polemic against Christianity. Entitled *The True Doctrine,* Celsus's polemic is known through quotations given in Origen's refutation *Against Celsus.*

26. Source unknown.

27. A document drafted by the French National Assembly on 4 August 1789 and sanctioned by Louis XVI on 5 October of that year. It created a constitutional monarchy in France, based on the rule of law and "liberty, property, security, and the right to resist oppression."

28. By "Scythians," Ivanov means nations that were not touched by classical culture, although the term has more Oriental connotations than "barbarianism" (used extensively in Ivanov's 1908 essay "On the Joyful Craft and the Joy of the Spirit"). Blok's 1918 poem "The Scythians" ("Skify") gave the term wide currency in Russian revolutionary discourse, although Ivanov himself had used the Scythian theme as early as 1891 in his poem "The Scythian Dances" ("Skif pliashet"), part of his cycle "Parisian Epigrams"

("Parizhskie epigramy"), included in *Pilot Stars* and quoted in "On the Joyful Craft and the Joy of the Spirit" in this volume, p. 121.

29. By "red culture affirmation" (*krasnoe kul'turtregerstvo,* from the German *Kulturträger*), Ivanov apparently means those revolutionaries (such as Lunacharsky and Gorky in Russia) who advocated preserving earlier cultural achievements in the new proletarian culture.

30. The phrase "proud man," from Pushkin's poem *The Gypsies* (1824), was quoted to great effect by Dostoevsky in his "Pushkin Speech" of 1880 (*A Writer's Diary*, 2:1284). "Mangodhood," the opposite of the concept of "godmanhood," also appears in Dostoevsky and is represented most notably by the character Kirillov in *Demons.* It is unclear whether Ivanov includes Dostoevsky among the "religiously paranoid."

31. Ivanov is referring to Plato's political philosophy in *The Republic.*

32. See Menelaus's fight against Hector for the body of Patroclus (*Iliad* XVII).

33. Cf. Sophocles' tragedy *Ajax.*

34. Cf. Euripides' *Bacchae.*

35. "The Nomads of Beauty" ("Kochevniki krasoty") is a poem from Ivanov's *Transparency.* An epigraph to the poem attributes the image to L. D. Zinov'eva-Annibal's drama *The Rings* (*Kol'tsa*).

36. "The Well-Tempered Clavier" is Johann Sebastian Bach's main collection of preludes and fugues for the keyboard. Its two parts are dated 1722 and 1738–42.

37. "Native chaos" is from Tiutchev's "Why are you howling, night wind?" ("O chem ty voesh' vetr nochnoi?" 1836).

38. Cf. Nietzsche, "Zarathustra's Prologue," pt. 1 of *Thus Spake Zarathustra.*

39. Source unknown.

40. On the image of Isis's veil, see note 64 to "Two Elements in Contemporary Symbolism" in this volume.

41. Argus was the herdsman the jealous Hera set to watch over Zeus's lover Io, whom Zeus had turned into a cow; he was covered with eyes (therefore named "Panoptes"), which after his death at the hands of Hermes were placed in peacocks' tails. Io later traveled to Egypt where she regained her previous form and, by some accounts, became Isis.

42. Ivanov's section title ("Po tu storonu gumanizma") clearly echoes the title of Nietzsche's *Beyond Good and Evil* ("Po tu storonu dobra i zla" in Russian translation).

43. Cf. Nietzsche's *The Case of Wagner* 1; see "The Symbolics of Aesthetic Principles" in this volume, p. 9; and "Nietzsche and Dionysus" in this volume, p. 186.

44. Cf. Lk 17:18.

45. See note 16 to "The Symbolics of Aesthetic Principles" in this volume.

46. Nikolai Fedorov (1829–1903)—Russian utopian philosopher whose writings were collected into a multivolume *Philosophy of the Common Task*. Fedorov combined a positivist spirit with Christian ideals, seeking practical means to overcome death and resurrect previous generations. Ivanov's transformation of "the common task" into "the universal task" may be tied to a book published under the latter title by the Fedorov-inspired Iona Brikhnichev (*Vselenskoe delo,* vyp. 1 [Odessa, 1914]). Ivanov had used "the universal task" for a 1914 article in support of the war ("Vselenskoe delo," *Russkaia mysl',* no. 12 [1914]: 97–107).

47. Solovyov's 1898 article "The Idea of Humanity in Auguste Comte" was an attempt to show the religious potential in the philosophy of the leading French positivist (1798–1857), in whose "religion of humanity" concrete humanity was taken as the Supreme Being (*le Grand Être*). Solovyov found this concept, shorn of its positivistic connotations, to be in harmony with his own notion of godmanhood, as presented in his 1879 *Lectures on Divine Humanity.* Cf. note 39 to "The Religious Task of Vladimir Solovyov" in this volume.

48. Jn 15:5.

49. Citing the poet's ability to "reincarnate" himself into all nationalities, Dostoevsky called Pushkin an "allman" or "panhuman" (*vsechelovek*); see Dostoevsky's "Pushkin Speech" in *A Writer's Diary,* 2:1294.

50. Aeschylus's *Agamemnon,* lines 121, 139, 159, 349; see "Manner, Persona, Style" in this volume, p. 61.

51. Heb 11:1.

52. Baal and Dagon, both prominent in the Old Testament, were gods of the Canaanite and Philistine nations, respectively.

53. Aeschylus, *Eumenides* 161–67. Ivanov proceeds to relate the plot of *Eumenides,* part of the trilogy *The Oresteia,* which he translated in full (1913–17, published only in 1988).

54. Goethe finished his drama *Iphigenie auf Tauris* in 1787.

55. "Ethical consciousness" is a stage in Hegel's account of the development of the spirit where the individual's actions are wholly directed toward the fulfillment of duty. The "terrible antinomy" arises from the fact that the "ethical consciousness" remains an unarticulated and "dark" ethical will that fails to recognize the truth of the actual world, i.e., it commits transgressions and incurs guilt. This stage is characterized precisely by the actions of Antigone in Sophocles' tragedy; cf. *The Phenomenology of Spirit,* sec. 444–77.

NIETZSCHE AND DIONYSUS

"Nietzsche and Dionysus" first appeared in the May 1904 issue of *Libra* (no. 5, pp. 17–30) and was reprinted with significant changes in *By the Stars* (pp. 1–20) and *Collected Works* (1:715–26). The 1909 version, the basis of this translation, introduced two new passages, several minor emendations, and a different division of the text. Originally, there were five sections entitled: "The Prophet of Dionysus"; "Two Gifts"; "How and What"; "The Superman"; "The Theomachist." Ivanov's German translation of the essay, which he worked on between 1929 and 1932 (unpublished manuscript, Rome archive), has been consulted for some of the notes.

Ivanov attributed great significance to this article, one of the first he published, "because it crystallizes all of my Yes'es and No's to Nietzscheanism" (*Literaturnoe nasledstvo,* vol. 85 [Moscow: Nauka, 1976], p. 442). His cult of Nietzsche is based almost wholly on his reading of *The Birth of Tragedy,* with its paeans to Dionysus and Richard Wagner, and an appreciation of *Thus Spake Zarathustra;* at various times, Ivanov intended to translate both of these works into Russian, but none of these plans saw fruition. He sees almost all of Nietzsche's subsequent works as stages in an increasingly grave betrayal of the original insight into the need to overcome worldly being. Ivanov singles out for pillory Nietzsche's concepts of the will to power and master morality.

Much of Ivanov's argument is clarified when one recognizes its striking resemblance to Vladimir Solovyov's account of Plato's life and works, "The Drama of Plato's Life" (1897). Solovyov held that Plato's philosophy was basically a liberating attempt to reconcile the ideal and real worlds through the power of Eros. Further, Solovyov found that Plato's later works, especially the collection known as *The Laws,* indicated that Plato had relinquished his striving for cosmic reconciliation and become satisfied with the lower world in its fallen state. If one substitutes Dionysus for Eros and makes allowances for the peculiar nature of Nietzsche's moral teaching, one sees the general contours of Ivanov's view of Nietzsche's regressive development from liberator to "legislator." Suffering, together with Eros, is for Ivanov a force that effects cosmic reunion, melting the barriers erected by individuation. In fact, Nietzsche's own struggle against his god results in salvific suffering and, in Ivanov's view, redemption. Ivanov finds Nietzsche to be not only a Platonist but also an unwilling and unbelieving Christian.

The personal feat of the "Dionysian philosopher," as Ivanov calls Nietzsche, leads Ivanov to compare him to Faust. Like Faust, Nietzsche's untiring efforts lead him to blessed images of divine reward, but, like Faust, he has "two souls" in his breast that prevent him from accepting God's gift. Ivanov refrains from referring to the finale of *Faust,* but despite all his references to tragedy, he obviously shares Goethe's aversion to tragic destruction.

1. The Skamander was a river near Troy.

2. Pausanius, *Description of Greece* III.24; VII.9. Much of the two paragraphs on Eurypylus is taken from Ivanov's *Hellenic Religion,* pp. 70–71.

3. Cf. Acts 17:22–23; Ivanov's *Pilot Stars* included a poem "To the Unknown God" ("Nevedomomu Bogu").

4. Rv 1:15 (referring to Christ at the Second Coming); Ez 1:24, 43:2 (referring to the "God of Israel"); cf. Ps 93:4.

5. A paraphrase (cited in English) of lines from Percy Bysshe Shelley's 1820 poem "The Cloud": "From my wings are shaken the dews that waken / The sweet buds every one, / When rocked to rest on their mother's breast, / As she dances about the Sun."

6. From Antistrophe 3 of Ivanov's "Rebirth" ("Vozrozhdenie"), first published in *Pilot Stars;* also quoted in *Hellenic Religion,* p. 228.

7. Ivanov probably borrows this Latin phrase meaning "the tragedy begins" from Nietzsche's *Gay Science,* sec. 342, 382; cf. "The Symbolics of Aesthetic Principles" in this volume, p. 7.

8. Cf. Pushkin's "The Prophet" (1826); the imagery of "The Prophet" is drawn largely from Is 6:5–10.

9. In his 1897 article "Belles-lettres or the Truth?" ("Slovesnost' ili istina"), his first statement about Nietzsche, Vladimir Solovyov called him "not a superman, but a super-philologist."

10. Gottfried Hermann (1772–1848)—classical philologist and literary historian.

11. Karl Otfried Müller (1797–1840)—historian of Greek religion, including the cult of Dionysus, who stressed the need to understand it on its own terms; see Patricia Mueller-Vollmer, "Dionysus Reborn: Vjaceslav Ivanov's Theory of Symbolism (Russia)" (Ph.D. diss., Stanford University, 1985), pp. 97–99.

12. Philipp August Boeckh (1785–1867)—classical philologist at Berlin University. In a methodological afterword to *Dionysus and Predionysianism,* Ivanov adheres to Boeckh's distinction between "lower philology" (textual criticism) and "higher philology" or hermeneutics (interpretation in the context of spiritual culture), which utilizes the faculty of divination; see Mueller-Vollmer, "Dionysus Reborn," pp. 84–85, 91–97.

13. Friedrich Gottlieb Welcker (1784–1868)—German philologist and archaeologist who adopted an attitude of empathy toward his object of study. He also specialized in the religion of Dionysus; see Mueller-Vollmer, "Dionysus Reborn," pp. 99–101.

14. Friedrich Ritschl (1806–76)—classical philologist and Nietzsche's teacher.

15. Subjects of early articles by Nietzsche, who was a classical philologist by training ("De Laertii fontibus," 1868–69, and "Der Florentische Tractat über Homer und Hesiod, ihr Geschlecht und ihren Wettkampf," 1870–73).

16. *Phaedo* 60E–61B. Nietzsche believed that the irrational element of music would inevitably emerge when Socratic reason and science reached their limits; see *The Birth of Tragedy,* sec. 14, 15.

17. The words of Zosima from Dostoevsky's *Brothers Karamazov* (pt. 2, bk. 6, chap. 3, sec. g: "On prayer, love, and the touching of other worlds").

18. Schopenhauer made wide use of terminology culled from Hindu sources, such as the term "Maya," which means quite literally the "haze of appearances." Schopenhauer also bequeathed to Nietzsche the scholastic term "individuation," which Nietzsche used as the principle that gives rise to illusory, "objectivized" existence, which Dionysus in turn dissolves back into the unified basis of being. However, at times, Nietzsche also identified individuation with Dionysus, who as the substratum of the world experiences creation as dismemberment and suffering (e.g., *The Birth of Tragedy*, sec. 9, 10). Ivanov likewise used the term inconsistently to denote both cosmic division and the sacrificial surrender of selfhood to the elements. Cf. "The Symbolics of Aesthetic Principles" in this volume, p. 6.

19. Ivanov perhaps has in mind Nietzsche's exhortation to discover the two principles—Dionysian and Apollonian—within oneself (e.g., *The Birth of Tragedy*, sec. 9).

20. Literally, "nonbeing"; the 1904 version lacks the Greek equivalent. On Ivanov's understanding of the term, see "The Testaments of Symbolism, p. 40 and note 32 in this volume.

21. "Spectrally" replaces "eternally" in the 1904 version. The following passage, beginning at "The eternal sacrifice" and extending through two full paragraphs down to and including the first sentence of the third (beginning with "The Dionysian principle . . ."), was added to the 1909 version. The sentence following the inserted passage, originally the second in the section entitled "How and What," also read slightly differently: "Therefore the Dionysian principle cannot be interpreted as any particular 'what.' In Dionysus *a* and *not-a*, sacrificial victim and high-priest, are united as an identity" (pp. 21–22).

22. According to Orphic cosmogonies, Dionysus Zagreus was the son of Zeus and Persephone; he was eaten by the Titans, who were then turned to cinders by Zeus; humanity sprang from their remnants. On the one hand, this myth explains the divine substratum of humanity; on the other, it leads to the thought that the unification of humanity would be the reformation of the god.

23. In the Orphic myth, Dionysus's heart was saved by Athena; after Zeus swallowed it, he joined with the mortal woman Semele, and from their union Dionysus Zagreus was born anew.

24. It is a commonplace that the classical Greeks had little appreciation of the virtue of hope; Ivanov hints that Dionysus's birth from a human mother (Semele, who was disintegrated in the process) indicates humanity's potential divinity and could have instilled the virtue of hope, as it did in Christianity. In Ivanov's German translation of this essay, this sentence

reads: "The Greeks knew no eschatological hope." This emphasizes that the Greeks lacked the redemption common to the Jewish and Christian traditions. Cf. "Ancient Terror" in this volume, pp. 160–62.

25. Cf. *The Birth of Tragedy*, sec. 21. The image was important to Ivanov, who even named one of his poetry collections *The Flaming Heart* (*Cor Ardens*). It first occurs in the *Iliad* XXII.460–61, with additional reference to chap. 3 of Dante's *Vita Nuova*; see Pamela Davidson, *Poetic Imagination of Vyacheslav Ivanov* (Cambridge and New York: Cambridge University Press, 1985), pp. 195–200.

26. "Unexpected joy" is the name of a venerated icon of the Mother of God.

27. Cf. Lk 1:40.

28. The first half of an untitled poem by Fedor Sologub (1902) from a cycle "Hymns of the Suffering Dionysus," printed immediately after the first installment of Ivanov's study "The Hellenic Religion of the Suffering God" in the first issue of *The New Path* for 1904; quoted by Ivanov with a minor inaccuracy.

29. Cf. *Faust* II.4715–27 (see also p. 187 in this volume).

30. From the last line of Giacomo Leopardi's poem "L'infinito" ("Endlessness," c. 1820), which Ivanov translated in 1887 (published in 1904 in *Transparency*): "And shipwreck is sweet for me in this sea." In the 1904 version of the essay, Ivanov omitted Leopardi's name (p. 23).

31. The following three paragraphs were inserted in the 1909 version of the essay.

32. Cf. Tiutchev's "Just as the ocean surrounds the earthly sphere" ("Kak okean ob'emlet shar zemnoi," 1830).

33. Cf. Nietzsche's view of Faust: "We have but to place [Faust] beside Socrates for the purpose of comparison, in order to see that modern man is beginning to divine the limits of this Socratic love of knowledge and yearns for a coast in the wide waste of the ocean of knowledge" (*The Birth of Tragedy*, trans. Walter Kaufmann [New York: Vintage Books, 1967], p. 111 [sec. 18]). Ivanov implies that it would be more Dionysian, and perhaps more Faustian, to experience tragic destruction in this ocean than to seek safe landing.

34. The sufferings (passion) of Dionysus.

35. "Love of fate"; cf. note 4 to "Presentiments and Portents" in this volume.

36. On the "good news" see note 24 to "The Symbolics of Aesthetic Principles" in this volume.

37. "Undivided and unconfused" is the formula given in the Athanasian Creed to describe the relationship between the two natures of Christ within His single hypostasis; see note 9 to "Thoughts on Symbolism" in this volume.

38. Nietzsche signed his final letters, written around the time of his final breakdown in January 1889, either "The Crucified One" or "Dionysus." The closest he came to identifying the two (as separate "incarnations" of himself) is in his 3 January 1889 letter to Cosima Wagner.

39. The lark usually sings in the morning, which explains why Tiutchev's lyrical hero is terrified by its evening song ("Dark and inclement evening, / Hark, is that the voice of a lark?" ["Vecher mglistyi i nenastnyi," 1836]).

40. In 1904, this phrase read: "Imbued by the Dionysian 'how'" (p. 23).

41. "Metanoia," traditionally translated "repent," literally means "change your mind"; Mt 3:2; cf. 6:10.

42. In 1904, this phrase read: "seen from its religious aspect" (p. 23). In some early poems and in *Hellenic Religion* (p. 227), Ivanov examined the epistemological role of "aspect"; see Davidson, *Poetic Imagination of Viacheslav Ivanov,* pp. 167–73.

43. For example, see Nietzsche's *The Antichrist,* sec. 43.

44. One of the names of Dionysus (in Greek, *Luaios*).

45. In *The Birth of Tragedy,* Nietzsche called Socrates the first "theoretical man" (sec. 15, 18).

46. Although Nietzsche criticized Socrates' absolute faith in knowledge, he soon began numbering himself among "those who know" or "the knowledgeable ones" ("die Erkennenden"); *The Gay Science,* sec. 344; *Towards a Genealogy of Morals,* preface, sec. 1, pt. 3, sec. 24.

47. Jonah was sent to Ninevah to prophesy, but he rebelled against God and was punished until he repented. He then rebelled against God for showing mercy to the Ninevans (Jon 1–3). In the New Testament, Jonah's punishment (three days spent in the belly of a whale) is taken as an archetype of Christ's resurrection (Mt 12:39–40).

48. The later Nietzsche was heavily influenced by eighteenth-century French thinkers, especially Rousseau and his concept of *ressentiment* (e.g., in the *Twilight of the Idols*).

49. From Pushkin's "At life's beginning I remember school" ("V nachale zhizni shkolu pomniu ia," 1830).

50. Cf. pt. 5 of "Zarathustra's Prologue," in pt. 1 of *Thus Spake Zarathustra.*

51. Nietzsche's final ideal of the "will to power" was first stated in *The Gay Science,* sec. 349, where it is defined as the "will to life," and then in "On Self-Overcoming," sec. 12 in pt. 2 of *Thus Spake Zarathustra.*

52. Dionysus was the god of moisture and fertility; Zarathustra often expresses the need to retire into the desert, which symbolizes the negation of this world (cf. "On the Three Metamorphoses," sec. 1 in pt. 1; "On the Famous Wise Men," sec. 8 in pt. 2 of *Thus Spake Zarathustra*).

53. Lk 12:27. "Nysa" was the mountain where Dionysus (son of Semele) was raised by nymphs. In *Hellenic Religion,* Ivanov calls Nysa "the ideal meadow or paradise of Dionysus" (p. 87; cf. p. 141).

54. Cf. Jn 15:1–6.

55. Mt 18:3: "Assuredly, I say to you, unless you are converted and become as little children, you will by no means enter the kingdom of heaven. . . . Take heed that you do not despise one of these little ones, for I say to you that in heaven their angels always see the face of My Father who is in heaven."

56. Cf. *Beyond Good and Evil,* sec. 195, *Towards a Genealogy of Morals,* pt.1, sec. 7, 10.

57. "The Dionysian fiend."

58. "The old God is dead." This idea occurs repeatedly in Nietzsche's works following its first occurrence in *The Gay Science* (sec. 109, 125). The occurrence closest to the form given by Ivanov is in "Retired," sec. 6 in pt. 4 of *Thus Spake Zarathustra.*

59. Max Stirner (1806–56) developed an atheistic philosophy founded on a theory of egoism; cf. Stirner's *Der Einzige und sein Eigenthum* (1845), translated as *The Ego and Its Own,* ed. David Leopold (Cambridge and New York: Cambridge University Press, 1995).

60. In the *Veda,* "Atman" can mean "I," "body," or an individual soul that is correlated to the world soul, and which appears as the substratum of being. Reality as "Atman" is, in a sense, the subjective aspect of objective Brahma, the creator and base of all.

61. See *Faust* I.490. Nietzsche claims Goethe for his own view; see the "Epilogue" to *The Case of Wagner.*

62. "Das Göttliche kommt auf leichten Füssen"; from Nietzsche's *Case of Wagner,* sec. 1; cf. "The Symbolics of Aesthetic Principles" in this volume, p. 9.

63. See especially "On Self-Overcoming," sec. 12 in pt. 2 of *Thus Spake Zarathustra.*

64. See especially bk. 3 of *Towards a Genealogy of Morals.*

65. *The Gay Science,* sec. 341.

66. Ibid.

67. *Faust* II.4704–14.

68. Cf. *The Birth of Tragedy,* sec. 5, 24.

69. This may be a defense of Wagner against Nietzsche's charge that the composer is a mere actor (*The Case of Wagner,* sec. 8, 9; cf. *Hellenic Religion,* p. 47).

70. In Ivanov's German translation, this last phrase reads: "by the vengeful Cassandra."

71. Lycurgus was the son of the king of the Edones in Thrace. Two separate myths portray him as a committed opponent of Dionysus (*Iliad*

VI.130–40; *Bibliotheca* [formerly attributed to Apollodorus of Athens], III.5.1). According to the *Bibliotheca,* Dionysus made Lycurgus mad so that the latter killed and mutilated his own son by mistake; when he came to his senses, Lycurgus found that his crime had made the earth infertile, and he was sacrificed as an appeasement to Dionysus.

72. Gn 32:24–30; cf. 27:22–29.

THE RELIGIOUS TASK OF VLADIMIR SOLOVYOV

"The Religious Task of Vladimir Solovyov," in its first publication (under the title "On the Significance of Vladimir Solovyov in the Fates of Our Religious Consciousness"), was dated 14 December 1910, the same day that Ivanov read a lecture at a meeting at the Literary Foundation of St. Petersburg in memory of the tenth anniversary of the death of Vladimir Solovyov (1853–1900), the great Russian philosopher and poet whom Ivanov considered his mentor. On 11 February 1911, Ivanov repeated his lecture at the Vladimir Solovyov Religious-Philosophical Society in Moscow, and it was included in a collection of essays on Solovyov, mainly by prominent members of that society (*Sbornik pervyi: O Vladimire Solov'eve* [Moscow: Put', 1911], pp. 32–44). It was reprinted with some significant changes in *Furrows and Boundaries* (pp. 95–115) and then in the *Collected Works* (3:296–306).

Ivanov's main aim in this essay is to present himself as a faithful follower of Solovyov. Though conscious of his mentor's inconsistencies and shortcomings, he is keen to continue his master's task. His appreciation of Solovyov's writings centers on the philosopher's "historiosophy," ecclesiology, and ontology, and therefore he mentions Solovyov's ideas of theocracy, the universal church, all-unity, and divine-humanity. Solovyov's poetry also serves as proof that his thought was based on mystical apprehension of the world. On the other hand, Ivanov shows that he himself has contributed significantly to the development of Solovyov's epistemological and aesthetic works. The essay contains Ivanov's most succinct and striking formulation of the "thou art" principle, based on the need to mediate knowledge through other people with whom one is joined in the love of God and in mutual love, the only earthly source of truth and being. At the same time, Ivanov seems to hint at the roots of this epistemology in the work of the Russian Slavophiles, with their key concept of *sobornost'*.

As is the case with Nietzsche in the essay on "Nietzsche and Dionysus," Ivanov is eager to defend Solovyov's basic inspiration against some of the ethical prescriptions he himself drew. Ivanov appears to compare Solovyov to the latter's own portrait of Plato in the 1898 article "The Drama of Plato's Life," where Solovyov reconstructs several periods in the Greek philosopher's creative life: an idealistic turn away from the practical reason of Socrates (*Gorgias, Phaedo, The Republic,* bk. 2, and so on); a reconciliation of the two realities through Eros (*Symposium, Phaedrus*), and later, in the *Timaeus*, through the world soul; and then a renunciation of lofty ideals in favor of their actual, but imperfect, realization (*The Laws*): "Plato's Eros, whose nature and general calling had been so wonderfully described by the poet-philosopher, did not accomplish its calling, did not connect the heavens with the earth and the underworld, did not build between them any real bridge, and it flew indifferently away empty-handed into the world of ideal contemplations. But the philosopher remained on the earth—also with empty hands—on the empty earth, where truth does not live" (Solovyov, *Sochineniia v dvukh tomakh* [Moscow: Mysl', 1988], 2:620).

Ivanov's final view of Solovyov is milder and more reverent. Solovyov's study of Eros brought him to appreciate "that place of the . . . contiguity of the two worlds, which is called *beauty*" (*Sochineniia*, 2:613). Aesthetics, Sophiology, ecclesiology, and the unfinished epistemology are all grounded in this realm of contiguity; Ivanov remains cautious of those instances when Solovyov seems to tip the scales in favor of "transcendentalism" or "immanentism," which result either in a nonsacramental church or the disengagement of ethics and politics from the demands of the absolute.

1. Sergei Trubetskoi (1862–1905) was a Russian philosopher, Solovyov's friend, and brother of Evgenii Trubetskoi, who wrote the first major study of Solovyov's thought. Solovyov died 30 July 1900 at the Trubetskoi estate Uzkoe.

2. Mt 7:7.

3. "The new religious consciousness" was the common goal of Russian religious thinkers contemporary to Ivanov, such as Nikolai Berdiaev and Dmitry Merezhkovsky. Below, Ivanov attributes the term to Solovyov himself.

4. *The Brothers Karamazov* ("On Prayer, Love and Touching Other Worlds," pt. 2, bk. 6, chap. 3, sec. g,); cf. "Nietzsche and Dionysus" in this volume, p. 180. Ivanov proceeds to characterize other themes from the same novel and from Dostoevsky's other late novels, namely: *Crime and Punishment, The Idiot,* and *The Demons.*

5. The Gorgon's head turned to stone all that met its gaze. Cf. "Lev Tolstoy and Culture" in this volume, p. 201.

6. "A sublime deceit is dearer to us than a mass of low truths" is a line from Pushkin's "The Hero" ("Geroi," 1830).

7. The mention of Sophia was added in the 1916 text.

8. Solovyov wrote that Plato rejected All-National Aphrodite, who represents carnal love, in favor of "true, or heavenly Aphrodite Urania" (Solovyov, *Sochineniia*, 2:609).

9. In the 1911 edition, this paragraph read:

Dostoevsky, in contrast to Tolstoy, is profoundly ecclesiastic in spirit; and here, once again, I do not mean Dostoevsky's Orthodox nationalism, but his contemplation of the Church as a mystical entity. He studied the crisis of the isolated personality with a profundity that will last the ages, imprinting it in his creations (Raskolnikov, Kirillov, Ivan Karamazov); he saw the only salvation of the personality and of humanity in living, mystical *sobornost'* (Raskolnikov's repentance, Zosima and Alesha).

But once and for all society agreed not to accept this writer in full. The abundance of genius grants the privilege of satisfying various people with various gifts, particularly to the artist; in Goethe's saying, anyone can find something for himself in one who brings much. (p. 35)

10. Ivanov refers particularly to *The Brothers Karamazov*, where the idea of theocracy is thematized in the characters of Ivan Karamazov and the boys who gather around Alesha.

11. *Faust* I.97–98 ("Prologue in the Theater").

12. Ivanov here repeats Solovyov's own evaluation of Plato's *Laws*, expressed in Solovyov's work "The Drama of Plato's Life." Ivanov's contemporaries largely concurred with Ivanov in seeing *The Justification of the Good* (1897, 1899) as a kind of fall into scholasticism.

13. Cf. the title of Nietzsche's essay "Schopenhauer as Educator" (1874), pt. 3 of *Untimely Meditations.*

14. Solovyov's complete title is *The History and Future of Theocracy* (1885–87).

15. Ivanov's quotation is from the first sentence of the foreword to Solovyov's *The History and Future of Theocracy* (*Sobranie sochinenii* [St. Petersburg: Obshchestvennaia pol'za, 1903–7], 4:214).

16. A reference to Solovyov's doctoral dissertation "Critique of Abstract Principles" (1880; *Sobranie sochinenii*, vol. 2).

17. From Solovyov's poem "Ex Oriente Lux" (1890).

18. "Thou shall not have false gods," i.e., it is wrong to absolutize the nonabsolute, conditional.

19. The best-known instance of Solovyov's social activity is his speech in 1881 in which he called for Christian charity to be extended to the assassins of Alexander II (for which he lost his teaching post at St. Petersburg University). Although Solovyov was the spiritual heir of the early Slavophiles, he consistently opposed nationalistic politicians and commentators.

20. "To each his own."

21. Cf. Col 1:15; Jn 14:2.

22. The idea that all of humanity and the cosmos will be redeemed at the end of time is called Apocatastasis and finds many exponents in Eastern Christian thought, although it is not a doctrine of the Church.

23. Source unidentified.

24. Reading *kafolichestvo* (*Furrows and Boundaries,* p. 106) over *katolichestvo* ("Catholicism," *Collected Works,* 3:301). The artificial distinction introduced into the pronunciation and spelling of the two words in Russian distinguishes Roman Catholicism (*katolichestvo*) from the idea of univer-

sality or "catholicity" (*kafolichestvo*), a quality that the Eastern Orthodox Church claims for itself.

25. Mt 3:15. The Russian word for "righteousness" (*pravda*) could also mean "truth."

26. Apart from *The History and Future of Theocracy,* Ivanov mentions Solovyov's famous propapal book *Russia and the Universal Church,* written in French in 1887 and published in Russian translation only in 1911; published in an English translation by Herbert Rees (London: Geoffrey Bles, the Centenary Press, 1948). Especially in the late 1880s, Solovyov sought contact with Catholics interested in the Orthodox East, and in 1894, he appears to have made a formal acknowledgment of papal authority, the significance of which is widely disputed.

27. "The Short Tale of the Antichrist" is part of Solovyov's polemical *Three Conversations* (1899–1900). At the end of the "Tale," representatives of the Orthodox, Catholic, and Protestant traditions unite to defeat the Antichrist.

28. Rv 12:1: "And there appeared a great wonder in heaven; a woman clothed in the sun, and the moon under her feet, and upon her head a crown of twelve stars." Solovyov interpreted this image as a symbol of Sophia–Divine Wisdom.

29. Solovyov, *Russia and the Universal Church,* pp. 179–86, 195–202. On Solovyov's use of the word "theurgy" (which corresponds to "prophecy" in *Russia and the Universal Church*), see note 51 below.

30. "Just as the Church is collectively organized piety, so the state is collectively organized pity"; V. S. Solovyov, *Justification of the Good,* trans. Nathalie A. Duddington (London: Constable, 1918), p. 448. Cf. Solovyov on Plato: "Plato is not satisfied with his role as theoretician of the social ideal. He wants most definitely to begin the practical fulfillment of his plan" (Solovyov, *Sochineniia,* 2:622).

31. Schopenhauer's metaphysics was based on the conflict between will and the "principle of individuation" (*principium individuationis*). This conflict entails suffering for humanity, and people can oppose the principle of individuation only by sympathizing with the common suffering of all humanity. See *The World as Will and Representation,* bk. 4, sec. 67. Solovyov was heavily influenced by Schopenhauer's metaphysics; see Solovyov's *The Crisis of Western Philosophy (Against the Positivists),* trans. and ed. Boris Jakim (Hudson, N.Y.: Lindisfarne Press, 1996).

32. 1 Jn 5:19: "We know that we are of God, and the whole world lieth in wickedness." See Solovyov's *Spiritual Foundations of Life* (*Sobranie sochinenii,* 3:270–382). In "The Drama of Plato's Life," Solovyov uses this phrase to characterize Plato's perception of the lower world after the death of Socrates; this negative view of practical life turned Plato's gaze to that which really is, the world of ideas (Solovyov, *Sochineniia,* 2:606).

33. Ivanov means the three articles published in 1897–99 under the common title "Theoretical Philosophy" (*Sochineniia,* 1:757–831).

34. Compare the usage of *speculum speculorum* in "The Testaments of Symbolism" in this volume, p. 47.

35. Cf. Mt 18:20.

36. A reference to Husserl's 1910 article "Philosophy as a Rigorous Science," which was published in Russian in 1911 in the journal *Logos.*

37. Possibly a reference to the thought of Nikolai Minsky (real name Vilenkin, 1855–1937), an early Symbolist or Decadent poet who developed a philosophical doctrine of Meonism (from the Greek *"mè ón"*—nothing), which postulated all things as merely potential being.

38. From the tract "On Non-Being" of Gorgias (c. 485–375 B.C.).

39. Cf. Solovyov's essay "The Idea of the Superhuman," where he radically reinterprets Nietzsche's idea of the superman, viewing it as an aspect of the Christian ideal of the divinization of humanity. See also the end of "The Drama of Plato's Life": "The weakness and fall of 'divine' Plato are important because they sharply underscore and clarify the impossibility for man to fulfil his calling, i.e. to become an actual *superhuman,* by the sheer force of his mind, genius and moral will—they clarify the need for a real, essential *divine-human*" (Solovyov, *Sochineniia,* 2:625); cf. note 47 to "On the Crisis of Humanism" in this volume.

40. Solovyov's irreconcilability with death owed much to the "philosophy of the common task" of Nikolai Fedorov, on whom see note 46 to "On the Crisis of Humanism" in this volume.

41. From Solovyov's poem "Three Labors" ("Tri podviga," 1882).

42. According to Eusebius's *Vita Constantini,* these words accompanied a vision of the cross in the sky preceding Constantine the Great's victory over his rival Maxentius at the Milvian bridge in 312.

43. See Vladimir Solovyov, *The Meaning of Love,* trans. Jane Marshall, ed. and rev. Thomas Beyer Jr. (Hudson, N.Y.: Lindisfarne Press, 1985).

44. From Solovyov's poem "We Met for a Reason" ("My soshlis' s toboi nedarom," 1892); quoted in "The Drama of Plato's Life" (Solovyov, *Sochineniia,* 2:610).

45. Cf. Solovyov: "The triumph of love is in the full resurrection of life. . . . The real task of love is actually to immortalize the object of love, actually to free it from death and corruption, and to grant it final rebirth in beauty" ("The Drama of Plato's Life," in *Sochineniia,* 2:615–16).

46. On Ivanov's use of the myth of Isis, see note 64 to "Two Elements in Contemporary Symbolism" in this volume.

47. From Solovyov's poem "The time of spring storms has not yet passed" ("Pora vesennikh groz eshche ne minovala," 1885).

48. Themes from Solovyov's lyrical poems.

49. Cf. Lk 1:41ff.

50. The Eternal Feminine leads us up; the final lines of Goethe's *Faust* II.

51. Solovyov first discussed the theurgical nature of art in *The Philosophical Principles of Integral Knowledge* (1877; Solovyov, *Sochineniia*, 2:156, 174, 199). He further developed the concept of theurgy in his "Three Speeches in Memory of Dostoevsky" (1881–83; cf. "Two Elements in Contemporary Symbolism" in this volume, p. 14) and aesthetic essays such as "Beauty in Nature" (1889) and "The General Meaning of Art" (1890; cf. "Scriabin's View of Art" in this volume, p. 221).

LEV TOLSTOY AND CULTURE

"Lev Tolstoy and Culture" originated in a lecture given in memory of Tolstoy at the St. Petersburg Religious-Philosophical Society on 16 November 1910. First published in the Russian philosophical journal *Logos* (bk. 1 [1911]: 167–78), it soon appeared in a German translation by Fedor Stepun in the German edition of the same journal, *Logos. Zeitschrift für Philosophie der Kultur* (vol. 2, bk. 2); an abridged German translation was later published in *Neue Zürcher Zeitung* (no. 1621 [9 Sept. 1928]: 3). A slightly changed version was included in *Furrows and Boundaries* (pp. 75–93) and in *Collected Works* (4:591–602).

Ivanov follows a conventional distinction between Tolstoy the writer and Tolstoy the thinker. Although Ivanov had great respect for Tolstoy's artistic writings, his image of Tolstoy is largely dependent upon the latter's moral, religious, and pedagogical works, which, with several notable exceptions, were all that Tolstoy published between 1880 and his death in 1910. Like most Symbolists and religious philosophers of the 1910s, Ivanov took great exception to Tolstoy's moral teachings, but the strength of his personality and the force with which he exposed negative elements in Russian religious life made Tolstoy an unavoidable fact of Russian culture. Thus, as with Nietzsche and Solovyov, Ivanov sets out to defend Tolstoy from himself and correct his intellectual path, showing that although Tolstoy overcame relativism through his ascetic and iconoclastic cultural ideal, he failed to make the next step up to "healthy and correct" Symbolism. If Tolstoy is like Socrates, then Symbolism is like Plato in that it seeks to transform culture and nature into "a created icon of the Sophianic world." Ivanov's formulation of theurgical Symbolism in the final section of the essay is notable for its directness; one clearly sees the parallels with Eastern Orthodox aesthetics (particularly in the use of the word "icon") but also the esoteric leanings of Ivanov's theurgy (e.g., the notion of freeing the captive world soul, which has parallels in Gnosticism).

Ivanov's account of Tolstoy's significance was also intended as a statement in the philosophical polemic between the journal *Logos* and the philosophers grouped around the publishing house Put', which had recently published Ivanov's essay on Solovyov. *Logos* was home to Russian neo-Kantians such as Sergei Gessen and Fedor Stepun, who had studied under Heinrich Rickert and Wilhelm Windelband. As in "The Testaments of Symbolism," Ivanov focuses on the concept of value as an area of common ground between himself and the neo-Kantians, but he further demonstrates that it is impossible to speak of value without premising its source in transcendent reality.

1. On the night of 27–28 October 1910, the eighty-two-year-old Tolstoy left his estate Yasnaya polyana in disgust at his wife's interference in his affairs. After visiting his sister at Shamardino convent near the famous monastery Optina pustyn', he traveled on to evade pursuit. On 31 October, Tolstoy was taken ill at Astapovo station, where he died on 7 November (20 in new style) 1910. Tolstoy's final ordeal was followed closely by the entire country.

2. Goethe, *Faust* II.11936–37.

3. A request for applause which ended classical Latin plays.

4. A reference to Tiutchev's "Silentium"; see especially "The Testaments of Symbolism" in this volume, pp. 36–37.

5. Cf. Mt 19:17.

6. Aeschylus, *Prometheus Bound* 250.

7. Cf. Aristotle, *Poetics* 1449b, 1453b.

8. Tolstoy's philosophy of simplicity and nonviolence spawned an entire movement of Tolstoyans, who often lived in communes, practiced abstinence, and educated peasants.

9. Tolstoy espoused not only pacifism but also a Taoist-inspired doctrine of abstention from action; see his 1893 essay "Non-Acting" (as the term was rendered by Tolstoy's translator Aylmer Maude).

10. Source unknown.

11. Apart from Tolstoy's general creed of simplification, Ivanov might have in mind the aesthetic intimated in the character of Mikhailov in *Anna Karenina* (pt. 5, chap. 9–12).

12. Ivanov echoes the formulations of Dmitry Merezhkovsky, who in his ground-breaking study *Tolstoy and Dostoevsky* (1900–2) called the former "prophet of the flesh" and the latter "prophet of the spirit."

13. In "The Kreuzer Sonata" (1889), a man who killed his wife puts the blame for his crime on the carnal ideals inspired by Beethoven's sonata and modern life in general.

14. Source unknown.

15. Tolstoy's Christian name "Lev" is also the word for "lion"; cf. Latin "Leo."

16. Weariness of the phenomenon; cf. *taedium vitae* (weariness of life) from Horace, *Odes* I.xi.8, quoted by Ivanov in "Ancient Terror" in this volume, p. 160.

17. A possible reference to Lermontov's "I walk out onto the road alone" ("Vykhozu odin ia na dorogu," 1841).

18. The word "ergon" is restored to the text according to *Furrows and Boundaries,* p. 80.

19. Cf. Lk 10:39–42.

20. A line from Fedor Sologub's "Lifeless Chamber" ("Bezzhiznennyi chertog," 1902).

21. Dulcinea was the heavenly inspiration of Don Quixote's quests, Aldonza her debased worldly counterpart. The use of the two names to symbolize the distance between ideal and reality was a commonplace in Russian literature beginning with Turgenev. Of the Russian Symbolists, the opposition is frequently found in the work of Fedor Sologub.

22. Ivanov's use of the word "phenomenology" may relate to Husserl's philosophy, which was becoming known in Russia at the time. S. L. Frank's translation of Husserl's *Logical Investigations* was published in 1909, and a Russian translation of Husserl's "Philosophy as a Rigorous Science" appeared in the same issue of *Logos* as Ivanov's essay.

23. Cf., e.g., Gn 28:12; Ps 139:8; Is 14:13–14.

24. Cf. Vladimir Solovyov's 1890 poem "Ex Oriente Lux," quoted in note 11 to "On the Russian Idea" in this volume.

25. *Ivanov's note:* I am obliged to my friend, Professor E. V. Anichkov, for the idea of Tolstoy's Westernism. [Evgeny Anichkov (1866–1937) was a prominent folklorist who, despite his involvement in radical politics, was close to Ivanov and other Symbolists.]

26. "Den Vereinigten Staaten," no. 29 of Goethe's "Zahme Xenien."

27. Ivanov's evocation of Socrates is reminiscent of Nietzsche's later critique of the Greek thinker as a "Decadent"; see Nietzsche's "The Problem of Socrates" in *The Twilight of the Idols.*

28. On the distinction between organic and critical (or analytical) epochs, see pp. 97–99 in this volume.

29. A paraphrase of Socrates' argument in Plato's *Apology* 22–23, esp. 23B.

30. Cf. Tiutchev's "The blue-gray shadows are merged" ("Teni sizye smesilis'," 1836).

31. Cf. Gn 3:5; Is 14:13–14.

32. Plato, *Apology* 20E.

33. Tertullian (died c. A.D. 220), *De carne Christi* 5.

34. From the tract "On Non-Being" of the Sophist Gorgias; see also "The Religious Task of Vladimir Solovyov" in this volume, p. 196; "On the Crisis of Humanism" in this volume, p. 168.

35. Attributed to the Sophist Protagoras (DK 80 B 14).

36. From Vladimir Solovyov's 1882 poem "The Three Labors"; see note 46 to "On the Limits of Art" in this volume.

37. This sentence was added in *Furrows and Boundaries*. The "Sophianic world of eternal archetypes" indicates Ivanov's allegiance with the Russian Sophiologists, from Vladimir Solovyov to Sergei Bulgakov and Pavel Florensky, who identified the cosmos with the feminine aspect of the Godhead, Sophia–Divine Wisdom.

38. *Phaedo* 60E–61B; cf. "Nietzsche and Dionysus" in this volume, p. 179.

39. "A reminder to die" (Latin).

40. "A reminder to live" (Latin).

SCRIABIN'S VIEW OF ART

The most extended of Ivanov's three published essays on the composer, "Scriabin's View of Art" was originally read as a lecture at the Scriabin Society in Petrograd on 11 December 1915, then in Moscow on 13 February 1916, and later in Kiev in April of that year. It was apparently intended to form part of Ivanov's contribution to a collection of essays in memory of Scriabin. This plan was never realized, nor was a separate book meant to include Ivanov's three Scriabin essays that was prepared by the publishing house Alkonost between 1919 and 1921. The text became known from the publication of two sets of corrected page proofs: in Ivanov's *Collected Works* (3:172–89); and in I. A. Myl'nikova, "Stat'i Viach. Ivanova o Skriabine," in *Pamiatniki kul'tury. Novye otkrytiia. Pis'mennost'. Iskusstvo. Arkheologiia. Ezhegodnik 1983* (Leningrad: Nauka, 1985), pp. 103–13, which represents a later stage of composition than the text in *Collected Works*. A facsimile of the page proofs used by Myl'nikova has recently been published in V. I. Ivanov, *Skriabin* (Moscow: IRIS-Press, 1996). The facsimile edition, which has been taken as the basis for our translation, forces one to question Myl'nikova's editing (she ignored Ivanov's corrections in the first five sections of the essay and misread numerous handwritten additions). Some of the passages eliminated or reformulated by Ivanov in this final text have been noted; we have also utilized some of Myl'nikova's commentary.

As Ivanov indicates in his essay, he always viewed Scriabin as "*the artist,*" despite the brevity of their close personal association (1914–15). Scriabin not only belonged to the theomachic and self-sacrificing race of Promethean artists so dear to Ivanov, he also shared Ivanov's philosophical belief that the contemporary world could only return to its religious roots through artistic activity. Ivanov portrays Scriabin's death as the beginning of a funeral celebration capable of growing into a realization of the unrealized Mysterium.

It is somewhat surprising, therefore, that Ivanov's appreciation of Scriabin is set loosely in the terms of his 1913–14 essay "On the Limits of Art," which rejects the art of sheer ascent and theurgy in favor of a more humble ideal of symbolization and maturation. There, Ivanov strove to limit the realm of art to the process of descent from mystical heights attainable only by the integral human being. He chastised Symbolism (himself included) for confusing the ascending man with the descending artist, which resulted in an aestheticist and solipsistic philosophy.

The apparent contradiction between Ivanov's mature aesthetics of descent and his coterminous fascination with the Promethean Scriabin can only be resolved by distinguishing between the art of Symbolism and the imminent synthesis of the arts envisioned by the composer. As Ivanov writes in both "On the Limits of Art" and "Scriabin's View of Art," Symbolism had shown itself largely incapable of exceeding the limits of art. Scriabin, in contrast, had burst through these limits and achieved his creations on a higher plane where such distinctions were no longer held to be valid. Ivanov views Scriabin as a true post-Symbolist, the messiah proclaimed by the Symbolist forerunners. This placing of Scriabin above and beyond Symbolism itself must be seen as the greatest compliment Ivanov could bestow.

1. Cf. a passage on Shakespeare from Dostoevsky's notebooks: "All reality is not exhausted by the everyday, for in its greatest part it is enclosed within the everyday in the form of a subsurface, unexpressed, future Word. Very rarely there appear prophets who guess and utter this integral word. Shakespeare is a prophet sent by God to proclaim to us the mystery of man, of the human soul" (F. M. Dostoevsky, *Sobranie sochinenii* [Leningrad: Nauka, 1972–90], 11:237).

2. Ivanov crossed out the continuation of this sentence: "lending it a semimystical explanation" (*Skriabin*, p. 7).

3. Ivanov originally named the "thinker"—Schopenhauer (*Skriabin*, p. 8). The precise source of Ivanov's paraphrase has not been identified but for similar thoughts, see Schopenhauer's *World as Will and Representation*, bk. 3, sec. 36–37.

4. From Lermontov's "The Prophet" ("Prorok," 1841).

5. *Symposium* 203B; see also Nietzsche's *Gay Science*, sec. 370.

6. Scriabin began work on the "Preliminary Act" ("Acte préalable," 1913–15) in preparation for the "Mysterium," which he felt would not only be his final work but would bring on the end of time. Although many memoirists recall hearing Scriabin play excerpts from the "Preliminary Act," after Scriabin's death, little written music was discovered. The poetic text of the "Preliminary Act" was published posthumously (*Russkie propilei*, vol. 6, ed. M. Gershenzon [Moscow: Izdanie M. i S. Sabashnikorykh, 1919]); it was clearly influenced by the poetry of Ivanov and other Symbolists (Myl'nikova, "Stat'i Viach. Ivanova o Skriabine," p. 91; cf. Scriabin's use of Ivanov's image "the tender mystery": *Russkie propilei*, 6:209, 240–41).

7. The Parcae are the Fates (also known as the Moirai).

8. Ivanov crossed out: "which captivates with the charm and majesty of its verse and which amazes with the profundity and subtlety of its speculation" (*Skriabin,* pp. 10–11).

9. The Pythia was the priestess of Apollo at Delphi. Seated on the tripod over a crevice in the rock, the Pythia uttered oracles, usually in an obscure and incoherent fashion. The image of the Pythia being drowned out by a jealous god may refer to the legend that, when the fourth-century emperor Julian the Apostate attempted to revive the oracle at Delphi, the Pythia merely cried out and refused to prophesy.

10. A paraphrase of the last two lines of Pushkin's "Only the roses wilt" ("Lish' rozy uviadaiut," 1825).

11. The second half of Scriabin's oeuvre, after about 1904, includes such works as *Prometheus* (1910), the composer's first step toward including visual material in his musical score.

12. Pushkin, "The Beauty" ("Krasavitsa," 1832).

13. From Pushkin's "To the Poet" ("Poetu," 1830).

14. *Natura naturata* means "created nature," while *natura naturans* means "creating nature." The terms appear in St. Thomas Aquinas (*Summa Theologicae* IIa–IIae) and were used by Spinoza and Schelling. *Natura naturans. Natura naturata* is also the title of an 1895 poetry collection by the early Symbolist or Decadent poet Aleksandr Dobroliubov (1876–1945?). In a later essay, Ivanov introduced the analogous terms *forma formans* and *forma formata;* these terms may have originated in S. T. Coleridge's *Literaria Biographia,* chap. 23.

15. Myl'nikova has an extra sentence of uncertain provenance: "We encounter such a view in the Pythagoreans and in Heraclitus" ("Stat'i Viach. Ivanova o Skriabine," p. 105).

16. The chorus leader (*choregos, koriphaios*), leader of the Muses (Musagetes) and of the Fates (Moiragetes), are epithets of Apollo. By capitalizing "God" (*Bog*) (a change introduced into the final proofs, p. 15), Ivanov would seem to associate Apollo with the Christian God or at least to raise him above the other heathen "gods."

17. Source unknown.

18. In his *Religion within the Limits of Reason Alone* (1793), Kant defined the church as an ethical commonwealth, governed by laws of virtue, that prepares the way for the Kingdom of God. Ecclesiastical religion is thus not a "constitutive principle" that reveals the noumenal realm but a means used by reason, a "regulative principle" (*regulatives Prinzip*) with subjective applicability, as Kant termed such concepts (*Religion within the Limits of Reason Alone,* bk. 2, sec. 1, C; bk. 3, div. 1, VII).

19. On Amphion, see note 42 to "The Testaments of Symbolism" in this volume.

20. Terpander was a musician from Lesbos, active in Sparta (also known as Lacedaemon) in the seventh century B.C., who was said to have replaced the four-stringed lyre (cithara) with a seven-stringed one. In the eighth and early seventh centuries B.C., Sparta was pursuing the conquest of Messenia. Cf. Ivanov's poem "Terpander" ("Terpandr") from *Pilot Stars*.

21. The Homerides were a clan of bards, purportedly descended from Homer, who wrote mainly on heroic subjects. Hesiod belonged to the rival Boeotian school of epic poetry, which concentrated on more practical matters of daily life and morality. See Hesiod, *Theogony* 1–35. Cf. Pushkin's "The Hero" ("Geroi").

22. Plato, *Phaedrus* 244A–245C, 249DE, 265AB.

23. Cf. Aristotle, *Poetics* 1449b; on the image of medicine for the soul, see also Plato, *Protagoras* 311B–313A, 356C–357A.

24. Ivanov crossed out the Latin phrase *transparentia formae* (the transparency of forms; *Skriabin,* p. 19).

25. *Paradise* XXXIII.145; cf. "Thoughts on Symbolism" in this volume, pp. 52–53. The mystical rose is a dominant image throughout Dante's *Paradise.*

26. In his *Critique of Judgment* (1790; sec. 15–17, 42, 58), Kant defines judgments of aesthetic taste as those based on the purposefulness of form, i.e., the ideal or purposeless purposefulness (*Zweckmässigkeit ohne Zweck*) of nature.

27. Cf. *Faust* I.6253. In the context of Goethe's work, this image is not explicitly a parody of Kant.

28. In his *Critique of Judgment,* extending his definition of the beautiful as "purposeless purposefulness" (see note 26), Kant uses such terms as "the free play of the powers of imagination," "the free play of the cognitive powers," or "the changing free play of feelings" (e.g., sec. 9, 22; note to sec. 55). The concept of play, as a force that mediates between matter and form, the world and the personality, sense and reason, was developed in Schiller's *Letters on the Aesthetic Education of Man;* see especially the "Twenty-Seventh Letter."

29. Herbert Spencer (1820–1903)—positivist philosopher, social Darwinist, and founder of sociology.

30. Here, Ivanov takes issue with the metaphysics and aesthetics of Schopenhauer, who, like Schiller, worked within a largely Kantian conceptual framework albeit with very different results.

31. Virgil, *Aeneid* VI.

32. On Schiller's *Letters on the Aesthetic Education of Man,* see note 28. "Beautiful soul" (*schöne Seele*) is a concept that appears in Schiller's article "On Grace and Dignity" ("Über Anmut und Würde"), especially in the section "Dignity."

33. Friedrich Schelling (1775–1854)—German idealist philosopher. The Romantics of the Jena circle include Ludwig Tieck (1773–1853),

Friedrich von Schlegel (1772–1829), and August Wilhelm Schlegel (1767–1845), in addition to Novalis (Friedrich von Hardenburg, 1772–1801).

34. In the table of contents for an unrealized German edition of his essays (held in Ivanov's Rome archive), Ivanov changed the title of "Scriabin's View of Art" to "Scriabin's Magical Idealism." Cf. note 54 to "The Testaments of Symbolism" in this volume.

35. 1 Kgs 7. Nothing is said of Hiram's death in the Bible.

36. Ivanov crossed out: "which I view as his lofty initiation" (*Skriabin*, p. 23).

37. Rv 22:20.

38. The Harpies, mysterious beings in ancient myth, often appeared as winds or birds. In reply to Pavel Florensky's interpretation of Phil 2:6–8, where Florensky tried to prove that the Harpies represent a particular kind of mystical experience, Ivanov wrote: "You were unable to prove that the Harpies are gods of [mystical] ecstasy. They are gods that steal one from the earth, after which there is no return to earth; therefore they are gods of death in all ways, and not only for the uninitiated. . . . Later among the esoterics and in their sphere of influence, just as may have been the case long before in communes of the orgiastic cults, with respect to certain marked individuals this was interpreted as being enraptured in grace from the earth into holy mansions" (P. A. Florensky, *Sochineniia v chetyrekh tomakh* [Moscow: Mysl', 1994–99], 2:748).

39. "Its strength is whole if it turns to the earth"; see note 54 to "On the Russian Idea" in this volume.

40. Ivanov quotes his sonnet "In Memory of Alexander Scriabin" (1915).

41. From Solovyov's "The General Meaning of Art" (*Sochineniia*, 2:404).

42. From the first of Solovyov's "Three Speeches in Memory of Dostoevsky" (*Sochineniia*, 2:293); see "Two Elements in Contemporary Symbolism" in this volume, p. 14.

43. From Dostoevsky's novel *The Idiot* (pt. 3, chap. 5); cf. "On the Limits of Art" in this volume, p. 90.

44. On the polemics about Symbolism, see the introductory notes to "The Testaments of Symbolism," "Thoughts on Symbolism," and "Manner, Persona, Style" in this volume.

45. Ivanov crossed out: "lacking ontological roots" (*Skriabin*, p. 27; cf. 3:183).

46. Originally the foregoing passage read: "That his theoretical postulates about *sobornost'* and the choral rite were full of the pathos of mystical realism and differed in essence from my hopes only in that for him they were also immediate practical tasks. We could, or rather needed to argue only about the highest forms of religious consciousness or confession.

We turned out to share the mystical basis of our worldviews, as well as many details of intuitive comprehension, and especially our view of the meaning of art" (*Skriabin*, p. 27; cf. III 183).

47. This poem by Ivanov ("Razvertyvalas' druzhby nashei zaviaz'") was first published within this essay.

48. Ivanov's "The Rose of the Sword" ("Roza mecha," pub. 1911) from *Cor Ardens*.

49. From Pushkin's "The Prophet" ("Prorok," 1826).

50. *The Divine Poem* is the title of Scriabin's Third Symphony (op. 43, 1902–4).

51. A quotation from Pushkin's "There lived a poor knight" ("Zhil na svete rytsar' bednyi," 1829).

52. Cf. Nietzsche, *The Birth of Tragedy*, sec. 5, 24.

53. Ivanov crossed out: "progression toward a spiritual assimilation of the profundities of Christianity" (*Skriabin*, p. 34).

54. "The One" replaces Ivanov's earlier variant "of the Divinity" (p. 34; 3:187); cf. "The Symbolics of Aesthetic Principles" in this volume, pp. 7–10.

55. From Scriabin's "Preliminary Act" (*Russkie propilei*, 6:202).

56. "In spirit" replaces Ivanov's earlier variant "before the face of the future Mysterium" (*Skriabin*, p. 36).

57. The "shaft of light" was a central image in Scriabin's texts for the "Preliminary Act."

58. Dostoevsky coined the word "allman" in his "Pushkin Speech"; cf. note 49 to "On the Crisis of Humanism" in this volume.

59. Ivanov's first sonnet on Scriabin's death ("Osirotela muzyka. I s nei," 1915); on this poem, see Michael Wachtel, "The 'Responsive Poetics' of Vjačeslav Ivanov," *Russian Literature* 44, no. 3 (1998): 305–15.

60. See "On the Crisis of Humanism" in this volume, pp. 163–64.

61. From sec. 2 of "Zarathustra's Prologue," pt. 1 of *Thus Spake Zarathustra*.

62. The last tercet of Ivanov's "Prooemion" in *Tender Mystery* (1912); on Scriabin's use of the image "tender mystery," see note 6.

Bibliography of Works
in English by Viacheslav Ivanov

"Annensky as Dramatist." In *The Russian Symbolist Theatre: An Anthology of Plays and Critical Texts*, translated and edited by Michael Green, 121–25. Ann Arbor, Mich.: Ardis, 1986.

"Čiurlionis and the Problem of Synthesis of the Arts." Translated by Tatiana Fedorow. *Lituanus* 7, no. 2 (June 1961): 45–57.

"Concerning the Ideology of the Jewish Question." In *The Shield*, edited by Maxim Gorky, Leonid Andreyev, and Fyodor Sologub, with a foreword by William English Walling, translated from the Russian by A. Yarmolinksy, 125–30. New York: Alfred A. Knopf, 1917.

[With M. O. Gershenzon.] "A Corner-to-Corner Correspondence." Translated by Gertrude Vakar. *Russian Intellectual History: An Anthology*, edited by Marc Raeff, 373–401. New York: Harcourt, Brace and World, 1966.

[With M. O. Gershenzon.] *Correspondence across a Room.* Translated by Lisa Sergio. Marlboro, Vt.: Marlboro Press, 1984.

[With M. O. Gershenzon.] "Correspondence between Two Corners." Translated by Norbert Guterman. *Partisan Review* 15, no. 9 (September 1948): 951–65, 1028–48.

"Correspondence between Two Corners of a Room." *Mesa*, no. 3 (winter 1947): 4–22.

"The Crisis of Individualism." In *A Revolution of the Spirit: Crisis of Value in Russia, 1890–1924*, translated by Marian Schwartz and edited by Bernice Glatzer Rosenthal and Martha Bohachevsky-Chomiak, 163–73. New York: Fordham University Press, 1990.

"[Dostoevsky and the Dionysiac.]" In *Utopias: Russian Modernist Texts, 1905–1940*, edited by Catriona Kelly, pp. 225–26. London: Penguin Books, 1999.

Freedom and the Tragic Life: A Study in Dostoevsky. Translated from the German by Norman Cameron. With a foreword by Sir Maurice Bowra. London: Harvill Press; New York: Noonday Press, 1952. Reprint, with an introduction by Robert Louis Jackson, Wolfeburo, N.H.: Longwood Academic, 1989.

319

"From 'On the Dignity of Women.'" In *Utopias: Russian Modernist Texts, 1905–1940,* edited by Catriona Kelly, pp. 156–57. London.: Penguin Books, 1999.

"Gogol's *Inspector General* and the Comedy of Aristophanes." In *Gogol from the Twentieth Century: Eleven Essays,* translated and edited by Robert A. Maguire, 199–214. Princeton, N.J.: Princeton University Press, 1974.

"The Inspiration of Horror." In *The Noise of Change: Russian Literature and the Critics (1891–1917),* translated and edited by Stanley Rabinowitz, 207–14. Ann Arbor, Mich.: Ardis, 1986.

"Jurgus Baltrušaitis as a Lyric Poet." Translated by Thomas E. Bird. *Lituanus* 25, no. 1 (spring 1979): 17–31.

"The Need for a Dionysian Theatre." In *The Russian Symbolist Theatre: An Anthology of Plays and Critical Texts,* translated and edited by Michael Green, 113–20. Ann Arbor, Mich.: Ardis, 1986.

"Our Language." In *Out of the Depths (De Profundis): A Collection of Articles on the Russian Revolution,* translated and edited by William F. Woehrlin, 119–24. Irvine, Calif.: Charles Schlacks Jr., Publisher, 1986.

"The Precepts of Symbolism." In *The Russian Symbolists: An Anthology of Critical and Theoretical Works,* translated and edited by Ronald E. Peterson, 143–56. Ann Arbor, Mich.: Ardis, 1986.

"Realism." Translated from the Italian by Thomas E. Bird. *Russian Literature Triquarterly* 4 (1972): 159–62.

"Symbolism." Translated from the Italian by Thomas E. Bird. *Russian Review* 25, no. 1 (January 1966): 24–34.

"Thoughts on Symbolism." In *The Russian Symbolists: An Anthology of Critical and Theoretical Works,* translated and edited by Ronald E. Peterson, 181–88. Ann Arbor, Mich.: Ardis, 1986.

"Thoughts on Symbolism." Translated by Samuel D. Cioran. *Russian Literature Triquarterly* 4 (1972): 151–58.

"Threefold Reality." In *Crime and Punishment and the Critics,* translated and edited by Edward Wasiolek, 43–44. San Francisco: Wadsworth Publishing Company, Inc., 1961.

Index

321

Index

Index

Sappho, xii

Saussure, Ferdinand de, viii

Savinkov, Boris, 273

Savonarola, Girolamo, 261

Schelling, Friedrich Wilhelm Joseph von, 219, 239, 314, 315

Schiller, Friedrich, viii, 24, 40, 97, 120, 218, 236, 242, 249, 265–66, 272, 275, 287, 289, 315; Works cited: "Der Pilgrim," 97

Schlegel, August Wilhelm von, 316

Schlegel, Friedrich, 260, 316

Schleiermacher, Friedrich, 256

Schopenhauer, Arthur, 114, 160, 180, 195, 232, 233, 235, 239, 241, 289, 300, 307, 313, 315

Schumann, Robert, 20

Scriabin, Alexander, x, xvii, 171, 211–28, 293, 312–13, 314, 317; Works cited: *Divine Poem,* 224; *Mysterium,* 213, 220, 224, 225, 226; *Poem of Ecstasy* (Fifth Sonata), 225; "Preliminary Act," 213, 220, 226; *Prometheus,* 225, 226; Tenth Sonata, 225

Second Isaiah. *See* Isaiah, Prophet

Semele, 81, 235, 263, 300, 303

Severianin, Igor, 258

Shakespeare, William, 21, 80, 102, 120, 174, 262, 272, 313; Works cited: *Hamlet,* 79, 173

Shchedrin, Mikhail. *See* Saltykov-Shchedrin, Mikhail

Shchetinin, Aleksei, 284

Shelley, Percy Bysshe, 177, 299; Works cited: "The Cloud," 177

Shestov, Lev, vii, 271

Shiva, 290

Shulamite, 243

Shvarsalon, Vera, x

Simeon, St., 13

Simonides, 50, 253

Sirens, 11, 17, 28, 84, 121, 201, 275

Slavophiles, 133, 282, 304, 306

Socrates, 18, 136, 179, 205–7, 209, 240, 283, 302, 304, 307, 309, 311

Solger, Karl, 239

Sologub, Fedor, 45, 181, 291, 301, 311; Works cited: "Lifeless Chamber," 203; "Orgiastic madness in wine," 181

Solomon, 25, 219, 243

Solon, 146, 147, 288

Solovyov, Vladimir, viii, xi, xii, xiv, xv, 9, 14, 32, 35, 43, 45, 87–88, 97, 117, 129, 172, 179, 189–99, 204, 208, 221, 234, 237, 239, 245, 246, 247, 255, 258, 259, 260, 261, 263, 266, 280, 281, 284, 285, 287, 288, 289, 298, 299, 306, 307, 308, 309, 311, 312, 316; Works cited, Poetry: "Ex Oriente Lux," 193; "In the Alps," 9; "In the morning mist with timid steps," 97; "The Three Labors," 87–89, 197, 208; "Three Meetings," 32; "The time of spring storms," 198; Philosophical works: *The History and Future of Theocracy,* 192, 193; *The Justification of the Good,* 192; *Russia and the Universal Church,* 194; "A Short Tale of the Antichrist," 194; "Three Speeches in Memory of Dostoevsky," 14–15, 32, 35, 239

Sophia–Divine Wisdom, 190, 198, 209, 245, 247, 249, 255, 258, 305, 312

Sophists, 18, 207, 217

Sophocles, 61, 64, 292, 295, 296, 297; Works cited: *Antigone,* 159, 167

Spencer, Herbert, 218, 315

Spinoza, Benedict, 273, 314

Stakhorskii, S. V., 264, 268

Statius, Publius Papinius, 122, 276

Stepun, Fedor, 230, 309, 310

Stirner, Max, 185, 303

Stoics, 161

Sulamith. *See* Shulamite

Sully-Prudhomme, René-François-Armand, 276

Swedenborg, Emmanuel, 24, 242

Swinburne, Algernon Charles, 243

Tantalus, 159, 166, 292

Tasso, Torquato, 114, 115, 271; Works cited: *Jerusalem Emancipated,* 115

Terence, 295

Terpander, 216, 315

Tertullian, 275, 284, 311

Themis, 159, 292

Theodoric, 120, 275

Theognis, 7, 235, 287

Theseus, 167, 295

Thetis, 292

Thomas à Kempis, 284

Thomas Aquinas, St., 314

Thyone, 235

Tiberius, Emperor, 240